CULTURAL PERSPECTIVES ON REPRODUCTIVE HEALTH

The International Union for the Scientific Study of Population Problems was set up in 1928, with Dr Raymond Pearl as President. At that time the Union's main purpose was to promote international scientific co-operation to study the various aspects of population problems, through national committees and through its members themselves. In 1947 the International Union for the Scientific Study of Population (IUSSP) was reconstituted into its present form.

It expanded its activities to:

- stimulate research on population
- develop interest in demographic matters among governments, national and international organizations, scientific bodies, and the general public
- foster relations between people involved in population studies
- disseminate scientific knowledge on population.

The principal ways through which the IUSSP currently achieves its aims are:

- organization of worldwide or regional conferences
- operations of Scientific Committees under the auspices of the Council
- organization of training courses
- publication of conference proceedings and committee reports.

Demography can be defined by its field of study and its analytical methods. Accordingly, it can be regarded as the scientific study of human populations primarily with respect to their size, their structure, and their development. For reasons which are related to the history of the discipline, the demographic method is essentially inductive: progress in knowledge results from the improvement of observation, the sophistication of measurement methods, and the search for regularities and stable factors leading to the formulation of explanatory models. In conclusion, the three objectives of demographic analysis are to describe, measure, and analyse.

International Studies in Demography is the outcome of an agreement concluded by the IUSSP and the Oxford University Press. The joint series reflects the broad range of the Union's activities; it is based on the seminars organized by the Union and important international meetings in the field of population and development. The Editorial Board of the series is comprised of:

Cultural Perspectives on Reproductive Health

Edited by
CARLA MAKHLOUF OBERMEYER

OXFORD
UNIVERSITY PRESS

*This book has been printed digitally and produced in a standard specification
in order to ensure its continuing availability*

OXFORD
UNIVERSITY PRESS

Great Clarendon Street, Oxford OX2 6DP

Oxford University Press is a department of the University of Oxford.
It furthers the University's objective of excellence in research, scholarship,
and education by publishing worldwide in

Oxford New York

Auckland Bangkok Buenos Aires Cape Town Chennai
Dar es Salaam Delhi Hong Kong Istanbul Karachi Kolkata
Kuala Lumpur Madrid Melbourne Mexico City Mumbai Nairobi
São Paulo Shanghai Taipei Tokyo Toronto

Oxford is a registered trade mark of Oxford University Press
in the UK and in certain other countries

Published in the United States
by Oxford University Press Inc., New York

© IUSSP 2001

The moral rights of the author have been asserted

Database right Oxford University Press (maker)

Reprinted 2004

ISBN 0-19-924689-0

Acknowledgements

The papers on which this book is based were presented at a seminar organized by the Reproductive Health Committee of the International Union for the Scientific Study of Population. The Committee membership was as follows: Carla Makhlouf Obermeyer and Axel Mundigo, co-chairs; members Oona Campbell, Sonalde Desai, Vincent Fauveau, Anastasia Gage, Maria Coleta de Olivera, and Kate Stewart. I would like to thank France Jans, secretary of the committee, for her help with the various administrative aspects of the committee's work over our three-year mandate.

The seminar took place in Kwa Maritane, South Africa in June 1997, and was jointly organized with the Department of Community Health of the University of Witwatersrand in Johannesburg. I am most grateful to William Pick, chair of the department, for generously taking time from his busy schedule to help with the organization of the seminar and the various activities that took place in connection with it, including the meetings with South African colleagues and the wonderful social programme that made this a most special occasion for all participants.

Funding for the seminar was provided by the Mellon Foundation, the Ford Foundation, and the Norwegian Ministry of Foreign Affairs. Their support is gratefully acknowledged.

I also wish to thank Robert Reynolds and Michelle Schulein for their editorial work on this volume.

Contents

List of Contributors

Didier Fassin, Professor of Anthropology, Ecole des Hautes Etudes en Sciences Socioles and Professor of Sociology, University of Paris North, Director of the Centre for Research on Public Health Issues, Bobigny, France

Susan Greenhalgh, Professor of Anthropology, University of California at Irvine, Irvine, California

Homa Hoodfar, Associate Professor of Social Anthropology, Department of Sociology and Anthropology, Concordia University, Montreal, Canada

Dale Huntington, Senior Associate, Associate Director ANE Region, Frontiers in Reproductive Health Project, Population Council, New Delhi, India

Inge Hutter, Associate Professor, Population Research Centre, University of Groningen, the Netherlands. Coordinator research programme HERA (HEalthy reproduction: Research for Action), PRC Groningen and NIDI (Netherlands Interdisciplinary Demographic Institute), The Hague, the Netherlands

Marcia C. Inhorn, Associate Professor, Department of Health Behavior and Health Education, School of Public Health, International Institute, and Department of Anthropology, University of Michigan, Ann Arbor, Michigan

Nora Jacobson, Research Scientist, Centre for Addiction and Mental Health, Toronto, Canada

Deborah James, Lecturer, Department of Anthropology, London School of Economics, London, United Kingdom

Carol E. Kaufman, Healthy Ways Project Director, University of Colorado Health Sciences Center, Denver, Colorado; Consultant, Population Council

Margaret Lock, Professor of Medical Anthropology, Department of Social Studies of Medicine and Department of Anthropology, McGill University, Montreal, Canada

Nancy Luke, Lecturer, Department of Sociology and Population Studies Center, University of Pennsylvania, Philadelphia, Pennsylvania

Soledad González Montes, Professor-Researcher, Interdisciplinary Women's Studies Program, El Colegio de Mexico.

Mark Nichter, Professor, Department of Anthropology, University of Arizona, Tucson, Arizona

Carla Makhlouf Obermeyer, Associate Professor, Department of Population and International Health, Harvard University; and Scientist, Department of Gender, Women and Health, World Health Organization, Geneva, Switzerland

Rosalind P. Petchesky, Professor of Political Science and Women's Studies, Hunter College, City University of New York, New York; Founder and Former International Coordinator of the International Reproductive Rights Research Action Group; and recipient of a Macarthur Fellow

Radhika Ramasubban, Director, Centre for Social and Technological Change, Mumbai, India

Bhanwar S. Rishyasringa, Senior Fellow, Centre for Social and Technological Change, Mumbai, India

Ina Warriner, Social Scientist, Department of Reproductive Health and Research, World Health Organization, Geneva, Switzerland

Susan Cotts Watkins, Professor, Department of Sociology and Associate, Population Studies Center, University of Pennsylvania, Philadelphia, Pennsylvania

Introduction

CARLA MAKHLOUF OBERMEYER

REPRODUCTIVE HEALTH AND CULTURE

The chapters in this volume explore, in various ways, the connections between reproductive health and culture. The notion of reproductive health, which gained a prominent place in discussions of population policies at the time of the 1994 Cairo International Conference on Population and Development, exemplified the shift that took place in global thinking about population, from the demographically driven provision of family planning to an expanded approach which places individual needs at the centre of an agenda concerned with the broader context of reproduction. Key to this approach is a greater emphasis on women's health for its own sake rather than as an instrument to achieve demographic goals or improve child survival, on the exercise of free choice in matters of reproduction, on sexuality, and on the social conditions which influence reproductive decisions, their health correlates, and their consequences (Sen et al. 1994; Tsui et al. 1997). Such concerns with understanding reproductive health in context coincide with those that have long guided sociological and anthropological research on the social construction of the body, local notions of illness and healing, and the connections between gender and health. Bringing together anthropologists whose work dealt with various dimensions of reproduction and health researchers concerned with reproductive health had the potential to generate valuable insights that would have relevance both within and across disciplinary fields, and in 1997 the Reproductive Health Committee of the International Union for the Scientific Study of Population organized a seminar to consider the common themes that would emerge from comparisons of reproductive health across cultures.

Two related questions form the background of discussion of reproductive health in this collective volume: (1) How does culture shape the particular ways in which reproductive events are associated with health outcomes? (2) To what extent does the notion of reproductive health, which emerged at a historical moment, and was moulded by the experience of specific groups—feminists concerned with the connections between gender and reproduction, and health activists worried about the potential abuses that family planning programmes had sometimes been associated with—have relevance in different circumstances?

These questions about the role of culture and the link between the global and the local have increasingly come to be the focus of attention among international researchers and policy makers in the field of population, in view of the diversity of settings in which the reproductive health approach is being applied. Because the notion of reproductive health represents the culmination of a process of consensus building that brought together researchers, activists, and practitioners from around the world, it has the potential to resonate with the concern of men and women everywhere. But since its power resides less in the rigour of the categories it defines than in its ability to incorporate the aspirations of diverse constituencies, the process of implementing the reproductive health agenda is as much a question of the adoption of a particular set of cultural values in various parts of the globe as it is a question of management and technical know-how, and hence must necessarily be informed by cross-cultural perspectives (Obermeyer 1999).

A CULTURAL PERSPECTIVE ON REPRODUCTIVE HEALTH: THEORETICAL ORIENTATIONS

Much has been written on the definition and implementation of the reproductive health approach in the years preceding and following the International Conference on Population and Development, and a number of useful reviews are available. While an exhaustive discussion of cultural perspectives on reproductive health is beyond the scope of this chapter, it is possible to provide a summary of the key elements that define a cultural perspective to health—these are indeed the principles that have guided my own research in this area and have provided the theoretical orientation to the planning of this volume.

The first principle is that health care is not simply about using health services for specific purposes, and reproductive behaviour is not simply about decisions to use or not use contraceptives or medications for gynaecological illnesses. Rather, behaviours related to health and reproduction are everywhere, associated with symbolic meanings beyond their immediate instrumental effects. They cannot be sufficiently explained by strictly rational models where information is directly linked to behaviour, or behaviour to clearly formulated goals, because they frequently express norms about appropriate social conduct, implicit views of the body, and profound orientations about life. In addition, because individuals frequently have to take decisions in light of incomplete information, make difficult judgements regarding future risks, or choose among imperfect alternatives, it is important to develop the conceptual and methodological tools that can capture the iterative process of decision making, and throw some light on the uncertainty that surrounds individual choices.

A second concept that would be central to a cultural perspective on health is that of medical pluralism, the existence of multiple alternatives for maintaining or restoring health and controlling reproduction. The expansion of biomedicine and modern contraception to all regions of the world creates situations where one or more models of health are coexisting—or colliding—and the areas of correspondence and inconsistency that result from these encounters pose important questions for researchers. For example, local notions of the body may be at odds with scientific models; or users may reinterpret medicines and therapies in a manner different from that intended by manufacturers; or individuals' ideas of risk and prevention diverge from the impersonal probabilistic assessments of public health professionals. Thus, a discrepancy may come to exist between professional recommendations and local practices. Conversely, as pragmatic users draw on multiple sources of care, eclectic combinations and unintended syntheses emerge—we now have clear evidence that even in countries of the North, individuals are not exclusive users of conventional health care, but alternate between a variety of providers. Understanding the multiplicity of views of health that exist in a given context, their convergence or divergence, the factors that shape such situations, as well as their health consequences, requires an approach that can draw on both public health models and social science explanations, and an ability to uncover the logic underlying practices that appear to contradict familiar models of health. Such a perspective can yield important insights into motivations and attitudes, improve communication practices, and promote the design of better health interventions.

A third concept that is, in my view, key to understanding health in general, and reproductive health in particular, is that of medicalization, the expanding use of medical models and practices to an increasing number of areas of life. An important contribution of medical anthropology and studies of science and technology has been to bring to light the influence of culture and history on the construction of biomedical knowledge and practice. The effectiveness of biomedicine in explaining health and reproductive processes, in controlling reproduction, and in preventing and treating ill-health has given biomedical models considerable power to define societal values and diagnose ills beyond strictly defined medical problems. Such models and the practices they support are increasingly authoritative, and health gradually acquires value as a moral good. Understanding the determinants and implications of the powerful and apparently inexorable process of medicalization generates both awe and humility, and fosters the development of a reflexive attitude towards public health as a global enterprise.

The chapters in this collection provide views of how reproductive health is conceived of by women and men in different parts of the world, mainly at the level of 'local communities'—villages and slums in India, Egyptian and South Asian cities, Kenyan and Mexican rural areas, or South African settlements—but also in the centres of power of China and Iran, and in modern (and post-modern) settings of the North and Far East. The particular topics covered by the different chapters centre around health events and conditions that surround reproduction—core topics such as pregnancy, birth and the post-partum, abortion, sexual behaviour, reproductive illnesses, infertility—as well as questions that are less directly tied to specific reproductive events, such as the problem of domestic violence, discourse about population, debates about women's bodies, state policies on women's health, and negotiations of reproductive rights. Although an effort was made, at the time the seminar was organized, to solicit contributions that would touch on most reproductive health problems and cover most regions of the world, inevitably in a collective work such as this one, some gaps remain: important topics such as female sexuality, female circumcision, menarche and menopause are not adequately covered and the geographic distribution of the countries discussed in the chapters is by no means even. The collection does however illustrate a number of key issues and brings out the complex processes surrounding reproductive decisions and behaviours, be it by individual women, by health providers, or by policy makers.

The approaches used by contributors to this volume to collect data for studying cultural factors are varied, and range from the classic methods of anthropology—participant observation, in-depth interviewing, and case studies—to questionnaire surveys, analyses of documents, and statistical analyses of demographic data. Several of the authors combine quantitative and qualitative analyses, a strategy that is especially appropriate to study the public health dimension and social context of reproductive health. Regardless of the particular method used however, all the papers have in common the effort to present the perspective of the actors. Whether the focus is on men and women seeking to protect themselves and their families and increase their well-being, or on providers of health services or policy makers, whose views reflect authoritative biomedical knowledge and religious or political ideologies, the studies included here seek to render the perceptions, decisions, and rationalizations that surround health and reproduction.

PROFESSIONAL AND LAY MODELS OF REPRODUCTIVE HEALTH, ILLNESS, AND THERAPY

A central theme of the book is the correspondence between professional and lay models of reproductive health. Medical anthropology has long been concerned with ethnophysiology, folk views of illness, the attribution of causality, and traditional practices of prevention and healing, but there have been few systematic investigations that would throw light on a recurrent finding of research on reproductive health, namely the discrepancy between women's perceptions and expression of their needs and biomedical assessments of their health. Careful validation studies of obstetric and gynaecological morbidity in contexts as diverse as Egypt, the Philippines, Indonesia, Bangladesh, and India have shown that the ability of women to recognize medical conditions and their potential complications and seek the appropriate services is limited (Younis *et al.* 1993; Zurayk *et al.* 1995; Bulut *et al.* 1996; Koenig *et al.* 1999; Ronsmans 1999).

Part of the discrepancy between objective indicators and subjective perceptions of morbidity is due to epidemiological and medical reasons: many conditions are asymptomatic and are discovered only upon laboratory testing, and thus are not always perceptible; in addition, because its manifestations are not life threatening, reproductive morbidity often does not receive a great deal of attention from health providers. Thus unless special efforts are made to identify them, reproductive morbidity conditions can remain invisible. More importantly perhaps, the discrepancy between medical measures and women's reports is a reflection of the cultural construction of gender. A number of health studies have shown that 'women's problems' frequently receive a low priority and tend to be surrounded by a 'culture of silence' (Khattab 1992; IWHC 1994). Where women expect some degree of suffering to accompany reproductive functions, they are less likely to define the conditions associated with these functions as pathological or unacceptable. Moreover, constraints related to economic factors, deficiencies in the infrastructure, and the quality of health services limit women's ability to obtain appropriate health care and generally keep reproductive health conditions away from medical attention. Even where the construction of gender is not grossly inegalitarian there remains a discrepancy between professional and lay models of reproductive health. While it is comforting to learn that improving the quality of obstetric services and providing outreach services can lead to improved recognition of potential complications and better use of services and to better health outcomes (Nwakoby *et al.* 1997; Olaniran *et al.* 1997; John Snow International 1998), we know less about the link between health education and the recognition of gynaecological morbidity, although it is likely that such efforts are successful to the extent that they are able to incorporate an understanding of local conditions into educational initiatives.

Several of the chapters in this volume elaborate on the particular ways in which culture shapes the formulation of reproductive health and illness in different contexts. Two papers focus on local concepts that have no exact equivalent in biomedicine but are central to an understanding of reproductive health. Ramasubban and Rishyasringa focus on *ashaktapana*, an illness found to be prevalent among slum-dwelling women of Mumbai, characterized by a generalized feeling of weakness, and associated with a variety of symptoms including bodily aches and vaginal discharge. Their analysis of material from in-depth interviews shows the connections between the different symptoms of weakness, the factors that constitute risks for reproductive ill-health and poor nutritional status, and the social conditions of poverty and gender inequality that constrain women's lives.

Luke, Warriner, and Watkins analyse the local concept of *rariu*, a reproductive illness found among rural Luo women of Kenya. *Rariu* does not correspond to any medical diagnosis but is partly suggestive of reproductive tract infections. Although the women in the study use clinics for various health conditions, they seek the exclusive services of traditional healers for *rariu*, and, conversely, clinic personnel are reluctant to acknowledge *rariu*—except if they are unable to offer another diagnosis. The chapter highlights the contrast between professional and lay perspectives on this illness, the association between the prevalence of *rariu* and lay referral networks, and the power and social distance that separate providers and clients. These findings raise questions regarding what an appropriate response from reproductive health services might be in cases of such 'culture-bound syndromes', and whether health professionals should recognize such an illness—thus running the risk of legitimizing a 'false' category—or ignore it and continue to encourage women to seek care from traditional healers.

Hutter's examination of nutritional practices among rural Indian women in Karnataka indicates that the reason women do not comply with experts' recommendations regarding increased food intake during pregnancy is not, as has frequently been argued, that they are trying to have a small child and hence an easy delivery. Rather, her detailed interviews and observations show that women feel the need to reduce food intake precisely because they perceive the baby as growing and needing space to move in the 'stomach'. Women's perception that their eating patterns are meant to minimize their own discomfort during pregnancy coincides with the emphasis in discussions of reproductive health that women's well-being be a goal of policies rather than a means to improved child health, even though, in this case, the outcomes of their behaviour during pregnancy do not fit with public health formulations.

The chapters in this volume consider the therapies and technologies that are available to deal with reproductive health problems from the perspective of the users, and contrast it with that of experts. In his discussion of patterns of self-care in South Asia, Nichter brings together observations from several projects that he and colleagues carried out in Thailand and the Philippines. Nichter documents disturbing patterns of prophylactic antibiotic use among commercial sex workers and their clients, as they attempt to protect themselves against sexually transmitted diseases. His analysis of the reasons why individuals engage in behaviour which appears harmful from a biomedical perspective provides insights into the connections between constructions of risk, varying perceptions of vulnerability, notions of purity and immunity, and attempts to control exposure to danger.

Differences in the way individuals are able to avail themselves of technologies and therapies are the focus of Inhorn's study of infertility among Egyptian women. Her analysis shows considerable class and gender differentials in the construction of infertility and in access to new reproductive technologies: while poor women are frequently limited to ineffective traditional methods or to suboptimal, and sometimes harmful, therapies dispensed in 'modern' facilities, women of the elite classes can seek advanced technologies such as in vitro fertilization either in Egypt or outside the country. The discussion highlights the way in which class, gender, and religion operate to constrain the reproductive options of Egyptian women.

DISCOURSE, PRACTICE, AND REPRODUCTIVE DECISIONS

While a number of contributions to this volume touch on the policies and politics of reproduction, some of the chapters deal specifically with reproductive behaviour and ideologies in the context of the state. Greenhalgh considers the population policies of China from a Chinese perspective, i.e. through the eyes of the leaders themselves. She examines how the question of the 'missing girls' fits in the context of discourse on population and development, and she shows the different ways in which son preference is constructed, as a remnant of the peasant past and as a peasant reality to be accommodated. She points out that although official views do not see the one-child policy as a contributor to the missing girls problem, Chinese policy makers have addressed the issue of discrimination against girls, but ironically some of their discourse has served to reinforce son preference.

Concern with the link between population policies and ideology is also central to Hoodfar's analysis of the women volunteer health workers and the variety of women's religious gatherings that take place in Iran under the leadership of female *mullahs*. While female preachers and health volunteers support the government's population policy and disseminate its health education messages, they have also very successfully initiated strategies to challenge their exclusion from power, and to reinterpret their role in society. This, in turn, results in a degree of ambivalence towards women's activism on the part of the state: on the one hand, the regime fully appreciates women's participation in an institution it created and financed, and recognizes its success in supporting its population policies; on the other hand, the authorities are concerned about the possibility of a threat against them by a powerful organization spread among the less privileged segments of the population.

Huntington's research project on post-abortion care in Egypt shows how, in a legal and religious context that is opposed to abortion, physicians and women manipulate official constraints to avoid unwanted pregnancy. Analyses of interviews reveal that women distinguish between deliberately inducing an abortion of a recognized pregnancy, compared to one that is merely suspected, and by maintaining a degree of ambiguity, find it easier to terminate a possible pregnancy. Huntington also shows that the morality underlying decisions of women and health providers is influenced by the value of motherhood and providing for children, by a doctrinally based distinction between abortion before and after ensoulment, and by a determinist position that sees God as having the final say in any outcome.

Kaufman and James explore the negotiation of identity within and across ethnic boundaries and the links between ethnicity and reproductive behaviour among two language/ethnic groups in South Africa (the Sotho and the Ndebele). Starting with demographic data showing an association between group affiliation and indicators of fertility, Kaufman and James use the results of ethnographic fieldwork to refine their analysis. They provide a nuanced understanding of the interaction between gender, socio-economic differences, and ethnic identification, their influence on expectations and behaviours regarding reproductive events, and the ways in which women use ethnic identity to gain some control over work, marriage and childbearing.

Jacobson's chapter brings together detailed information about the formulation of professional and legal policies regarding silicon breast implants in the United States, along with feminist critiques of the medicalization of women's reproductive experiences. Her case study focuses on the debates surrounding implants, shows conflicting 'expert' views of technology, and highlights important issues in reproductive health, in particular those that relate to choice versus coercion in women's use of their bodies.

REPRODUCTIVE HEALTH, CULTURE, AND HUMAN RIGHTS

The other chapters in this volume further elaborate on the dilemmas that confront individuals regarding reproductive decisions, and illustrate complex processes of negotiation, adaptation, and manipulation.

Montes' presentation of the results of a project that sought to design interventions to reduce violence against women in a rural area of Mexico brings out the difficulties that emerge from efforts to involve health providers in an issue that was, until recently, not considered a health issue. It provides a keen analysis of medical personnel's views of domestic violence, and their opinions regarding its health consequences, in particular the effects of sexual coercion, and the impact of violence on contraceptive behaviour and pregnancy outcomes. Practitioners' limited responses when confronted with cases of violence against their female patients seem to stem both from their lack of training and from a professional notion that their area of competence is medical, while violence is a social problem.

Lock focuses on the dilemmas that emerge from the new diagnostic and genetic techniques available to monitor and assist reproduction in Japan. She uses case studies to illustrate the influence of the extended family on reproductive decisions, and the ways in which discourse about reproductive technologies and the new genetics is shaped by culturally informed ideas about kinship and the social and moral order. Lock also reviews the ideologies that have historically shaped reproduction and notions of the planned family in Japan, and shows their continuing influence on contemporary values related to the production of a healthy normal family.

The chapter by Petchesky explores a question that is fundamental to discussions of human rights in general, as well as to post-Cairo initiatives regarding indicators of progress in reproductive health: How are reproductive and sexual rights negotiated in the everyday life of women around the world? Petchesky brings together the results of a research project which covered seven countries. Several common themes emerge from the findings, including the ways in which women negotiate among the different dimensions of rights, the pragmatism that they demonstrate in dealing with religious ideology, and the greater importance they give to the right not to be subjected to violence than to 'positive' rights such as sexual enjoyment. These similarities point to what may be fundamental characteristics of the societal construction of rights across cultures and provide rich material to reflect on the conditions that favour or hinder the existence of a shared 'politics of the body.'

Fassin draws on his experience with projects in Ecuador and among African immigrants in France to critique 'culturalist' explanations of behaviours that do not fit with the expectations of health professionals. Culturalism reifies culture and denies the Other the universality of her aspirations, her right to difference, her rationality, and the influence of social conditions on her decisions. Fassin argues that culture should only be invoked after an examination of the socio-economic conditions that sustain it, and that cultural explanations should by definition be political. The chapter invites a general reflection on the place of cultural explanations in analyses of reproductive health and thus provides an appropriate conclusion to the volume as a whole.

Taken together, the chapters in this volume exemplify research that seeks to take account of the multiple dimensions of reproductive health and its embeddedness in culture, and contribute important insights to our understanding of its meaning for individuals in a variety of contexts.

References

Bulut, A., Yolsal, N., Fillippi, V., and Graham, W. (1995), 'In search of truth: Comparing alternative sources of information on reproductive tract infections', *Reproductive Health Matters*, 6: 31–9.

International Women's Health Coalition (IWHC) (1994), *Challenging the Culture of Silence: Building Alliances to End Reproductive Tract Infections*, New York: International Women's Health Coalition.

John Snow International (JSI) (1998), Report on Safe Motherhood. Rabat, Morocco, unpublished report.

Khattab, H. (1992), *The Silent Endurance: Social Conditions of Women's Reproductive Health in Egypt*, Amman: UNICEF, and Cairo: The Population Council.

Koenig, M., Jejeebhoy, S., Singh, S., and Sridhar, S. (1996), 'Undertaking community-based research on the prevalence of gynaecological morbidity: lessons from India'. Paper presented at the International Union for the Scientific Study of Population Seminar, *The Assessment of Reproductive Health: Innovative Approaches*, Manila, September 1996.

Nwakoby, B., Akpala, V., Nwagbo, D., Onah, B., Okeke, V., Chukudebelu, W., Ikeme, A., Okaro, J., Egbuciem, P., and Ikeagu, A. (1997), 'Community contact persons promote utilization of obstetric services', *International Journal of Gynaecology and Obstetrics*, 59 (Suppl. 2): S219–24.

Obermeyer, C. M. (1999) 'The cultural construction of reproductive health: Implications for monitoring the Cairo agenda', *International Family Planning Perspectives*, 25 (S): 50–55.

Olaniran, N., Offiong, S., Ottong, J., Asuquo, E., Duke, F. (1997), 'Mobilizing the community to utilize obstetric services', *International Journal of Gynaecology and Obstetrics*, 59 (Suppl. 2): S181–9.

Ronsmans, C. (1999), 'Studies validating women's reports of reproductive health: How useful are they?'. Paper presented at the International Union for the Scientific Study of Population Seminar, *The Assessment of Reproductive Health: Innovative Approaches*, Manila, September 1996.

Sen, G., Germain, A., and Chen, L. (eds.) (1994), *Population Policies Reconsidered: Health, Empowerment and Rights*, Cambridge: Harvard Center for Population and Development Studies, and New York: International Women's Health Coalition.

Tsui, A., Wasserheit, J., and Haaga, J. (eds.) (1997), *Reproductive Health in Developing Countries: Expanding Dimensions, Building Solutions*, Washington DC: National Academy Press.

Younis, N., Khattab, H., Zurayk, H., El-Mouelhy, M., Fadle, M., and Farah, A. (1993), 'A community study of gynecological and related morbidities in rural Egypt', *Studies in Family Planning*, 24 (3): 175–86.

Zurayk, H., Younis, N., Khattab, H. (1995), 'Rethinking family planning policy in light of reproductive health research', in C. M. Obermeyer (ed.), *Family, Gender and Population in the Middle East: Policies in Context*, Cairo: American University in Cairo Press.

PART I

PROFESSIONAL AND LAY MODELS OF REPRODUCTIVE HEALTH, ILLNESS, AND THERAPY

1

Weakness ('*Ashaktapana*') and Reproductive Health among Women in a Slum Population in Mumbai[1]

RADHIKA RAMASUBBAN AND BHANWAR RISHYASRINGA

INTRODUCTION

Since the late 1980s and early 1990s growing interest in women's reproductive well-being has brought to the fore for the first time the considerable burden of reproductive morbidity carried by poor women in developing countries (Dixon-Mueller and Wasserheit 1991; Germaine *et al.* 1992).

Community-based studies in developing countries to estimate the incidence of reproductive tract infections (RTIs) among poor women have revealed that this morbidity and general ill-health is, for the most part, silently endured by women, due to a combination of forces which serve to keep women's sufferings invisible: cultural restrictions and gender inequalities in the form of lack of autonomy over mobility, finances and decision making, low educational levels, poor awareness about their bodies, about their health and about available services, and infrastructural shortcomings in the form of lack of good quality and sensitively tuned health and counselling services (Bang *et al.* 1989; Wasserheit *et al.* 1989; Khattab 1992; Younis *et al.* 1993; Brabin *et al.* 1995; Gittelsohn *et al.* 1994; Bhatia *et al.* 1997; Streehitakarini 1995; Baroda Citizens' Council *et al.* 1995; Oomman 1996). It is notable that a number of these studies have been conducted in India, with more underway (Koenig *et al.* 1996).

The insights from these exploratory studies have only served to highlight how much more we need to know—particularly about the underlying socio-cultural and behavioural factors which bring about reproductive morbidities, and which constitute obstacles to improved health. Do solutions lie in the direction of medical interventions, i.e. providing more visible reproductive health care facilities and improving their quality in terms of both technical and human resources? Or are they to be sought in devising mechanisms that can effectively enhance women's care seeking capabilities through raising awareness and facilitating access? Or, is there a range of reproductive illnesses which defy direct medical intervention alone, and which require more broad-based approaches?

WEAKNESS AS ILLNESS

Several Indian community-based studies seeking to understand how rural women rank their health problems in order of severity and the way they group common illnesses, have revealed that women perceive vaginal discharge and weakness to be among the most severe and common afflictions (Patel 1994; Narayan and Srinivasan 1994; Oomman 1996; Bang and Bang 1994). Studies on vaginal discharge highlight the close link, in women's perceptions, between vaginal discharge and feelings of weakness, with one seen to be causing the other and vice versa, but there are no analyses of the phenomenon of 'weakness'. Yet weakness was an important complaint among women. Among the women in Oomman's study, weakness and vaginal discharge were the most frequently mentioned illnesses, with menstrual problems coming a close third. Weakness here was seen as playing a dual role: as an illness in itself as well as the root cause of the other two illnesses. And the factor seen by women to be responsible for the state of weakness was poverty, described as 'weakness in the house'. The lack of enough foods and lack of nutritious foods was seen as its most obvious symbol (Oomman 1996).

There is a reciprocal relationship between weakness and reproductive health: weakness impacts upon reproductive health, for example through anaemia during pregnancy and through lowered immunity and greater susceptibility to infections of the reproductive tract; it can result from particular reproductive problems such as problematic pregnancies and difficult deliveries or sterilization.

The association of weakness and poor reproductive health with socio-economic conditions is complex. Poverty enhances the synergism between poor nutrition and lowered immunity to infectious diseases, complications of pregnancies and maternal deaths, low-birth-weight infants and low child survival, high fertility, thus putting women at risk. Gender relations leading to nutritional discrimination against women in the household impede the realization of genetic potential in body size, which in turn impacts upon reproductive success. Lower caloric intake coupled with high energy expenditures on physical work can, particularly at the time of pregnancy and lactation, drain the body of energy and lead to weakness, persistent feelings of physical distress. Social problems such as unemployment in the household, male alcoholism, and abuse including wife beating can also contribute to the weakness and sickness load experienced by women. The prevailing patterns of health-seeking behaviour may be another factor that reduces women's ability to cope with weakness and to bolster their own reproductive health. Finally, certain reproductive episodes—problems during pregnancy, delivery, the post-partum period, abortions, child loss, and sterilization—and the social contexts within which they take place, shaped by prevailing gender and age hierarchies, may also play a role in causing weakness.

Women's perception that vaginal discharge and weakness are associated, and result from poverty-induced malnutrition[2] underscore the importance of further exploring the role of the social and physical environment in which women live, and the link between reproductive morbidity and the feelings of 'weakness' among poor women.

This chapter focuses on the problem of weakness or *ashaktapana* as it is referred to in Marathi (it is referred to as *kamjori* in Hindi and Gujarati, the other languages of northern and western India), and analyses the links that exist between conditions of poverty, poor reproductive health, and women's subjective experience of weakness. This is done through an in-depth study of a small number (25) of poor urban slum-dwelling women, who report this as the most common and nagging health problem they suffer from. The study is set in Mumbai (until recently known as Bombay), one of India's largest metropolises and one of the most populous cities in the world, where over 60 per cent of the population live in slums/slum-like conditions characterized by overcrowding, poor quality housing, and lack of access to adequate infrastructure.

The reason for focusing on *ashaktapana* as a 'weakness as illness' was that the word was frequently mentioned in the reproductive narratives of women. Many problems were attributed to *ashaktapana* and the illness was often mentioned in connection with other health problems. Our observations on the problems of *ashaktapana* in these women are drawn from a larger ongoing research into the socio-cultural and behavioural determinants of reproductive health among women in poverty, and may be seen as one of the second generation of studies on women's reproductive health, with a greater emphasis on qualitative investigation of the meanings of states of reproductive health, illness, and morbidity. The study is based on repeated intensive, individual interviews with around 60 ever-married women belonging to three ethnic groups—neo-Buddhist, caste Hindu, and Muslim—living in poverty in Mumbai. The interviews collected information on menstrual, pregnancy and obstetric histories, experience of illness and morbidity, health service use, and family and neighbourhood support in daily life and during crucial reproductive events and health crises in the family. The study asked women specifically about their experience of *ashaktapana* and sought to place reproductive health and weakness within the context of household dynamics—family size, gender and age hierarchies, male employment/unemployment, alcoholism and domestic violence, and communication between marital partners on health-related issues.

The women in the larger study are distributed over four slum pockets of around 5,000 households each. A list of around 300 women in the age group of 20–45 years was prepared, from which a sample of 60 women was selected randomly. A first round of interviews collected life histories, pregnancy and obstetric histories, patterns of health service use and support systems, and a second round probed into specific illnesses and morbidities relating to vaginal discharge, menstruation, urinary problems, prolapse, back pain and other pains, weakness, sexual problems, mental tension, etc. Clinical investigations are currently underway to provide medical treatment to women suffering from remediable problems. We are also continuing to study reproductive health, in particular health-seeking behaviour and family dynamics, and are conducting key informant interviews with local health care providers, older menopausal women, and adolescent girls.

The structure of this chapter is as follows. The setting of the study is sketched, to evoke the physical and social environment within which this discussion of weakness is located. This is followed by the delineation of categories used by the women in the study to describe illness, weakness, and the perceived causes of this condition. We then discuss the risk factors for weakness as they emerge from the life history, pregnancy history, and reproductive illness history narratives. The conclusion considers health-seeking behaviour for weakness and possible directions for intervention if this problem is to be addressed.

THE SETTING

The women in our study are drawn from large slum settlements in the suburbs and extended suburbs, where environmental quality is generally poor. Each settlement may consist of several pockets, and each of these pockets houses a community of between 2,000 and 5,000 households whose inhabitants come from different parts of the country.

While there is considerable diversity among the slum-dwelling households themselves in terms of income levels, assets, skills, physical environment, and ethnic identity, individual slum pockets are relatively homogeneous in terms of ethnic identity, economic levels, and micro-environmental conditions. The women on whom this discussion of *ashaktapana* focuses, speak Marathi, the language of the region, they are neo-Buddhist by religion, and belong to what are called the scheduled castes (known as 'untouchables' in pre-independent India). They reside in two slum pockets in M Ward in the northeastern suburbs of the city, the ward with the highest concentration of scheduled caste population living in the city. This social group has traditionally been among the poorest and socially most underprivi-leged in the country. In their socio-economic, demographic, and cultural profile, these women may be said to be fairly representative of this underclass.

Their average age ranges from 28 years (in pocket A) to 35 years (pocket B). The average age at menarche was 13 years and the average age at marriage was 16 years. Social expectations are that the young bride should become pregnant within three months of marriage. Within a year of marriage, i.e. before they turned 18, these women were mothers. However, 40 per cent of these women went through their first pregnancy when they were 15 and became mothers even before they turned 18. The average number of pregnancies was 4.0 and the average number of living children was 2.5. Although free municipal school services up to class 7 are now available, the educational levels of the women in the study are low. Around a third of the women are illiterate, and the majority of those who are literate have only between 2 and 5 years of schooling and can barely read and sign their names. Less than a fourth have between 8 and 10 years of schooling, broadly the level required for absorption and retention of health-related information (Ramasubban *et al.* 1990). Many women were taken out of school with the onset of menstruation.

Families have strong links with their villages of origin. In fact, the village is in the city, as observed from the cultural norms governing the daily lives of these women and the pattern of their interaction within their extended families and neighbourhoods. Marriages are universally arranged by families, brides are regularly brought to the city from the village, and an overwhelming proportion of marriages are arranged within the close kin group (mainly cross-cousin marriages) or arranged between migrants hailing from the same or proximate villages.

The husbands of these women are relatively better educated than their wives, almost three-fourths having done between 8 and 10 years of schooling, and the rest having done between 10 and 11 years. But they are by and large unskilled. Only a very small number have permanent jobs (e.g. as sweepers or watchmen with the municipality or private commercial establishments). The majority are in unstable jobs or are self employed: unskilled workers in the conservancy department of the municipal corporation, in textile mills, and casual workers on rail and road works, or driving autorickshaws. Almost all of them have experienced short or prolonged periods of unemployment at some time or other, and a few are currently unemployed or laid off due to alcoholism or advanced TB.

A negligible minority of the women work for wages. It is only in the direst of circumstances, as when the family is threatened with prolonged economic hardship and disorientation due to the husband's prolonged unemployment, or when the husband's wages go into buying liquor, that women seek work outside the house. In this case, the options open are: piece work which they carry out sometimes with the help of other women members of the family such as sewing buttons, ironing and folding ready-made garments, making electric light switches, etc.; wage work in small workshops in nearby locations; part-time domestic paid work; carrying headloads at fishing wharves; or retailing dried fish and vegetables in the local (slum) market. The majority of the women stay at home, and their lives are totally absorbed by household duties and social interaction with immediate neighbours or visiting relatives.

All births take place in municipal hospitals/maternity homes that offer free services. Institutional delivery is accepted by all in this community, even the most illiterate, as crucial for child survival, probably because of constraints on care imposed by poor housing conditions. Safety at least during delivery is thus ensured, but it is to this environment that mothers return within three days of the delivery.

Generally, contact with the health system is only in the last trimester of pregnancy. Antenatal care before the seventh month is limited, since childbirth is seen as a natural phenomenon and not one requiring medicalization. Most women register only in the seventh month, which is when government policy recommends giving women their two tetanus toxoid injections, prescribing iron, folic acid and calcium supplements and doing a routine blood and urine test. Women with a history of difficult pregnancies and those with obvious problems earlier in their pregnancy (sudden bleeding, pain, or inexplicable swelling of the body) generally seek care from private doctors or private maternity homes or one of the larger public hospitals before the seventh month.

The average birth weight of babies born to these women is around 2.5 kg. Fourteen out of 25 women have experienced foetal and infant loss. Adverse pregnancy outcomes may result from induced abortions to terminate a pregnancy, violent assault by the husband, prolonged labour, and caesarian deliveries performed because of cephalopelvic disproportions.

The most frequently used method of contraception is sterilization. Over half (56 per cent) of the women have undergone tubectomy, and only five (one-fifth) have had any experience at all with other contraceptive methods (pill, condom, and IUD) for spacing their pregnancies. Given the early age at marriage and the pressures to start childbearing early, it is not surprising that the average age at sterilization is only 24 years, as families realize that they cannot sustain a large number of children. Also, as a result of government policy, the pressure on them is high in the municipal hospitals that they access for childbirth. All but 11 women were not sterilized; of those, two women were not cohabiting with their husbands and the rest have decided that they will undergo sterilization after they complete their families.

THE CONSTRUCTION AND VOCABULARY OF WEAKNESS

The most commonly used word for weakness among this community is *ashaktapana*. *Ashaktapana* is an antonym for the word *shakti* (strength) derived from Sanskrit, and the Marathi word *pan* is added to mean a state of weakness or 'feeling of weakening'. *Ashaktapana* is very specific in its connotation. It is not used to convey a generalized state of economic helplessness, or powerlessness *vis-à-vis* others, or a loss of control over established gender equations. These circumstances are conveyed through the use of different expressions, such as *ghara madhey garibi hai* ('there is poverty in our house'), *navara taabya madhey thewula nahi* ('she has not been able to entice her husband into her grip' implying the woman's own vulnerability), and *bai ko taabya madhey thewuli nahi* ('he has lost control over his wife' implying a husband's failure to wield authority firmly).

There is a striking consistency in the manner in which *ashaktapana* is described and experienced in this community. The descriptions of the feeling of being debilitated are several and used in more or less the same way by all the women. The most frequent description is that of sheer exhaustion when doing any work; resulting in slow body movements and inability to get through with the housework briskly; of headaches, heaviness in the head, giddy spells, and blackness before the eyes; and of wanting to lie down and sleep and to never get up. Other descriptions are: the inability to go out into the sun due to blackouts and giddiness, and blurring of vision and blackouts when bending over (as in housework such as sweeping and cleaning), or when working at heights (as when fixing/repairing leaking roofs), when doing heavy work, or lifting heavy objects (water for household use has to be filled and brought in from public taps), or when climbing stairs; the inability to walk a lot, and breathlessness and exhaustion while climbing stairs or lifting weights; and the feeling of wobbliness in the arms and legs, or a sense of them dissolving or becoming lifeless, numb or heavy. Women also mention the persistent feeling of being physically ill all the time, a feeling of having a mild fever always; of being tired most of the time (sapped of body energy), the feeling of no life being left in the body; of terrible *ashaktapana* as a constant feeling; and *ashaktapana* and exhaustion after sex. Some women speak of *ashaktapana* as both a physical and mental problem, about persistent lethargy bringing on a feeling of helplessness and depression, and the low self-esteem arising out of the feeling that one is a sickly person. Sunanda (38 years and mother of two children), who is the wife of a skilled factory worker, describes her condition thus:

Yes, I feel *ashaktapana*. . . My *ashaktapana* is both a physical problem and also causes me a lot of mental distress. It does not allow me to do much housework, and when I do any work I feel exhausted . . . due to this problem I always feel that I am ill and just want to stay in bed. . . I have this problem for the last five years . . . Because of this *ashaktapana*, I get bad thoughts in my mind. I am alone all day in the house and I keep brooding all the time.

Manda (35 years) who works as a domestic help in several houses to support the family (since her husband, who is an alcoholic and in a state of advanced tuberculosis, is unemployed) says:

I have *ashaktapana* for the past three years. . . I feel physically ill all the time. But I am also mentally worried. . . Due to the weakness, when I go out in the sun or walk much, I get *chakkar* (feel giddy) and blackness in front of my eyes. I also get back pain and pain in my thighs, calves and heels. . . I don't sleep well at night . . . my hands and legs tremble.

The word *ashaktapana*, therefore, is used specifically to connote a sense of weakness with particular physical symptoms and mental states. Among the women who report this illness, most complain of acute *ashaktapana*, i.e. enumerate between three and nine symptoms each. *Ashaktapana* does not appear to be a state of ill-health characteristic of advancing age. Mention of symptoms by women below 30 years of age is found to be proportional to their distribution in the sample, i.e. roughly 40 per cent.

Almost all the women who say that they suffer from *ashaktapana* also mention other accompanying illness conditions (Table 1.1). There is no evidence that the condition is related to age.

Accompanying conditions include: white discharge; a variety of aches and pains all over the body especially acute low back pain; insomnia or disturbed sleep; and mental stress. It is interesting to note that only three women mentioned white discharge as associated with weakness, although 14 women admitted, upon probing, that they were suffering from a problem of white discharge. Five of the women complaining of white discharge related it to their unfavourable experience of sterilization, four to tension, and two to overwork. While menstrual problems are not cited as the specific cause of the weakness being experienced, some women mention *ashaktapana* as an associated illness symptom with problems during

Table 1.1. *Symptoms associated with* ashaktapana *among the 25 women in the study*

Symptoms	Number of women mentioning symptom
Headaches, giddy spells, and blackness before eyes	18
Exhaustion while doing any work	17
Inability to walk a lot, breathlessness while climbing stairs/lifting weights	15
Wanting to sleep all the time	12
Blackouts when out in the sun, blurred vision/giddiness while bending over	10
Feeling of arms and legs dissolving/becoming lifeless	7
Feeling of being physically ill all the time	5
Weakness and exhaustion after coitus	4
Terrible weakness as a constant feeling	3
Feeling of no strength in the body	3
Weakness as both a physical and mental problem	3
Women who mention weakness and associated symptoms	Number
Total number of cases	25
Cases mentioning weakness	22
With 6–9 symptoms	7
With 3–5 symptoms	11
With 1–2 symptoms	4
No symptoms	3

menstruation such as painful menstruation; feelings of tremendous exhaustion just before and during menstruation, excessive bleeding (for over ten days); severe abdominal pain due to late or delayed periods; and tension during the menstrual period leading to exhaustion.

WOMEN'S PERCEPTIONS OF *ASHAKTAPANA*

Interviews with women and the analysis of narratives of pregnancy and illness show that women's feelings of weakness are embedded in both conditions of poverty and unfavourable gender relations, and while there are some risk factors which women are able to perceive directly, there are others which culture renders invisible.

When asked about perceived causes of weakness, most women (18) are able to identify some reasons (Table 1.2) and most relate it first to the physical difficulties of day-to-day living and management of the household, second to the stress inherent in the insecure economic and social conditions of the existence, and third to sterilization. Although the association with individual aspects of reproductive health, other than sterilization, is relatively weak, the constellation of factors surrounding pregnancy and childbearing when put together becomes the second

Table 1.2. *Perceived causes of weakness and its accompanying symptoms*

Causes mentioned	Number of women mentioning cause
Excessive housework/caring for family members	12
Tension/stress/brooding	7
Sterilization	6
Burden of childbearing	5
Tendency to neglect diet/erratic eating habits	5
Suffered neglect since childhood	4
Neglect of diet during pregnancy	3
Post-delivery neglect	3
Weakness of recent origin, but unable to understand cause	2
Recent neglect of health	2
White discharge	1
Low blood pressure	1
Difficulty in combining paid work and housework	1
Aging	1

most important set of perceived risk factors for *ashaktapana* after 'burden of housework'. Women describe the set of factors variously as the burden of childbearing—neglect of diet (both in quantity and quality) during pregnancy, too many and too closely spaced pregnancies, caesarian deliveries—in their pregnancy narratives. The burden of childbearing lends itself to direct description. A greater elaboration of how these reproductive causes work is provided in the pregnancy narratives. Women are able to elaborate on the causes of *ashaktapana* and to identify which one of their pregnancies sparked off the problem of weakness: when the 'lack of blood in the body' as diagnosed during pregnancy set in; overwork during pregnancies; the experience of an accident during pregnancy; or the lack of rest after deliveries. Women also mention the tendency to neglect themselves, and their experience of early neglect in childhood, as a root cause of current feelings of *ashaktapana,* and the results of clinical tests for anaemia (done as part of this study) lend support to these views of the causes of *ashaktapana.*

Women view their excessive household responsibilities in several ways. Prominent among these is the belief into which they have been socialized, that a woman is responsible for looking after each and every need of husband and children. The burden of this ideology of marital responsibility becomes unbearably difficult as they themselves grow older and as their growing children's demands and needs advance. The women do not explicitly elaborate on this as they see it as an inseparable and irremediable part of their lives. It is a drudgery from which there is no escape, since this is a woman's lot. But they do speak about the sheer inability to do housework during extreme bouts of weakness. It is the sum total of this overwork, in their view, that exacerbates the other symptoms of physical distress such as low back pain, giddiness and blurred vision, body pains in general, and insomnia, all of which are mentioned as conditions accompanying the feeling of weakness. The capacity to do housework is also described as being affected by mental stress, leaving no will to work. Indeed, the two—excessive housework and mental stress— together account for almost 40 per cent of the causes cited for *ashaktapana.*

Pushpa (40 years), who battled her way through seven pregnancies of which she lost five, who has lived all her life in poverty and deprivation with no support from her alcoholic and unstably employed husband, and who does part-time paid domestic work in three houses, says:

My hands and legs feel heavy. Just thinking about getting through with the housework makes me feel ill. My hands, feet, thighs, knees and calves pain from time to time. But the back pain is constant. These other pains are on account of the *ashaktapana.* Heavy work is beyond me, like filling water and carrying it home. My head, too, pains sometimes. Walking in the sun for a little while gives me *chakkar* (giddiness), blackness before my eyes, my throat feels parched. . . I am weak in my body, but mental stress is also there. There is no one to share my burden of housework, to cook or to look after me. I some- times think that it is better to die than to live like this.

Shohha (27 years), who has done 5 years of school, says:

When one is in a bad problem and doesn't know how to get out of it, one is bound to have a lot of tension. My tension is mostly due to my husband and children, because my husband works for daily wages lifting goats in the slaughter house, sometimes he gets work and sometimes he doesn't . . . often we have to sleep with empty stomachs because there is no food in the house. . . That is what I keep worrying about. What is going to be the future for me and my children . . . my husband is never going to get a good permanent job . . . that is why I got myself operated after two children. When we are unable to feed two children, where would we have gone for supporting a third?

While mental stress and the tendency to brood is cited by the women as among their most important health problems along with *ashaktapana,* the relationship between the two, particularly where stress is also perceived as one of the causes of weakness, is a complex one and is discussed later in this chapter when we contextu- alize 'weakness' in women's life history narratives. Here we may just mention that the main factors cited as raising stress levels are: poverty; worries about how to make both ends meet; husband's alcoholism; TB or some major disease in the family; unemployment of the husband and grown-up sons; and worries about the future of the children. Women with chronic reproductive problems, such as prolapse (*aang baahar nikalna* or 'protrusion of a part of the body'), continuous white discharge (*safed pani*) accompanied by burning and pain, or urinary incontinence (*lagvicha rog*), say that they worry continuously about their own health, even as they refrain from actively seeking definitive medical care for the problems, on grounds of fear of the unknown or what they justify as extremely busy domestic schedules. Occasional visits are made to the nearest local practitioner (whether qualified or not) when the distress becomes unbearable. Their brooding, they say, brings on dark fears about cancer and death, and sometimes leaves them with a sense of hopelessness.

Sterilization (or 'operation' as it is locally referred to), although more closely linked in women's minds with the experience of white discharge and low back pain, is also a frequently cited cause of *ashaktapana*. All the women who attributed the onset of low back pain to sterilization, explained that it was the anaesthetic spinal injection which was the triggering factor. There was a high agreement that sterilization was the cause of abdominal pain, generalized back pain, and a feeling of lack of strength in arms and legs, all of which the women associated with severe *ashaktapana*. Although dismissed by medical professionals as a figment of imagination among illiterate populations, this is quite clearly a frequent mode of explanation among those who say that they suffer from these after-effects. The most explicit overlap of descriptions of *ashaktapana* symptoms with descriptions of other reproductive health problems is when the women talk about sterilization, tending to attribute almost all feelings of physical distress to this episode: weakness, white discharge, severe low back pain, deep abdominal pain, giddiness and blackouts and blurred vision particularly when walking in the sun, a feeling of weakness in the hands and legs; aches and pains all over the body, particularly in the thighs and calf muscles; and irregular menstruation. Many of these perceived symptoms of post-sterilization ill-health—particularly white discharge—are in turn seen to be exacerbated by *ashaktapana*. Even the women who talked at length about their pregnancy and obstetric histories, some of them difficult ones and causing much trauma, became emotional when it came to talking about their experience of sterilization, and unhesitatingly cited the latter as the main cause of their present feelings of *ashaktapana* and ill-health.[3]

Chhaya (27 years) works as a coolie at the fishing wharves, on daily wages. Her work involves lifting heavy headloads of fish brought in by trawlers.

Ever since I had my operation (sterilization), my periods have become irregular, coming once in two or three months. They are accompanied by tremors in my hands and legs, my body feels weak and tremulous and I get blackness before my eyes. I suffer every now and again from a foul smelling vaginal discharge, and I get a pain deep inside my abdomen during and after *sambandh* (intercourse). I get pain in my vagina sometimes, and I have seen boils there sometimes. I also have acute back pain and tremendous *ashaktapana*. All these problems have started only since the operation. . . . I am sure that the operation is a culprit. I was happy to get myself operated. But when I came home I felt weak. I get severe chest pain, sometimes. It is two years since my operation and I have become the victim of pains all over my body.

The importance of diet is less frequently recognized as a possible cause of *ashaktapana*. Fewer women mention the routine neglect of diet as a significant cause of their feelings of weakness. This would appear to be because few women consciously recognize this relationship. Maya (35 years), who recounts how weak and sickly she had always been even as a child and how she had contracted TB from her father in childhood, says when asked a direct question about her *ashaktapana*, 'I eat well twice a day, so I can't understand how I have this *ashaktapana*.'

As will be discussed later in this chapter, these women's diets have always been meagre and they themselves are not conscious about this fact, which might be one reason why poor nutrition is not perceived by them to be at the root of many of their poor health conditions. On probing, however, some women admit in their life history narratives that neglect of diet could be a cause: the historical neglect of not having been properly fed from childhood due to poverty, and frequent starvation due to poverty in the husband's house; neglect of health—diet and rest—from the start and now being faced with the inability to take care of oneself due to the demands of a growing family; loss of appetite due to sheer exhaustion; and not being able to eat on time due to the demands of housework.

WEAKNESS, POVERTY, AND GENDER INEQUALITY

The life histories, pregnancy narratives, and reproductive health histories allow us to see *ashaktapana* in the broader context of the lives of these women and to consider the links between conditions of poverty (including poor nutrition, inadequate health services) and inequitable gender relations (i.e. young women's special vulnerability within the household) and the experience of particular reproductive events, including pregnancy and sterilization, with poor reproductive health and women's subjective experience of weakness.

The narratives are replete with mentions of mental stress, the main form of which arises from the conditions of poverty—worry about how to keep the house going on the basis of the meagre and unstable earnings of the husband; how to repay loans taken (mainly for major health care problems involving hospitalization, or house repair, or house purchase); how to get daughters married; etc. Every contingency leads to mental stress, since the day-to-day expenses permit no leeway to plan for major or minor crises. But most worrying is the feeling of lack of control, particularly in planning for the future of the children—education of sons and marriage of daughters, in that order.[4] When the husband is an alcoholic, women's worries compound. And where alcoholism is accompanied by violence against the wife and children, mental stress becomes a physical fact as well. In such cases, the lack of dialogue between the marital partners and the emotional gulf between them is a cause of distress to the women. Women speak of their husbands spending their earnings on drinking and on friends, and as evincing little interest in how their wives manage to run these precarious households.

Women cite both housework and stress as important contexts for *ashaktapana*. Our own observation shows that the nature of the physical infrastructure around which slum life revolves, makes house management an exhausting task for women, thus adding to the difficulty of getting through with the daily routine. Women have to queue up at the water tap and fetch water, lift heavily loaded containers of clothes to be washed and pots and pans to be cleaned, and carry these and other heavy loads up steep flights of stairs in the case of households occupying 'rooms' above ground level. The efforts are harder during bouts of weakness, other illnesses, menstruation, pregnancy and the post-partum period, and during extreme seasonal conditions. Due to the woeful lack of physical amenities, when the quantum of housework increases, the other symptoms of physical distress also get exacerbated, such as low back pain, giddiness and blurred vision, body pains in general, and insomnia (another frequently mentioned complaint). The psychological burden of having to run a household on a meagre budget makes housework appear even heavier than otherwise. Lata (33 years) describes it:

I get exhausted doing the housework. Nor can I lift heavy weights. I always feel that I am unwell and want to just lie down and sleep. Walking a lot and climbing stairs makes me tired. I always ate well and never had a problem of weakness. But in the last two to three years, I have been having this problem. . . Perhaps it is due to my worrying about all the members of the family, looking after them, their food and school, trying to make the house run on one person's earnings . . . probably this is why I am weak ...

Women find it difficult to overcome their weakness, which is a realistic assessment of their situation in the context of space availability in the city, and the constraints on their ability to upgrade the quality of shelter. *Ashaktapana* due to housework (intensified by the psychological burden of catering to the needs of household members) is accepted as an inexorable part of their lives, of which they will be rid only when the life leaves their bodies. The only relief that women see for themselves is when their daughters reach pubertal age and are taken out of school at this age so they can share in the burden of housework. Daughters' educational needs are secondary even in the eyes of their mothers who are themselves disadvantaged. Although most women want to see their daughters go on to lead better lives than themselves, and acknowledge that education is a key to a better future, it is only in those households where women have gone to high school that daughters are kept in school beyond the age of 13 or so. Less educated women (who also belong to relatively more deprived households) seem unable to sustain their daughters in school, and take their help in housework, in care of younger children, or management of the house when they themselves are in income-earning activities or, alternatively, send them out for jobs pending the arrangement of their marriages.

The somatization of stress would seem to be evident in the way some women speak about *ashaktapana*, tension, and body pains, particularly pain of the lower back ('My back feels as though it will break'). Women use the word *tensun* to describe the mental distress they have to suffer in this regard. They speak of brooding when alone in the house, and the consequent neglect of their own health due to the feeling of despair ('Since I brood, I don't notice things about myself '). Weakness or *ashaktapana* is itself seen as a cause of brooding and 'bad thoughts' (*vaayeet vichaar*; 'what would happen to my children if something were to happen to me'). Sometimes it is almost a death wish, as symbolized in the phrase 'I wish I could just sleep and never get up'. Brooding may also be a cause of domestic accidents, as in the case of one woman whose sari caught fire as she sat before the burning kitchen stove totally lost in her own gloom after a brutal beating from her husband. Lack of sufficient time and physical rest to recover from accidents or sickness episodes further exacerbate feelings of *ashaktapana* and keep the vicious link between *ashaktapana*, depression, and the feeling of having lost control. Women speak of feelings of frustration and despair over having to put up with their intermittent bouts of sickness, their persistent aches and pains, the feeling of being debilitated in the midst of so much domestic responsibility, and yet being able to do nothing about it. 'I feel so weak, but I cannot afford to buy milk for my tea.' They speak of fears that their symptoms of vaginal itching or discharge could mean cancer or some terrible tumour, about which they feel they neither know what to do nor are in a position to do anything anyway. 'I can't go to the doctor, because he will say take this or that tonic and there is no money to buy these things. So it is better not to go at all.'

Women's feelings of weakness are rooted in their poor nutritional status. However, they themselves do not easily admit to suffering from any nutritional deficiencies. In their own eyes, their food is adequate in quantity and quality even when they suffer from chronic illnesses like TB and are prescribed better food to be able to ingest the powerful antibiotics. Nor are they conscious of the implications of their poor diet during pregnancy. The importance of diet and nutritional supplements during lactation is poorly understood by them, although several say that they are generally aware that a diet rich in greens and fruits has benefits. Only a few of the women mention that neglect during childhood and during pregnancies could be a deep-rooted cause of their weakness.

Women's state of under-nutrition can be gleaned from their life histories. The narratives describe a continuous experience of poverty in the natal family followed by poverty in the husband's home. Over and above poverty during childhood and there being simply too little food to go around, early death of a parent sometimes exacerbates this neglect. When women describe a continuous existence of poverty, they do not generally make any connection with physical debility. It is significant that despite probing, not a single woman mentioned any conscious experience of unequal food sharing between girls and boys in the natal home. Despite the poverty, the happiest memories for almost all the women are childhood memories of growing up in the natal home.

Poverty in the husband's home combines with cultural expectations of what constitutes a proper wife and daughter-in-law, to determine food intake. In the early years of marriage, the husband is often unemployed or unstably employed, and dependent upon the pooled earnings of his father and brother(s). So the young wife must play out her pregnancies, which follow in quick succession during these early years, as best as she can. Where he is employed and contributing to the family expenses, it is culturally impermissible for him to be showing interest in his wife's eating habits or in the allocation of food in the household by his mother. Even where parents-in-law are affectionate and supportive (and this is not rare), the importance of diet during pregnancy and lactation is simply not understood.

All women say it is not possible for them to make a separate dietary provision during pregnancy, despite problems of vomiting, and most find it natural to have eaten minuscule quantities during their pregnancies due to vomiting, giddy spells, and disinclination for food. Some of the more extreme cases describe themselves as having subsisted on tea and *pau* (bread made from refined flour and bought cheap from the market) throughout their pregnancies. Detailed probing into eating habits reveals a 30 per cent deficiency in caloric and protein intake.

Visits to private health providers in the neighbourhood for vomiting and giddiness during pregnancy may be sanctioned by the decision makers in the husband's home, since these symptoms are seen as pathological if they persist. Doctors' prescriptions that special or more nutritious food be eaten during pregnancy are ignored, and only prescriptions of pills to stop the vomiting are acted upon. Where, additionally, tonics and *takat golis* (tablets for strength) are prescribed, they are not bought, both for reasons of expense and because it is not becoming of a woman to be seen to be hungry and to eat 'a lot', since women's experience of the tonics is that they increase the appetite (in-laws and even husbands closely watch the amount of food the young wife eats, and 'eating too much' can bring on negative reactions). Tonics are also seen as making women fat, also a sign of eating too much, and thus drawing negative attention to oneself in a situation of economic precariousness. Even the vitamin supplements given free by municipal hospitals to antenatal women are not always consumed.

Women are not supposed to make demands on the resources of the husband's home. Short of being admitted to the hospital for rest, supervision, or saline administration (which some of the women report doing with the husband's support under the doctor's insistence), all advice (to eat special foods or reduce housework) other than the most minimal medical intervention (anti-vomiting pills) is not acted upon either by the woman concerned or supported by other members of the family. The woman's status within the household simply does not permit this preferential treatment.

But the most efficient self-censors are the women themselves, who do not easily admit to eating less than they should. When households have to be run on slender and uncertain earnings, women's early socialization leads them first to minimize their own food intake. Women are conditioned to give greater priority to providing for the needs of children and husband over their own needs and their responsibility for their own health. Women need both relative freedom from poverty and tremendous support from the husband/his family to be able to act on advice regarding their own health, particularly during their pregnancies and lactating periods. Men in these communities are socialized into thinking that their own needs and pleasures come before those of their families, and their earnings frequently go into buying liquor and marketed snacks for themselves, leaving wives to run the household on extremely slender budgets. Even when it is possible for women to provide better food for themselves, the notion that a household is built upon a woman's sacrifice confirms to all men that this is what they have a right to expect. Ideologically, redistribution where women are the takers is not accepted either by them or by others in the household. Even when women are the earners, they do not stake claim to their earnings, not even when the situation makes it imperative as during pregnancy or lactation. Since others' needs cannot be denied, and even the drunk and unemployed husband must get his food first, redistribution whereby women too get a greater share must await a much more bountiful scenario.

As regards *ashaktapana* in relation to pregnancy and childbirth, a number of associations emerge from the narratives, which give us insights into the social context of long-standing reproductive morbidities. Most women start childbearing early and do not know about the physiological changes during pregnancy, and the need for continuous monitoring and improved diet. Households have the fixed notion that the hospital is to be accessed only in the seventh month, i.e. when registration officially begins (even then, compliance is mainly for the tetanus toxoid injections and urine and blood tests, whilst other prescriptive supports such as tonics are mostly ignored or are taken haphazardly, as elaborated earlier). This may partly be rooted in the cultural practice of the pregnant woman being taken to her natal home in the seventh month to stay there for the remainder of the pregnancy; indirectly, therefore, her well-being during pregnancy and delivery is the responsibility of her parents. It is only when women experience major problems, such as acute swelling of the body, sudden pain, sudden and heavy bleeding, or unbearable weakness of the kind that keeps them in bed, that they seek health care before the seventh month. The reasons for this are a combination of ignorance about the dangers of pregnancy in a state of anaemia, a wait-and-watch approach, the belief that childbirth is a natural process which should not be needlessly medicalized, as well as the hesitancy to spend money.

Women who make the strongest association between problems during pregnancy and the onset of a chronic feeling of *ashaktapana* are those who have experienced spontaneous abortions, perinatal child loss, or delivered stillborn babies. Around half the women in this subgroup have experienced perinatal child loss or spontaneous abortions. By contrast, women who had to be admitted to a public hospital or a private nursing home early in their pregnancy on account of complications, were able to bolster their body reserves through injections, tablets (*golis*), and saline drip (referred to as *glucose* in Marathi) given during hospitalization.

In some cases successive spontaneous abortions, stillbirths, or perinatal deaths follow invasive measures such as *pishwi saaf* (literally, cleaning of the 'bag' or uterus), which is sometimes resorted to as a fertility-inducing measure when young wives do not conceive within two or three months of marriage and mothers-in-law claim that this is a problem of infertility. It is a commonly held belief in this community that *pishwi saaf* is a panacea for many ills. In a city, it is only when even *pishwi saaf* does not work that holy men and temples are visited to ask for the boon of a child. Even 12-year-olds may be subjected to this procedure, as happened to Pushpa who was married at 10 and brought to her husband's house at 12 upon attaining menarche. When by 13 she had still not become pregnant, her mother-in-law took her to the municipal hospital for a *pishwi saaf*.

Despite the doctor's advice against it, saying that I was too young for it and that I would conceive in due course, and his warning that future pregnancies may become difficult to sustain, I was made to undergo this procedure at my in-laws' insistence. My first pregnancy did not go beyond the seventh month. Because of the *pishwi saaf* my stomach pains started. . . After the delivery the doctor had told me that the mouth of the cervix (*pishwi la tond*) had expanded and that the next baby may not be able to stay inside easily. And that if I did heavy work or went out too much, I would have a miscarriage. He warned that if I became pregnant again, I would have to be very careful after the delivery. He also stitched up the *pishwi* and advised us against intercourse (*sambandh*) for one and a half years.

Pushpa went on to suffer two perinatal child losses, both cases of premature births. In all, she had seven pregnancies.[5] Among women with an early history of unsuccessful pregnancies, the pregnancies that were brought to full term were those that were medically monitored from the early months.

Foetal wastage, leading to a progressive problem of *ashaktapana*, may also be the result when ignorance among young mothers combines with physiological factors. There is considerable ignorance among women of this community of what might be the danger signs in early and late pregnancy. Nanda (24 years), married to a kinsman at the age of 15 and pregnant with her first child within three months of marriage, was brought to her natal home by her parents and registered at a private maternity home in the seventh month. In the eighth month she developed a sudden severe pain in her abdomen. Ignorant of what to expect, she describes herself as having tried to suppress the pain by pressing hard on her abdomen. She stayed in this position and did not tell anyone about the problem. When the pain subsided a few hours later and she noticed that the child did not seem to move, she told her parents who panicked and took her to the hospital. The child was found to be dead and was delivered using forceps (those might have been labour pains, and it may have been a case of obstructed labour leading to hypoxia). After this experience, Nanda went through four spontaneous abortions, all in their second trimester, and finally brought only two pregnancies to term resulting in two live children, after which she underwent sterilization. Nanda complains of a constant feeling of *ashaktapana*, she gets tired easily, and gets a pain in her chest when she exerts herself. Her strength is at its lowest ebb during her monthly periods. She reports visiting a local health provider every month, for administration of two bottles of glucose intravenously to treat the weakness and to help her cope with her menstrual periods.

Women describe post-delivery weakness (*balantarog*) as something that can be brought on by several reasons: lack of blood in the body, giddiness, TB, mental tension due to lack of access to good food, or ill-treatment by the mother-in-law, or due to the husband's drinking and violence against the wife. From the narratives, yet other causes may be gleaned for post-delivery weakness, such as when a woman gives birth to a second or third daughter, or to a weak or sickly child, or to a stillborn child, or faces perinatal child loss. Spontaneous abortions, too, could result in neglect and ill-treatment with the resultant mental stress.

From the narratives, the experience of *balantarog* emerges as a nightmare which every woman dreads, and which many women actually die of if not supported emotionally and financially through access to prompt health care by their parents.

Women particularly stress the mental trauma involved, which they refer to as *dimaag mey jhatkaa* (a state of shock). Many women start observing fasts voluntarily, they grow progressively thinner, and there is a death wish at work. 'If I have to die, let me die. I will do what is expected of me and it doesn't matter if I die in the process.' They become reckless and start lifting heavy weights in their precarious state of health, such as filling large water containers at the public tap and carrying them home, or bathing or working in cold water such as washing the household's clothes, or eating very small meals. All these activities are traditionally proscribed for post-partum women as the root cause of later ill-health.

The crucial importance to the young mother of bringing her pregnancy to full term and of delivering a live child which survives, is poignant in more ways than one. Whereas municipal hospitals keep a woman for up to three or four days if she delivers a live infant, she is sent home in one day in the case of infant/foetal loss. Where the foetal loss takes place at home, and where it occurs successively, a health facility may not be accessed, and even when a woman receives care, she generally goes back to her husband's home directly, and is generally put to work immediately whether it is a joint household—this is particularly so in the case of young couples who cannot afford to be on their own—or a nuclear household where she must perforce shoulder the burden of house management. It is only in the case of the first pregnancy that she may be taken back to her mother's home where she gets the rest and mental peace to recover. Within a few months of her return after an unsuccessful pregnancy, the woman is usually pregnant again. Husbands who are willing to wait for 45 days after a live birth to resume sex with their wives, are not willing to wait at all after a foetal or infant loss. Much of the debility and *ashaktapana* that such women with problematic pregnancy histories complain about, have their roots in this cultural context of motherhood.

After my first child was born dead, I was brought home to my parents' place in a state of tremendous weakness. I had become very thin. After one month my husband took me back to my in-laws. The people there were nice to me for just two days. Then they started mistreating me. My mother-in-law said just what came to her, and when my husband came back home from work she filled his years with complaints about me and urged him to beat me. He would get enraged with me and would beat me. It happened every day. Whenever I heated water for my bath, my mother-in-law would taunt me, 'Look at her heating water for her bath as though she had a live child.' I would get angry and have my bath in cold water from the *matka* (there was no tap in the house and water was stored in earthen pots). I started a fever. One day my father came to see me and took me to a private doctor. I was given capsules for *takat* (strength). They never gave me enough food to eat and I was often forced to go hungry. Despite all these torments, I never told anyone in my *maike* (mother's house). Within fifteen days of my coming back home my husband resumed sex. I was so weak that it hurt. But I never thought of protesting. It was part of the daily beating and starvation. Six months later I found that I was pregnant again. (Nanda about her first pregnancy when she was 15 years old).

Three unsuccessful pregnancies followed, each time accompanied by profuse bleeding and giddiness. But no health care was accessed. Further abuse and ill-treatment at the hands of the mother-in-law, threats of divorce, pressure on her to demand money from her father, and brutal beating by the husband, all continued until the next pregnancy. During her fourth pregnancy, which was being medically monitored by her natal family, Nanda says:

. . . my husband continued to threaten me with divorce if the baby did not stay in my stomach for nine months, or if it turned out to be a girl. He threatened alternatively to beat me and to divorce me. I lived in dread. More than him, it was his mother who kept his attention on me in this manner.

While *balantarog* is the extreme expression of post-delivery weakness, such weakness can also occur due to resumption of heavy household duties in a state of general under-nutrition. Whenever women have got the mandatory post-delivery 45 days rest, it has been due to supportive natal homes.

Often, foetal loss may be attended by severe physical and mental trauma, such as a violent assault on the pregnant wife by the husband who loses his self-control due to the influence of liquor or who is egged on by family conflicts. Or the violence may be perpetrated by another male member of the family such as the husband's brother who becomes the violent face of the conjugal home. In such situations, women suffer heavy blood loss and may have to undergo further invasive procedures at whatever health facility—generally where too many questions will not be asked—is accessed by panicking family members.

Maya (32 years), married to a kinsman when she was 15 and the victim of harassment by her parents-in-law for her inability to take complete responsibility for all the housework of the joint family, gave birth to two children in quick succession (a girl whose birth weight was 1.5 kg and a boy who weighed 2 kg at birth), and was pregnant for a third time within two months of the second child's birth.

One day, when I was eight months pregnant, my husband in a fit of rage due to the constant fights between my in-laws and I, took out his anger on me. He pushed me down a steep flight of 16 steps outside the house. The child in my stomach died. My husband picked me up and carried me in. At that time I didn't feel any pain. But I was aghast that my husband, too, had left my side and had joined my tormentors. But he was weeping as he carried me in and told me that he had done it in anger, unable to bear the conflict around him. The next day a terrible pain started in my stomach which lasted for two days and then, just as suddenly, it stopped. My husband took me to a private nursing home in Worli. But they wouldn't take me in because I looked bad and they didn't want a problem. It was only when one of my husband's aunts pleaded with them telling them that we had just come to Bombay from the village, that the hospital agreed to admit me. I was taken to a cot and made to lie down. A doctor came up to me and carelessly looked at my eyes and face and said, 'if you don't deliver, we will do a caesarian and take the baby out.' At midnight, the senior lady doctor came in. She examined me thoroughly and said something angrily to the doctor in English. On her instructions, I was given three bottles of glucose and an injection for the pain. My pain stopped and the dead child in my stomach was taken out with the help of forceps. If that senior doctor had not come when she did, I would have died. . . I became pregnant immediately after that. It was a boy and he was 1.5 kg. The delivery was normal. . .

HEALTH CARE FOR *ASHAKTAPANA*

It is clear that *ashaktapana* or weakness as an illness is a very real part of the lives of these women, and is perceived by them as being among their most pervasive health problems. Although some researchers have drawn unilinear links between weakness and white discharge (Patel 1994; Bang and Bang 1994) and others have highlighted the 'worry pains' syndrome (Emmel and O'Keefe 1996), this chapter has tried to demonstrate that adverse reproductive health history, stress, and poor diet resulting in anaemia all reinforce each other in making for *ashaktapana*. Women's voices describing *ashaktapana* permit us to see that while poverty is the overarching condition determining their lives, the unequal gender relations and the cultural contexts within which women play their reproductive roles constitute an important window through which to view states of wellness and illness. And the fact that they speak of *ashaktapana* as a complex of feelings of physical illness along with feelings of mental exhaustion, makes this health problem symbolic of poor women's overall situation.

This cultural and economic context creates conditions for the onset of *ashaktapana* while women are still very young, sometimes as early as the first pregnancy. Subsequent pregnancies and growing household and child care responsibilities, often inadequately supported financially and emotionally by their husbands, worsen the illness. Among those with the experience of sterilization, which again comes early in the lives of these women, the illness seems to get cast into a lifelong mould.

It is possibly for this reason that women hardly report accessing doctors for this problem. Since the symptoms have no unambiguous outward manifestations of any morbidity, and since women's cultural conditioning impels them to carry out their household duties whatever the difficulties, they are not perceived by other family members to be ill for as long as they are not in a state of total collapse. Routine health-seeking behaviour for *ashaktapana*, as for other problems such as chest pain, blood pressure, and vaginal discharge, remains episodic and haphazard, and only those women with some family support would go to a doctor at all. Such a doctor must necessarily be someone located very close to the woman's house, since her services can be spared, both in her own eyes and in the eyes of the family, only for the barest minimum time. Local doctors dispensing allopathic medicines (whatever their qualifications) are resorted to.

Of the 22 women complaining of persistent *ashaktapana*, only seven reported ever having accessed a local doctor for this specific problem. They were not given any clinical check up and were treated on the basis of verbal descriptions alone. These providers generally dispense allopathic pills for one day and/or give injections (both administered without any explanation or other factual information such as the name of the drug), for which a fee is charged, and the patient is asked to come back the next day. If the acute symptoms persist, she may go back the next day, but more often than not, she does not go. Since the fees and medicines/injections are on a daily basis, it gives the sufferer the chance to decide how far she wants to go with the 'cure'. The providers are therefore seen as being friendly and understanding, and some even permit credit. But, as the women say, 'Even he has to be paid some day', so visits are kept to the minimum and take place only when the distress is so acute that housework becomes impossible. When the problem is seen as severe, a few bottles of tonic may be consumed, if available free of cost from a government health facility. In extreme cases, intravenous glucose might be seen as the only alternative.

While the dimension of nutrition is totally ignored by both the women and other household members and that of rest neglected in overcoming illness symptoms brought on by weakness, attention is paid when *ashaktapana* is accompanied by heavy bleeding during menstrual cycles, complications during pregnancy, or surgeries (as, for example, sterilization operations). The bolstering of women's survival by and large takes place only when they approach the health system in a state of virtual crisis, on which occasions they are administered saline intravenously or, in extreme cases, given blood transfusions. The narratives reveal that almost every major contact with hospitals—during pregnancy crises, deliveries, and sterilizations—is an occasion for administration of a few bottles of glucose.

Attempts at seeking relief from *ashaktapana* during the post-delivery period are mediated by success or failure of the outcome of pregnancy. Adverse outcomes, i.e. foetal or infant loss, birth of a sickly child or birth of a girl child successively, may result in withdrawal of sympathy, medical attention, rest, and care. In frustration, many women resort to self-flagellation through overwork, reducing food intake, and recklessness in self-care.

There is thus a rank order in the perception of problems relating to women's health, which influences when health care will be sought. Sudden onset of problems to do with menstruation, pregnancy, and delivery rank highest. Next in importance for contact with the health system comes sterilization (which reflects the family's acceptance that the family size and gender composition of offspring is as desired). Other reproductive illnesses such as white discharge, low abdominal pain, etc. come last. Health care seeking in this case takes place only when any of these sets of problems puts women into dire straits, i.e. when they are unable any more to carry out their household responsibilities.

CONCLUSION

The foregoing discussion of *ashaktapana* highlights the importance of accessibility, quality of care, and understanding by providers of the prevailing perceptions of illness and disease among specific populations, in the planning of medical services for them. Particularly noteworthy here is the need to take antenatal services to women very early in the pregnancy. Equally, it highlights the importance of addressing the issues of social counselling and public education (desirable age at first pregnancy, understanding the various stages in a pregnancy, awareness of danger signs, importance of nutrition, impact of mental and physical violence and cruelty). The narratives point quite clearly to the importance of awareness raising about adequate and nutritive diets for women, both to meet general requirements of body energy, and in specific situations like pregnancy, lactation, and morbidity episodes. The importance of rest, accompanied by a lowered psychological burden of responsibility for housework, at least during the critical episodes related to their reproductive role, are also of equal importance. Complementing these is the need for more supportive attitudes on the part of men and their greater awareness of their own responsibilities, for both women's reproductive health and freedom from unduly high stress levels.

It is evident that efforts in these directions must concentrate as much on family members—the husband in a nuclear family, mothers-in-law and sisters-in-law in joint families—as on the woman herself. It becomes crucial for awareness raising strategies to balance an other-centred slant with a self-centred one, because ideologically and culturally a woman is not supposed to be seen as caring for herself. Fortunately, our observations suggest that supportive mothers-in-law and sisters-in-law do exist in the community. Among men, however, self-centredness is deep rooted. Seeking supportive roles from husbands/fathers/brothers in the fulfilment of the health of women of the household requires change in this attitude among men.

In sum, lower nutritional intake, gender relations, individual behavioural factors, and institutional arrangements all seem to work in tandem to add to the incidence and severity of *ashaktapana* and mental stress among women during their reproductive years.

Notes

1. The study on which this paper is based has been made possible by a grant from the Ford Foundation (grant no. 95-1012 to the Centre for Social and Technological Change, Mumbai). Thanks are due to Michael Koenig of the Ford Foundation, New Delhi, for his sustained interest in the study; to Sujata Khandekar of CORO for facilitating access to the area; to Kamal Bansode and Maya Pawar, both residents of the area, for assistance in investigation; and to the women in the study for consenting to be interviewed. An earlier draft of the paper was presented at the IUSSP seminar on Cultural Perspectives in Reproductive Health in South Africa in June 1997. Apart from useful discussions at the seminar, the authors have benefited from comments from Bert Pelto, Peggy Bentley, Shireen Jejeebhoy, Zoe Matthews, and the anonymous reviewer(s) of the manuscript.

2. In discussions following the first draft of this paper, it has been repeatedly pointed out to us that weakness as a reported problem may be found even among middle-class women and among adolescent girls with no experience of economic hardship. Counsellors working in urban settings, and counting middle- and upper middle-class women among their clientele, report encountering this illness. Doctors working in multicultural societies say that they have found it to be a peculiarly 'Indian' problem as compared with clients belonging to other racial groups, e.g. among Gujarati women working in family-run grocery stores in South Africa (William Pick, personal communication). While wrong eating, lack of sufficient exercise and, among shopkeepers perhaps, long hours of work suggest themselves as possible causes, the problem is intriguing.

3. The recurring reference among the women in this study to sterilization, as virtually symbolic of their weakened condition, raises two questions for further research. One relates to the physical and social conditions under which this intervention takes place

among this class of women, the overwhelming majority of whom resort to municipal health services to meet this need. Is the procedure performed under hygienic and sterile conditions? Further, are women counselled before and after the procedure, along with their mothers-in-law/husbands who are the main sources of emotional and economic support? Given the anaemic status of these women and the heavy burden of housework they go back to, what is the advice regarding post-operative rest and care that is given by service providers? The other question that calls for analysis relates to the primacy accorded by the women to sterilization in the order of explanation, over poor nutritional history or unfavourable pregnancy histories. It is important to keep in mind that women desire to put a halt to their fertility, and that sterilization is seen as the only option, since the general opinion regarding IUDs is an unfavourable one. Nevertheless, they see sterilization as the beginning of the decline in their health. Is it that sterilization is seen as a negation of what it is to be a woman (i.e. fertile), or as an uneasy compromise between this fertility and the economic difficulties of coping with its consequences? Or is it that household dynamics and unequal gender relations (among the deep-rooted causes of *ashaktapana*) are so internalized that they elude identification, while sterilization is seen as an 'external' intervention, something that is outside of the received culture and therefore an avoidable but necessary evil? The symbolic dichotomy between the internal and external can be seen, in a different context, in Chhaya's (27 years) statement, 'What is the option to marriage? Where one man beats you, a hundred men can lay their hands on you and a hundred women can speak evil about you. Here, at least there is only one person to contend with.' Or, when women complain to others about the violence meted out by their husbands, the common response is, 'Why are you complaining? It is only your own husband who is doing this to you. Do you want a man from outside to come to beat you?'

4. Manda (35 years), who works as a domestic help in several houses to support the family since her husband (an alcoholic and advanced TB sufferer) is at home, says, 'I have *ashaktapana* for the past three years. The reason for this is exhaustion due to too much housework. Due to this weakness I always feel ill and want to be left alone to lie down and sleep all the time. I feel physically ill all the time. But I am also mentally worried. I keep worrying about my husband's drinking, whether my son will do well in school and get a better life, my daughters, their marriage, the expenses involved . . . Due to the weakness, when I go out in the sun or walk much, I get *chakkar* (feel giddy) and blackness in front of my eyes. I also get back pain, and pain in the thighs, calves and heels. I have low blood pressure for the last two years and I don't sleep well at night. This makes my hands and legs tremble.'

Nandita (35 years), who has had ten pregnancies and who makes paper bags at home to earn a little extra money to supplement her husband's income from a contract job, counts *ashaktapana* as one of her major problems. 'From the very start I have not been careful about my health and now I have also had lots of children. This has made me even more weak. Ever since I started having children I have been weak. Because of my weakness, I have in turn not cared much about eating and drinking and before I knew it I had 10 children, five of whom died and 5 are living. Now because the children are growing, I am even less able to care for my health and diet. This is the reason for my *ashaktapana*.'

5. 'We did not have *sambandh* as he had advised, and I got pregnant only two years later. From the third month, I started getting vomiting and giddy spells, but no other problems. I did the lighter chores in the house and did not lift heavy weights. My mother-in-law and sister-in-law (husband's sister) did that. This pregnancy lasted for eight months. In the eighth month the pains started. My mother-in-law who was living with us came with me

to Rajawadi Hospital. Within a hour I delivered. The child died within an hour of birth. I don't know the cause. They kept me in hospital for one day and I was sent home after that. I rested for two days, and after that I had to resume all the housework. I was deeply sad. But my family members consoled me saying, "So what if the child died, you still have the first child. Whatever had to happen happened. What will you gain from continuing to grieve? Stop crying and concentrate on the living child." I did as I was told. I bottled up my sorrow within me and worked hard at my household chores. Within a year I was pregnant for the third time.'

Pushpa also talks of her history of malnutrition. 'My mother having died early, my diet was never anybody's concern. I was always poorly fed, often going hungry, eating whatever I could and whenever. I never learnt to care for my health. . .'

And about her many pregnancies, 'The reason for my weakness are my repeated and quick pregnancies. During my pregnancies and after my diet was very poor. Often I just didn't get any food to eat. Because of my circumstances I couldn't eat properly then. Now I get more to eat but am unable to do so. I am able to cook and feed everyone else but cannot benefit from it myself. I was always weak but feel that I have worsened in the last 2 years.'

References

Bang, R. A. *et al.* (1989), 'High prevalence of gynecological diseases in rural Indian women', *The Lancet*, 14, 1 (8629): 85–8.

Bang, R., and Bang, A. (1994), 'Women's perceptions of white vaginal discharge; ethnographic data from rural Maharashtra', in J. Gittleshohn, M. Bentley, and P. Pelto *et al.* (eds.), *Listening to Women Talk about Their Health: Issues and Evidence from India*, New Delhi: Har-Anand Publications, pp. 79–94.

Baroda Citizens' Council, Child in Need Institute, SEWA-Rural and Streehitakarini (1995), 'Prevalence of clinically detectable gynaecological morbidity in India: Results of four community based studies', (mimeo).

Bhatia, J. C., Cleland, J., Bhagvan, L., and Rao, N. S. N. (1997), 'Levels and determinants of gynaecological morbidity in a district of South India', *Studies in Family Planning*, 28 (2): 95–103.

Brabin, L., Kemp, J., Obunge, J. *et al.* (1995), 'Reproductive tract infections and abortions among adolescent girls in rural Nigeria', *The Lancet* 4, 345 (8945): 300–4.

Dixon-Mueller, R., and Wasserheit, J. N. (1991), *The Culture of Silence: Reproductive Tract Infections among Women in the Third World*, New York: International Women's Health Coalition.

Emmel, N. D., and O'Keefe, P. (1996), 'Participatory analysis for redefining health delivery in a Bombay slum', *Journal of Public Health Medicine*, 18 (3): 301–7.

Germaine, A., Holmes, K. K., Piot, P., and Wasserheit, J. N. (1992), *Reproductive Tract Infections: Global Impact and Priorities for Women's Reproductive Health*, New York: Plenum Press.

Gittleshohn, J., Bentley, M., Pelto, P. *et al.* (eds.) (1994). *Listening to Women Talk about Their Health: Issues and Evidence from India*, New Delhi: Har-Anand Publications.

Khattab, H. A. S. (1992), *The Silent Endurance: Social Conditions of Women's Reproductive Health in Rural Egypt*, Cairo: UNICEF.

Koenig, M., Jejeebhoy, S., Singh, S., and Sridhar, S. (1996), 'Undertaking community-based research on the prevalence of gynaecological morbidity: Lessons from India', Paper presented at IUSSP Seminar on Innovative Approaches to the Assessment of Reproductive Health, Manila, Philippines, September 24–27.

Narayan, N., and Srinivasan, S. (1994), 'Some experiences in the rapid assessment of women's perceptions of illness in rural and urban areas of Tamil Nadu', in J. Gittlesohn, M. Bentley, and P. Pelto *et al.* (eds.), *Listening to Women Talk about Their Health: Issues and Evidence from India*, New Delhi: Har-Anand Publications.

Oomman, N. (1996), 'Poverty and pathology: Comparing rural Rajasthani women's ethnomedical models with biomedical models of reproductive morbidity: Implications for women's health in India', Dissertation thesis submitted to Johns Hopkins University, Baltimore, USA.

Patel, P. (1994), 'Illness beliefs and health seeking behavior of the Bhil women of Panchmahal District, Gujarat State', in J. Gittlesohn, M. Bentley, and P. Pelto *et al.* (eds.), *Listening to Women Talk about their Health: Issues and Evidence from India*, New Delhi: Har-Anand Publications.

Ramasubban, R., Crook, N., and Singh, B. (1990), 'Educational approach to leprosy control: A study of knowledge, attitudes and practices in two poor slum localities in Bombay', Bombay: Centre for Social and Technological Change.

Ramasubban, R., Crook, N., and Singh. B. (1996), 'Urban health and researcher-NGO coalition in Bombay', in P. R. Jimenez and K. T. Silva (eds.), *Towards Better Health: Building Partnerships between Health Scientists and Social Scientists in the Asia Pacific Region*, Manila: De La Salle University.

Streehitakarini (1995), 'Gynaecological diseases and perceptions about them in a Bombay slum' (mimeo).

Wasserheit, J. *et al.* (1989), 'Reproductive tract infections in a family planning population in rural Bangladesh', *Studies in Family Planning*, 20 (2): 69–80.

Younis, N. H. *et al.* (1993), 'A community study of gynecological and related morbidities in rural Egypt', *Studies in Family Planning*, 24 (3): 175–86.

2

Nutrition and Reproduction: The Socio-cultural Context of Food Behaviour in Rural South India

INGE HUTTER

INTRODUCTION

This chapter is about the social and cultural context of nutritional behaviour of women in rural South India. It focuses on women's nutrition during pregnancy, delivery, and the first month after delivery, and makes a comparison between biomedical recommendations and the practices and explanations of Indian women.

Research on women's food behaviour during pregnancy has found that in many developing countries[1] women reduce their food intake at the end of pregnancy contrary to prevalent biomedical recommendations. Quantitative evidence of a reduction in food intake during the last trimester of pregnancy has, however, been limited. A number of studies have argued that the reason behind this custom is that women hope to have a small child and thus an easy delivery (cf. Hytten 1980; Ministry of National Planning and UNICEF 1984; Kusin *et al.* 1984; de Vries 1987; Djazayery *et al.* 1992), while other studies (Pool 1983; Nichter and Nichter 1983) have explored other more complex reasons.

Nichter and Nichter have criticized the explanation of reduced food intake during the last trimester, stating that it 'tend(s) to underestimate pregnant women's concern for the health of their babies' and 'tends to gloss over a complex of ideas associated with notions of ethnophysiology and preventive health' (1983, p. 236). They have argued that women reduce their food intake because they want to have a large, not a small, child. In their research in South India, these authors found that most women associated a reduction in food intake in the last trimester of pregnancy with a large rather than a small child. If the women eat too much, there would not be enough room for the child to grow.

I argue here that even this conclusion is too simple: other factors play a role and relationships are even more complex. Among women in the study population, the first reason to reduce food intake at the end of pregnancy is not related to size or health of the child, but to feelings of unwell-being of the women themselves. I also discuss practices during the post-partum period and the local meaning associated with women's health during this time.

THE RESEARCH PROJECT

The present chapter is part of a collaborative project between PRC (Population Research Centre) Groningen and NIDI (Netherlands Interdisciplinary Demographic Institute) The Hague, the Netherlands, which seeks a better understanding of reproductive health and develops educational materials.[2] The general approach adopted by the project is a process-context approach which situates reproductive behaviour in the context of a woman's reproductive career, particularly during delivery and the post-partum, and relates it to women's beliefs and perceptions of the body, social pressures and to the general economic and social constraints of their lives.

This chapter is based on findings from a longitudinal study of nutrition and health during pregnancy and well-being of children, which included fieldwork of 20 months duration (December 1990 to August 1992) in 11 villages in Dharwad taluka, Karnataka, India. A total of 186 women were followed throughout pregnancy up to one month after delivery (Hutter 1994). The villages are all located in the western part of Dharwad District, in the semi-malnad area, which is a rugged, hilly landscape at higher elevation, moderately forested, with moderate rainfall. Most villages are multi-religious and multicaste, with only a few consisting of one caste (e.g. the stone crushers). Most are accessible by road except for three villages, which cannot be reached by buses in the rainy season. A household census conducted in the beginning of 1991 showed that the total population amounted to almost 12,000 people with the population per village ranging from 110 to 4,000 people. The study population is poor; the level of literacy very low. Most women (82 per cent) had not received any formal education at all. The majority of the women are Hindus of various castes (86.0 per cent), while 10.2 per cent are Muslim. Another 3.2 per cent belong to the tribal people Gouli, and one woman is Christian.

Both quantitative and qualitative research methods were used. A census of 2,040 households reported the demographic and socio-economic characteristics of the total research population. From this census, women who might become pregnant during the course of the study were selected (women who were married, actually living with their husband and who had not yet undergone a sterilization). This group of potentially pregnant women ($N \pm 1000$) was followed on a monthly basis, with height, weight, and date of last period recorded at each visit. As soon as a woman reported a pregnancy, she was enrolled in the longitudinal study. A total of 186 women were enrolled in the study. Data on pregnancy histories, food intake and nutritional status of women, birth weight of children, as well as women's beliefs and perceptions were gathered through several surveys. Information on beliefs and women's perceptions were collected through regular visits, participant observation, in-depth interviews, and key informant interviews (for more details, see Hutter 1994).

Most of the women selected (65.4 per cent) were aged 14–24 years. The average parity (the number of live births) was 1.8, and 18 per cent were pregnant for the first time. The women married young—the average age at consummation of marriage was 15.7 years. Most women (69 per cent) lived in the joint family of their husbands. Women were light and short. They weighed on average 41 kg (± 4.6) before pregnancy; the average height was 151 cm (± 5.5). More than half of the women appeared to be malnourished even before they became pregnant (chronically energy deficient (CED) measured by the Body Mass Index: pre-pregnancy weight/height2). In addition, 62.3 per cent had Hb-levels ≤ 11.0 g/dl (which is the cutoff point for anaemia used by UNICEF India) (UNICEF 1991) in the last trimester of pregnancy.

FOOD INTAKE DURING PREGNANCY: BIOMEDICAL
RECOMMENDATIONS AND LOCAL PRACTICES

The diet of most of our respondents did not vary much, consisting of the same meal pattern and food items with some seasonal variation in the availability of vegetables and fruit. Especially among lower socio-economic status women, the variety of foods consumed was limited. The standard daily food pattern consisted of tea, a breakfast (if available and affordable), and two meals—a meal consists of *rotti* (bread) made of sorghum with vegetable curry or pulses, and rice plus curry. Milk was rarely consumed. Even if buffaloes or cows were available to the household, most milk was sold to the milk cooperative, leaving only a small quantity for use in the household. About 30 per cent of the study population was vegetarian. But even among non-vegetarian women, the actual consumption of chicken, fish, or mutton was very limited because of its expense. Eggs were eaten more commonly and the caste group Bovi, traditionally the fishermen, ate fish more frequently. The consumption of fruit was also low, despite the common availability of bananas and, in the months of April and May, mangoes. When asked about fruits eaten during pregnancy, women mentioned a number of different types; however, when asked how often they ate them, women reported eating fruits only three or four times during their entire pregnancy.

International standards recommend that pregnant women eat more than they normally do throughout their pregnancy, with an extra 285 kcal per day recommended (FAO/WHO 1985). This recommendation has been formulated based on a theoretical total energy cost during pregnancy of 85,000 kcal (Hytten and Leitch 1971), where women gain on average 12.5 kg during pregnancy and the average birth weight of children is 3.4 kg. Indian recommendations differ slightly; women weighing around 40 kg should consume 1,957 kcal plus 300 kcal extra during the last two trimesters of pregnancy (ICMR 1990).[3] Most of our respondents did not reach the recommended levels of energy intake—or even those of non-pregnant women. In addition, few women gained the theoretical average weight gain and the weights of their live born children were consistently below average. The average daily intake during pregnancy in general was 1,700 kcal, average weight gain 6.4 kg (± 3.2), and average birth weight of children 2,646 g (± 464). Twenty-six per cent of the children were of low birth weight (LBW < 2,500 g).

Among our study population, we found a trend of declining energy intake over the whole period of pregnancy. The biggest change took place between months five, six and seven and months eight and nine of pregnancy—energy intake declined from 1,749 kcal (± 312) to 1,662 kcal (± 279). The change in energy intake was apparently not related to ecologic or economic factors; intake during pregnancy was reduced regardless of season or time of year when the pregnancy took place. The major determinants of change in energy intake in our study were pre-pregnancy weight-for-height and length of last birth interval. Women who were better nourished before pregnancy were more likely to reduce energy intake than women who were undernourished. When stratified by two levels of chronic energy deficiency (CED), women in the undernourished group (BMI ≤ 18.4) hardly changed energy intake and remained at a level of energy intake around 1,660 kcal. The well-nourished women (BMI ≥ 18.5) showed a decline in energy intake from a level of more than 1,800 kcal in months five, six, and seven to 1,630 kcal in months eight and nine, an average reduction of 170 kcal. This finding might indicate that women realize—whether consciously or not—that there is a limit to reduction of energy intake during pregnancy: only women who can 'afford' to eat less actually do.

Biomedical recommendations also encourage pregnant women to eat a diverse range of foods, particularly those rich in proteins, vitamins, and minerals. Iron, obtained from foods such as beans, groundnuts, milk, meat, and dark green leafy vegetables, is especially important during pregnancy. It is recommended that the normal intake of protein of 1 g/kg be increased by 15 g during pregnancy, that intake of calcium reach at least 1,000 g/day, and intake of iron reach 38 mg/day. The respondents' diet deviated from biomedical recommendations with regard to most nutrients. The average daily intake of proteins throughout pregnancy totalled 47.3 g (± 7.34). Given an average pre-pregnancy weight of 41 kg, 74 per cent of the women in the study population achieved the recommended normal level of protein intake while only 11.4 per cent consumed an extra 15 g as recommended during pregnancy. Compared with other nutrients, the amount of proteins consumed was relatively high, which is probably related to women's daily consumption of *dal* and *gram*. The average daily intake of calcium throughout pregnancy amounted to 288 mg (± 118), which is much lower than the recommended intake of 1,000 g/day. The average daily intake of iron amounted to 24.7 mg (± 7.63). Only 4 per cent of women in our study achieved the recommended intake of 38 mg/day.

When asked what food items were added during pregnancy to their normal diet, most women reported they did not increase their intake significantly. Some women took extra buttermilk and curds in order to reduce the heat of pregnancy (see below) while others ate more vegetables during pregnancy, because they liked them and not for a specific health-related reason. In addition, 11.4 per cent of the women reported consumption of more green vegetables during pregnancy. Here, too, the main reason mentioned was that they liked them more, and a small number ($n=4$) associated increased intake of green vegetables with improvement of health of mother or child. These women generally explained that eating green vegetables increased the secretion of breastmilk. Given that 36.6 per cent of all multiparae women breastfed their previous child during pregnancy, it is probable that women consumed more green vegetables not for the benefits to the foetus but to increase milk lactation for the youngest child.

Several women reported that they just ate what they liked and, of course, what was available in the household. The affordability and availability of food in the household was one of the constraints on eating extra food. Many respondents reported that they wanted to drink more milk, curds, or buttermilk during pregnancy, but there was either no cow or buffalo in the household or no money to buy the milk. Women also reported similar constraints for the consumption of fruits. Even when economic circumstances were more favourable, pregnant women ate whatever the family ate. The pattern of food distribution within the family and the dependence of women on others for provision of food items represent further constraints on women's ability to eat extra food during pregnancy. Only after men and children finished their meals did women eat the food that was left over. In addition, most women were dependent on men (more than 80 per cent)—either the husband, father, or brother-in-law—or the mother-in-law (12 per cent) to bring food from the marketplace.

When asked whether women could request that their husbands or another person go to the marketplace to bring back a special food because they were pregnant, a giggle was usually the first response. Several women remarked, 'how can I ask?', their position in the household being one of paying respect to elders and their husbands. A few women, however, especially those living in a nuclear family, mentioned that they were able to ask their husbands to bring back a requested food item.[4]

Many women remarked that in their mother's house they ate better food than when they were with their husbands. The custom of 'sending' women to their mother's home during late pregnancy, and the fact that women go even at high parities, is thus positive for its effect on women's health. Almost 70 per cent of women in our sample left their husband's family in order to deliver in their mother's house (*tavaru mane*). Leaving in month seven (for some first pregnancies), or more typically in month eight or nine of pregnancy, women are able to rest more and eat better than they would in their husband's house. As the mother of one of the respondents said (a quarrel was going on between the families and the respondent had fled from her husband's house): 'How could she eat more? There the first preference is given to the husband.' Pressures to conform were felt more by women living in joint families rather than in nuclear families and also varied with parity. Women of lower parity, who were just married, who had to get used to a new family and had to prove their fertility, definitely experienced more psychological pressure.

LOCAL CATEGORIES OF FOOD AND THEIR PERCEIVED EFFECTS ON THE HEALTH OF PREGNANT WOMEN

Among the food items avoided during pregnancy are papaya (mentioned by 72 per cent of the respondents), fresh coconut (65 per cent), banana (46 per cent), white sesame (37 per cent), sweet potato (32 per cent), peanut (18 per cent), pumpkin (16 per cent), and jackfruit (10 per cent).[5] Although the kind of food items to be avoided were generally agreed on, the perceived consequences of consumption were more diverse. Some food items were believed to have one effect only. For example, all respondents related banana and fresh coconut to illnesses of the child after delivery. Perceived consequences of other food items, however, varied. Thirty per cent of the respondents classified papaya as 'hot' and to be avoided because it would induce a spontaneous abortion. A third of the respondents categorized the fruit with food items such as banana and fresh coconut, believed to have an adverse effect on the health of the child. A smaller group of women classified papaya with other 'hot' foods reporting that it causes either rashes and birthmarks on the skin of the child or possibly swelling in the body of the mother. These three effects, heating, childhood illnesses, and allergic reactions, are further discussed below.

The concept of heating (*ushna* in Hindi, *kaavu* in Kannada) is an integral part of the Ayurveda medical system, with food and other items being classified according to their effects on the human body. The dichotomy of hot versus cold is only one of the many potential attributes of food, and the avoidance of hot food is related to the ethnophysiology of pregnancy (Nichter and Nichter 1983). In general, pregnancy is believed to be a process of increasing heat in the body, which is felt as a burning sensation. One respondent described this sensation: 'My body is burning . . . like *kara* (chili) it is burning . . . it is burning inside the stomach and legs, from stomach to bottom; a burning sensation. Like chili powder.' During pregnancy this burning sensation in the body is considered to be quite normal; this includes a burning sensation with urination, burning eyes, and cracks in the feet. Since the child is growing, activity is taking place in the body, implying that heat is created. As one respondent explained: 'I went to the doctor, but the doctor said, "So now you are completing nine months of pregnancy, it is like that, it is normal." '

Too much heat, however, is considered to have adverse effects, including termination of pregnancy. Excess heat can be created by season (summertime), body constitution, or particular foods such as papaya which traditional birth attendants use to induce abortion. Too much heat can also be created by having sexual intercourse during pregnancy. Even more heat is created during intercourse if men have bad habits like smoking and drinking alcohol (which are considered to be extremely heating). In general, it is believed that sexual intercourse should stop after four or five months of pregnancy. Excess heat can also be created by allopathic medicines; tablets taken for headaches (Anacin) are associated with excess heat as are tetanus injections provided during pregnancy. Furthermore, hard work or carrying heavy things can create too much heat, especially during summertime.

Excessive heat is thought to be neutralized by eating foods which have a cooling quality (*tampu*) such as curds or buttermilk. Women who have spontaneous abortions, stillbirths, or severely malformed children are believed to have a hot body constitution. These women often take a special herbal medicine with cooling qualities to counterbalance the heat. The medicine is called *beevin rasa* and is a juice made of neem leaves with water that is taken every morning.

Some women avoid heating food items like papaya, sweet potato, jackfruit, pumpkin, or *ginna* because they are thought to lead to swelling and pain in the hands, legs, or face (*baavu*). These food items are said to cause *barsna*, a kind of allergy, and lead to rashes, pimples, prickly heat, or birthmarks on the skin of the child after delivery. The notion that the health status of the child is affected even after delivery is even more strongly evidenced by women's avoidance of banana and fresh coconut, which are believed to cause *barsna*. Food is *barsna* during specific time periods. During pregnancy, banana and fresh coconut are *barsna*, while in the period of lactation, other food items are considered to be *barsna*. The etiology is such that if women eat banana and fresh coconut, classified as *tampu*, during pregnancy they have a cooling effect on the body of the foetus (not on the body of the pregnant woman). If eaten, the child's body constitution is influenced, pro- voking cold-like symptoms and coughs, breathlessness, fever and fits, commonly identified as pneumonia. Moreover, the oil contents of sesame and peanut, and also of fresh coconut, lead to the same imbalance in body constitution. The illness *hotte andu*, evoked by specific foods intake during pregnancy, can occur during the whole period of childhood (up to 12 years).

Women's avoidance of certain foods and the addition of other foods to their diet during pregnancy are influenced by several key individuals, including the mother- in-law and the mother (each reported by about half of the respondents as influenc- ing their behaviour), neighbours (about one-fourth), and other family members (about one-third of the respondents). Very few women (*n*=3) mentioned a medical doctor or nurse. Women who were pregnant for the first time knew the foods they should not eat, but rarely knew why, while higher parity women were freer to choose which foods they ate and were less dependent than women of first parity on others' recommendations.

Social norms, however, are not necessarily predictive of actual behaviour, and rules about food avoidance were not always followed. For example, while the survey found that almost all women stated that they avoided bananas during pregnancy, in the interviews it became clear that more than 50 per cent ate banana during pregnancy. Conversely, some women reported avoiding banana during interviews whereas they had reported consuming banana in the survey. Several respondents stressed that a little banana does not have a bad effect on the health of the child, but too much certainly would. The difficulty in knowing how women actually act is related to the importance of the social context. In a social context where showing respect to elders is very important, it is difficult to obtain information on whether women really do as they say and conform to their mother-in-law or others.

Case studies (see Hutter 1994) indicate that women do eat some of the food items they are told to avoid, but perhaps only in small quantities. If a child becomes ill or dies due to cold or cough or *hotte andu*, people will say, 'It is because [the mother] ate banana during pregnancy.' Many women probably reason as these two respondents did: 'It is better not to take any risks, it is just a precaution' and '. . . it is better to observe the rules for if the child becomes ill, we will be blamed for it.'

PRENATAL CARE AND FOOD BEHAVIOUR

The health workers in the villages, i.e. the auxiliary nurse midwives (ANMs) and the *anganwadi* (kindergarten) worker, provide mother and child health care, and their recommendations focus on food supplementation and the provision of iron tablets during pregnancy. The *anganwadi* worker registers the pregnant women in the village, from month five of pregnancy onwards, and keeps a record of their pregnancy and birth. The information gathered is used to identify women at risk who need supplementary feeding. Women considered to be vulnerable receive supplementary food (a small snack, a *tiffin*) from the *anganwadi*, up to six months after delivery. These vulnerable women include those who are poor, living on wage labour only and in need of some extra food, or women who belong to a scheduled caste or tribe, women with a history of many spontaneous abortions or stillbirths and women pregnant at an older age.

When questioned whether they were selected to receive food supplementation during pregnancy, the majority of our respondents responded negatively. Women selected to participate in the programme (*n*=29) did not always participate. A few women (*n*=2) mentioned that they were selected but did not go to collect the food from the *anganwadi*. They felt ashamed to go there while the whole village watched them. They felt that they would be openly admitting to being poor. In most villages, children attending the *anganwadi* bring the *tiffin* home. Sometimes, too, only the powder is provided, but this is an exception, as it does not guarantee consumption by the pregnant woman herself.

Even if the *tiffin* is provided at home, the proportion of women who actually ate the food was low. Only 7 out of 29 women ate the extra food without any restriction. Others ate the food only sometimes. Some respondents (*n*=5) indeed received the food, but used it as a substitution rather than a supplement. If they ate the *tiffin*, they skipped another meal. Others (*n*=12) reported that they received the food but did not eat it. They either did not like the taste, or gave it to the children.

Women mentioned that they received the supplementation at such a time that the *tiffin* was cold and no longer tasty. The supplementary food was prepared early in the morning, and when the children brought it home at the end of the morning it had cooled down. Good food is supposed to be fresh or just-prepared hot food, and this is a problem for women working in the fields and coming home late in the afternoon. The fact that the *tiffin* is cold by the time women receive it is even more a constraint after delivery, since this is considered to be a time during which all cold foods should be avoided (see below).

Women also receive iron tablets as part of prenatal care to prevent anaemia (Werner 1996, p. 129). When women are asked whether they took iron tablets, most confirm that they did. However, in the in-depth interviews it became clear that most women did not really take the tablets—or tonic tablets as they are called by the villagers. Of all the women, 15 per cent stated they took the tablets. The majority, almost 80 per cent, did not take the tablets at all and instead reported throwing them out. This high percentage of non-compliance is related to perceptions regarding the effects of the tablets. Most (90 per cent) of the women who did not take the iron tablets stated that the tablets would lead to a large child causing labour problems. Fear of pain and economic reasons were important considerations, in particular the costs of a caesarean delivery at the hospital due to the size of the child. It is quite logical that women associate the tablets with the health of the child and not with their own health. A health worker of a local NGO mentioned: 'They reason, "If these tablets are only given to women who are pregnant it should be meant for the child." ' Other reasons for not taking iron tablets were related to the concepts of heating and cooling. Because tonic tablets are reported as heating, drinking milk is considered necessary for its cooling effect, but milk is often not available in the household. In addition, the iron tablets are associated with contraceptives, because oral pill packages contain 21 contraceptives and 7 iron tablets.

Women are more likely to take iron tablets if they purchase them from the pharmacy on the recommendation of their doctors. These tablets are nicely packaged, while the iron tablets given by the ANMs were given by hand and often bled colour in rainy and warm weather.[6] In addition, the doctor prescribing the tablets has much more social status than the ANM. But above all, respondents pay for these tablets while the others are given free. As was reported by a respondent: '. . . for those tablets we did pay. So that is why we take them.' However, although these tablets were taken more often, it was still quite common to buy tablets and consume only half the number.

THE ETHNOPHYSIOLOGY OF FOOD INTAKE AND FOETAL GROWTH

We asked women how much they ate at the end of pregnancy compared with their normal food intake. Most women (54.4 per cent) reported eating less than normal in the last trimester. Another 42.4 per cent mentioned that they ate just as normal. Only five women mentioned that they ate more than normal, as international standards recommend. We subsequently asked women in the first two categories (the latter five women have been left out of the analysis) why they did not eat more during pregnancy.

For a few women ($n=3$) economic circumstances made them eat just as they normally did. They reacted: 'How can we eat more? We are poor people.' Two women mentioned that they did not eat more because of the distribution of food in the family. Most women (52 per cent) answered that eating more during pregnancy would lead to problems. 'If we eat more, we women will have problems (*namge tras agati*).' Different types of problems were identified. Due to acidity, women reported (35 per cent) they did not feel able to eat more. Acidity is a common, although minor, problem during pregnancy (Werner 1996, p. 264). In the study population, the perceived etiology of acidity is an interesting one. Women believe acidity starts because the foetus has a lot of hair all over its body. One of the respondents said: 'Do you know why I eat less? The child is there, it has a lot of hair. Then there is *hulsudu* (acidity) and therefore I eat less.' The local remedy against acidity is application of lime on the outside of the throat. A few women reported drinking milk, buttermilk, or curd against acidity.

Women also reported eating less because of *khapsu dilla*. *Khapsu* can be translated as 'capacity' (*dilla* is the negative form). A better translation, however, is digestion. During the last months of pregnancy, there was no digestion and women could not eat more. In some cases, this factor was also associated with constipation. Some respondents related digestion to strength. If there is more strength, then there is more digestion and one can eat more food. On the other hand, women who are weak have less digestion and, as a consequence, eat less. Almost half of the women mentioned at least one of these related problems.

One-third of the women reported that if they ate more, *ekase* would occur.[7] The Mysore Kannada word *kakassa* seems to reflect the same idea as it is described as trouble (heavy breathing, etc.) arising from an overloaded stomach, or from running fast, etc. In the villages, *ekase* is associated with eating too much. One respondent said: '. . . 1.5 to 2 hours after having meals *ekase* occurs. *Ekase* means some problems: not being interested in working or doing anything.' *Ekase* has been further described as a problem (pain) occurring between the heart and the stomach, i.e. in the chest. Respondents mentioned symptoms like a feeling of heaviness in the stomach because both child and food are there, acidity, breathlessness, heart beatings, no digestion, gas problems, vomiting, feeling tired and dull (*aiasse*), and not being able to work and walk freely. *Ekase* is related to several other factors. Several women ($n = 21$) said they did not eat more because then they would not be able to work and walk freely. The social environment plays a role here—especially in their husband's place women should be able to work. A respondent mentioned: 'Eating more *ekase* occurs. We feel tired, like to sleep and sit and are not able to do the work. And in our husband's house we have to work . . . . Eating less, there are no problems and we just work more and better.' In addition, it is difficult for a pregnant woman who has a 'tight stomach' to bend and cut the paddy. Women in the lower economic classes must be able to work in either the fields or stone quarry since they have to earn an income. One respondent remarked: 'the child is there in the stomach . . . and gives too much weight . . . eating more food makes it more heavy: we cannot work and walk freely.' Everybody can have *ekase*. Among pregnant women, however, it occurs sooner because the child is there in the stomach. Women often mentioned: 'The child is there in the stomach, therefore I eat less.'

In local Kannada a pregnant woman is referred to as *avulu hotte yalli adaale*, literally meaning 'she is with a stomach' (*hotte*). Many other words related to the reproductive process refer to the stomach. A spontaneous abortion is called *hotte hoitu* (the stomach died) or *hotte mugitu/bittu* (the stomach is finished, has stopped). An induced abortion is called *hotte tolesuvudu* (the stomach has been washed). A sterilization operation is called *hotte kooyudu* (the stomach has been cut). Also food goes to the *hotte*. Nichter and Nichter (1983) reported women to believe that both food and child are in the same place—the stomach. Many of our respondents did not have any idea of the location of the child and food in the body. One of the poor respondents said laughingly: 'How do we know? We are no doctors! We just work and eat, that is it.' Some believed the child and food to be together in one place. But quite a few mentioned that the child is in a separate place: in the *kusin chilla* (literally: bag for the child). Educated women also mentioned the Sanskrit word *garbha kosha* (uterus). But in general, the part of the body where the stomach, belly, and uterus are located together is called the *hotte*.

Thus, as pregnancy progresses, more space in the stomach is occupied by the child and less place is left for food. Some women explicitly said that at the end of pregnancy the child is big and 'if the baby is big . . . it occupies more place . . . then, if eating more, we will have stomach problems.' This is an important statement, indicating a reversed relationship between food intake and size of the child; this directly contradicts literature that states that women in developing countries eat less because they do not want a big baby. Here women stated that because the child is big at the end of pregnancy, they eat less. If more space is occupied by the child, logically there is less space for food. The statement that women eat less because the child is there, must further be related to the local notion that one should eat until the stomach is full. If people eat too much and the stomach becomes too full, problems like pain or tightness of the stomach occur. Eating too much also means that there is no room left for the child to move or rotate. If the child does not move the mother is believed to have problems. One respondent: '(if I eat more) . . . there will be problems for us (women) . . . the child will not turn around. When I eat less I feel very well. And if the child turns, also the child is okay.' A few women said they did not eat more because eating more would result in a small child.

Remarkably, none of the women stated that they did not eat more as they feared the child would be large. The idea that women eat less during the last trimester of pregnancy because the child will be too large, this leading to a difficult delivery, has not been confirmed in our study. On the contrary, women said that they eat less because the child is big at the end of pregnancy and occupies more space. When women were asked what would be the consequence for their child of eating the normal amount or less—not more as international standards recommend—at the end of pregnancy, almost 30 per cent of the women believed that the child would have more space to move around in the stomach. Rotation is considered to be good not only for the child but also for the woman. However, there is a limit. If not enough food is eaten, women complain about the child kicking too much, giving them a feeling of being unwell. If they eat a small snack (*tiffin*) at that moment, the kicking stops. Rotation or movement of the child was an important signal for the respondents. If the child moved, the women knew that everything was okay.

In addition, women believed that the child would have more space to rotate and as a consequence would be better developed (17.6 per cent) or larger (only 4.0 per cent). The concept of being better developed is considered different than being large, and the distinction is important. While eating less makes it possible for the child to develop well (in Kannada 'the child will grow like a crop in the fields'), as mentioned previously iron tablets are believed to lead to a large and fat child, giving problems at the time of delivery. Most respondents, however, explained that if they ate the way they did, i.e. normally or less, the child would be fine. Some women (12 per cent) said their actual amount of food intake did not have any effect on the child. They did not see any relationship between food and the size or health of the child. Moreover, women said, 'How can it be; it is natural. It is God's blessing whether the child will be big or small. It does not depend on food.'

LOCAL BELIEFS ABOUT QUANTITY OF FOOD INTAKE IN BIOMEDICAL PERSPECTIVE

While women acknowledge that they are highly influenced by other people in their immediate environment regarding food avoidance, they perceive themselves as deciding on the amount of food they ate. Are the reasons our respondents report determined by culture or do physiological factors play a role? If physiological factors do play a role, would not women in industrialized countries also face similar physical problems at the end of pregnancy? None of the scientific reviews (see Hutter 1994) mention physiological changes during pregnancy which influence energy intake. However, personal communication with medical professionals and pregnant women in the Netherlands suggests that similar feelings of unwell-being are experienced there as well. At the end of pregnancy the foetus presses against the stomach leaving women with less appetite and more acidity. The data found by van Raay *et al.* (1986, 1987) and Spaay (1993) in the Netherlands indicate an average daily increase of only 57 kcal, and 44 kcal, respectively, during pregnancy. In the latter study, the high variation in energy intake during pregnancy indicates that some of the respondents did show a reduction in food intake at the end of pregnancy. It would be interesting to study beliefs regarding quantity of food intake during pregnancy among Dutch women as well and compare them with the findings of this study.

Another consideration might be that women in industrialized countries, if they face these kinds of physical problems at the end of pregnancy, are more able to vary the quality of their diet. Women in our study population had little possibilities for variation—they consume the same bulky food every day. It would certainly make a difference whether one can consume, for example, only a little more cream (and thus add a certain amount of extra kilocalories) instead of one more *rotti*.

The recommendation that women consume 300 extra kilocalories per day may not be absolutely justified. Studies in the Netherlands and Scotland (van Raay *et al.* 1986, 1987; Durnin 1986, 1987; Durnin *et al.* 1986) indicate that the recommendation might be too high. The studies indicate that 'the pregnant body is able to save energy and bridge the energy cap by adjustments in physical activity, an increase in work efficiency and an adaptation of the metabolic response to food.' (van Raay *et al.* 1987, p. 953). Durnin concluded that 'in industrialized countries extra energy requirements during pregnancy might be much lower than thought before. Instead of the recommended 300 kcalories per day extra, an addition of 100 kcalories per day would be more than adequate.' (Durnin 1987). This indicates that recommendations, based on the biomedical model, also change, and in fact professional recommendations have fluctuated through the centuries. The formula 'eating for two' is only one example. During the last decades, food recommendations for pregnant women have varied from a daily energy intake of 2,700 kcal in 1953 to 2,200 and 2,400 kcal/day in the sixties and seventies, respectively (NAS 1990).

At present, Indian pregnant women are advised to eat more frequently and consume smaller quantities of food which are readily available (personal communication, Dr. Rama Naik, Home Science College, Dharwad). The data in our study strongly supports this kind of a recommendation. However, one wonders to what extent Indian women in the reproductive period (who are young, recently shifted to their husband's house, and have limited decision-making power) are able to cook small portions for themselves, and eat before other family members do.

FOOD BEHAVIOUR DURING BIRTH AND
THE POST-PARTUM

Of the 186 women, 175 gave birth to 176 live births (one set of twins were born). The percentage of girls was 52 per cent and boys 48 per cent. Eleven women had a stillbirth. Of all newborns, four died almost immediately after birth either as a consequence of complications during delivery (such as the umbilical cord twisted around the neck) or because of congenital malformations. These data indicate a relatively high perinatal mortality rate in the population. Some of these deaths could have been prevented. For example, a woman with breech delivery could not reach the hospital as transport facilities were not available at night, and her child died. Another woman lost her child due to the fact that the medical personnel of the PHC in her parents' village did not refer her in time to the hospital. During the first month of life, two more children died. One woman died a few days after pregnancy due to complications associated with an indirect cause of maternal mortality, viral hepatitis. This maternal death could also have been prevented, as will be described.

Most women in the study population (83 per cent) gave birth at home, either at their parents' or their husband's house. A small number of deliveries ($n=33$) took place in the hospital. Six women were referred to the hospital due to complications. The other women who delivered in the hospital were of lower parity and had a higher level of education. Most women, however, preferred to deliver at home. Economic reasons played an important role—a hospital delivery is quite expensive. Moreover, mothers of the respondents told us they preferred their daughters to deliver at home because only there appropriate care for both mother and child is provided (see below).

Most of the deliveries which took place at home were assisted by a traditional birth attendant (65 per cent), the *dai*. Most *dais* living in the 11 research villages have received some biomedical training. In addition, a relatively high proportion of deliveries were assisted by a family member, often the mother (30 per cent). Only a small number of the respondents got help from a village health worker (15 per cent). Here, again, economic reasons played a role. One of the key informants, an older Madiga woman who conducted many deliveries in her family, remarked that poor women preferred a *dai* rather than modern health workers. She related this to the attitude of government nurses and doctors to give injections in order to induce and speed up labour. Injections are quite expensive. The data indicate that at least 30 per cent of all deliveries were attended by a person untrained in biomedicine.

Some special food items were known to speed up the process of birth. Cumin boiled with water and sugar is commonly taken in all villages, while women in the forest area drank a concoction made of a fruit grown in the forest. In addition, ghee (clarified butter) was believed to quicken delivery due to its heating qualities. Hot tea is commonly drunk during the process of delivery. Some women add butter as it is supposed to make 'the birth canal more slippery, so the child will come out more easily'.

While pregnant women should avoid excess heat caused by food, work, season, allopathic medicines, or sexual intercourse, heat is needed at the time of delivery in order to accelerate the process. Hot foods, like ghee or hot tea but also other items, are applied, for example a warm bath or massages with coconut oil or warm water. After delivery, mother and child are bathed with warm water. From the first moment onwards, the child stays with its mother on a special bed or sleeps in a small hammock attached to the bed. Only later it sleeps in a cradle. The mother and child being together facilitates breastfeeding on demand.

After delivery, biomedical recommendations are that the mother can and should eat every kind of nutritious food she can get. Foods which are especially good for her are milk, cheese, meat, fruits, vegetables, grains, groundnuts, etc. (Werner 1996, p. 294). The Indian Council of Medical Research (ICMR 1990) advises Indian women lactating to consume 550 kcal extra per day during the first six months after delivery. Based on a small number of observations (42 respondents), we believe that in the post-partum period the majority of women do not reach these normal levels of energy intake. In the first two months after delivery, average energy intake amounted to 1,658 kcal, a level similar to the average energy intake in the last month of pregnancy. In months three to five after delivery, average energy intake slightly increased to 1,710 kcal. Regarding other nutrients, intake likewise did not meet recommendations. For example, the average protein intake in the first five months after delivery amounted to 45 g while the recommended intake is 1 g/kg body weight per day plus 25 g extra in the first six months after delivery. Given the average weight of 41 kg, it is clear that only a few women in the study population reached the extra level of protein intake.

However, in contrast with the period of pregnancy—when almost no extra food was added to the normal diet of women—in the post-partum period special food items are provided to the mother. Most important is that this special food should be hot. During the first five days after delivery, women eat only sweets made of wheat with milk and *jaggery* (all are heating). At *aidesi* (the fifth day), special food is prepared: *kobri kara*. The ingredients depend on economic status of the household, but commonly consist of dried coconut and sugar or *jaggery*. Other heating food like dried dates, gum, ghee, cashew nuts, and spices like cloves or cardamom can be added. A special sweet, *ladu* (made from heating foods like wheat, dried fruit, dried coconut, nuts, and gum), which can be bought at the city market is eaten by women from higher socio-economic classes since only they can afford to buy it.

Some time after delivery, rice and *rotti* (bread) are eaten again. However, in the period after delivery *rotti* and rice are eaten immediately after their preparation, while they are still hot and fresh. Food that is kept after preparation is considered to be cold and hard and to be avoided as it causes stomach problems for both mother and child. Due to this belief, lactating women often do not consume the food supplementation provided by the *anganwadi* (see above). In addition to hot rice and *rotti*, in the period after delivery other heating foods like eggs, mutton, and ghee are consumed more often.

While heating food is thus considered to be essential, cold food should be avoided in this period after delivery. Women drink warm water only and avoid cold water and cold food like curds and buttermilk. Water intake is restricted: women indicated they drank about one-third of the normal amount after delivery. Too much water is believed to dilute the breastmilk and to lead to cramps in the stomach of the child.

Several of the customs of food avoidance observed during pregnancy are continued after delivery. Along with other *tampu* (cooling) food such as buttermilk and curds, these food items are avoided (especially in the cold season) because they lead to illnesses like colds, coughs, and pneumonia. Besides cooling food, other foods are avoided: fresh green chilies, pumpkin, *brinjal*, sweet potato, lady fingers, *arecanut*, and *ginna* (colostrum of the cow). These were said to be *barsna* for both mother and child: they lead to an adverse reaction of the body. Other foods were believed to cause swelling in the body of the mother, especially in her legs, hands, and face. Some women classified *brinjal* together with cold *rotti* and fresh coconut and banana as hard food—hard to digest. Only soft food should be consumed in this period after delivery.

Several foodstuffs are believed to influence the production of breastmilk: *galactogogues* were the seeds of fenugreek boiled in warm water with sugar, garlic, and green vegetables. Fresh chilies are believed to lead, via the breastmilk, to dysentery for the child. The same effects were created by cold and hard food like cold *rotti*. Warmth, in addition to all its beneficial effects for the mother, was also believed to increase breastmilk.

We thus see that while during pregnancy heating food has to be avoided as too much heat will lead to, among other things, an induced abortion, and during delivery extra heating food is provided to induce delivery, in the post-partum period, heating food is needed and cold food is to be avoided. Beliefs about food to be added (heating, soft) and food to be avoided (cooling, hard, *barsna*) in this period after delivery are related to perceptions of the body.

THE CONCEPT OF *HASI MAY*

After delivery, the mother's bed is placed in a separate room or in a corner which is secluded from the rest of the house by curtains made of bags or blankets. These prevent wind, cold and dirt, and also bad influences of people and evil spirits from reaching mother and child. Under the bed, a charcoal fire is placed. Mother and child stay in this dark and warm place for some time. The mother is said to be in *hasi may*, literally a fresh, raw or tender body. *Hasi may* can be thought of as a local notion of vulnerability. The concept is not only used for women who have delivered a live birth, but also for women who have had a miscarriage or stillbirth (although the period is shorter). It is also used to describe the period when girls reach maturity. Many similarities in the kind of food to be eaten and care to be taken among these different periods exist.

During *hasi may*, the body of the woman is vulnerable, weak and, above all, cold. Respondents said that 'all the heat has gone during delivery, a lot of blood has gone so there is no heat anymore in the body.' The woman's body is easily affected not only by cold or wind but also by the evil eye or evil spirits and ghosts. Warmth and heat are essential in this period after delivery. In addition to consuming more heating foods, heat is created by the seclusion by curtains, the charcoal fire under the bed, and by hot water baths and massages with oil and turmeric, neem and garlic. Moreover, warmth is preserved by the cap or scarf which women wear on their heads.

It is believed that during *hasi may* heat gives back the strength and energy which is lost during delivery. Heat is believed to freshen the blood and to create new blood. Moreover, warmth relieves the pain suffered at the time of delivery. Warmth, too, is believed to be good for the 'open stomach' and to tighten the stomach again. For this, women also 'bind the stomach' with a cotton cloth tied around the underbelly 'to get the stomach down and to close the open stomach again'. Women explained that due to pregnancy their belly had expanded and by binding the stomach it would return to its normal shape. In addition, 'the birth canal is open after delivery and should be closed again.' The cotton cloth worn after delivery speeds up this process. Stomach binding is also believed to be good to get rid of the waste blood.

Ideally, the period of *hasi may* after delivery lasts for three months and is concluded with a special *puja*. In reality, the length of the period of seclusion and rest depends on several factors. Women who have given birth for the first time are commonly given time to recover and only return to their husband's place after five months. Economic circumstances often determine whether a woman can afford to stay idle. The length of *hasi may* also depends on season. In the summer, when there is more heat from the sun, the period of seclusion can be shorter.

The concept of *hasi may* protects the health of both mother and child after delivery. It was often mentioned that this kind of care cannot be given in the hospital. It is also a perfect time for women to get some rest and refrain from work, especially if they stay at their parents' house. But there are also some disadvantages. In our sample, one woman died after having given birth. While she developed jaundice, her parents did not allow her to go to hospital, as she was in *hasi may* and thus vulnerable to evil spirits. When the symptoms became worse and they finally allowed her to go, she died on the way to the hospital.

CONCLUSIONS

It is useful here to consider how health educational campaigns aimed at improving the nutritional and reproductive health status of women can combine practices and explanations of the two different meaning systems? This is an important question, given that the findings of the research presented above have been translated into health educational material in cooperation with the local NGO, the India Development Service (IDS) in Dharwad. The results of this translation of research into a health educational campaign are described elsewhere (Hutter, forthcoming).

It is evident from our comparison of biomedical recommendations and local practices that most of our respondents did not comply with the recommended levels of food intake, during pregnancy or in the first months after delivery. Most of them did not even reach the recommended level for non-pregnant or non-lactating women. The health educational campaign, in a series of flashcards, first of all tries to make women aware of how much they do eat during pregnancy, as the research indicated. The amount of food eaten is not indicated in kilocalories or proteins. Those are concepts used in the biomedical model which do not have any meaning to the respondents living in the villages. Instead, the amount of food intake is indicated in the amount of *rottis* or number of local vessels of rice eaten. The same flashcard then indicates also how much is recommended for pregnant women to eat. The differences immediately become obvious to the women: that they do not consume the leafy green vegetables they need during pregnancy, nor do they get enough calcium by drinking more milk. This example illustrates how biomedical practices and explanations are used—but translated in local concepts—to try to improve the nutritional status of women.[8]

Another example illustrates that while a traditional practice appears to comply with the biomedical model, the explanation for why it is followed differs from that offered in biomedicine. The research indicated that women avoid food that has a heating (*kaavu*) effect on their body and would lead to a pregnancy termination. Excess heat can be created by season (summertime), body constitution or particular foods such as papaya, by having sexual intercourse during pregnancy, and by allopathic medicines. Furthermore, hard work or carrying heavy things can create too much heat, especially during summertime. Remarkably, all these items classified by the respondents as heating and thus to be avoided during pregnancy, are similar to items which are identified by the biomedical model as having negative health. Alcohol, drugs, smoking, and too many medicines are all items that the biomedical model recommends avoiding during pregnancy (see Werner 1996, p. 263). The health educational campaign builds on this convergence to reinforce local practices and does not go into the discussion whether the explanation—heating or not?—is true.

Another example is the custom of *hasi may*, where women are given special care after delivery: they get extra rest, extra food, and are cared for by others. The health educational campaign shows a series of flashcards in which the first card shows a woman who obviously has delivered. As the research indicated: she is sitting on the bed, a curtain around it, a charcoal fire is under her bed. In the campaign it is told that the custom of *hasi may* is a good custom and one to be continued. However, sometimes, when women are secluded like this, there is hardly any fresh air in the room, so one could now and then open a window. This example illustrates how the custom—which is good—is reinforced, but some information from the biomedical model is added.

In addition, a disadvantage of the custom is that women are believed to be extra vulnerable for evil spirits, and are sometimes not allowed to visit the hospital while being in *hasi may*. As indicated above, one of the respondents died because she was not allowed by her mother to visit the hospital as she could be attacked on the way by the evil spirits. The health educational campaign shows a card that depicts this situation, and then provides information that women in these circumstances should go to the hospital, and then elaborates on certain harmless practices—generally done in the villages—to protect against evil spirits.

These are only a few examples of how the two different meaning giving systems can be combined in a health educational campaign. For sure, not everything can be dealt with so easily. But the basic plea in this chapter is that health education ought to relate to local practices and concepts—which can only be discovered by listening to people—and to recognize that people are not empty vessels and have knowledge and reasons for doing what they do. Education that does this can be more effective.

Notes

1. The custom has been reported to exist in, among others, Kenya (Kusin *et al.* 1984; de Vries 1987), Oman (Baasher 1979), Ethiopia (Beddada 1979), Sudan (El Shalazi 1979), Iran (Djazayery *et al.* 1992), Somalia (Ministry of National Planning and UNICEF 1984), and India (Nichter and Nichter 1983; Pool 1983; Nichter 1989).
2. The results from this research are currently being translated into a health education intervention project where the integration of food practices, women's perceptions, and biomedical recommendations is a major concern. Health educational materials are being developed by the local Indian NGO, the India Development Service (IDS) in Dharwad. The project is financed by the Ministry of Foreign Affairs of the Netherlands.
3. The recommended daily energy intake for Indian women, weighing 50 kg and conducting moderate work, amounts to 2,225 kcal per day plus 300 kcal extra during the last two trimesters of pregnancy. given that the average weight of women in the study population is 41 kg, non-pregnant Indian women, ages 18–30 years, weighing 35, 40, or 45 kg should consume 1,824, 1,957, and 2,090 kcal, respectively (ICMR 1990).
4. Women reported specific beliefs of foods that have special effects during pregnancy. In a society where light-coloured skin is highly valued, several food items are known to result in a fairer complexion, among them *badaami* wheat, or saffron mixed with milk or cumin with aniseed. The desired effect may be questioned, but at least the pregnant woman is consuming an extra cup of milk. Another custom mentioned by respondents was *pica* and *geophagia*, i.e. the consumption of items like mud, charcoal, sacred ash, and chalk during pregnancy. Special cravings consisted of sour things like raw mango, pickles, raw fruits, and cucumber. Also vegetables and fruits like sweet lime, grapes, and apple were mentioned.

5. Other food items reported, but by less than 10 per cent of the respondents, were *ginna* (colostrum of the cow or buffalo from which a special sweet is made), fresh green chilies, watermelon, *kekkerhannu* (musk melon), and non-vegetarian food (meat, fish, and eggs).
6. Recently, the government has changed its programme and now provides iron tablets that are nicely packaged and colourfast (personal communication, IDS 1997).
7. *Ekase*, a typical of village Kannada word, is not included in the standard Kannada–English dictionary written by Kittel (1894).
8. The health educational campaign also includes two puppet shows on food intake during pregnancy and the post-partum period. A puppet play is an excellent tool to emphasize the role of members of a social network. This particular puppet play describes a story of two women who were both pregnant. One of them was taken care of very well by her husband and mother-in-law: she got extra food and care. The other woman was not being taken care of by her in-laws: she had to work and eat as normal. In the puppet play, which lasts for three hours, many related aspects are discussed and included in songs. After the play is over, the content is discussed with the audience.

References

Baasher, T. (1979), 'Psychological aspects of female circumcision', WHO/EMRO Technical Publication No. 2 (2), Alexandria, pp. 71–105.

Beddada, B. (1979), 'Traditional practices in relation to pregnancy and childbirth', WHO/EMRO Technical Publication No. 2 (2), Alexandria, pp. 47–56.

Dixon-Mueller, R. (1993), 'Population policy and women's rights', London: Praeger.

Djazayery, A., Siassi, F., and Kholdi, N. (1992), 'Food behavior and consumption patterns in rural areas of Sirjan, Iran: Dietary patterns, energy and nutrient intake and food ideology', *Ecology of Food and Nutrition*, 28: 105–17.

Durnin, J. V. G. A. (1986), 'Energy requirements of pregnancy. An integration of the longitudinal data from the 5-country study', in *Nestle Foundation Annual Report 1986*, Lausanne: Nestle Foundation, pp. 147–54.

—— (1987), 'Energy requirement of pregnancy: An integration of the longitudinal data from the five country study', *The Lancet*, 14: 1131–3.

—— McKillop, F. M., Grant, S., and Fitzgerald, G. (1986) 'Energy requirements of pregnancy. A study on 88 Glasgow women', in *Nestle Foundation Annual Report 1986*, Lausanne: Nestle Foundation, pp. 39–74.

El Shalazi, H. (1979), 'Nutritional taboos and traditional practices in pregnancy and lactation including breastfeeding', WHO/EMRO Technical Publication No. 2 (2), Alexandria, pp. 100–13.

FAO/WHO (1985), 'Energy and protein requirements. Report of a Joint FAO/WHO/UNU Expert Consultation', Technical Report Series 724, Geneva: WHO.

Gelis, J. (1984), *L'arbre et le fruit. La naissance dans l'Occident moderne*, Paris: Fayard.

Hutter, I. (1994), *Being Pregnant in Rural South India; Nutrition of Women and Well-being of Children*, Amsterdam: Thesis Publishers.

Hytten, F. E. (1980) 'Nutritional aspects of human pregnancy', in H. Aebi and R. Whitehead (eds.), *Maternal Nutrition during Pregnancy and Lactation*. A Nestle Foundation Workshop, Lausanne, Verlag Hans Huber, Bern, pp. 27–38.

—— and Leitch, I. (1971), *The Physiology of Human Pregnancy*, 2nd edition, Oxford: Blackwell Scientific Publications.

Indian Council of Medical Research (ICMR) (1990), Nutrient requirements and recommended dietary allowances for Indians. A report of the expert group of the Indian Council of Medical Research, New Delhi.

Kusin, J. A., van Steenbergen, W. M., Lakhani, S. A., Jansen, A. A. J., and Renquist, U. (1984), 'Food consumption in pregnancy and lactation', In J. K. van Ginneken and A. S. Muller (eds.), *Maternal and Child Health in Rural Kenya*, London: Croom Helm, pp. 127–42.

Ministry of National Planning and UNICEF, Somalia (1984), Women and children in Somalia: A situation analysis, Mogadishu: UNICEF.

National Academy of Sciences (NAS) (1990), *Nutrition During Pregnancy*, Washington, DC: National Academy of Sciences.

Nichter, M. (1989), *Anthropology and International Health. South Asian Case Studies*, Dordrecht: Kluwer.

—— and Nichter, M. (1983), 'The ethnophysiology and folk dietetics of pregnancy: A case study from South India', *Human Organization*, 42 (3): 235–46.

Pool, R. (1983) 'Food avoidances and the hot/cold syndrome. A case study in rural Gujarat, India', Doctoral dissertation, Cultural Anthropology, Universiteit van Amsterdam.

van Raay, J. M. A., Peek, M. E. M., and Hautvast, J. G. A. J. (1986), 'Maternal energy requirements in pregnancy in Dutch women', in *Nestle Foundation Annual Report 1986*, Lausanne: Nestle Foundation, pp. 53–75.

—— Vermaat-Miedema, S. H., Schonk, C. M., Peek, M. E. M., and Hautvast, J. G. A. J. (1987), 'Energy requirements of pregnancy in The Netherlands', *The Lancet*, 24: 953–5.

Spaay, C. J. K. (1993), 'The efficiency of energy metabolism during pregnancy and lactation in well-nourished Dutch women', Thesis, Landbouw Universiteit Wageningen.

UNICEF (1991), *Children and Women in India. A Situation Analysis 1990*, New Delhi: UNICEF India Office.

de Vries, M. W. (1987), 'Cry babies, culture, and catastrophe: Infant temperament among the Masai', in N. Scheper-Hughes (ed.) *Child Survival*, Dordrecht: D. Reidel Publishing Company, pp. 165–86.

Werner, D. (1996), Where There is No Doctor. The Hesperian Foundation, Palo Alto, London: MacMillan Education Ltd.

3

'Rariu Doesn't Rhyme with Western Medicine': Lay Beliefs and Illness Networks in Kenya

NANCY LUKE, INA WARRINER, AND
SUSAN COTTS WATKINS

INTRODUCTION

In the course of research on the role of conversational networks in women's health behaviours and family planning usage in South Nyanza District,[1] Kenya, we uncovered a reproductive health condition that rural Luo women call *rariu*.[2] Women refer to this cluster of symptoms by placing their arm across their abdomen, often bending at the waist. When asked about women's health problems in semi-structured interviews, one-third of the women mentioned *rariu* and described its symptoms.

When one is pregnant and she's just about to give birth, then the *rariu* wants to come out first.

I feel so bad. This place [stomach] becomes so painful that I cannot do anything.

When I am pregnant, I have stomachaches continuously, just above my private parts. It is a big mass that just moves about in one's stomach.

Data from a household survey given to 453 women reveal that 61 per cent of the respondents have suffered from *rariu*, and 69 per cent know someone who has; 84 per cent of the respondents either had *rariu* or knew someone who did. *Rariu* is a broad illness category that does not parallel any single condition in biomedicine, although the collection of symptoms is associated with women's reproductive health, and maternal morbidity in particular. *Rariu* is a culture-specific illness, one that is understood in the local culture and holds distinct meaning for the local women (Low 1985; Kleinman 1980).

In our sample of Luo women, 96 per cent of those who suffered from *rariu* sought some kind of treatment. Although the range of treatment possibilities is large, from self-treatment to traditional healers to diviners to hospitals, we focus on health-seeking behaviour for the two predominant health care systems used for *rariu*: traditional and biomedical.[3] In this study, the specific traditional healers consulted are herbalists, also called traditional midwives or *nyamrerwa*, and are mostly women.[4]

At first glance, it would seem appropriate for rural Luo women to seek treatment for *rariu* from formal health services, as there is little reluctance to use modern health services in general in this region (Brass and Jolly 1993; Nyamwaya 1986), and for pregnancy and childbirth services in particular.[5] Formal medical services have been available in South Nyanza for over 70 years (Nyamwaya 1986). However, when asked whether they sought treatment at a clinic/hospital or from a *nyamrerwa*, 73 per cent of the respondents who sought treatment visited a *nyamrerwa*,[6] and 27 per cent went to a clinic or hospital.

Why do so many women seek treatment from a traditional healer for *rariu*? We believe the answer lies in the social function of *rariu* and significant factors affecting its recognition and treatment, including the influences of social interactions and available treatment options. A particularly important aspect of social interaction is the influence of women's social, or lay referral, networks. We use the term 'lay referral network' to refer to women, their families, and social networks who are involved in illness decision making. We find that women's lay referral networks are mostly elderly women and *nyamrerwa* in the rural Luo women's community. The women's community has customarily held authority in the realm of 'women's illnesses', and it uses this power to legitimate the suffering from *rariu* and deflect the stigma of role deviation, such as infertility and miscarriage.

Biomedical clinicians, on the other hand, have a different type of interaction with rural women: their power, symbolized by their uniform, English language skills, and education, makes it possible for them to enforce their biomedical model of disease. Conflict arises when the Luo women present at the clinic with the symptoms and label of *rariu*. From the clinicians' perspective, *rariu* is not a legitimate illness because its cluster of symptoms does not parallel any specific condition in biomedicine. Thus, clinicians delegitimate women's illness experience. This perception often contributes to incomplete or ineffective treatment, or even no treatment at all. The lack of fit between local notions of *rariu* and available biomedical services is what may have led one nurse to comment, 'This *rariu*, it doesn't rhyme with Western medicine.'

The treatment and perception issues surrounding *rariu* provide an enlightening case study of the interaction between the formal health care system and rural understanding of disease. Questions like this have been of enduring interest to anthropologists and sociologists and have recently received international attention. The 1994 International Conference on Population and Development held in Cairo stated that advances in women's reproductive health should be a major goal for countries around the world. Structural factors, such as technological, economic, and physical problems, are often highlighted by health planners when designing reproductive health interventions. The case of *rariu*, however, reveals that the questions are more involved than that. Focusing attention on social interactions and lay definitions of disease will aid in reaching the Cairo objective of improving women's reproductive health in ways sensitive to local circumstances and context.

THE RESEARCH SITES

As part of a larger study of the role of social interaction in fertility behaviour, the data on *rariu* were collected in four sublocations (similar to counties in the United States) in Nyanza Province, southwest Kenya. The sublocations Obisa, Kawadghone, Owich, and Wakula South are all in South Nyanza District.

A brief description of the social system provides the necessary background for understanding the characteristics of the respondents. There is considerable homogeneity by socio-economic characteristics and cultural patterns within and across the four study areas. The economy is predominantly subsistence agriculture. None of the four sublocations is connected to the electric grid or has a general store or similar establishment, and telephones are few. Although these areas are relatively isolated and remote, there is nonetheless considerable interaction with others outside the area. Men leave the area to work and their wives go to live with them or visit. Visitors also come back for funerals, which are important social gatherings.

Nyanza Province is predominantly Luo, one of the largest ethnic groups in Kenya, and almost all of the respondents are Luo.[7] About one-fifth of the sample speaks English, which is the language of secondary schooling. Nearly 80 per cent of the women in the household survey had attended school; of those, only 14 per cent had attended secondary school, and slightly less than half of those had finished. In Nyanza, households are extended, with parents and their married sons and grandchildren often sharing the same compound. The Luo practise polygyny and are patrilineal, patrilocal, and exogamous. In principle, husbands gain both domestic and sexual rights over their wives at marriage (Watkins *et al.* 1997; Cohen and Odhiambo 1989; Parkin 1978). Reproduction is a central concern, and women's status depends on producing many children, especially sons (Shipton 1989; Ndisi 1974; Blount 1973).

Most people live in mud huts with thatched roofs, although a minority with higher incomes have metal roofs. Similarly, possession of a radio distinguishes the somewhat wealthier from the somewhat poorer. Women do most of the time-consuming subsistence farm work, and most women also earn what they call 'something small' by selling such items as small surpluses of corn or vegetables or hand-made baskets (Watkins *et al.* 1997). Since the early colonial days, men from Nyanza have migrated in search of cash income; about one-third of middle-aged men in this area may live outside their compounds as they migrate within Kenya or to other East African countries (Francis and Hoddinott 1993; Shipton 1989; Ndisi 1974). Other sources of money are local wage labour by the men (e.g. fishing and working in stone quarries, either on a regular or an occasional basis) and cash crops, which are typically marketed by men (Shipton 1989; Ndisi 1974).

Overall, rural Luo women are held to demanding physical and social responsibilities regarding production and reproduction. Women continue to carry out these responsibilities in lieu of threats of beating or divorce or separation (Miruka 1997; Hay 1982; Potash 1978). If divorce or separation occurs, a woman must leave her husband's compound and return to her natal home, where she has no cultivation rights to support herself through farming. Her children are not permitted to accompany her, and she is disgraced. The threat of losing her children ensures a woman's adherence to the norms of faithfulness, industriousness, and submissiveness.

DATA AND METHODS

Data for this study were collected during 1994–5 using a variety of methods ranging from standard survey approaches to field observations (for a complete description of the data collection process, see Watkins *et al.* 1996). We use qualitative data from 40 semi-structured interviews with randomly selected ever-married women of reproductive age, ten interviews from each of the four sites, and nine focus groups.[8] We also use data from informal interviews with additional women, clinic personnel, and traditional herbalists. The field notes of the research team from observations in the villages and at clinics are included where applicable.[9] Follow-up information is also included from interviews with women, traditional herbalists, and clinicians, which was gathered during subsequent research trips to South Nyanza.

We also use household survey data collected from a random sample of 977 women in the four sites, about 200 women in each site. Each respondent was asked background characteristics and a battery of questions concerning family planning knowledge, usage, and the woman's informal social networks. Additionally, about half of the women (453) were asked questions from a module focusing on conversations about *rariu*. These respondents were also asked to name a maximum of four network partners with whom they talked about *rariu*, where, how frequently, and the characteristics of those with whom they talked.[10]

We analyse the formal and informal interviews and the research team's field notes using content analysis and interpretation. These qualitative data provide information on the content of conversations, information that could not be satisfactorily obtained from the household survey. Analysing this type of data involves considerable interpretation, and the authors took steps to ensure reliability of explanation. Each author read all the interviews and field notes. *Ethnograph* was used to perform content analysis and provide a systematic basis for assessing the distribution and frequencies of views expressed by the respondents. The codes for *Ethnograph* were developed jointly by two of the authors, Nancy Luke and Ina Warriner. They then coded ten interviews independently and a high consistency was found between their coding. Subsequently, all interviews and field notes were coded and checked by these two authors. Grids were constructed for each code or theme that emerged from the semi-structured interviews. By comparing grids for each respondent and group of respondents, it was possible to determine, for example, which opinions were typical and which were not, thereby enhancing the quality of the content analysis of the data.

LABELLING AND LEGITIMATE SUFFERING

We use social labelling as the theoretical framework for illness categorization, which emphasizes the role of social interactions and social factors in illness identification and decision making. This approach provides the greatest insight and most useful framework for understanding the perpetuation of *rariu* and its treatment from traditional medicine in the rural Luo context.

Social labelling theory offers an explanation of how specific illnesses are defined as legitimate in various cultures. The theory proposes that 'who is to be called "ill" is determined by the beliefs and norms of society, individual characteristics, and one's social network rather than by universal and objectively defined signs and symptoms' (Waxler 1981, p. 283; Conrad and Schneider 1992; Pescosolido 1992). This lies in contrast to the biomedical model of disease based on the medical practitioner examining and interpreting the patient's symptoms as objective facts and trying to link them to textbook descriptions of disease. The social labelling perspective also considers the power relations between 'labellers' and the 'labelled' central to the legitimation process.

Being recognized as legitimately ill is necessary to attain the rights that accompany illness, a central tenet to Parsons' concept of the sick role.[11] In Parsons' model, biomedicine plays a substantial role in social control. The physician legitimates an individual's sickness as well as prescribes action to heal the individual and bring her back to her normal role in society. In rural Kenya, however, biomedicine is not the dominant medical system. The domestic realm of women's and children's illnesses has traditionally been the domain of traditional midwives, herbalists, and the elder women in the larger women's community (Kawango 1995; Sargent 1989). Traditional medical treatment, both preventive and curative, has ensured women fulfil their social obligations, for example, by ensuring healthy pregnancy and curing infertility. With *rariu*, elder women maintain some traditional authority in a context where some of this authority has been appropriated by modern medicine in terms of childbirth services and family planning. They use this limited power to legitimate the suffering from *rariu* to other women and, especially, to husbands, thus creating a space for gender solidarity across generations. Nonetheless, biomedicine plays an important role in women's treatment, as it offers an alternative route to relief. We will see how biomedicine—which is utilized for other women's conditions—may alleviate suffering but nevertheless is not supportive of women's suffering and does not cure women of *rariu*. As a result, the majority of women advocate traditional healing as treatment for *rariu*.

LAY PERCEPTIONS OF *RARIU*

Now we offer a brief discussion of *rariu* and its meaning for rural Luo women. When women and *nyamrerwa* discuss *rariu*, they usually begin by situating it during pregnancy, although when questioned, they also say that any woman can get it, regardless of pregnancy or age. The symptoms women cite for *rariu* are varied, but common words or idioms appear. The following are some representative descriptions of *rariu* from rural Luo women (common idioms are italicized and sublocations and the respondent's number are given in parentheses):

It is a *big mass* that just moves about in one's stomach. (Obisa, woman 7)

Something settles in the abdomen so that when it is time for giving birth, *something blocks the child's outlet.* It can delay the child's birth for another one or two weeks. (Owich, focus group 2)

When I'm heavy like this [late pregnancy] my *lower abdomen hurts* me a lot. It even makes me walk slowly. . . . When you are going for 'long call' [defecate] and when trying to push, *it feels like coming out,* that is what it is. (Wakula South, woman 8)

One who is suffering like I'm suffering from that disease, I get my periods three times a month. Sometimes when the pain comes *I can't even stand straight.* I can't go to the river or perform heavy duties. (Obisa, focus group 1)

The symptoms women report for *rariu* in individual and focus group interviews are summarized in Table 3.1. The *nyamrerwa* use similar language to describe *rariu*: 'something coming out' and 'blocks' the birth; something that can be touched or felt in the lower abdomen; and something 'hard in the abdomen'. Waxler notes that 'each society has its own peculiar definitions for the kinds of behaviours, dysfunctions, even feelings that are to be called and treated as "illnesses" ' (1981, p. 289). The high amount of inter-informant agreement about the general symptoms of *rariu*, the repetition of idioms describing it, and the use of common hand and arm gestures suggest a shared meaning of the illness among rural Luo women.

Many of the idioms surrounding *rariu* are connected to a belief in a 'thing' or worm in the body that, when moved from its normal position, causes pain in the lower abdomen. This parallels other Luo concepts of illness. For example, Luos believe that there are beneficial worms located in the body that sustain life. When provoked by occurrences in the natural or social environment, the worms cause illness. Herbal remedies are needed to appease these worms, and biomedical treatment can be fatal if the worms are harmed or killed (Geissler 1998; Ndisi 1974).

When the 'thing' *rariu* is out of position, it affects a woman's ability to fulfil her expected roles. *Rariu* can affect all stages of reproduction. It can 'block' conception, nourishment to the foetus (causing miscarriage), or delivery of a baby. *Rariu* also impairs a woman's ability to fulfil her productive duties, including farming or completing domestic tasks for her husband. There is consensus among the women and *nyamrerwa* that when one is affected by *rariu*, it is so painful that one cannot work or walk or have sexual intercourse: one 'cannot do anything'.

Although *rariu* is categorized as a single, distinct illness by the rural Luo women, its symptoms may be translated into numerous conditions in biomedicine.[12] To our knowledge, there has been no systematic attempt to diagnose the variable cases of *rariu* clinically. The symptoms, however, suggest possible biomedical diagnoses. Women who complain of difficulties with urination may have urinary tract infections (UTIs) or pelvic inflammatory disease (PID). The 'big mass' that 'moves about in one's stomach' may be prolapsed uterus or PID. The high levels of HIV/AIDS in this area suggest the presence of sexually transmitted infections

Table 3.1. *Symptom frequency for* rariu *noted in individual interviews (N= 13) and focus groups (N= 7)*

Symptom	Number of women reporting	Number of focus groups where symptom was discussed
Pain in stomach, lower abdomen, or lower stomach	11	4
(this symptom when pregnant)	(7)	(2)
Problems walking, working, standing, doing anything	4	2
Thing comes out of rectum, blocks rectum, difficulty defecating	4	1
Problems urinating	2	3
Problems with menstruation: bad menstrual cramps, frequent periods	2	3
Backache	2	2
Overall pain	1	1
Tired	1	1
Pain in legs	1	0
Breasts swell and crack during breastfeeding	1	0
Blocked delivery	0	4
Delayed delivery	0	3
Prevents pregnancy	0	2
Pain after sex	0	1
Womb has moved downward	0	1

(STIs). Women who cannot 'do anything' may also be anaemic. Some of the symptoms of *rariu* suggest harmless biomedical conditions, such as braxton hicks contractions or simply a foetus pushing on nerve endings. In sum, *rariu* appears to be an umbrella term for any condition in the lower abdominal region. As one nurse explained, the traditional women give everything the name *rariu*, whereas clinicians try to pinpoint the specific problem. *Rariu* is similar to other culture-specific illnesses, where local illness categories 'may not correspond with scientific categories, and in fact are often broader', encompassing numerous diseases in biomedicine (Green 1992, p. 125; Nichter 1994; Erwin 1993).

There are local names for STIs, including *segete* and *nyach*, and women distinguish between these and *rariu*. It is likely that many women with *rariu* do have STIs, but as STIs are not 'respectable' because they are associated with extramarital affairs, some respondents may want to make it clear *rariu* is not an STI (Tsui *et al.* 1997). *Rariu* appears to be a non-stigmatizing illness label, which may be an explanation for its application to a broad array of symptoms (Erwin 1993). The neutral label *rariu* may be invoked instead of a more specific, but stigmatizing, label such as *segete*.

There is little spontaneous mention of the causes of *rariu* by the women; when asked they frequently say they do not know, and it is evident that this aspect does not seem to be important to them. Similar to what Nichter (1994) found with 'weak lungs' in the Philippines, the respondents in this study speak more about factors predisposing one to *rariu* than specific etiology. *Rariu* is not associated with supernatural causes like other Luo illnesses but with more natural causes. *Rariu* is associated by *nyamrerwa* and some clinicians with frequent childbearing, hard work, or carrying heavy loads on one's head—all of which rural Luo women do. The physical exertion and frequency of tasks, such as procuring water and fuel wood or weeding, can lead to symptoms similar to *rariu*, including fatigue, sore hips and legs, and conditions such as prolapsed uterus (Paolisso and Leslie 1995). In addition, physical and mental abuse has been linked to chronic pelvic pain (Heise 1994).

We believe that *rariu* is an illness interpretation specific to rural Luo culture. *Rariu* can clearly be quite painful, but it is also a means for women to gain a temporary respite from their social obligations, be it hard work or continued childbearing. A legitimate label *rariu* given by the women's community deflects the stigma of incomplete role expectations. With *rariu*, women who are infertile, subfecund, or need a rest from work are not stigmatized; their bodies are not deficient because the illness is at fault. Had women readily committed these offences, these would be justifiable reasons for husbands to reprimand them. With *rariu*, the women's community has granted a certificate of illness, and this serves as a defence from threats of sanction, including divorce and physical abuse. From this description of the symptoms and meaning of *rariu*, we find both physical and social factors that predispose a woman to suffer from it. We investigate these factors further in the next section.

CHARACTERISTICS OF RESPONDENTS WITH *RARIU*

The characteristics reported in the qualitative interviews of those who suffer from *rariu* are wide ranging: sufferers may or may not have children; they may or may not be pregnant during the episode; they may or may not have ever had sexual intercourse; and they may be of any age. We now turn to data from the household survey, which provide a systematic overview of the individual characteristics and patterns of social interaction associated with *rariu*.

Table 3.2 presents bivariate relationships between individual characteristics of respondents and the probability of ever suffering from *rariu*. Although the rural Luo women themselves do not consider age a factor, older ages may be associated with traditional beliefs (Fosu 1981) or increase the length of exposure to the probability of ever having *rariu*. According to Table 3.2, however, age does not have a significant influence on suffering from *rariu*. This suggests that *rariu* is widespread among rural Luo women and is not in the process of disappearing. With respect to pregnancy, we suspect that some of the conditions that the term *rariu* includes may be more frequent among older and high-parity women who have had greater numbers of pregnancies (e.g. prolapsed uterus). Table 3.2 shows that women who have ever been pregnant are indeed more likely to have suffered from *rariu*.

Table 3.2. *Percentage of women who reported suffering from* rariu *and seeking treatment from a* nyamrerwa, *by characteristics*

Characteristic	N	Percent who reported *rariu*	N	Percent who reported visiting a *nyamrerwa*
Demographic				
Age				
15–19	50	56.0	27	70.4**
20–24	116	62.1	65	73.8
25–29	88	60.2	44	70.4
30–34	83	62.6	47	83.0
35–39	50	60.0	28	53.6
40–44	42	66.7	24	66.7
45–60	24	58.3	14	57.1
Ever having been pregnant				
Yes	424	62.3$^+$	237	70.5
No	29	44.8	12	75.0
Sublocation of residence				
Obisa	128	66.4	74	81.1*
Owich	99	70.7*	65	80.0$^+$
Kawadghone	114	65.8	67	43.3***
Wakula South	112	42.0***	43	81.4$^+$
Social network				
Speaks English				
Yes	98	51.0*	45	66.7
No	355	63.9	204	71.6
Number of funerals attended				
More than average	152	71.7***	99	65.7
Average or less than average	301	55.8	150	71.6
Belongs to income generating group				
Yes	117	70.1*	73	68.5
No	335	58.2	175	72.0
Belongs to church group				
Yes	354	62.1	194	72.7
No	98	58.2	54	68.5
Sells at the market				
Yes	221	67.0*	129	71.3
No	232	55.6	120	70.0
Knows others who have suffered from *rariu*				
Yes	315	67.6***	192	71.4
No	138	46.4	57	68.4
Number of network partners				
0	79	26.6***	19	57.9
1–2	155	65.2	92	78.3

Table 3.2. *Continued*

Characteristic	N	Percent who reported *rariu*	N	Percent who reported visiting a *nyamrerwa*
3–4	151	74.2	98	69.4
5+	68	63.2	40	62.5
Mother in woman's network				
Yes	43	79.1*	33	63.6
No	410	59.3	216	71.8
Mother-in-law in woman's network				
Yes	84	77.4***	53	66.0
No	369	57.5	196	71.9
Co-wife/sister-in-law in woman's network	-			
Yes	210	55.2***	137	57.4
No	243	44.8	112	42.6
Nyamrerwa in woman's network				
Yes	41	87.8***	34	85.3*
No	412	58.5	215	68.4
Economic status				
Metal roof and owns a radio	63	57.1	35	42.9***
Metal roof only	22	63.6	14	57.1
Radio only	171	60.2	90	66.7
Neither metal roof nor radio	192	63.0	106	85.9
N	453		249	

$^+p < 0.1$. $^*p < 0.05$. $^{**}p < 0.01$. $^{***}p \leqslant 0.001$; chi-square test.

Rariu is associated with rural Nyanza. Urban Luo women who were asked about *rariu* informally either had not heard of it or were embarrassed by the topic. However, since *rariu* is a locally defined illness, it is possible that there are differences across our research areas in the extent to which it is acknowledged. We see from Table 3.2 that sublocation of residence is an important indicator of suffering from *rariu*. The remote sublocation Wakula South on an island in Lake Victoria shows fewer women reporting *rariu*. We interpret this finding to be evidence of different circles of interaction working in the sublocations. It is also possible that environmental or other community effects are influencing the prevalence of *rariu* symptoms or the acceptability of recognizing the illness. The availability of biomedical treatment does not appear to affect recognition of the illness, as women with the best and worst access to the services (Kawadghone and Owich, respectively) are both more likely to suffer from *rariu*.

We include in our analysis measures intended to capture a variety of dimensions of the respondent's social network, and we find in Table 3.2 that most of them are significantly associated with suffering from *rariu*. We include information on whether a woman reported that she speaks English because we believe it captures the effect of how women interact with the wider world around them and how they view themselves.[13] Our interactions with urban Luos and clinic personnel suggest that the more cosmopolitan women are less likely to acknowledge *rariu*, perhaps because they find other ways of labelling their illness, such as trusting biomedical diagnoses, or that such women may not want to acknowledge to the research team that they have had *rariu*, out of concern that we would not understand or would associate them with uneducated rural women. Education may also lead respondents to behave in ways that are less likely to produce *rariu*, such as less carrying of heavy burdens or seeking treatment for infections earlier.

Attending funerals, belonging to an income generating group, selling at the market, and knowing others who have had *rariu* are significantly associated with *rariu* prevalence. In addition, network size has an effect. Some network partners are probably more crucial in identifying *rariu*; thus, we use information on the specific network partners named, including their mother-in-law,[14] mother, co-wives and sisters-in-law,[15] and a *nyamrerwa*. These network partners are significantly associated with suffering from *rariu*. The in-laws typically live in the same compound and have an immediate concern for the woman's health. Mothers typically live elsewhere (marriage is exogamous), but we believe the significance of a mother in the network may show that women follow the advice of trusted network partners and seek them out whether or not they are nearby and available for frequent conversation. Economic status is not significantly associated with suffering from *rariu*. These bivariate results suggest that suffering from *rariu* depends on a woman's social interaction, and her lay referral network in particular.

LAY REFERRAL NETWORKS: LABELLING WOMEN AS ILL AND TREATMENT ADVICE

The initial labelling of Luo women as ill usually happens within the family compound (Parkin 1972)—numerous studies document the importance of the family as the place where early treatment decisions are made (Fosu 1995; Christakis *et al.* 1994; Pescosolido 1992; Anyinam 1987; Feierman 1985; Kleinman 1980, 1988). From semi-structured interviews, it is evident that women most commonly tell their husbands, mothers-in-law, mothers, women friends, and *nyamrerwa* about their symptoms. Newly married women move into their husband's extended-family compounds and often maintain only limited contact with their blood kin; thus they are most likely to speak to related and nearby women due to proximity.

More than two-thirds of the women in the semi-structured interviews reported speaking to their husbands about *rariu*. The following are some discussions regarding husbands' responses to the illness (I = interviewer, R = respondent).

I have talked to my husband, explaining to him how my lower abdomen hurts. He tells me to go to some elder mother who has already given birth, so she can explain what I can do. (Kawadghone, woman 3)

I: Do you talk with your husband about such problems?

R: Yes, of course. When you are sick and in bed he has to ask you. It hurts you so that you can't wash his clothing and can't cook. He has to ask you, 'How are you sick?' But even if you tell him, he can't know because he also doesn't know. If I don't know it must be that he also doesn't know, and that is why I went to ask my mother-in-law. (Obisa, woman 6)

In Luo society, a husband must be informed of his wife's health status, especially if she cannot complete her family obligations or if it involves money for treatment. In most cases, husbands do not know what to do about *rariu* and tell their wives to ask an older or more experienced woman for advice. Here, husbands recognize the authority of the women's community with regard to *rariu* and sanction treatment advice given by the women in the lay referral network. But with regard to treatment decisions, these husbands act as gatekeepers, as they have control over the household's resources.

After informing husbands, women seek the advice of other women to help them give meaning to their symptoms and decide on treatment options. The input of mothers-in-law appears to be particularly important for *rariu*, and 20 per cent of the women in the household survey and one-third of the women in semi-structured interviews reported that their mother-in-law is in their *rariu* network. All women who reported talking to a mother-in-law followed her advice about treatment.

I: Why did you choose to tell your mother-in-law?

R: You see, when it was hurting I had not had such an experience, but you know your grandmother [mother-in-law] is like your mother, so she is the one you have to go to. (Obisa, woman 6)

R: When I told my husband he dismissed me, that I should tell his mother because he was still young, he didn't know much about these things. So I went and told his mother, who advised me to go for treatment [from the traditional healer] at Kaksingri. (Wakula South, woman 3)

Like husbands, mothers-in-law need to be informed of a woman's illness status, but unlike husbands, they know what to do about illness. Women trust the opinion of a mother-in-law with regard to *rariu*, and the mother-in-law is an important legitimator of illness.[16]

Nyamrerwa are also part of women's lay referral networks and share the rural Luo women's beliefs about *rariu*: they understand the women's complaints, they use the same language and gestures to describe it, and they invoke the same illness labels. They also legitimate suffering and offer medicines specific to *rariu*. For these reasons, the *nyamrerwa* are believed to embody a form of technically competent help.

Women talk mostly to other women about *rariu*. This stems from a situation where women have traditionally had little access to formal education and outside information (for example, about the biomedical model of disease), and knowledge about reproduction and illness is passed down from older, more experienced women (March and Taqqu 1986). Older women and traditional healers such as midwives become the most reliable sources of information (Newman 1985; Sukkary-Stolba 1985) because 'they saw the world before us'.

Networks also function as a means of support for sick women: they cover duties and care for children, offer advice, and bring medicine. This creates female solidarity in a context of strict gender roles by both validating suffering and supporting ill women until they are well.[17]

HEALTH-SEEKING BEHAVIOUR

Treatment given by *nyamrerwa* for *rariu* consists of herbs that the *nyamrerwa* believe are specific to this illness or palpating the abdomen area to 'return' the 'thing that blocks' to its proper position. *Nyamrerwa* also prescribe abstention from women's duties, such as avoidance of frequent childbearing, hard work, or sexual intercourse, sometimes for months at a time. A *nyamrerwa*'s services are less expensive relative to formal medical treatment, and, unlike the clinics, *nyamrerwa* accept in-kind payment, such as a chicken, or delayed payments.

Treatment from formal medical services in South Nyanza District includes various levels of health care services: government dispensaries, health care centres, and hospitals, in addition to various private (mission and for-profit) clinics and hospitals.[18] There are, however, problems of distance to, and long waiting lines at, health care facilities, as well as complaints about the rudeness of clinic staff. Preventive care is free from government facilities, although, as a result of structural adjustment programmes, cost sharing has been introduced for curative services (Okoth-Owiro 1994; Sindiga 1990). Private facilities have even higher costs.

Most clinic personnel prescribe Panadol (paracetamol), a common non-aspirin painkiller, for *rariu*. They may also prescribe antibiotics if they believe a woman suffers from a UTI or an STI, although clinics often do not have medications in stock. Most clinicians also report that they refer women to a district hospital if they believe *rariu* is serious, if any tests are inconclusive for their specific diagnosis or for further testing, or if a patient does not respond to antibiotics. Clinicians may also refer women to a *nyamrerwa*.

Although women's lay referral networks advise treatment from traditional medicine, we find that some women seek treatment from both biomedicine and traditional medicine either simultaneously or consecutively.[19] Seeking treatment from biomedicine in addition to the *nyamrerwa* is not a rejection of traditional beliefs but indicates 'considerable pragmatism' to find relief from distress (Erwin 1993, p. 145; Last 1992; Osero 1990; Obeyesekere 1978). Once inside the clinic, however, rural women's beliefs conflict with those of the clinicians' biomedical model of disease. The women's reception in the clinic contributes to their perception that they are not treated well and subsequently are not cured.

WOMEN'S DISTRUST OF BIOMEDICINE

Women offer an abundance of comments as to why formal health services cannot effectively treat *rariu*. These comments can be grouped into three categories. First, there is the belief reported in numerous studies of African healing that traditional medicine is believed to eliminate the root cause of an illness, while biomedicine only addresses the symptoms (Mbiti 1990). *Nyamrerwa* know how to 'return' *rariu* to its proper position and bring back normal functioning, whereas biomedicine can only temporarily relieve the pain, or worse, may cause more harm than good. Women and *nyamrerwa* note that incorrect treatment of *rariu* by the hospital can be detrimental or even fatal, as several biomedical procedures do not 'rhyme' with *rariu*. For example, if *rariu* is operated on (and therefore cut), the patient could die or be rendered infertile. This parallels Luo concepts of the body referred to earlier: *rariu* is seen as a natural part of the body whose presence sustains life, and 'killing' it could cause actual death, or social death through infertility (Geissler 1998). Traditional medicine is therefore less risky; it can cure infertility from *rariu*, not cause it.

Second, many women believe that the clinics or hospitals do not give the proper medicine or they do not have medicine available (Osero 1990). Whereas the *nyamrerwa* give herbs they believe are specific to treating *rariu*, the formal system gives medicines easily available on the open market rather than something special. For example: '[The hospital] did not give me any medicine because they didn't have them. . . . They don't even give proper treatment. They give Panadols, aspirin, and chloroquin' (Wakula South, woman 3).

Third, formal health services are associated with large costs. Curative services and prescriptions are relatively costly for rural Luos and must be paid for on delivery. In addition, transportation to the hospital may involve large monetary and time costs: 'Me, I do have a problem with *rariu*, and you know, nowadays if one has to go to the hospital one has to have money' (Obisa, woman, focus group 3).

An analysis of the household data with respect to health-seeking behaviour reveals the importance of these monetary concerns as well as other factors in women's decisions about treatment. Table 3.2 presents bivariate relationships between individual characteristics and visiting a *nyamrerwa*. The findings show that the influences on the recognition of suffering from *rariu* and its treatment are different. For treatment choice, the most important factors are age, sublocation of residence, and economic status. Younger women appear more likely to seek the treatment of a *nyamrerwa*, which we believe reflects the greater influence of their lay referral networks on their illness decisions. Sublocation is significant, where Kawadghone is negatively associated with visits to a *nyamrerwa*. Although this may be due to location of biomedical services (there are two hospitals in Kawadghone), Obisa also has relatively easy access to a hospital, suggesting that treatment choice is not associated merely with geographic distance to and availability of hospitals.

Although formal schooling is associated with use of biomedical services (Csete 1993; Kleinman 1980), speaking English is not a significant predictor of treatment choice. Somewhat surprisingly, there is only one network variable showing a significant association with treatment: the presence of a *nyamrerwa* in a woman's lay referral network. This finding may be interpreted as an indication that *nyamrerwa* may push their own services, or, more likely, reflects the fact that the respondent did consult her. We know from the qualitative interviews, however, that network partners frequently give advice on treatment and often advocate seeking help from a *nyamrerwa*. Table 3.2

also shows that those with higher economic status are less likely to seek treatment from a *nyamrerwa*. Other studies have found that treatment at a hospital or traditional healer in Africa is not dependent on individual income or education but on the shared view of illness reality of the entire family (Feierman 1985). Our results contradict this assertion and suggest that although women's lay referral networks usually advise treatment at the *nyamrerwa*, a woman may attend treatment at the clinic if her household—usually husband—has the money for payment.

CLINICIANS' PERCEPTIONS OF *RARIU*

When women present at the clinic, they have been labelled by those in their lay referral networks with *rariu* and this diagnosis may have little to do with biomedical reality (Feierman 1985; Waxler 1981). The clinicians are committed to the biomedical model of disease, and because *rariu* does not fit into their textbook definitions of disease, they delegitimate women's illness experience and many times end up minimizing their treatment of it. Delegitimation is the experience of having one's perception of illness systematically disconfirmed (Ware 1992). Clinicians accomplish this in various degrees.

First, clinicians may reject *rariu* as legitimate suffering. Clinicians have expressed doubt that the symptoms of *rariu* are 'real' or that *rariu* is 'mainly psychological'. In this manner, they believe the women are malingerers who are not seriously ill but 'just want to get out of work'. This dismissal may also be gender specific: doctors and nurses may not take *rariu* seriously because it represents common 'women's ailments'.

Second, clinicians reject the label *rariu* because it does not 'rhyme' with Western medicine. They tell us that *rariu* is 'not in English' or 'there is no medical term for it'—which means that it has no equivalent in Western biomedical language. Alternatively, they attempt to fit the condition to a specific diagnosis they recognize and can try to treat. When asked to describe *rariu*, the clinicians initially use the rural women's symptom idioms. They describe it as 'something pressing' in the uterus or 'the child doesn't come out the way it should'. However, they then quickly translate these symptoms into formal biomedical terms—terms they are comfortable with.

Although there may be no overall biomedical equivalent for *rariu*, each episode of *rariu* could be one of numerous biomedical conditions. Interestingly, most clinicians interviewed insisted on one, specific diagnosis for all the cases of *rariu* they have seen. For example, one doctor maintained that *rariu* is always PID. Another insisted it is prolapsed uterus, and yet another, STIs. The discrepancy in diagnoses may reflect the interaction of clinicians with a foreign research team: the medical personnel may have felt compelled to quickly put a distinct, Western medical label on the condition. More likely, clinicians tend to stick to one biomedical diagnosis, perhaps based on their initial experiences.

Third, clinicians admit that some cases of *rariu* confuse them; they do not know what it is and cannot treat it. One nurse explained, 'If a condition is something they know they can treat, like malaria, that's one thing, that's something real, tangible.' *Rariu*, on the other hand, is vague in the sense that its symptoms could be anything in the lower abdominal region, it may be difficult to diagnose, and women's description of the symptoms and problem may not be very helpful for a diagnosis. In addition, a complaint of *rariu* is a red flag that the patient is a 'rural, ignorant' woman who believes in traditional things like *rariu*; hence clinic personnel may perceive them as difficult patients.

Despite clinicians' difficulties with *rariu* patients, the power of clinicians over rural women—due to class, educational, and rural/urban differences—ensures that their view of medical reality must be accepted inside the clinic. Although most clinic personnel are Luo, some are trained locally and the higher-level nurses have national training. They are more educated and of a relatively higher socio-economic status than the rural Luo women. Clinicians have worked hard to become trained medical personnel, and they wish to maintain their distinction as an educated elite. Women do not report that nurses or doctors are part of their *rariu* networks— people with whom they 'chat' about *rariu*. The social distance between clinicians and the rural women is great and carefully maintained by the clinicians (Rutenberg and Watkins 1997; Bender and Ewbank 1994). Clinicians use this power to promote their biomedical diagnoses—and delegitimate women's experience with *rariu*.

STRATEGIES TO TREAT *RARIU*

Clinicians use treatment strategies that reinforce biomedical labels and often clash with Luo women's understanding of *rariu*. Following are some examples.

Clinicians believe many cases of *rariu* are STIs; nonetheless, some of the procedures designed to treat women with STIs are incompatible with women's concepts of *rariu*. For example, one nurse requested an infected woman to bring in her partner before she was provided treatment. Women see men as 'carriers' of *rariu* who transfer it from one woman to another, but men do not usually contract it themselves. Thus, women are confused when asked to bring in their partners, as they do not see what this has to do with *rariu*. In addition, in their eyes it is a waste of time and money to return another day with a partner. This strategy appears to delay and even discourage treatment altogether.

In another case, a nurse gave a woman medicines for an STI and the symptoms initially disappeared. But they reappeared, perhaps because she did not complete the course of medicine correctly or was reinfected (Caraël 1994). The woman interpreted her 'new' symptoms to mean that the nurse's diagnosis of an STI was wrong, and it reaffirmed her belief that she had *rariu*.

Other clinicians have tried to convince women that *rariu* does not exist. When a patient told one nurse, 'Me, I've got *rariu*. I can't push the child', the nurse responded, 'There is nothing like that, just listen to me. That one, it is just a belief.' Comments like these are usually said in a condescending tone and do not appear to dissuade women from their commitment to *rariu*.

Some treatments recommended by the clinicians are not accepted by *rariu* patients. In addition, women may not follow through with their course of medication if they do not receive instant relief. They often resort to herbs instead of the prescribed drugs or take them at the same time. Herbs are often smuggled into the hospital or given immediately after women have been diagnosed and given biomedical drugs at the clinic. Clinicians are frustrated when women take herbs while under the clinic's care. Some nurses also believe that particular herbs will make a condition worse (including some cases or *rariu*) or nullify biomedical prescriptions. Herbs are usually discouraged or taken away without explanation.

These failed strategies naturally frustrate most clinicians and lead them to minimize their treatment of *rariu*. They repeatedly prescribe Panadol, do not examine women completely, and refer them to the hospital or *nyamrerwa*. For example, one nurse commented that government health centres cannot test for UTIs and would not do it because it is easier to give the women Panadol and 'send them away'. A doctor admitted that he could not treat *rariu* (whatever the symptoms); he gives women Panadol and sends them to a *nyamrerwa*. Half the clinicians report that they refer women to a district hospital—advice they recognize women will not follow—if they cannot diagnose or cure *rariu*. Most clinicians do not deny women treatment or referral for *rariu*; their measures, however, may be a means of declining responsibility if the women are not effectively healed. Even the most sympathetic clinicians may feel helpless if they do not know what *rariu* is or if they cannot treat it. The less patient clinicians are often rude or patronizing, calling women 'ignorant' or 'simple' (Vlassoff 1994). As a result of these interactions, women do not readily revise their belief in *rariu*, and clinicians and women remain at odds in understanding the illness.[20]

The efficacy of herbs specific for *rariu* is not known, although some clinicians say they work for certain cases.[21] The efficacy of biomedical pharmaceuticals is highly regarded, assuming the correct diagnosis is made and women follow through with treatment. The symptoms associated with *rariu* may be temporarily eliminated or clear up on their own (such as those of an STI or premature labour pains, for example) (Green 1992), and thus women may believe they have been cured by herbs. Nevertheless, our purpose is not to discern the physiological nature of the treatment from either the clinics or the *nyamrerwa*; what we are interested in is women's perception of cure, which most say is only possible from the *nyamrerwa*. In our study of the social interactions between healers and patients, we have tried to uncover some obstacles to achieving a biomedical diagnosis and cure, leaving aside the issue of efficacy of the Western drugs. Although we cannot show the physiological difference between the efficacy of biomedicine versus traditional medicine, we can, nonetheless, highlight how they differ in other ways. We argue that the traditional medicine's connection to the social aspects of illness experience makes a great difference for women with *rariu*, for two reasons.

First, the *nyamrerwa* share traditional beliefs and offer ill women support and understanding. *Nyamrerwa* are part of illness networks and most *nyamrerwa* are also rural Luo women of similar educational attainment and socio-economic status. One rural nurse commented, 'The *nyamrerwa* are attached to us, they know more about us.' Fosu explains that 'the traditional healer's approach to diagnosis and treatment seems quite effective because of its very personal and supportive nature'

(1981, p. 479). This support validates women's experiences with *rariu* as 'real', needing appropriate treatment. In a study of health-seeking behaviour among the Luo, Osero concludes:

Certain indefinite complaints and chronic ailments are often a means of securing the attention of those around and of justifying some personal deficiency such as sterility or social failure. However, what matters is the [reintegration] of the patient in the group, [those] who sympathise with his miseries and provide him at the same time with both explanation of them and compensation for them (Osero 1990, p. 90).

Second, biomedicine can only offer women a relief from suffering; it does not cure women and more importantly it does not offer all the functions provided by the traditional system, such as legitimation for a respite from social obligations and reintegration into society (Kunstadter 1978). The biomedical diagnoses clinicians pin on *rariu* are not accompanied by a certificate of legitimate illness in the rural community—in fact, a diagnosis such as an STI would be stigmatizing and unfavourable for rural women instead of validating their suffering.

CONCLUSION

This chapter has focused on the social nature of illness and the role of social interactions in illness legitimation and treatment. We have described *rariu*, a culture-specific illness that serves to legitimate rural Luo women's temporary respite from social obligations. Women's lay referral networks are crucial in identifying and validating suffering, thus creating a form of female solidarity surrounding 'women's illness' .

Despite *rariu*'s location within the traditional realm, we have described how women seek treatment from both the *nyamrerwa* and clinics. There is great pragmatism on the part of women when it comes to relieving pain, and those with the money to do so are more likely to try biomedical treatment, in spite of the advice of their networks. But their experiences at the clinic, combined with the lack of equipment and drugs, reinforce their belief in the effectiveness of traditional medicine. Rural women are willing to expend resources on biomedical care if they believe they will get results: they do this for other issues, such as childbirth and immunizations. They are not willing to risk paying such high costs, especially if they believe the clinicians cannot adequately diagnose and treat *rariu*.

The structural shortcomings of biomedical practice in the developing world are well known (Christakis *et al.* 1994). Our study probes further, concentrating on social interactions and women's experiences with *rariu* as determinants of treatment choice. Clinicians, who are dedicated to the biomedicine model, do not concentrate on these social aspects in their healing; indeed, they are likely to dismiss them as spreading 'myths and rumours'. Our study provides insight into rural Luo women's point of view and suggests that improving the social interactions surrounding treatment could go a long way to improve care.

More consideration should be given to understanding lay definitions of illness and the meaning of *rariu* for rural women. As we have seen, women's reactions to biomedical procedures and instructions are shaped by these local meanings. Health workers need an understanding of lay knowledge and practices so as to 'better tailor their program to local contexts' (Yoder 1995, p. 212; Erwin 1993; Osero 1990). It is doubtful that rural Luo women will readily embrace the biomedical model of disease. We saw that explanations do not always fit lay concepts of the body, and prescribed treatments may fail. Nonetheless, clinicians can place biomedical explanations in terms understandable to rural women and help them make informed choices about treatment (Vlassoff 1994; Sherwin 1998), and they can involve lay referral networks— in addition to husbands who control the money for treatment—in health education messages and treatment consultations. Biomedical explanation should not just be relayed mechanically, but through respectful, positive interactions that foster patient confidence and compliance (Jaffre and Prual 1994; Vlassoff 1994).

Although the clinic does not offer the same degree of legitimation and support as the women's community, biomedicine can go a long way to cure *rariu*. With greater sensitivity to local complaints and illnesses that may not 'rhyme' with biomedicine, new initiatives would be able to encourage rural Luo women to bring these complaints to the clinics. With training, clinicians may be able to diagnose underlying biomedical conditions and to diminish their insistence on maintaining social distance between themselves and their clients.

Women are not simply pawns, however, of either the medical establishment or their lay referral networks. The availability of multiple treatments empowers the ill woman to make her own decisions regarding labelling and treatment. Currently, rural Luo women overwhelmingly choose treatment from a *nyamrerwa*. In order to deliver effective reproductive health care to these women, health planners need to widen their theoretical thinking beyond the biomedical model and the standard factors that determine health care utilization and incorporate into their model the social nature of illness.

Notes

1. At the time of the fieldwork, an administrative reorganization had created Homa Bay District, roughly coterminous with the former South Nyanza District. Another reorganization occurred a few years later. Since the area is still referred to as South Nyanza, however, we use that term here.
2. In all research sites, women recognize the term *rariu* although they also use other local names, such as *ruoth* in Owich and *mgongo* in Wakula South. The spelling of these terms is uncertain, as *rariu* does not appear in the Luo-English dictionary (Blount 1977).
3. The semi-structured interviews do not ask about self-treatment of *rariu* nor do the respondents mention this option spontaneously. Although Kleinman argues that 'self-treatment by the individual and family is the first therapeutic intervention resorted to by most people across a wide range of cultures' (1980, p. 51), there is little evidence of this for *rariu*. For this reason, the option of self-treatment was not included in the survey question concerning treatment sought.

4. *A nyamrerwa* is a minor medicine man or woman who does not possess *bilo*, or magic power, but knows how to obtain drugs from specific plants used for curing ill people. If the *nyamrerwa* is a woman, she usually specializes in women's and children's conditions, particularly pregnancy and child care (Nyamwaya 1986; Ocholla-Ayayo 1976; Hauge 1974). We use the terms biomedicine or formal health services to encompass what some researchers refer to as Western, scientific, or modern medicine.

5. The 1994 Kenya Demographic and Health Survey also supports the claim that there is little reluctance to use formal health services in Kenya, especially for pregnancy and childbirth: 95 per cent of the respondents obtained antenatal care from a doctor or trained nurse/midwife (table 8.1); 90 per cent of those who gave birth in the last 5 years had a tetanus toxoid injection (table 8.3); 44 per cent gave birth in health facilities (including public health facilities, mission hospitals and clinics, and private hospitals and clinics) (table 8.4) (NCPD, CBS, MI 1994).

6. Regarding reported use of a traditional healer, other studies have shown that under-reporting the use of traditional medicine is common in Africa (Csete 1993; Green 1992). Due to the high percentage of women reporting the use of a *nyamrerwa* in the household survey and due to the spontaneous disclosure of belief in the efficacy of traditional medicine from the individual and focus group interviews, we do not believe this occurred in this study.

7. A small proportion of the respondents in one sublocation are Basuba, a group long-settled in the community, and a few were women from other ethnic groups who had married a Luo man. All spoke Luo, although a few Basubas spoke it rather poorly.

8. The respondents for the semi-structured interviews were systematically selected with respect to the geographical location of their homes. Focus group participants were selected by the local chiefs, who the research team believes gathered what they considered their 'most presentable' women: many had at least some secondary education, many belonged to income generating 'women's groups', and some were relatives of the chief or subchief. As a consequence, the women who participated in the focus groups are not representative of the communities (Watkins *et al.* 1996). Despite these biases, we include focus group data in this paper because the dynamics of group conversations provide a useful counterpoint to interviews of individuals.

9. The semi-structured interviews and focus groups were conducted in Luo and taped and then simultaneously transcribed and translated into English. University educated Luos from the University of Nairobi served as interviewers for the qualitative phase and as supervisors for the survey. All transcripts, surveys, and field notes are available from Susan Watkins, University of Pennsylvania.

10. The respondents in these areas were not familiar with surveys or survey procedures, which probably had some effect on the way the interview was conducted. For example, respondents rarely seem to have simply answered the questions but rather asked for clarification or gave their own opinions. Many made it clear that they expected some benefit to come from the interview, either to their Luo clan or the larger community or, preferably, to themselves personally. In addition, although all the interviewers were Luo, the interviewers were distinguished by their education, and all respondents were well aware that behind the Luo interviewers were the Ministry of Health and the 'white' foreigners. Although the connection to the Ministry of Health was slight, the vehicles used by the team were marked as belonging to the Ministry. It is hard to know how these inside–outside interactions affected the responses, but they should be kept in mind. For example, it may be that women exaggerated the extent of their suffering from *rariu* in the hopes that the research

team or the Ministry of Health would provide more medical care, either specifically for this ailment or generally; on the other hand, others may have felt that outsiders do not understand or even denigrate *rariu*, and thus they may have been reluctant to report it.

11. Parsons (1951) studied illness in the American context in particular; the concepts of illness rights and obligations are also helpful to understand illness in Luo society and the thoughts and actions of women, their lay referral networks, and the health practitioners. Rights include 'exemption from normal social role responsibilities' (Parsons 1951, p. 436), by which the individual is not held morally responsible for her temporary respite due to illness (Annandale 1998; Conrad and Schneider 1992). Parsons thus added a social dimension to sickness, connecting illness to a deviation in the normal patterns of behaviour and connecting healing to the integration of the individual back into society (Annandale 1998). The responsibilities of sickness include the obligation to get well and to seek '*technically competent* help' (italics in original, Parsons 1951, p. 437), or the assistance believed to be best trained to provide treatment.

12. Although it is not possible to diagnose *rariu* without clinical examinations, we asked Kenyan biomedical personnel, as well as numerous other biomedical experts working in developing countries on reproductive health issues, to translate the symptoms of *rariu* into what they believe could be biomedical equivalents.

13. Speaking English is correlated with education in our sample, $r = 0.57$.

14. Luo women often refer to older women as 'mothers'. The interviewers tried to maintain the distinction between older women, biological mothers, and mothers-in-law when interviewing.

15. Because the same word is used for co-wife and sister-in-law, we suspect that the interviewers sometimes confused them; thus, we combine them in our analysis.

16. This contrasts with the findings of Watkins *et al.* (1997) with respect to family planning usage in South Nyanza. The rural Luo women reported opposition to family planning by mothers-in-law, but this did not seem to be influential in dissuading them from using family planning. Watkins *et al.* hypothesize this could be due to a shift in generational power, perhaps because family planning is seen as an innovative practice. In dealing with *rariu* and indigenous illness knowledge, on the other hand, the advice of mothers-in-law appears to be an integral factor in illness decision making.

17. This type of female solidarity was also evident in Donaldson's study of women's support networks in the South African homeland of Bophuthatswana. She found that the majority of women made health care decisions with other women. Their networks provided the opportunity for 'women's mutual reinforcement within an informal gender-specific support network [and] provide the basis for the continued, functioning female solidarity' (1997, p. 271).

18. In the sublocation of Obisa, which contains the town of Oyugis and the Oyugis Health Center, there is a Catholic health centre (10 km away) and a government health centre (about 13 km away). The drive to the district capital of Homa Bay and Homa Bay District Hospital takes about one hour. The sublocation of Owich lies in a very remote location. A new road was recently built to Homa Bay, which takes about one or more hours. There is, however, very little traffic on the road and it may be difficult to catch a bus or a ride. Kawadghone is the site of the Kandiege Health Center. The Homa Bay District Hospital is about one-half hour away on a busy road. There is a good private Seventh Day Adventist hospital in Kendu Bay, not far away. Wakula South is a site on Mfangano Island in Lake Victoria. It is also the site of a health centre although the beds are not available for patients.

An hour-long boat ride to the mainland and then another hour on roads brings one to Homa Bay. There is a private Catholic hospital at the other end of the island.

19. Luo women do not necessarily make a choice between only seeking help from formal medical services or a *nyamrerwa*. In many studies of health-seeking behaviour, researchers note the presence of patterns of treatment (Pearce 1993; Green 1992; Mwabu 1986; Feierman 1985), such as visiting more than one healer simultaneously or consecutively for a particular illness episode. The data from the household survey used in this study are problematic with regard to patterns of treatment. The survey does not ask information on concurrent or consecutive treatment, and the responses permit only one treatment option to be reported. Data from the qualitative interviews, however, provide more information on treatment patterns.

20. This contrasts to Low's findings regarding the culture-specific illness 'nervosa' in Costa Rica. Here, the use of the term by patients 'elicited doctors' attention to social and emotional aspects of the patient's illness and enhanced doctor–patient interaction' (1985, p. 190). In contrast, presentation with *rariu* appears to exacerbate the already great social distance between clinicians and rural women and lead women back to traditional medicine.

21. Anyinam (1987) notes that traditional medicine is often very effective; however, more studies need to be completed regarding its efficacy. Green (1992) believes that traditional medicine is not effective in treating STIs, as evidenced by the continued high rates of them in Africa.

References

Annandale, E. (1998), *The Sociology of Health and Medicine*, Cambridge, United Kingdom: Polity Press.

Anyinam, C. (1987), 'Availability, accessibility, acceptability, and adaptability: Four attributes of African ethno-medicine', *Social Science and Medicine*, 25 (7): 803–11.

Bender, D. E., and Ewbank, D. (1994), 'The focus group as a tool for health research: Issues in design and analysis', *Health Transition Review* 4 (1): 63–80.

Blount, B. (1977), *Luo-English Dictionary*, Nairobi: Institute of African Studies.

Blount, B. G. (1973), 'The Luo of South Nyanza, Western Kenya', in A. Molnos (ed.), *Cultural Source Materials for Population Planning in East Africa*, Vol. 3, Nairobi: East African Publishing House.

Brass, W., and Jolly, C. L. (eds.) (1993), *Population Dynamics of Kenya*, Washington, DC: National Academy Press.

Caraël, M. (1994), 'The impact of marriage change on the risks of exposure to sexually transmitted diseases in Africa', in C. Bledsoe and G. Pison (eds.), *Nuptiality in Sub-Saharan Africa*, Oxford: Clarendon Press.

Christakis, N. A., Ware, N. C., and Kleinman, A. (1994), 'Illness behavior and the health transition in the developing world', in L. C. Chen, A. Kleinman, and N. C. Ware (eds.), *Health and Social Change in International Perspective*, Boston: Harvard School of Public Health.

Cohen, D. W., and Odhiambo, E. S. A. (1989), *Siaya: The Historical Anthropology of an African Landscape*, London: James Currey.

Conrad, P., and Schneider, J. W. (1992), *Deviance and Medicalization: From Badness to sickness*, Philadelphia: Temple University Press.

Csete, J. (1993), 'Health-seeking behavior of Rwandan women', *Social Science and Medicine*, 37 (11): 1285–92.

Donaldson, S. R. (1997) , ' "Our women keep our skies from falling": Women's networks and survival imperatives in Tshunyane, South Africa', in G. Mikell (ed.), *African Feminism: The Politics of Survival in Sub-Saharan Africa*, Philadelphia: University of Pennsylvania Press.

Erwin, J. O'Toole (1993), 'Reproductive tract infections among women in Ado-Ekiti, Nigeria: Symptoms recognition, perceived causes and treatment choices', *Health Transition Review*, vol. 3 (Suppl.): 135–49.

Feierman, S. (1985), 'Struggles for control: The social roots of health and healing in modern Africa', *African Studies Review*, 28 (2/3): 73–134.

Fosu, G. B. (1981), 'Disease classification in rural Ghana: Framework and implications for health behaviour', *Social Science and Medicine*, 15B: 471–82.

—— (1995), 'Women's orientation toward help-seeking for mental disorders', *Social Science and Medicine*, 49 (8): 1029–40.

Francis, E., and Hoddinott, J. (1993), 'Migration and differentiation in Western Kenya: A tale of two sub-locations', *The Journal of Development Studies*, 30 (1): 115–45.

Geissler, P. W. (1998), ' "Worms are our life", part I: understandings of worms and the body among the Luo of western Kenya', *Anthropology and Medicine*, 5 (1): 63–79.

Green, E. C. (1992), 'Sexually transmitted disease, ethnomedicine and health policy in Africa', *Social Science and Medicine*, 35 (2): 121–30.

Hauge, H.-E. (1974), *Luo Religion and Folklore*, Oslo: Universitetsforlaget.

Hay, M. J. (1982), 'Women as owners, occupants, and managers of property in colonial Western Kenya', in M. J. Hay and M. Wright (eds.), *African Women and the Law: Historical Perspectives*, Boston: Boston University Papers on Africa, VII.

Heise, L. L. (1994), 'Gender-based violence and women's reproductive health', *International Journal of Gynecology & Obstetrics*, 46: 221–9.

Jaffre, Y., and Prual, A. (1994), 'Midwives in Niger: An uncomfortable position between social behaviours and health care constraints', *Social Science and Medicine*, 38 (8): 1069–73.

Kawango, E. A. (1995), 'Ethnomedical remedies and therapies in maternal and child health among the rural Luo', in I. Sindiga (ed.), *Traditional Medicine in Africa*, Nairobi: East African Educational Publishers, Kenya.

Kleinman, A. (1988), *The Illness Narratives*, New York: Basic Books, Inc., Publishers.

—— (1980), *Patients and Healers in the Context of Culture*, Berkeley: University of California Press.

Kunstadter, P. (1978), 'The comparative anthropological study of medical systems in society', in A. Kleinman, P. Kunstadter, E. R. Alexander, and J. L. Gate (eds.), *Culture and Healing in Asian Societies*, Cambridge, Massachusetts: Schenkman Publishing Company.

Last, M. (1992), 'The importance of knowing and not knowing: Observations from Hausaland', in S. Feierman and J. M. Janzen (eds.), *The Social Basis of Healing in Africa*, Berkeley: University of California Press.

Low, S. M. (1985), 'Culturally interpreted symptoms or culture-bound syndromes: A cross-cultural review of nerves', *Social Science and Medicine*, 21 (2): 187–96.

March, K., and Taqqu, R. (1986), *Women's Informal Associations in Developing Countries: Catalysts for Change?* Boulder: Westview Press.

Mbiti, J. S. (1990), *African Religions and Philosophy*, 2nd edition, Oxford: Heinemann International.

Miruka, O. (1997), 'Gender perspectives in Luo proverbs, riddles and tongue-twisters', in W. M. Kabira, M. Masinjila, and M. Obote (eds.), *Contesting Social Death*, Nairobi: Kenya Oral Literature Association.

Mwabu, G. M. (1986), 'Health care decision at the household level: Results of a rural health survey in Kenya', *Social Science and Medicine*, 22 (3): 315–519.

National Council for Population and Development (NCPD), Central Bureau of Statistics (CBS) (Office of the Vice President and Ministry of Planning and Development [Kenya]), and Macro International Inc. (MI) (1994), *Kenya Demographic and Health Survey, 1993*, Calverton, MD: NCPD, CBS, and MI.

Ndisi, J. W. (1974), *A Study in the Economic and Social Life of the Luo in Kenya*, Lund: Berlingska Boktryckeriet.

Newman, L. (ed.) (1985), *Women's Medicine: A Cross-cultural Study of Indigenous Fertility Regulation*, New Jersey: Rutgers University Press.

Nichter, M. (1994), 'Illness semantics and international health: The weak lungs/TB complex in the Philippines', *Social Science and Medicine*, 38 (5): 649–63.

Nyamwaya, D. (1986), 'Medicine and health', in G. S. Were, B. E. Kipkorir, and E. O. Ayiemba (eds.), *South Nyanza District Socio-cultural Profile*, Nairobi: Government of Kenya, The Ministry of Planning and National Development and the Institute of African Studies, University of Nairobi.

Obeyesekere, G. (1978), 'Illness, culture, and meaning: Some comments on the nature of traditional medicine', in A. Kleinman, P. Kunstadter, E. R. Alexander, and J. L. Gate (eds.), *Culture and Healing in Asian Societies*, Cambridge, Massachusetts: Schenkman Publishing Company.

Ocholla-Ayayo, A. B. C. (1976), *Traditional Ideology and Ethics among the Southern Luo*, Uppsala: Scandinavian Institute of African Studies.

Okoth-Owiro, A. (1994), 'Traditional health systems: Issues and concerns', in A. Islam and R. Wiltshire (eds.), *Traditional Health Systems and Public Policy*, Proceedings of an International Workshop, International Development Research Centre, Ottawa, Canada, March 2–4.

Osero, J. O. (1990) , 'Health seeking behaviour in a rural setting: The case of Ukwala Division in Siaya District', M. A. Thesis, Nairobi: Institute of African Studies.

Paolisso, M. and Leslie, J. (1995), 'Meeting the challenging health needs of women in developing counties', *Social Science and Medicine*, 40 (1): 55–65.

Parkin, D. (1978), *The Cultural Definition of Political Response: Lineal Destiny among the Luo*, London: Academic Press.

Parkin, D. J. (1972), 'The Luo living in Kampala, Uganda, and Central Nyanza, Kenya', in A. Molnos (ed.), *Cultural Source Materials for Population Planning in East Africa*, Vol. 3, Nairobi: East African Publishing House.

Parsons, T. (1951), *The Social System*, New York: The Free Press.

Pearce, T. O. (1993), 'Lay medical knowledge in an African context', in S. Lindenbaum and M. Lock (eds.), *Knowledge, Power, and Practice*, Berkeley: University of California Press.

Pescosolido, B. A. (1992), 'Beyond rational choice: The social dynamics of how people seek help', *American Journal of Sociology*, 97 (4): 1096–1138.

Potash, B. (1978), 'Some aspects of marital stability in a rural Luo community', *Africa*, 48 (4): 380–97.

Rutenberg, N. and Watkins, S. C. (1997), 'The buzz outside the clinics: Conversations and contraception in Nyanza Province, Kenya', *Studies in Family Planning*, 28 (4): 290–307.

Sargent, C. (1989), 'Women's role and women healers in contemporary rural and urban Benin', in C. S. McClain (ed.), *Women as Healers: Cross-cultural Perspectives*, New Brunswick, New Jersey: Rutgers University Press.

Sherwin, S. (1998), 'A relational approach to autonomy in health care', in S. Sherwin (coordinator), *The Politics of Women's Health*, Philadelphia: Temple University Press.

Shipton, P. (1989), *Bitter Money: Cultural Economy and Some African Meanings of Forbidden Commodities*, American Ethnological Society Monograph Series, No. 1.

Sindiga, I. (1990), 'Health and disease', in W. R. Ochieng' (ed.), *Themes in Kenyan History*, Nairobi: East African Educational Publishers.

Sukkary-Stolba, S. (1985), 'Indigenous fertility regulating methods in two Egyptian villages', in Newman, L. (ed.), *Women's Medicine: A Cross-Cultural Study of Indigenous Fertility Regulation*, New Jersey: Rutgers University Press.

Tsui, A. O., Wasserheit, J., and Haaga, J. G. (eds.) (1997), *Reproductive Health in Developing Countries*, Washington, DC: National Academy Press.

Vlassoff, C. (1994), 'Gender inequalities in health in the third work: Unchartered ground', *Social Science and Medicine*, 39 (9): 1249–59.

Ware, N. C. (1992) , 'Suffering and the social construction of illness: The delegitimation of illness experience in chronic fatigue syndrome', *Medical Anthropology Quarterly*, 6 (4): 347–61.

Watkins, S. C. with Rutenberg, N., Green, S., Onoko, C., White, K., Franklin, N., and Clark, S. (1996), *'Circle no Bicycle': Fieldwork in Nyanza Province, Kenya, 1994–1995*, University of Pennsylvania. Unpublished paper.

—— Rutenberg, N., and Wilkinson, D. (1997), 'Orderly theories, disorderly women', G. W. Jones, R. M. Douglas, J. C. Caldwell, and R. M. D'Souza (eds.) , *The Continuing Demographic Transition*, Oxford: Clarendon Press.

Waxler, N. E. (1981), 'The social labeling perspective on illness', in A. Kleinman and L. Eisenberg (eds.), *The Relevance of Social Science for Medicine.* Dordrecht, Holland: D. Reidel Publishing.

Yoder, P. S. (1995), 'Examining ethnomedical diagnoses and treatment choices for diarrheal disorders in Lubumbashi Swahili', *Medical Anthropology*, 16: 211–47.

4

Money, Marriage, and Morality: Constraints on IVF Treatment-Seeking among Infertile Egyptian Couples

MARCIA C. INHORN

INTRODUCTION

Consider two births: one of Louise Brown, the world's first 'test-tube baby', conceived and born in England in 1978, and the other of Heba Mohammed, Egypt's first test-tube baby, born less than a decade later in 1987. The lives of these two girls, one Western and one Middle Eastern, are connected by a modern technology, in vitro fertilization (IVF), that allowed their parents to overcome otherwise intractable infertility. It is their global connection and the ways in which Western-generated technologies such as IVF are received in places like Egypt that provides the major focus of this chapter.

Since Louise's birth more than two decades ago, the new reproductive technologies (NRTs) including IVF have become widely available in the West for couples with once hopeless infertility problems. As this technology has proliferated, so have its critics, particularly bioethicists, technology assessment specialists, and feminist theorists and activists. They worry about issues ranging from future 'genealogical bewilderment' (Humphrey and Humphrey 1986) to 'technopatriarchal' control over women's reproductive bodies (Mies 1987; Rowland 1987), which are being used increasingly as 'test-sites' for new drugs and surgeries (Klein and Rowland 1989). Yet, a clear Western bias is evident in such reproductive technology discussions, focusing as they do either explicitly or implicitly on the Western, white, socio-economically advantaged couples who are able to afford high-tech reproductive medicine and who thus provide the material and data for commercial and academic exchange (Sandelowski and de Lacey, forthcoming). In such discussions, the issue of the global spread of NRTs to the so-called 'developing world' is rarely acknowledged—a scholarly erasure that may be due to unexamined, Eurocentric, even neo-Malthusian prejudices surrounding the 'hyperfertility' of non-Western subjects and their inherent unworthiness as candidates for these technologies.

Nonetheless, significant infertility problems exist in the developing world—particularly on the African continent, which is considered to have an 'infertility belt' wrapped around its centre (Collet *et al.* 1988; Ericksen and Brunette 1996; World Health Organization 1987). Thus, it should come as no surprise—despite the lack of Western concern and commentary—that 'high-tech' reproductive technologies *are* being marketed to and consumed by those in the developing world on a massive scale. For example, limited reports indicate that these technologies have spread to several parts of Latin America, Asia, and Africa. But perhaps nowhere is this globalization process more evident than in the Muslim Middle East, where IVF centres have opened in countries as small as Bahrain and Qatar to those as large as Saudi Arabia and Egypt.

Egypt provides a particularly fascinating locus for investigation of this global transfer of new reproductive technologies because of its ironic position as one of the poor, purportedly 'overpopulated' Arab nations. Egypt was among the first Middle Eastern Muslim countries to establish a national population programme (through family planning) in the 1960s; as in the vast majority of the world's societies, infertility was not included in this programme as either a population problem, a more general public health concern, or an issue of human suffering for Egyptian citizens, especially women. Nonetheless, a recent World Health Organization-sponsored community-based prevalence study of infertility, based on a random sample of married women aged 18–49 in 20,000 rural and urban Egyptian households, placed the total infertility prevalence rate among married couples at 12 per cent (Egyptian Fertility Care Society 1995). Of this total, 4.3 per cent of cases suffered from so-called 'primary infertility', or the inability to conceive in the absence of a prior history of pregnancy. The remaining 7.7 per cent of the infertile study population suffered from 'secondary infertility', or the inability to conceive following a prior pregnancy (whether or not it resulted in a live birth).

Given this considerable infertile population and the strong culturally embedded desire for children expressed by virtually all Egyptian men and women, it is not surprising that Egypt provides a ready market for the new reproductive technologies. Indeed, with its long history of colonially inspired Western medicine (Inhorn 1994), Egypt has been on the forefront of IVF development in the Middle East, now hosting more than 35 IVF centres in full operation or development, more than any other Muslim or non-Muslim country in the region.[1]

In other words, less than 10 years after the birth of Louise Brown in England, IVF had already spread to Egypt, and in the decade following Heba Mohammed's IVF conception and birth, the new reproductive technologies have come to flourish in the country. However, these technologies are not transferred into cultural voids when they reach places like Egypt. Local considerations, be they cultural, social, economic, or political, shape and sometimes curtail the way in which these Western-generated technologies are both offered to and received by non-Western subjects. In the case of Egypt, infertile women and men willing to consider the use of new reproductive technologies face a series of culturally specific considerations and constraints—making it a remarkable fact that Egyptian *aṭfāl l-anābīb*, or

literally 'babies of the tubes', are born on an almost daily basis in some IVF centres
there. As will be highlighted in this chapter, these 'arenas of constraint' range from
class-based barriers to access, to gender dynamics within marriage, to local versions
of Islam, which legislate upon the appropriate use of these technologies and thus
restrict how 'babies of the tubes' are to be made. Such culturally specific considerations speak to the need for greater historical and cross-cultural expansion of
Western-based bioethical, feminist, and technological debates surrounding the
various impacts of new reproductive technologies. For, as the ethnographic research
presented in this chapter suggests, the use of new reproductive technologies in
Egypt involves not only a unique history, but different understandings of the role
of money, marriage, and morality, all of which profoundly influence Egyptian
women's and men's decisions about whether or not to utilize these technologies.

THE ETHNOGRAPHIC SETTING AND STUDY POPULATION

The research upon which this chapter is based encompasses two distinct time
frames. The first period is the late 1980s, or what may be called the 'early IVF
period' in Egypt. The first Egyptian IVF centre had just opened in an elite suburb of
Cairo in 1986, and hence the new reproductive technologies were neither widely
available nor widely understood in the country. In these early days, I conducted
15 months of anthropological fieldwork on the problem of infertility in Egypt,
basing my research in Alexandria, Egypt's second largest city. Working through the
University of Alexandria's large, public, ob/gyn hospital, popularly known as
'Shatby', I conducted in-depth, semi-structured interviews with 100 infertile
women and a comparison group of 90 fertile ones. Eventually, I made my way into
the communities and homes of these women, where I conducted less formal
interviewing and participant observation. With few exceptions, these women were
poor, uneducated, illiterate or only semi-literate housewives, who were not employed
in wage labour and were economically dependent upon their unskilled, labouring
husbands. It is extremely critical to note here that many of these urban poor women
were seeking treatment at Shatby Hospital not only because the infertility services
there were free, but specifically because of the hospital's widely publicized claims to
a 'free', government-sponsored IVF programme. Yet, by the end of the 1980s, when
I completed this initial fieldwork, it had become apparent to all of my poor, IVF-
seeking informants that an IVF programme at this public hospital had yet to arrive.
Furthermore, it appeared likely that IVF was not going to be the promised government 'freebie' for poor infertile women lacking the resources to seek IVF in the
private sector.

Moving ahead, the second period of research is the mid-1990s, or what may be
characterized as the 'IVF boom period' in Egypt. To wit, Egypt is now in the midst
of massive reproductive technology transfer, with new urban IVF centres cropping
up in private hospitals and clinics on a regular basis. In the midst of this IVF
explosion, I spent the summer of 1996 in Cairo conducting participant observation
and in-depth, semi-structured interviewing with 66 middle- to upper-class women

and their husbands; all of them were undergoing IVF or related technologies at two of the major IVF centres in this city of nearly 20 million inhabitants. Both of these IVF centres were situated in private hospitals in Heliopolis and Maadi, elite neighbourhoods on the outskirts of Cairo. These two clinics were among the three most established and respected clinics in the city, and received a daily influx of new patients, especially during the summer months, which were the busiest and were therefore ideal for my research. The patients presenting to these IVF clinics were generally well educated, professional, comparatively affluent women, who were often accompanied by their husbands. Indeed, in 40 per cent of the interviews conducted in these IVF clinics, husbands were present and participated, often enthusiastically, in discussions. Moreover, whereas interviews in my first study were conducted entirely in the Egyptian colloquial dialect of Arabic, many of the women and men who participated in the second study spoke fluent, even flawless, English as a result of their advanced educations, and they chose to conduct the interview in their second language.

Thus, my work on this subject incorporates both a diachronic perspective and a class-based comparison of infertile women seeking treatment in the two largest cities of Egypt. It reveals how the treatment experiences of poor and elite infertile women differ dramatically by virtue of education, economic resources, and power within their marriages, and how a time span of less than a decade has dramatically altered the infertility treatment landscape in Egypt. Let me illustrate these points by first telling two contrasting stories, one of Fadia and Osman, a poor infertile couple who I met in the late 1980s, and the other of Amira and Galal, a wealthy couple seeking IVF in the summer of 1996.[2]

THE STORY OF FADIA AND OSMAN

Like so many of the poor migrants to Egypt's northern cities, Fadia was born and raised in the south of Egypt, home of the major monuments of Egypt's pharaonic past and a place of renowned cultural conservatism. A divorcee from an early arranged marriage to her first cousin, Fadia fled to the home of her dissolute father living in Alexandria, only to find that he physically and verbally abused her. Needing a way out of another intolerable situation, Fadia sought refuge in a marriage proposal from Osman, a neighbour who had spotted the raven-haired beauty as she walked home from the market. Although Fadia found the balding, chain-smoking Osman unattractive and too old (he was 10 years her senior), she sensed that he might be kind to her. Yet, Osman's marital track record was not good. He had already wed five women, including one who turned out to be a true hermaphrodite, and all of these serial marriages had ended quickly and inauspiciously without children resulting from the unions. With the young, lovely Fadia, Osman hoped that his marital and procreative luck would improve.

Within her first 2 years of marriage to Osman, Fadia became pregnant three times, but she miscarried each time in the first trimester. Following the third miscarriage, Fadia did not become pregnant again. Osman, vexed over Fadia's failure to bear his children, became increasingly short-tempered—smoking as many as four packs of cigarettes a day, suffering severe impotence problems, and insulting, threatening, and beating his wife from time to time out of frustration over yet another ill-fated marriage.

Yet, Fadia convinced Osman to let her seek treatment for her infertility, which Fadia helped Osman to finance by joining neighbourhood savings clubs and selling off all her bridal gold. Like most other women of her class background, Fadia tried many traditional remedies, including, among other things, stepping over the gravedigger's tools in a local cemetery; sitting on a freshly delivered placenta; wearing glycerin-imbued vaginal suppositories; placing Qur'anic amulets under her pillow; and visiting spiritist healers who prescribed elaborate animal sacrifices. However, when none of these remedies worked to make her pregnant, Fadia stopped them altogether and started going from one doctor to another. Several of them requested a semen analysis from Osman, which he grudgingly underwent three times. The semen analyses revealed a chronic prostate infection and poor sperm motility, for which Osman was prescribed expensive drug therapy. Fadia, meanwhile, underwent both drug therapy and invasive procedures, such as cervical electrocautery, in which her cervix was thermocauterized by a heated instrument. Eventually finding her way to the university's Shatby Hospital, Fadia was diagnosed as having a large ovarian cyst, a severe pelvic infection, and blockage of both fallopian tubes. She underwent surgery to remove the cyst and 'clean out' the fallopian tubes, but a young physician, being uncharacteristically straightforward, told Fadia that her chances of conceiving normally without the help of IVF were minimal.

When Fadia broached the subject of IVF with Osman, he was adamantly op-posed—not only because of the extraordinary expense, which was well beyond the means of a poor carpenter, but also because Osman considered IVF to be *ḥarām*, or forbidden by Islam. According to Osman, who reinterpreted for Fadia the message of a popular televised cleric, the sinfulness of this procedure certainly derived from the fact that 'another man's sperm' might be introduced during the IVF procedure. Thus, 'a man would be raising someone other than his own child.'

Although Fadia herself was willing to try IVF, which she believed was imported from America, she realized her chances of undergoing this treatment were remote, given the delays in the public IVF programme at Shatby, her husband's moral opposition to the procedure, and their relentless poverty. With few treatment options left open to her, Fadia hoped that Osman's own male infertility problems and lack of children from his previous marriages would 'keep him silent' on the subject of divorce. For, if Osman divorced her, as was his right under Islamic personal status law, she would truly have nowhere else to go.

In the fall of 1992, I received a letter from Fadia, which she had dictated to one of the physicians at Shatby Hospital, who sent it on to me. Because of Fadia's failure to bear his children, Osman did, in fact, divorce her in August 1991. But, fortunately for Fadia, now a two-time divorcee, she was remarried in November of the same year, to a city bus driver who she described as a 'beautiful and decent man'. Best of all, Fadia reported that they loved each other, with the great affection that she had missed in both of her previous marriages. Unfortunately for me, I have since then lost touch with my friend and informant Fadia, as my letters to her have never been answered. But I can only hope that Fadia's newfound happiness has continued, and that, with or without the help of test tubes, she becomes an Egyptian mother of the children she so desires.

THE STORY OF AMIRA AND GALAL

Amira and Galal represent the other face of Egypt—one in which wealthy elites are able to purchase the fruits of globalization, including high-cost, high-tech medical services such as IVF. I met Amira and Galal on a hot July morning in the IVF clinic of an ex-movie star turned distinguished university ob/gyn professor named Mohamed Yehia.[3] Dr. Yehia was unusually supportive of my anthropological research—more than any of the Egyptian physicians I have worked with over the years. He not only read both of my books on Egyptian infertility (Inhorn 1994, 1996), but he also enjoyed discussing and debating my research, including the issues that were emerging through my work in his centre. He also arranged for me to have a private hospital room where I was able to conduct confidential interviews, as confidentiality turned out to be a major issue of concern for many IVF patients. And he introduced me to couples like Amira and Galal, encouraging them to participate in my study.

As it turned out, Amira and Galal were relatively new to Dr. Yehia's clinic, but as a transnationally sophisticated couple, they were already 'old pros' at IVF, which they had tried 2 years earlier in Los Angeles. Amira had married Galal 4 years before their first IVF attempt, knowing that Galal, her first cousin, suffered from a surgically irreparable varicocele, or a cluster of dilated veins in his testicles causing him to have a very poor sperm count. Although Amira's parents were deeply opposed to her marrying a man known to be infertile, even if he was her cousin, Amira loved Galal, a kind man who was also a handsome, rich factory owner. In part to escape family pressure and in part to seek medical advice, Amira and Galal decided to emigrate to the United States in 1992, where Amira had a sister living in Los Angeles. Once settled, they sought treatment for Galal's infertility and were told that they should undergo artificial insemination using donor semen from a sperm bank. Incredulous, Amira and Galal explained to the American physician that 'we are Muslims and this is forbidden.' So he referred them to an Egyptian Muslim physician running his own LA-based IVF clinic. This was the first time either Amira or Galal had heard of IVF, but, once they talked with the Egyptian doctor, they were soon convinced that IVF was allowed by Islam as long as both sperm and eggs came from husband and wife. Furthermore, they felt fairly certain that a good Muslim doctor would never allow any laboratory mix-ups to occur—even in LA. So Amira and Galal went ahead with one trial of IVF, which cost them $16,300. When the in vitro fertilization process produced extra embryos that were not to be transferred to Amira's uterus, she was given three choices: freezing, destroying, or donating to another couple. As Amira explained: 'We said, "destroy". It is our religion. We do not believe in a mixture of relations.'

Unfortunately for Amira and Galal, the trial of IVF was unsuccessful, as were Galal's real estate ventures in LA. So they decided to return to Egypt in 1995, where Amira proceeded to open a children's fashion boutique. Upon their return to Egypt, relatives on both sides of their family began urging them to go to doctors in Egypt, where 'science is constantly advancing'. But Galal had his doubts that doctors in Egypt were competent to carry out IVF without making major errors. It was not until they read two news articles—one in the major daily newspaper, *Al-Ahram*, and the other in a news magazine, *Nus id-Dunya*—that Amira and Galal changed their opinion about their potential to undergo successful IVF in their home country. Namely, the media were covering the successful introduction in Egypt of intracytoplasmic sperm injection (ICSI), a new variant of IVF in which the sperm of men with very poor fertility profiles are actually injected directly into the ovum, thereby 'helping along' the in vitro fertilization process. Amira and Galal decided that ICSI—or 'the microscopic injection' as it is called in Egypt—might be the solution to their childlessness, and they proceeded to the clinics of two physicians offering this newest technology. One, a notorious curmudgeon with exceptionally poor bedside manner, made Amira and Galal feel like 'he was just in it for the money'. So they chose Dr. Yehia, who, as Amira put it, 'pats you and says, "OK, it will be all right." '

Indeed, Amira needed Dr. Yehia's reassurance after her first trial of ICSI was cancelled. After going to great lengths to obtain the hormonal agents necessary to stimulate her ovaries—including having friends and relatives bring the drugs from Alexandria and Saudi Arabia—these agents did not succeed in producing an adequate number of ova for retrieval. As Amira explained, 'It costs your body and your feelings and your money. It's not easy. But my husband always supports me; it's very, very helpful for me. You feel like you're desperate and after that, he says, "We will try again." ' When Amira told the doctor that she did not think she could go through the emotional roller coaster of another failed trial, he told her to remain hopeful, and this time he provided her with the hormonal drugs from his own clinic supply. On their second try, the drugs worked, and Amira and Galal were able to go forward with the ICSI procedure. Although ICSI is the most expensive new reproductive technology available in Egypt, it cost Amira and Galal only $2,700—or less than one-fifth of what it had cost them to undertake one trial of IVF in the United States.

Luckily for Amira, she became an Egyptian mother of a test-tube baby, a beautiful little girl named Dalia, in the spring of 1997. Amira explained, 'Even if they have all these facilities now for IVF and ICSI in Egypt, after everything, if God wants me to have a child I will, and if not, I won't.' Clearly, God has decided in favour of Amira's motherhood—with the help of test tubes.

'ARENAS OF CONSTRAINT': CLASS, GENDER, RELIGION

Class

The contrasting stories of Fadia, Amira, and their husbands point to many issues. But what is especially clear from these two stories is the importance of structural constraints: namely, that one's class position in Egyptian society is often *the* major determinant of who receives IVF treatment services.

As seen in Fadia's story, the new reproductive technologies are absolutely unaffordable for most poor and even many middle-class Egyptian patients, even though they are often aware and highly desirous of such treatments. With only one exception, all Egyptian IVF centres today are *private* concerns, charging comparatively high prices for the procedures and drugs that patients pay for out-of-pocket—since health insurance in Egypt is new and not widespread. The one exception to this rule is the University of Alexandria's Shatby Hospital, where I conducted my initial research on infertility in the late 1980s. Shortly after I left Egypt, Shatby Hospital did open its own IVF centre, and the first Alexandrian 'baby of the tubes' was born and heralded in the Egyptian media in early 1992. However, since those early publicity-driven days of 'free', government-sponsored IVF, fewer and fewer test-tube babies have been born to poor Egyptian women such as Fadia. As Egypt's one and only *public* IVF programme, the Shatby Hospital IVF clinic continues to run, but on such a low volume that very few patients receive treatment and success rates are compromised. For the most part, the physicians charged with running this public clinic put their energies into their private IVF practices—which, as is typical for Egyptian physicians working in the public sector, they run 'on the side'.

As with Dr. Yehia, the Egyptian doctors who own and operate private IVF clinics comprise a small, elite corps of highly educated and biomedically sophisticated reproductive medicine specialists. Most of them have utilized their own economic resources to seek training in IVF in either Europe or the US. And, although many of these physicians have some sympathy for less affluent patients, occasionally taking on IVF charity cases, they generally feel justified in charging high prices for their services and subsequently purchasing the lifestyles—including, in some cases, BMWs and Mercedez-Benzes—that the profit from these services brings to them.

Not surprisingly, their patients also tend to be educated elites such as Amira and Galal, who are sophisticated about their medical options and can afford to pay for high-tech therapies. In a society where the majority of women remain illiterate and do not work in the formal sector, the women patients who present to IVF clinics today tend to be highly educated professionals, who are employed as doctors, lawyers, architects, engineers, accountants, businesswomen, professors, tourism officials, and even movie stars. Furthermore, many of these women and their husbands are members of the Egyptian 'brain drain' generation; namely, they increase their wealth by working in the petro-rich Arab Gulf countries, returning home annually on month-long summer vacations in order to undertake a trial of IVF. Some, like Amira and Galal, are true globe-hopping migrants, moving temporarily to Western countries in order to try IVF, often before they become convinced to seek IVF at home.

In other words, over a relatively short time span of a decade, the IVF scene in Egypt—once touted as being open to even the poorest public-hospital patients such as Fadia—has become extremely class based and exclusionary, the arena of a handful of elite doctors and their high-class patients. This does not mean that elites—both doctors and patients—are without feeling for the poor and even middle-class women who cannot afford IVF therapy. For example, Dr. Yehia described his futile, 10-year campaign to introduce IVF at Cairo's largest public, ob/gyn teaching hospital, bemoaning the lack of political will that had frustrated his efforts. Furthermore, affluent women themselves lamented the high cost of IVF therapy and the need to repeat the therapy if it did not succeed. They agreed that such therapy is exceedingly expensive, especially in light of what they view as a poor salary structure in Egypt and a generally low standard of living in this developing country. Yet, most of these patients also admitted that they and their husbands could afford repeated trials of IVF. And many stated bluntly during interviews that these therapies are 'not for everyone'—the 'everyone' in this case tacitly meaning poor women such as Fadia, who are often known to wealthy women only in their capacity as domestic servants.

Indeed, echoed in this exclusionary discourse is the same kind of Eurocentric prejudice which, as noted earlier, seems to underlie much Western discourse on infertility and the new reproductive technologies, and which is certainly rife in the Western-generated population discourse on Egypt. Namely, the new reproductive technologies to combat infertility *should not* be 'for everyone', because, as the equation goes, those who cannot afford these technologies certainly cannot 'afford children'. To wit, poor women do not deserve to be mothers—and especially not 'test-tube mothers'. And any reproductive technology directed at them should be to inhibit—not facilitate—their fertility.

So where does this leave infertile women such as Fadia? As her story highlights, most poor Egyptian women *do* seek treatment for their infertility, but not at IVF centres in Cairo or Alexandria. Rather, most poor women obtain help from both traditional 'ethnogynaecologists' and 'biogynaecologists' not specializing in IVF (Inhorn 1994), and they may employ their services simultaneously. Indeed, given Egypt's 5,000-year history of shifting medical traditions (Millar and Lane 1988; Inhorn 1994), numerous healing philosophies are still present in Egypt, leading to a multifaceted array of etiological, diagnostic, and therapeutic beliefs and practices regarding the nature and treatment of infertility.

Throughout urban poor neighbourhoods and rural communities in Egypt, healers such as lay midwives and herbalists treat the infertile with the materia medica and power of beliefs derived from these earlier traditions. As seen in the case of Fadia and her pursuit of a variety of traditional remedies, the vast majority of lower-class women continue to rely on these popular, indigenous practitioners at least as a first line of resort; for it is these healers, and not doctors, who recognize, diagnose, and treat ethnogynaecological causes of infertility (Inhorn 1994). These include, inter alia, reproductive 'binding' via ritual pollution; utero-ovarian humidity; an 'open back'; a severe shock or fright; sorcery; and the spirit-sister under the ground, who renders women infertile when angered. Although poor women are variable in the degree and extent to which they accept these ethnoetiologies and act upon them in their treatment quests, suffice it to say that ethnogynaecological beliefs, treatments, and practitioners are alive and well in Egypt among the urban underclass, providing an 'alternative' therapeutic realm for poor infertile women that is rich and varied in its content.

For many poor women such as Fadia, ethnogynaecology remains an especially appealing avenue for therapy, because of the considerable constraints to proper infertility care posed by Egyptian biomedicine. To wit, in Egypt today, those women who cannot afford IVF and the other new reproductive technologies are typically subjected to an array of outdated, inefficacious, and even iatrogenic, or disease-producing, therapies that are widely practised by Egyptian biogynaecologists. In many cases, the subjects of these iatrogenic practices are poor, minimally educated women, who, having been convinced of the superiority of biomedicine or simply desperate to be cured, may sell virtually everything they own in order to finance their biomedical quests to doctors who can only be described as 'second-rate'. Typically, these physicians engage in the blatant abuse of fertility drugs—overprescribing them to patients and failing to monitor sometimes serious side effects which may lead to additional infertility problems. Furthermore, as seen in Fadia's story, infertile Egyptian women typically undergo multiple, often painful invasive procedures—such as tubal insufflation, to purportedly 'blow open' blocked fallopian tubes; dilatation and curettage (D&C), to purportedly 'clean' the uterine cavity; and cervical electrocautery, to purportedly treat an 'eroded' cervix—that are not indicated in the modern treatment of infertility and are potentially dangerous.

Although a detailed cultural critique of Egyptian biogynaecological practice is beyond the scope of this chapter and is presented elsewhere (Inhorn 1994), suffice it to say here that an indigenous critique is beginning to emerge from within the Egyptian biogynaecological community itself. It involves the subversive discourse of younger, often university-based physicians, who rail against the irrational, inefficacious, and harmful practices of many of their community-based colleagues. According to these critics, most Egyptian biogynaecologists continue to perform these procedures for two reasons: (1) because of their outdated medical knowledge, which derives from an antiquated, colonially produced system of medical education in Egypt (El-Mehairy 1984; Sonbol 1991) and which is accompanied by a blatant lack of physician accountability through any form of systematic continuing medical education or malpractice; and (2) because of physicians' frank greed for money in a climate of economic uncertainty and stiff competition for paying clientele. Poor infertile women, who are uneducated and often too easily impressed by male physicians' authority, constitute easy prey for unscrupulous physicians, who may justify their largely inefficacious treatments as a harmless form of hope for their desperate female patients. As physicians practising in a developing country, they realize all too well that it is such poor patients who will never be able to afford IVF and other NRTs. Thus, the 'old' reproductive technologies, which are applied in a cavalier and harmful fashion, are even justified as a form of 'mercy' treatment by physicians who are incapable of offering the newer reproductive technologies to their poor patients.

Gender

Whereas most poor patients such as Fadia typically undergo these deleterious therapies, elite patients such as Amira rarely encounter them, as they tend to make their ways directly or through referral to infertility specialists. However, even Egyptian elites may find themselves limited in their avenues to IVF family formation for reasons having little to do with social class and subsequent access to high-quality medical care. In addition to class-based constraints, gender relations and conjugal dynamics come into play when Egyptian wives and husbands, together or alone, seek IVF services.

Indeed, gender politics can be an arena of great contestation, for infertility is highly threatening to both men and women and is often destabilizing of otherwise comfortable, companionate marriages. Generally speaking, however, women experience the threat of infertility more keenly. To wit, women who are unable to achieve entrance into the 'cult of motherhood' (Bouhdiba 1985) in Egypt are seen as being less than other women, as depriving their husbands and husbands' families of offspring, and as even endangering other people's children through their uncontrollably envy. Typically, they are also blamed for the infertility, and they are expected to seek treatment. Thus, in Egypt, infertile women of all backgrounds tend to face tremendous social pressures, ranging from marital duress and dissolution, to stigmatization within the extended family network, to outright ostracism within the larger community of fertile women. Indeed, of all the types of persons that one could be, there are very few less desirable social identities than that of the infertile woman, or *Umm Il-Ghayyib*, 'Mother of the Missing One', as Egyptians sometimes call her, giving this particular identity all of the classic features of a stigma (Goffman 1963).

Paradoxically, whereas infertility always mars a woman's social and gender identity, male infertility does not typically redound in the same way on a man's masculinity or personhood. Although male infertility is profoundly emasculating, given its conflation with problems of virility or sexual potency, having a child does not 'complete a man like it does a woman'. Whereas a woman's full adult personhood can only be achieved through attainment of married motherhood, a man's sense of achievement as an adult human being has other potential outlets, including employment, education, religious attainment, leisure activities, and the like.

Furthermore, men such as Osman and Galal who are infertile need not fear much for their masculine reputations, for male infertility is rarely 'exposed' to others in Egyptian communities. Why? For one, the diagnostic enterprise of semen analysis is fraught with difficulty in Egypt; some men refuse to undergo semen analysis, others disbelieve their negative results, others hide their bad results from their wives and families, and some are even known to bribe laboratory technicians for highly inflated, false reports. Furthermore, infertility specialists in Egypt bemoan the technical quality of semen analysis in their country, which varies considerably from lab to lab and thus may be highly unreliable. In other words, even though male infertility contributes to at least half of all infertility cases globally, diagnosing it in Egypt remains highly problematic and is exacerbated by men's abilities to hide the problem from others.

'Hiding' male infertility is abetted by wives such as Amira, who typically 'cover' for their husbands and publicly accept the 'blame'. Why? For one, many women continue to assume that there must be something wrong with them, too, and the degree of internalization of self-blame, even when it is not merited, is often quite remarkable in women's discourse about their reproductively fragile and malfunctioning bodies (Inhorn 1994). Furthermore, wives such as Amira who know of their husbands' infertility typically express profound sympathy and care for their husbands—rarely deeming the infertility to be a striking blow to their marriages. In fact, marriages such as Amira and Galal's that are affected by male infertility are often some of the best. This is because infertile husbands usually feel profound guilt over 'depriving' their wives of children; therefore, they treat their wives exceptionally kindly. Women, for their part, often feel great relief in knowing that their childless marriages are nonetheless secure by virtue of a male reproductive failing. Thus, they generally (although not always)[4] reciprocate their husbands' kindnesses with mutual affection and even public acceptance of the 'blame' for the infertility.

Infertility stemming from a wife, on the other hand, typically affects marital dynamics and outcomes in deleterious ways, sometimes leading to polygynous remarriage or outright divorce, as in the case of Fadia and Osman. Although many men are reluctant or totally unwilling to replace their infertile wives with a fertile woman, their extended family members are usually vociferous about the need to perpetuate the patrilineage (Inhorn 1996). Thus, a wife's infertility tends to lead to marital turmoil at some point in her marriage, usually through pressure exerted by in-laws. As a result, infertile women live in fear that their marriages will 'collapse', for Islamic personal status laws consider a wife's barrenness to be a major ground for divorce. Although Islam also allows women to divorce if male infertility can be proven, a woman's initiation of a divorce continues to be so stigmatizing in Egypt that women rarely choose this option unless their marriages are truly unbearable (Inhorn 1996).

Although most husbands of infertile Egyptian women do *not* divorce their wives, thereby resisting tremendous family pressure, divorces over childlessness do occur, as seen in the case of Fadia and Osman. Indeed, even among the presumably 'enlightened' upper classes, some men would rather divorce their infertile wives than undergo the trials, tribulations, moral uncertainties, and expenses surrounding IVF. Furthermore, during the IVF treatment process, marriages sometimes come unglued under the intense physical and psychological pressure that this therapy typically exacts on couples.

But perhaps the saddest new twist in marital politics in Egypt has occurred as a result of the recent introduction of ICSI, the 'newest' new reproductive technology that allowed Amira and Galal to have their baby. Namely, with ICSI, cases of seemingly intractable male infertility can now be overcome. Thus, ICSI heralds a revolution in the treatment of male infertility, and its arrival in Egypt has led to the flooding of IVF clinics with male-infertility cases—for example, 70 per cent of those couples I interviewed in the summer of 1996.

But, unfortunately, many of the wives of these Egyptian men, who have 'stood by' their infertile husbands for years, even decades in some cases, have grown too old to produce viable ova for the ICSI procedure. Because Islamic law forbids any kind of ova donation or surrogacy, couples with a 'reproductively elderly' wife face four difficult options: (1) to remain together permanently without children; (2) to foster an orphan, since adoption per se is not allowed by Islam; (3) to partake in a polygynous union with a younger, more 'fertile' woman;[5] or (4) to divorce outright so that the husband can remarry such a woman. Unfortunately, more and more highly educated, upper-class Egyptian men are choosing the latter option—believing that their own reproductive destinies may lie with younger 'replacement' wives, who are allowed to men under Islam's personal status laws.

Although it is arguable whether Islam is more or less patriarchal than any other world religion, many Middle Eastern feminist scholars have nonetheless pointed to Islam's personal status laws governing divorce and polygyny as glaring examples of the nexus between patriarchal ideology and practice in the Middle East (e.g. Badran 1993; Coulson and Hinchcliffe 1978; Hatem 1986; Smock and Youssef 1977; White 1978). Certainly, these laws—coupled with the Islamic position on the need for biological parenthood in the practice of IVF and ICSI—place infertile Egyptian women and the 'old' wives of infertile Egyptian men in an extremely precarious position *vis-à-vis* their reproductive and marital futures.

Religion

Indeed, Islam, along with the class-based constraints to IVF already described, poses perhaps the other most serious constraint on the practice of IVF in Egypt, both in terms of its restrictive legislation and in the anxieties over religious matters that it creates. Egypt is a decidedly Muslim country, with more than 90 per cent of its citizens Sunni Muslims and with public expressions of religiosity increasing under a two-decade long wave of Islamic revivalism. Although Egyptian Muslims are certainly heterogeneous in terms of religiosity and degree of religious expression, it is also true that Islam provides a source of guidance for many, if not most, Egyptian Muslims in a variety of arenas of human activity, including beliefs and practices regarding health and medicine. Instruction which informs or regulates the everyday activities of Muslims can be found in a number of theological documents which make up the body of Islamic jurisprudence. Those issues, such as the introduction of new reproductive technologies, which are not discussed in the legal texts are regularly legislated upon by the most venerable Islamic legal authorities in the form of written religious proclamations called *fatwas* (Lane and Rubinstein 1991).

Even before IVF emerged on the scene in Egypt, the Grand Sheikh of Egypt's world-renowned Al-Azhar University issued a *fatwa* on the religious permissibility of IVF. Namely, he declared that IVF and similar therapies were an acceptable line of treatment—as long as they were carried out by expert scientists with sperm from a husband and ova from a wife with 'no mixing with other cells from other couples or other species, and that the conceptus [the embryo] is implanted in the uterus of the same wife from whom the ova were taken' (Aboulghar *et al.* 1990). In other words, this *fatwa*, which is widely viewed as authoritative by physicians and patients in Egyptian (and other Middle Eastern) IVF centres today, clearly spells out which individuals undergoing reproductive therapies have the right to claim the status of 'mother' and 'father'—namely, only the *biological* mother and father, who thereby maintain 'blood ties' to their IVF offspring. Sperm, ova, and embryo donation are strictly prohibited, as is surrogacy.

Although this *fatwa* on IVF was issued as early as 1980, uncertainty about the Islamic position on IVF reigned throughout the rest of the decade in Egypt, as evident in Fadia's husband Osman's belief that IVF was *ḥarām*, or religiously prohibited. By the mid-1990s, however, some of this moral uncertainty had given way to a kind of moral clarity among the Egyptian women and men undergoing IVF and ICSI. Stating that the religious aspect of IVF is its 'most important' element, Egyptian IVF patients interviewed in my 1996 study were relative experts on the religious dimensions of IVF. As they explained, sperm, egg, or embryo donation leads to a 'mixture of relations'. Such mixing severs blood ties between parents and their offspring; confuses issues of paternity, descent, and inheritance; and leads to potentially incestuous marriages of the children of unknown egg or sperm donors. Thus, for Egyptian women like Amira with infertile husbands, the thought of using donor sperm from a 'bank' was simply reprehensible and was tantamount in their minds to committing *zina*, or adultery. Surrogacy, in addition, was believed to tamper with the 'natural maternal bond', which is meant to be an exclusive link between one mother and her biological children.

Furthermore, much of this righteous discourse is now constructed in relation to discourses about the moral corruption occurring in the Christian West. In Egypt, news stories and television movies imported from America and Europe show women who 'rent their wombs', only to struggle over the custody of the children they bear; or infertility doctors who impregnate hundreds of women with their own sperm, only to be sent to prison; or IVF mothers who bear black and white twins by two fathers because of careless sperm admixtures in Western IVF laboratories. Proclaiming that this would never happen in Egypt—where patients can trust that their IVF doctors are good, religious Muslims—patients in Egyptian IVF centres described these stories, all of which happen to be true, with a kind of righteous incredulity. They concluded, often apologizing to the American anthropologist researcher, that 'each society has its own traditions and customs'.

But such claims of moral superiority belie the fact that many Egyptians who are either contemplating or actually undertaking IVF in Egyptian IVF centres spend long hours worrying about 'accidental donation'—namely, unintentional laboratory 'mix-ups' of semen, ova, or embryos. In some cases, these fears and suspicions may prevent couples from undertaking IVF altogether, for once the products of conception leave one's body, it is virtually impossible to know for sure whether these products will be returned untainted.

Given these anxieties, the paramount concern for patients such as Amira and Galal is the trustworthiness of the physicians who provide the new reproductive technologies. Are they in it for the money? Are they technically competent? Are they good Muslims? Do they care about their patients? Some IVF providers, such as Dr. Yehia, realize the importance of good doctor–patient relations and spend considerable time in patient counselling, including on the religious aspects of IVF. In Dr. Yehia's case, furthermore, he and his laboratory counterpart have attempted to quash fears about laboratory accidents by providing each patient couple with a tailor-made videotape of the laboratory aspects of their own in vitro fertilization procedure. Other IVF physicians attempt to accentuate their own Muslim religiosity, peppering their speech with religious idioms, holding prayer beads, and reading passages from the Qur'an as their patients are wheeled into the embryo transfer room. Such physicians tend to develop saint-like reputations and, not surprisingly, attract large patient followings. Thus, physicians themselves must negotiate their multiple and sometimes conflicting roles as both providers of lucrative, high-tech global technologies and upholders of local religious and cultural traditions that restrict how these technologies are utilized.

As an American anthropologist interested in understanding the 'local moral worlds' (Kleinman 1992) of Egyptian IVF patients and their physicians, I would suggest that there may be a paradoxical 'down side' to Islam's restrictive moral code—one that affects women in particular, but which few infertile Egyptian Muslim women are willing to contemplate or discuss. On the one hand, Islam glorifies motherhood and all it entails (Schleifer 1986), insisting that women are endowed with a 'natural maternal instinct' and that children are the 'decorations of worldly life'. Yet, infertile women who attempt to achieve glorious motherhood through resort to reproductive technologies are narrowly limited in their technological options by virtue of a religion that prohibits any form of ova donation or surrogacy. Moreover, these constraints seem even greater when one considers that Islam also prohibits adoption for the same reasons it disallows IVF donation practices—thereby further restricting how families are to be formed and motherhood realized.

CONCLUSION

It seems appropriate to conclude this chapter with a particularly trenchant comment from a recent essay on 'Anthropology and the New Reproductive

Technologies' (Shore 1992, p. 301), which states, 'The lesson from anthropology is that every society has a vested interest in controlling reproduction, and in each, we tend to find dominant institutions—the church, the state, the medical profession, or whatever—competing to monopolize the discourses through which legitimate reproduction is conceptualized.'

Through my own anthropological work in Egypt, I hope to have shed some light on the ways in which the reproductive destinies of infertile Egyptian women are being constrained, if not always directly controlled, by deeply entrenched class divisions and gender hierarchies and by the state religion, which, in the case of the new reproductive technologies, directly informs the practices of the medical profession. Clearly, much is at stake here, 'not only traditional definitions of family, disability, parenting, kin connection, and inheritance, but the conventional understandings of nature, life, humanity, morality, and the future' (Franklin and Ragone 1998, p. 9). For some infertile Egyptian women such as Fadia, their futures remain uncertain and their chances of becoming Egyptian mothers of test-tube babies remain slim, given the myriad constraints that confront them. For others, such as Amira, they are only too happy to be living in a society in which the global has become the local, and the fruits of globalization are literally the test-tube children they bear.

Notes

1. Israel, the only non-Muslim country in the Middle East, now hosts 24 IVF centres, the greatest number per capita in the world, according to anthropologist Susan Kahn (personal communication).
2. These names are pseudonyms.
3. This name is not a pseudonym, as neither the author nor the doctor wish that he remain anonymous.
4. From his long-term experience as an Egyptian infertility specialist, Dr. Yehia warns that not all elite women are so kind to their infertile husbands and may, in fact, exert considerable power over them by reminding them of their threatened masculinity.
5. Polygynous remarriage is rarely practised, as few Egyptian women today wish to remain as an elder infertile co-wife in a polygynous union.

References

Aboulghar, M. A., Serour, G. I., and Mansour, R. (1990), 'Some ethical and legal aspects of medically assisted reproduction in Egypt', *International Journal of Bioethics*, 1: 265–8.

Badran, M. (1993), 'Independent women: More than a century of feminism in Egypt', in J. E. Tucker (ed.), *Arab Women: Old Boundaries, New Frontiers*, Bloomington: Indiana University Press, pp. 129–48.

Bouhdiba, A. (1985), *Sexuality in Islam*, London: Routledge and Kegan Paul.

Collet, M., Reniers, J., Frost, E., Gass, R., Yvert, F., Leclerc, A., Roth-Meyer, C., Ivanoff, B., and Meheus, A. (1988), 'Infertility in Central Africa: Infection is the cause', *International Journal of Gynecology and Obstetrics*, 26: 423–8.

Coulson, N., and Hinchcliffe, D. (1978), 'Women and law reform in contemporary Islam', in L. Beck and N. Keddie (eds.), *Women in the Muslim World*, Cambridge: Harvard University Press, pp. 37–51.

Egyptian Fertility Care Society (1995), *Community-based Study of the Prevalence of Infertility and Its Etiological Factors in Egypt: (1) The Population-based Study*, Cairo: The Egyptian Fertility Care Society.

El-Mehairy, T. (1984), *Medical Doctors: A Study of Role Concept and Job Satisfaction, The Egyptian Case*, Leiden: E. J. Brill.

Ericksen, K., and Brunette, T. (1996), 'Patterns and predictors of infertility among African women: A cross-national survey of twenty-seven nations', *Social Science & Medicine*, 42: 209–20.

Franklin, S., and Ragone, H. (1998), 'Introduction', in S. Franklin and H. Ragone (eds.), *Reproducing Reproduction: Kinship, Power, and Technological Innovation*, Philadelphia: University of Pennsylvania Press, pp. 1–14.

Goffman, E. (1963), *Stigma: Notes on the Management of Spoiled Identity*, Englewood Cliffs, NJ: Prentice-Hall

Hatem, M. (1986), 'The enduring alliance of nationalism and patriarchy in Muslim personal status laws: The case of modern Egypt', *Feminist Issues*, 6: 19–43.

Humphrey, M., and Humphrey, H. (1986), 'A fresh look at genealogical bewilderment', *British Journal of Medical Psychology*, 59: 133–40.

Inhorn, M. C. (1994), *Quest for Conception: Gender, Infertility, and Egyptian Medical Traditions*, Philadelphia: University of Pennsylvania Press.

—— (1996), *Infertility and Patriarchy: The Cultural Politics of Gender and Family Life in Egypt*, Philadelphia: University of Pennsylvania Press.

Klein, R., and Rowland, R. (1989), 'Hormone cocktails: Women as test-sites for fertility drugs', *Women's Studies International Forum*, 12: 333–48.

Kleinman, A. M. (1992), 'Local worlds of suffering: An interpersonal focus for ethnographies of illness experience', *Qualitative Health Research*, 2: 127–34.

Lane, S. D., and Rubinstein, R. A. (1991), 'The use of *fatwas* in the production of reproductive health policy in Egypt', Paper presented at the 90th Annual Meeting of the American Anthropological Association, December 1991, Chicago.

Mies, M. (1987), 'Why do we need all this? A call against genetic engineering and reproductive technology', in P. Spallone and D. L. Steinberg (eds.), *Made to Order: The Myth of Reproductive and Genetic Progress*, Oxford: Pergamon Press, pp. 34–47.

Millar, M. I., and Lane, S. D. (1988), 'Ethno-ophthalmology in the Egyptian delta: An historical systems approach to ethnomedicine in the Middle East', *Social Science & Medicine*, 26: 651–7.

Rowland, R. (1987), 'Of women born, but for how long? The relationship of women to the new reproductive technologies and the issue of choice', in P. Spallone and D. L. Steinberg (eds.), *Made to Order: The Myth of Reproductive and Genetic Progress*, Oxford: Pergamon Press, pp. 67–83.

Sandelowski, M., and de Lacey, S., 'The uses of a "disease": Infertility as rhetorical vehicle', in M. C. Inhorn and F. van Balen (eds.), *Infertility around the Globe: New Thinking on Childlessness, Gender, and Reproductive Technologies*, University of California Press, Berkeley (in press).

Schleifer, A. (1986), *Motherhood in Islam*, Cambridge, England: Islamic Academy.

Shore, C. (1992), 'Virgin births and sterile debates: Anthropology and the new reproductive technologies', *Current Anthropology*, 33: 295–301.

Smock, A. C., and Youssef, N. H. (1977), 'Egypt: From seclusion to limited participation', in J. Z. Giele and A. C. Smock (eds.), *Women: Roles and Status in Eight Countries*, New York: John Wiley, pp. 34–79.

Sonbol, A. (1991), *The Creation of a Medical Profession in Egypt, 1800–1922*, Syracuse, New York: Syracuse University Press.

White, E. H. (1978), 'Legal reform as an indicator of women's status in Muslim nations', in L. Beck and N. Keddie (eds.), *Women in the Muslim World*, Cambridge, MA: Harvard University Press, pp. 52–68.

World Health Organization (1987), 'Infections, pregnancies, and infertility: Perspectives on prevention', *Fertility and Sterility*, 47: 964–8.

5

Risk, Vulnerability, and Harm Reduction: Preventing STIs in Southeast Asia by Antibiotic Prophylaxis, a Misguided Practice

MARK NICHTER

We see things not as they are, but as we are. (Immanuel Kant)

Recognition of risk, production of knowledge about risk, and management of risk have been identified as core features of late modernity by several notable social theorists.[1] Globally, the public is being exposed to an increasing stream of information about risk to disease (accidents, ecological disasters, etc.). This information is provided by a number of different sources ranging from public health experts engaged in disease surveillance to politicians engaged in the justification of public policy, newspaper reporters in search of headlines to marketers pitching products. Information about risk is typically presented to the public as 'objective fact' backed up by statistics which highlight correlations commonly misinterpreted by the public as causal relationships. As many social scientists have pointed out, what masquerades as 'objective fact' is often 'social fact.' Knowledge about risk is far from neutral and often motivated by subtle and not so subtle social, political, and economic forces. Assumptions guide research (and research funding), who is to be compared to whom (e.g. groups defined by race or ethnicity instead of social class or environment), what is singled out as potential risk or protective factors to be measured, and the manner in which data is analysed as well as presented. The rhetoric of risk assumes a sense of determinacy which provides those in fields like public health with a 'model of' as well as a 'model for' action justifying as much as guiding recommendations.

An issue worth investigating is how messages about risk are interpreted and responded to by members of the general public.[2] Social theorists writing about risk as a feature of modernity often tend to speak in monolithic terms leading one to believe that concerns about risk lead whole populations to engage in self-discipline and personal surveillance (Foucault 1979, 1980), or some form of passive if not active reflexivity (Beck 1992a,b, 1995).[3] Missing is a close examination of practice and expressions of agency exercised by those exposed to risk by choice or circumstance. Nowhere is this research more needed than in the study of sexual and reproductive health.

Existing research has made it abundantly clear that familiarity with messages about risk to sexually transmitted infections (STIs) does not predict compliance with recommended courses of behaviour which protect one from STIs.[4] This apparent disjuncture between knowledge and behaviour invites investigation of popular interpretations of risk messages, personal perceptions of vulnerability, and practices adopted to reduce risk or decrease harm from STIs which lie outside the purview of public health guidelines (and wisdom). A prudent starting point for such an investigation is the recognition that public health messages about risk may be at odds with local knowledge, experience, and perceptions of self-identity. For most people, risks do not appear to be democratic. All people exposed to a source of danger do not think themselves equally at risk to harm. Furthermore, risks are rarely thought about abstractly or in isolation. They are understood subjectively and in context (Gifford 1986; Maine *et al.* 1995; Rhodes 1995; Ramos *et al.* 1995; Sobo 1993).[5] When individuals think about risks related to sexual activity, they tend to do so in relation to: (1) their personal sense of strength and relative sense of vulnerability; (2) their immediate needs versus the possible long-term consequences of their behaviour; (3) fears of physical harm as well as concerns about compromising social relations; and (4) harm reduction practices they have heard about which serve as a means of 'damage control'. A rational-man approach to the study of sexual decision making affords only limited insight into how individuals respond to information about risk. Concerns about health are often eclipsed by more pressing matters, social relations and self-identity, dreams of possible futures, fantasies which rule the moment, leaps of faith, and acts of desperation.

In this chapter, I will consider perceptions of risk and vulnerability among Southeast Asian commercial sex workers (CSW) and their clients.[6] I will highlight the practical logic (Bourdieu 1990)[7] of local harm reduction (damage control) practices employed by members of these high-risk groups to protect themselves from STIs (as they are classified locally). Using data sets from the Philippines and Thailand, I will make a case for studying: (1) local perceptions of vulnerability to STIs; (2) those actions taken to prevent and/or reduce the risk of contracting STIs (before or after sexual acts); and (3) the extent to which these practices are undertaken to protect not only one's own health, but the health of significant others as an expression of social responsibility. It is my contention that such research constitutes an important and necessary complement to public health studies of 'groups at risk', risky behaviours, and environments conducive to risky behaviour.[8]

During the last 15 years, the rapid spread of AIDS has moved concern about sexually transmitted infections from the margins to the centre of public health programmes in Southeast Asia. In their rush to promote the use of condoms as a means of preventing AIDS and other sexually transmitted infections (Aral *et al.* 1996; Royce *et al.* 1997; Wasserheit 1992), public health professionals have failed to pay adequate attention to those actions taken by local populations to reduce their chances of experiencing STIs or passing them on to significant others. In the review of research which follows, I will make note of several practices adopted as a means of harm reduction, but will focus on one practice in particular, the prophylactic use of antibiotics. I will argue that this is an important, albeit misguided, form of preventive self-help behaviour popular in Southeast Asia.

Prophylactic use of antibiotics is flagged for attention for two reasons. The first reason is that this potentially dangerous behaviour is more common than most health officials suspect. To correct this misconception I document the prevalence of this behaviour among CSW in different work environments (in the Philippines) as well as men attending STI clinics (in Thailand). The second reason for focusing on this behaviour is that it is more complex than it first appears. An ethnographic study of the prophylactic use of antibiotics affords us important insights into 'preventive and protective' health behaviour as it is understood by local populations. It also offers us insights into pharmaceutical practice and the appropriation of curative medicines for preventive health purposes.

THE PHILIPPINES

Data Set One: Mindoro [Nichter 1989]

In 1989, during an ethnographic study of tuberculosis in a town on the island of Mindoro, I discovered that travelling salesmen, drivers, etc. who engaged in the services of commercial sex workers commonly consumed antibiotics as a prophylaxis against STIs (Tagalog: *sakit sa babae*—literally disease of women).[9] A small pilot study of 20 men was undertaken to explore the range of behaviours associated with antibiotic prophylaxis (Nichter 1996). To collect data on sexual behaviour I camped at two popular small hotels where men would drink and bring women back to their rooms. After initial interviews with this convenience sample, I re-interviewed each man following a night in which he had sex with a commercial sex worker.[10]

During the initial interview, 70 per cent of the men reported using antibiotics in the past to prevent STIs, and 80 per cent reported using condoms with commercial sex workers. Morning-after interviews revealed marked differences in condom and antibiotic use depending on the marital status of the man and his familiarity with the commercial sex worker. Six of the nine men 'short timing' a commercial sex worker (i.e. paying for sex by the hour or ejaculation) had used a condom during their one and only act of intercourse. All three married men in this group took or planned to take a prophylactic antibiotic. Of those three men who 'short timed' commercial sex workers and did not use a condom, two stated they knew the woman and trusted her to inform them if she was ill. One of the three men reported that he had taken an antibiotic already and another intended to do so in the next 24 hours.

An important methodological issue arose during morning-after interviews with the 11 men who spent the entire evening with a commercial sex worker engaging in several 'rounds' of intercourse. This issue involves the frequency of intercourse and the way in which researchers typically frame questions about condom use. When first asked if they had used a condom with their partner the night before, eight men responded that they had. However, follow-up questions revealed that three of these men had not used a condom during all 'rounds' of intercourse.[11] Familiarity with the commercial sex worker influenced condom use. None of the five men who used a condom during all rounds of sex were familiar with their partner. Curiously, two members of this group also planned to take an antibiotic within the next 24 hours. Of the three men who used a condom during one, but not all rounds of sex, two were 'somewhat familiar' with the commercial sex worker.

What do these data suggest beyond the fact that 30 per cent of the sample of 20 men used or planned on using antibiotics before or after sex with a commercial sex worker? Two distinct patterns of prophylactic antibiotics use emerged. Antibiotics were taken either as a primary form of STI prevention when risk was not deemed to be great, or as a supplementary, second line of STI protection in addition to condom use when the perceived risk was higher. Notably, five of the six men who had taken or planned on taking an antibiotic reported being able to identify a woman who had an STI by some sign or symptom (e.g. skin rash, body temperature, vaginal smell, or pain when pressed beneath the belly button—referred to as pus-on).[12] They spoke of antibiotics as immediate protection as well as 'just in case' insurance.

When the entire sample of 20 men was asked if STIs could be asymptomatic, there was little consensus. One of the most prominent ideas was that a woman could have a latent disease[13] which could manifest if she were weak or engaged in 'too many vices'. This was one reason why Filipino males say they prefer sex with younger commercial sex workers—they perceive them to be safer and less likely to have a hidden disease.

Informants reporting a history of prophylactic antibiotic use were asked if they took antibiotics because their own resistance was weak, or because the health of a sexual partner was suspect? Probed were ideas about both one's state of vulnerability and fears that a latent illness might reoccur if one did not protect himself from further risk. Two men related experiences of having taken antibiotics to prevent STI because they suspected that they had a latent illness or were vulnerable to illness. In the first case, the man had a history of STI diagnosed and treated by a private doctor who did not test the patient prior to or following the remission of symptoms. The man stated that sometimes he felt uneasy because his urine did not look or smell normal. He spoke of occasionally having a minor discharge, *tulo*, which he was afraid would develop into a more serious illness.[14] He did not experience any pain and had no lesions, but felt vulnerable to illness acquired through having sex. In the second case, the informant did not have manifest symptoms of an STI, but spoke of feeling excessive heat in his body because he sat in front of a hot engine all day as the driver of a small truck. He felt vulnerable to *pasma*, a body state associated with shocking the body by moving from a hot to cold state post-sex. In addition to taking antibiotics, this informant and several of the other men spoke of taking vitamins to increase resistance.[15]

Table 5.1. *Perception of antibiotics as a means of preventing STIs**

Population	Sample size	Per cent who believed antibiotics are useful in preventing STIs
Registered CSW	211	36
Unregistered CSW	89	37
Men who have sex with men	300	26
Male STI patients	100	19

*Knowledge, Attitude, and Practice Survey, Cebu, the Philippines (1992).

Data Set Two: Cebu City [Abellanosa 1992]

A knowledge, attitude, and practice (KAP) study of high-risk behaviour associated with STIs and AIDS was carried out in Cebu City, the Philippines, in 1992. Interviewed were samples of registered and unregistered (freelance) commercial sex workers, men who have sex with men, and male STI patients attending the Cebu City Social Hygiene Clinic. Informants were questioned primarily about condom use and the range of behaviours that they thought could place them at risk to AIDS (from kissing to mosquito bites). Abellanosa, a doctor at the Social Hygiene Clinic, had observed that several of her patients self-medicated themselves with antibiotics as a means of preventing STIs. To measure local perceptions about the efficacy of this practice, she included a question about the prophylactic use of antibiotics on her survey. Responses to this question are presented in Table 5.1. Between 19 and 37 per cent of four convenience samples of commercial sex workers registered at the Cebu City Social Hygiene clinic, unregistered freelancers, men having sex with men, and male STI patients reported that antibiotics were useful in preventing *sira*, the Cebuano term encompassing a wide range of STIs. Notably, commercial sex workers reported the highest rate of familiarity with and faith in antibiotic prophylaxis.

Data Set Three: Cebu City [Abellanosa and Nichter 1994–5]

A third more methodologically rigorous study was undertaken to examine the harm reduction behaviour of commercial sex workers in Cebu City in 1994–5 (Abellanosa and Nichter 1996). Central to this study was an investigation of the extent to which commercial sex workers perceived prophylactic antibiotic use to be an effective form of both STI and HIV prevention, the prevalence of this practice in different work environments, and the manner in which this practice affected condom use.

A survey instrument was developed and pretested following three months of intensive ethnographic research on sexually transmitted infections and AIDS in Cebu. This 144-item survey was then verbally administered to 200 commercial sex workers

Table 5.2. *Characteristics of 160 commercial sex workers, Cebu City, the Philippines**

Characteristics	High-class *casa* ($N=49$, $GC=9$)	High-class bar; massage ($N=40$; $GC=11$)	Low-class bar; massage ($N=31$; $GC=12$)	Freelancers ($N=40$)
Median age	22	23	23	18
Origin (%)				
Urban	43	40	45	50
Rural	57	60	55	50
Education (%)				
Elementary	12	10	26	48
High school	73	70	71	52
College	14	20	3	
Has child	59	58	74	63
Mean number clients/week	3	3	3	10
Median amount earned/week (dollar equivalent)	$120	$80	$60	$60

*Commercial sex workers are classified by work environment with those having a history of gonorrhoea (GC) assigned to their respective work site category.

between July 1994 and April 1995. A multi-stage sampling procedure was followed to ensure that commercial sex workers from four distinct sex work environments and commercial sex workers having a history of gonorrhoea would be represented. Work sites were classified on the basis of the cost of alcoholic beverages and services offered: high-class *casas* (houses of prostitution), high-class bars (as well as massage parlours, etc.), low-class bars (massage parlours, etc.), and freelance street soliciting. Following the classification of 108 hospitality establishments registered with the Cebu City health office, random samples of 40 commercial sex workers, ages 18–28, were selected from lists of women employed in each of the first three work environments and required to receive weekly clinic examinations for STIs.[16] A convenience sample of 40 freelance (unregistered) commercial sex workers, ages 15–28, working the streets (or in illegal low-class *casas*) comprised the fourth sample. These women rarely, if ever, receive an STI checkup unless suffering from painful symptoms. Forty registered commercial sex workers who had tested positive for gonorrhoea during the past year following a cervical Gram stain that detects Gram-negative diplococci comprised a fifth sample. This sample drawn from registered commercial sex workers was fairly evenly distributed across the first three work sites.

Of the 200 commercial sex workers initially interviewed, 120 of the 160 registered commercial sex workers and all 40 freelancers had engaged in vaginal sex with one or more customers in the last two weeks. A profile of this group of 160 commercial sex workers is provided in Table 5.2.

In-depth interviews documented that these women engage in a wide range of practices to reduce their chances of becoming infected with an STI,[17] beyond the use of condoms. The following list summarizes the 12 most common practices engaged in by these informants.

Practices engaged in to reduce the chances of experiencing an STI (N= 160)
Taking antibiotics
    before sex
    after sex
    occasionally
    routinely (i.e. weekly)
Washing the vagina
    with water after sex
    with soap/shampoo after sex
    with toothpaste
Douching
    with vinegar or Bedadin/Lactacyd
    with soda water or Coca Cola
Inspecting and washing a partner's penis prior to sex
Urinating after intercourse
Drinking soapy water or laundry detergent
Taking vitamins

The 160 commercial sex workers who had had sex with customers in the last two weeks were asked whether they: (1) had ever used antibiotics as a prophylactic against STIs; and (2) had used antibiotics for this purpose in the last two weeks.[18] When asked about the use of antibiotics for STI prophylaxis, 20 per cent reported that they took antibiotics for this purpose occasionally and another 18 per cent stated that they did so routinely. Among occasional and routine users, 24 per cent reported using prophylactic antibiotics after having sex with each customer, 9 per cent before having sex, and 4 per cent before and after having sex. Fifteen per cent reported taking antibiotics for prophylaxis two or three times a week, 6 per cent once a month, and 31 per cent when they felt like some illness might be developing in their body. This body state was left unspecified, but was distinct from manifest symptoms associated with the actual occurrence of an STI. The median number of antibiotic pills or capsules taken for prophylactic purposes was one per treatment event and the most common antibiotics used were ampicillin (55 per cent), rifampicin (16 per cent), and amoxycillin (15 per cent).

Differences in occasional and routine prophylactic antibiotic use were not found to be statistically significant with regard to a commercial sex worker's place of origin (rural/urban), level of education (above/below high school), age (above/below 22 years), and whether or not the commercial sex worker had a child. Significant differences did emerge, however, when rates of commercial sex workers ever-using antibiotics were examined in relation to work site and registration at the Social

Hygiene Clinic that required routine tests for STIs. Notably, among those commercial sex workers who had ever taken prophylactic antibiotics, freelancers were four times more likely than registered commercial sex workers to have done so (OR 3.6, 95 per cent CI 1.75–9.0). A closer analysis of ever-use data revealed that 63 per cent of freelance commercial sex workers reported either regular (40 per cent) or occasional (23 per cent) antibiotic use compared to a 29 per cent use rate among registered commercial sex workers (19 per cent occasional use and 10 per cent routine use).

These differences were further examined in relation to the self-medication behaviour of CSW during the last two weeks. Two-week point-prevalence data was gathered on prophylactic antibiotic use. Thirty-one per cent of all CSW having a customer in the last two weeks reported the use of antibiotics as a prophylaxis against STIs. Among registered commercial sex workers having a customer in the last two weeks ($N=120$), those working in a high-class *casa* were twice as likely to have used an antibiotic for prophylaxis as all other registered commercial sex workers (OR 2.48, 95 per cent CI 1.03–6.03). When registered CSW were compared to freelancers, freelancers were found to be five times more likely to have used antibiotics for prophylaxis than registered CSW (OR 5, 95 per cent CI 2–10). A high prophylactic antibiotic use rate among freelancers was further validated by a followup study of a convenience sample of 100 freelancers attending an outreach clinic in 1995 (Abellanosa). The two-week prophylactic antibiotic use rate among this sample of freelancers was 62 per cent. This finding is nearly identical to the percentage of freelancers who reported routine or occasional antibiotic use in our 1994 study.

Prophylactic antibiotic use was next examined in relation to condom use. Table 5.3 summarizes condom use and antibiotic use across work environments and Table 5.4 compares the condom use of registered and non-registered CSW. Of the 160 commercial sex workers having a customer in the last two weeks, condoms were used with a median of 80 per cent of customers. CSW who used condoms with at least 80 per cent of their customers were compared to CSW who used condoms with less than 80 per cent of customers. Freelancers were seven times less likely to use condoms than all other commercial sex workers with at least eight out of ten or more of their customers (OR 7.4, 95 per cent CI 3.02–18.3). Further analysis revealed that they were 16 times less likely to use condoms with eight out of ten of their customers (at least during one round) than commercial sex workers working in high-class *casa*. Freelancers were also three times less likely to use a condom with a regular (*suki*) customer than registered commercial sex workers (OR 2.6, 95 per cent CI 1.15–5.97).

In order to assess whether the use of prophylactic antibiotics was associated with non-condom use, we examined factors, beyond work environment, which might have influenced low condom use (<80 per cent of last ten customers) and prophylactic antibiotic use. We tested the association of low condom use and antibiotic use with several variables, namely age, rural or urban background, having a steady boyfriend or husband, education, having a child, number of customers per

Table 5.3. *Per cent of commercial sex workers at different work sites who use prophylactic antibiotics and condoms to protect against STIs, Cebu City, the Philippines (N= 147*)*

Characteristics	High-class *casa* (N = 49)	High-class bar; massage (N = 40)	Low-class bar; massage (N = 31)	Freelancers (N = 40)
Prophylactic antibiotic use, last two weeks	13 (27%)	8 (20%)	5 (16%)	23 (58%)
Condom use in eight or more of the last ten customers	45 (91%)	31 (77%)	19 (62%)	14 (35%)

*13 of the 160 commercial sex workers reporting having sex with a customer during the last two weeks chose not to respond to questions about condom use (three freelancers and ten registered CSW).

Table 5.4. *Registered versus unregistered commercial sex worker use of condoms to protect against STDs, Cebu City, Philippines (N= 147)**

Characteristics	Freelancers (N = 37)	All other registered CSW (N = 110)	Total (N = 147)
Condom use in eight or more of the last ten customers	13 (35%)	88 (80%)	101 (69%)
Condom use in seven or less of the last ten customers	24 (65%)	22 (20%)	46 (31%)

*Freelancers are seven times less likely to use condoms than registered CSW with 80 per cent or more of their customers (OR 7.4, 95 per cent CI 3.02–18.3).

week, and smoking as a measure of general risk. Variables which proved to have statistical significance (chi square $p < 0.05$) were then employed in a stepwise multivariate logistic regression analysis to assess the relationship between low condom use and the taking of prophylactic antibiotics in the presence of confounding variables.

Using high-class *casa* as our comparison group, only work group was found to be significantly associated with low condom use (low-class bar: OR 7.1; $p = 0.0025$; freelance: OR 16.5; $p < 0.001$) while work group (freelance: OR 4.5; $p = 0.0004$) and number of customers (> 5 customers per week: OR 2.6; $p = 0.0286$), was associated with antibiotic use. For each of the work groups, separate analyses were next performed to assess the relationship between antibiotic use and condom use. Odds ratios larger than unity were found indicating a larger risk of non-use of condom for the antibiotic users compared to non-antibiotic users in all groups, but due to the small size of the samples they were not significant. Follow-up work with larger samples is called for to test this association further.

What did we learn from conducting followup ethnographic research about the relationship between antibiotic use and condom use? Data from in-depth interviews with five impoverished freelance commercial sex workers revealed that they were in a weak position to negotiate condom use with customers (all of whom were Filipino) and that they received little medical care. None had ever had an internal exam although three stated that they had received treatment for an STI. The number of customers each serviced weekly was high when compared with other CSW. Interview data suggested that they were more inclined to take antibiotics as a matter of routine over a two-week period regardless of condom use, to protect themselves from STIs and to give them some sense of personal control. These women did not choose between using condoms and antibiotics. They used condoms whenever feasible, took antibiotics to protect them against the ill-health of clients, and took vitamins to enhance their own health (when money was available). One woman spoke of antibiotics as protecting her from customers with TB as well as STIs. Her antibiotic of choice was rifampicin, an important drug in TB short-course therapy.

Interviews with 12 registered commercial sex workers taking prophylactic antibiotics revealed several reasons why they took antibiotics: (1) to cope with feelings of vulnerability following a self-assessed high-risk sexual encounter; (2) to ward off feelings of personal vulnerability to STIs related to their declining health status; (3) to reduce a sense of anxiety after hearing that a friend had an STI; (4) to enhance their sense of resistance to STIs by periodically taking medicine; and (5) to keep their jobs—some brothel or bar managers encouraged CSW to take antibiotics to increase their chances of being able to 'pass' the Social Hygiene Clinic's weekly checkup.[19] Women who did not pass mandatory weekly checkups and have their identity cards stamped were ineligible to work at commercial establishments.

Among the 12 informants, three were commercial sex workers employed in high-class *casas*. This group of commercial sex workers was found to have the highest rate of condom use and the second highest rate of antibiotic use (second only to freelancers). During an interview with one of these women who serviced a wealthier clientele, including foreigners, another reason for taking antibiotics emerged. Taking antibiotics was talked about as a way of hedging her bets against AIDS, an illness she associated more with foreigners than local Filipino males. During our initial interviews with 200 commercial sex workers, we asked informants if they thought taking antibiotics would protect them against AIDS 'if they had a doubt about a customer'. While only 18 per cent strongly felt antibiotics would offer some protection, another 34 per cent stated that antibiotics might help prevent one from getting AIDS. Notably, a higher percentage of informants (52 per cent) thought taking prophylactic antibiotics might be useful in preventing AIDS than in preventing other STIs (39 per cent).

Did having an experience with a serious STI (gonorrhoea) requiring treatment with antibiotics affect CSW's belief in and use of prophylactic antibiotics? No statistically significant difference was found between commercial sex workers with and without a history of gonorrhoea with respect to either: (1) prophylactic antibiotic use patterns or (2) perceptions about the efficacy of antibiotics in preventing STIs and AIDS.

A final issue raised with commercial sex workers was whether they thought their boyfriends were completely monogamous and, if not, whether they thought that their boyfriends used condoms with other lovers. Half of our sample of CSW doubted that their boyfriends were completely monogamous and few thought that they were likely to use a condom with other lovers.[20] When asked if they ever took prophylactic antibiotics to protect themselves against STIs when they suspected that their live-in boyfriends had had sexual relations with another woman, only 15 per cent replied that they had ever done so. Five women who reported that they had 'butterfly' (non-monogamous) boyfriends were interviewed. I asked them why they took antibiotics to protect themselves against diseases from customers, but did not take antibiotics to protect them from diseases from their boyfriend when they suspected he had slept with another woman. Curiously, responses to this question rarely focused on antibiotics. When I asked what they had done the last time their boyfriend was unfaithful, a range of protective health measures were noted. In two cases, the women stated that they were more careful to douche and urinate after sex. In a third case, the woman refused to have sex with her boyfriend for a few days as a safety period to see if symptoms manifested. She stated that she waited for four days before having sex, but had wanted to wait for seven days. In a fourth case, the informant stated that she always knew when her boyfriend had slept with someone else because he would not sleep with her for a few days to make sure he was not sick first. In the fifth case, the informant stated that she once asked her boyfriend to use a condom when having sex with her for a few days because he had visited another woman. This had resulted in a big fight. The informant reported that she would rather deal with a disease than her boyfriend's anger and violence. Later in the interview she revealed that she once experienced an STI which she 'probably got' from her boyfriend inasmuch as she had not had sex with a customer for a few weeks.[21] The social hygiene doctor asked her to bring her boyfriend in for an examination, but as he did not complain of any symptoms, she did not do so.[22] She told her boyfriend that she had a urinary complaint (*sakit sa kidney*) as a means of avoiding sex for some days until she felt she was no longer contagious. The last time she suspected that her boyfriend was unfaithful, she once again complained about a urinary infection and managed to avoid having sex with him for five days.

THAILAND

Case Studies by Kanato et al. [1993, 1994, 1995] and Boonmongkon, Nichter, and Chantaposa [1996, 1997]

In 1993, Kanato and his team conducted a study in four field sites in different regions of Thailand (East, Northeast, North, and South), where they interviewed five categories of people (construction workers, factory workers, tricycle rickshaw drivers, male students, and female commercial sex workers) having a recent history of an STI treated at a government clinic ($N=531$). Roughly half of all males interviewed had taken prophylactic antibiotics, with no significant differences found between field sites or among categories of men interviewed. Notably, almost all men reporting antibiotic use took rifampicin as their drug of choice.[23] Kanato found a common belief among Thai men that impurities and residues of illness build up in the body over the course of multiple sexual encounters.[24] Antibiotics were taken both after sex to protect them against illness transmitted during the current sexual encounter and prior to sex to reduce their cumulative risk to STIs incurred from sexual contact with women over time. In other words, antibiotics were taken both to protect them from a single powerful exposure to an STI, and to reduce their cumulative level of impurity and illness-substance so they did not exceed some threshold leading to manifest illness.[25] Kanato further found that Thai men believed taking antibiotics after sex was an effective means of 'killing the germ, which was still weak'. Several practices were documented (such as the consumption of various types of alcohol, fruits, or seafood) to hasten a 'young' illness to manifest itself so it might be treated while still in a weak state.

In 1996, while conducting research on reproductive morbidity in Northern Thailand (the area of highest AIDS prevalence in the country), Boonmongkon and I encountered men who thought of AIDS as a dominant STI which was so powerful that it displaced all other STIs in an ecological sense (like a new weed that overtakes other plants). These men stated that it was now necessary to protect themselves against AIDS by using condoms when having sex with any unknown woman, but they were not much concerned about STIs. One man made reference to a newspaper article he had read stating that the number of STI cases in Thailand was falling.[26] Five to ten years ago, these men reported that taking prophylactic antibiotics was a common practice in their locale, but not at present. Later, we observed a poster visibly displayed at the local district hospital warning the public that the taking of medicines (specifically bags of assorted medicines known as *ya chud*, sold at grocery shops and pharmacies) was not an effective way to prevent STIs.

In 1997, during a subsequent study of reproductive complaints in Northeast Thailand, we decided to test whether the availability of medicine to 'protect' against STIs had changed much in this region since Kanato's 1993 study. Working with Chantaposa, a pharmacy professor from Khon Kaen University, we conducted a surrogate patient study at 20 rural drugstores in three districts of Khon Kaen Province (Boonmongkon *et al.* 1998). At each drugstore a surrogate patient asked for a *ya lang tai* (purifying and cleansing medicine) to take following sex with a friend (as distinct from a prostitute encountered at a brothel). In 18 out of 20 drugstores the surrogate patient was prescribed one or more drugs to protect his health. In contrast to Kanato's data in 1993, a wide variety of medicines were sold for this purpose.

Drugs to protect against STIs (ya lang tai, ya kap lum klung)
Single drugs
    Rifampicin
    Ampicillin

Norfloxacin
Pondnamycin
Pyridium

Drugs sold in combination with others
Erythromycin
Pondnamycin
Pyridium
Cotrimoxazole
Ampicillin
Oreomycin (Chlortetracycline)

Four unidentified drugs reported to be diuretics by pharmacy attendants
Uposed (Tetracycline 125 mg, Sulfamethizole 250 mg, Phenazopyridine 50 mg)
Mazin
Paracetamol 500 mg
Chintamycin

Findings from a second study carried out by Kanato may be briefly noted in light of shifting patterns of sexual behaviour in Thailand and patterns of prophylactic antibiotic use. Over the last 5 years, Kanato has documented a marked decrease in brothel patronage and an increase in condom use by men when doing so. On the other hand, there appears to be a marked increase in sexual relations with 'pick-up' girls met at food stalls and bars who engage in sex for enjoyment, the chance of becoming girlfriends/minor wives, or as opportunistic sex work. Kanato has documented that condom use during sexual encounters with such women is much lower than with commercial sex workers working in brothels.

In 1995, Kanato examined antibiotic use among 85 sexually active male secondary school students and 104 adult males interviewed at an STI clinic, by type of sexual partner (unpublished data). As in the earlier study, approximately 50 per cent of those in both groups who had visited a commercial sex worker had taken prophylactic antibiotics prior to or following their most recent visit to a brothel. What was noteworthy to Kanato was the number of men who used antibiotics following sex with a pick-up girl or girlfriend. During interviews with 19 students and ten adult men who had sex with pick-up girls, 90 per cent had taken antibiotics. Another 10 per cent of both groups of males also noted that they had taken antibiotics prior to sex with established girlfriends.

These findings raise several issues. If substantiated by community-based studies, how should we interpret high rates of antibiotic use following sex with pick-up girls when condoms have not been used? Does antibiotic use reflect Thai men's mistrust of these women as potential carriers of disease, or does it rather reflect a perception that pick-up girls are less likely to have AIDS than prostitutes (Havanon *et al.* 1993; Lyttleton 1994*b*; Van Landingham *et al.* 1995)? If the rate of condom use is low with pick-up girls, is antibiotic use thought to provide good enough protection for the types of illness they are likely to harbour? Or is it social risk (risk of embarrassment, risk to male identity) or practical difficulties in acquiring a condom (e.g. when drunk) which lead men to engage in sex without a condom, and engage in methods of harm reduction later? Was the antibiotic taken in anticipation of a planned sexual encounter or following an unplanned sexual event?

Similar questions arise with respect to student populations. Data from the Thai Family and Youth Survey (Podhisita and Pattaravanich 1995) and recent research in the Philippines (Festin and Nichter 1998) suggest that approximately one-third of teenage boys claim knowledge of medicines which will prevent them from getting STIs.[27] In contexts where youth are exposed to AIDS educational campaigns which focus largely on prostitutes, how do they view members of their immediate sexual networks? Do students view fellow students as relatively safe from AIDS, but not from STIs? Does taking antibiotics mark a student's recognition that they may have engaged in risky sex (a negative act) or is it a positive expression of self-efficacy and control?[28] In urban Northeast Thailand, it is not common for youth to use morning-after pills to prevent pregnancy instead of condoms. Does the use of antibiotics follow a similar practical logic?

Little is known about the social responsibility side of harm reduction. Condom or prophylactic antibiotic use can signal mistrust of a partner. By the same token, it can constitute an act of concern for a long-term partner. Ten per cent of Kanato's (1995) sample reported using antibiotics before sex with girlfriends. An issue worth probing is whether antibiotics are taken only to protect oneself when one has slept around (*pai thiaw*) or whether one takes medicines to protect a primary sexual partner. For the man, does taking antibiotics constitute some exercise of male responsibility, however misguided? We need to examine more closely how men attempt to reduce their chances of infecting their wives or girlfriends after they have engaged in risky sex.[29]

Ethnographic research in both Thailand and the Philippines suggests that when faced with uncertainty, men engage in several practices to minimize the chances of infecting their wives or long-term girlfriends with STIs. These practices include: observing a waiting period from the time they have risky sex to the time they engage in sex with their primary partners; consuming specific foods and drinks to hasten symptoms so they may avoid sexual contact until they 'know' they are safe; and taking antibiotics to reduce risk. An additional practice recently documented among migrant workers in both the Philippines and Thailand is to take an HIV test upon returning home. The problem with this behaviour (medically speaking) is that men often have little knowledge about how long they have to wait following risky sex before taking the test in order for it to be accurate.[30] One layperson's perception which I have encountered in both countries is that the HIV test is very sensitive because it can diagnose 'even the weakest case' of disease—months, if not years before symptoms manifest. For this reason, men have told me the test is useful even if they have engaged in risky sex within the last one to two weeks. Further research is needed to determine: (1) whether impressions of the HIV test positively or negatively affect condom use among these men; (2) if they view the taking of this test as an expression of male responsibility; (3) whether test-taking and/or results are shared with their wives; and (4) if so, how women interpret the actions of their husbands. Is taking the test the best women feel they can hope for in contexts where it is deemed unacceptable to ask a husband to use condoms for weeks, let alone three months after his return home from migrant work?

CONCLUSION: HARM REDUCTION, RISK, AND VULNERABILITY

In this chapter, I have documented how CSW and their clients in two Southeast Asian countries attempt to minimize their risk to STIs. Special attention has been drawn to the prophylactic use of antibiotics to protect against STIs and possibly AIDS.[31] In addition to citing disturbing statistics about a form of behaviour which is clearly misguided from a public health perspective, I have presented ethnographic research providing insights into why different types of people engage in this practice at different times. Prophylactic antibiotic use cannot be dismissed as merely an expression of blind faith in the power of antibiotics.[32] This form of self-help needs to be understood in terms of gender and power relations, concern about social as well as physical risk, local perceptions of vulnerability and expressions of responsibility, agency, and the need to cope with uncertainty in a world where social influences often lead one to do things they regret the next day.

Let me conclude this chapter by highlighting a few lessons which I have learned about harm reduction, risk, and vulnerability during the course of this research. Vulnerability proved to be a more complex concept than I first imagined. At first blush, the distinction between vulnerability and risk appears analogous to that of illness/disease wherein illness refers to the subjective, lived dimension of ill-health and disease is an empirical reality identified by a therapy system through some kind of codified inclusion and exclusion criteria (Young 1982).[33] Like disease, being 'at risk' has assumed the status of a diagnostic category.[34] Unlike 'disease', risk is not a thing (pathogen, physiological state, humoral imbalance, etc.) waiting to be discovered. Risk, as the term is used in epidemiology and the biosciences, is a probability derived from calculations relating levels of exposure to disease outcomes. What is measured is the probability of any member of a defined population becoming ill when exposed to increasing levels (doses) of a risk factor, all else being equal.[35] In real life, few people think of themselves as having an equal chance of becoming infected (or addicted, likely to have an accident, etc.) as all those around them.[36] They observe that not everyone who engages in risky behaviours suffers negative consequences. The question is, why not? Why don't all people who have unprotected sex with multiple partners become infected with STIs? Why are some people more likely to become ill (or seriously ill) than others? 'Why' questions often lead to 'who' questions which raise issues about individual and group identity. How such questions are answered is vital to an understanding of vulnerability and cultural responses to risk messages. Indexed by people's answers are cultural perceptions of what renders individuals and groups weak, open, and therefore susceptible to illness (and other misfortune) as well as strong and resistant to illness.

In order to understand how risk to illness is understood in context, it is important to investigate both: (1) predisposing states leading up to illness and (2) causal factors directly associated with illness; instrumental factors seen as necessary, but not necessarily sufficient to cause illness. All too often researchers mistake informants' statements about vulnerability and susceptibility for disease-specific ideas about causality. For example, when narrating an illness story about an STI, informants may associate their illness with a state of overheat or impurity. Are the informants describing what predisposed them to become ill by rendering them vulnerable, or identifying the instrumental cause of their illness? Is this important to know? Let us consider the case of 'germs', a term making its way into local vocabularies as a gloss for external causes of illness previously associated with such things as minute worms, insects, fungus, etc.

In many narratives about STIs which I have collected in South and Southeast Asia over the years, informants dwelled upon more than one sexual encounter with a specific partner when talking about their illness. Other factors emerged in their illness stories—things which left them open and susceptible, unbalanced, polluted, or weak. These factors ranged from heat and blood impurity to contact with the dangerous secretions or excretions of others. In some cases, vulnerability was thought about in terms of cumulative or incremental risk (such as the buildup of impurities) or the presence of latent residual illness. These factors were identified as contributing to one's personal sense of susceptibility, a state of vulnerability which enabled 'germs' to have the impact they did at that time.[37] A state of vulnerability clearly contributed to their illness, but when asked directly what caused their illness, 'germs' was typically the answer. Probing whether a population knows that germs and sexual intercourse causes STIs tells us less than half the story about how people think about their risk to STIs.

Risk is not experienced as a constant. People feel more or less vulnerable at different times subject to life experience as well as things which remind them that risk is present. Such reminders may be the illness of a friend or newspaper headlines. For example, in the Philippines, Abellanosa and I found that many people perceived the threat of STIs or AIDS to be greater following a newspaper article on the subject. Adopting an epidemic rather than an endemic mind set, some people we interviewed imagined that epidemics of grave diseases moved through the community periodically.[38] At such times, these people felt vulnerable and adopted preventive practices to decrease their risk to disease until, in the words of one informant, 'the typhoon passed and the flags (designating an impending storm) were lowered'.

Risk messages are interpreted both in terms of individual feelings of susceptibility and a group's perception of 'their' vulnerability to a problem. Epidemiological assessments of STIs focus on routes of transmission, sexual networks, and types of behaviour that increase a population's chances of experiencing such diseases as gonorrhoea, hepatitis, or HIV/AIDS. Popular assessments of vulnerability to illness are based more on perceptions of which type of people are more likely to have a particular disease. Responsibility for dreaded diseases tends to be distanced by members of one's own group and displaced onto 'dangerous others'. At the same time, responsibility for less serious types of illness may be accepted by the group despite the fact that both types of illnesses are recognized as sharing a common route of transmission. This is the case in the Philippines where AIDS is associated with foreigners (and foreign-returned migrant workers) while STIs are accepted to be a local phenomenon.[39] One unintended ramification of local newspaper reports in the early 1990s which played up the foreign origin of AIDS cases detected in the Philippines was that sex between Filipinos appeared to be relatively safe.[40] Many Filipino CSW exclusively serving local customers felt vulnerable to STIs, but not to AIDS. By the mid-1990s this impression began to change as a result of increasing media coverage about AIDS, which brought the problem home.

In a world where risk is increasingly thought to be present as a result of health education messages and newspaper headlines, how does one pursue desired (or required) courses of action marked as risky without feeling overly anxious? If risk cannot be avoided, at least harm may be reduced. Practical logic drives harm reduction practices and draws upon whatever material and conceptual resources are at hand. Forms of behaviour, like the taking of prophylactic antibiotics to prevent STIs (using curative medicines to prevent or reduce harm), mark perceptions of vulnerability as well as index streetwise attempts to exercise agency. Those in public health who wish to engage local populations in meaningful dialogue about STI prevention need to do more than talk about risk in aggregate terms. More effective communication requires a more grounded understanding of popular health culture (Awaasthi *et al.* 2000). This chapter has suggested that investigations of vulnerability and harm reduction are essential to broaden our understanding of how people both experience and respond to risk.

Notes

1. Social theorists such as Beck (1992*a,b*, 1995, 1996), Giddens (1991), and Hacking (1990) have argued (in different ways) that thinking in terms of calculated risks is a salient feature of late modernity. In late modernity, life is increasingly organized around managing risks, many of which are recognized to be by-products of modernization (Beck, ibid.). Foucault (1979, 1980) has proposed that expert knowledge constitutes a form of 'biopower' or productive power over our lives. Once someone knows better, there comes a responsibility to act accordingly. Knowledge about risk makes social institutions as well as individuals accountable. Biopower affects both the ways populations are monitored and the ways individuals engage in self-surveillance and bodily discipline. Ways of measuring risk (even traces of risk such as the presence of genetic receptors which may never be expressed) alter our sense of what is normal. While the aforementioned theories are insightful on a general level, they fall short in explaining the variety of responses to scientific pronouncements about risk. Missing from the literature is an appreciation of how vulnerability is experienced and responded to in context. When is public health

advice listened to and how is it interpreted, when do people feel vulnerable, and what guides acts of harm reduction?

2. Scientific use of the term 'risk' as a calculated probability poorly reflects popular use and understanding of the term which has multiple layers of meaning including doubt and uncertainty (Douglas 1985; Douglas and Wildavasky 1982; Hansson 1989; Slovic 1987). Expert knowledge about risk may not be believed in a world of competing and rapidly changing messages which lead to the mistrust of science and technocratic projects (Winder 1993; Wynne 1996). In some cases, communication about risk may be considered to be a source of risk in its own right if: (1) people come to dwell on misfortune; or (2) the risk factor or problem appears so common as to appear acceptable and as the cost of living in a particular environment (adopting a lifestyle, etc.).

3. Engaging in self-surveillance is only one of many possible responses to information about risk. For example, routine diagnostic tests may be avoided so as not to stir up latent problems one hopes will not manifest (Kavenaugh and Broom 1998; Mathews *et al.* 1997). Communications about risk may be distanced, met by ambivalence or compartmentalized. Evidence suggests that when health statistics are made available to a population, this data may have limited impact on behaviour for a number of reasons including the challenge it poses to moral identity (Shiloh and Saxe 1989), perceptions of self-efficacy (Bandura 1990), and the inclination to accept a source of risk as a trade-off for a desired lifestyle.

4. Many scholars have pointed to a lack of congruence between public comprehension of AIDS and STI messages and behaviour change (e.g. Fisher and Fisher 1992; Lear 1995; Stall *et al.* 1986).

5. Researchers studying sexual and drug use behaviour related to HIV transmission have drawn attention to ways individuals distance danger through personal interpretations of 'relative risks' which are socially situated (Clatts 1995; Parker 1995; Pilskin 1997; Ramos *et al.* 1995; Sibthorpe *et al.* 1991; Sobo 1993, 1995).

6. I use the term 'commercial sex worker' as a heuristic device in this chapter with some trepidation. While commonplace in the literature, this term essentializes the many types of women and men engaged in the exchange of sex for money, glosses over differences in the social relations and meanings of sexual exchanges by assuming that all events are alike (i.e. commercial), and blurs important differences between the settings in which such exchanges occur (de Zalduondo 1991; de Zalduondo and Bernard 1995; Standing 1992). The term also has dehumanizing connotations. As Ratliff (1996) has convincingly argued of commercial sex workers in the Philippines, to reduce all sexual exchange between these women and their partners to a set of contractual relations having no future or 'real' emotional dimension is to deny to these women any sense of agency. In support of Ratliff's argument, it may be noted that 21 per cent of 200 commercial sex workers surveyed by Abellanosa and Nichter (1996) lived with a boyfriend who was previously a customer. When asked if their current 'work' would hurt their chances of finding a husband or long-term partner, 44 per cent of commercial sex workers interviewed said it would enhance their chances, 27 per cent said it would make no difference, and 29 per cent said it would hurt their chances. Such data calls into question the position that commercial sex workers only delude themselves in thinking they have 'real' emotional ties to 'customers' (Chant and McIlwaine 1995). On a blurring of distinctions between customers and boyfriends and the fluidity of potential relationships in Thailand, see Maticka-Tyndale *et al.* (1997).

7. Practical logic, as Bourdieu (1990) employs the term, is driven by expediency, disposition, and improvization. It is not rational because agents rarely possess the information

that rational action would presuppose. Practical logic is polythetic, capable of sustaining a multiplicity of meanings assembled in response to situational contingencies.

8. My focus on the phenomenology and social relations of vulnerability, and the practical logic of harm reduction complements recent advances in what is being termed 'new geography' (e.g. Kearns 1993, Pile and Thrift 1995) and 'eco-epidemiology' (e.g. Koopman 1994a,b; Koopman and Longini 1994; Krieger 1994; Susser and Susser 1996a,b; Wing 1994). Advocates of these paradigms invite those studying health risk to move beyond a limited tracing and cataloguing of behaviour within physical spaces to a consideration of wayfinding which demands an appreciation of the context of experienced place, interactional flows, performance, and positionality. On the need for situational analysis of sexual networks as a means of understanding STI transmission, see Bond (1995) and Zwi and Cabral (1991). On the need to take into consideration political economic as well as cultural factors which have an impact on how and when agency can/cannot be expressed in different interactional spaces, see Clatts (1995), Farmer (1995), Kendall (1994), and Thomas and Thomas (1999).

9. The term *sakit sa bahae* is commonly used by men to refer to STIs. Some women use the term in this way, while others use the term to refer to menstrual problems.

10. Men often drank with friends and met women later. In some cases they returned to their friends between 'rounds' of sex with a commercial sex worker. In a few cases, a woman was shared by more than one man. Women rarely spent the entire night and men could be interviewed while taking breakfast and getting ready to go to work the next morning. I told men I was carrying on research on sexuality in different cultures as well as doing research on tuberculosis. In about half of the cases, I was able to confirm data on condom use through the help of a waitress who knew many of the commercial sex workers visiting one hotel.

11. This finding raises doubts about how existing survey data on condom use may be interpreted. Just because informants respond that they have used a condom the last time they had sex does not necessarily mean they used a condom the entire time they had sex.

12. Men spoke to me of making friends with CSW so they would care enough about them to inform them if they were sick, and both CSW and their male customers spoke to me of the importance of checking out potential sexual partners as a means of selecting out those with STIs. Potential partners were assessed on the basis of their dress, hygiene, education, and bodily signs and symptoms associated with STIs. Ethnographic research suggests that despite overtures made about being able to choose safe partners, or turn CSW into friends, subjunctive ('what if') reasoning often followed heat of the moment (or heat of the money) sexual liaisons. At such times, the possibility, if not the promise, of medicinal fixes to prevent full-blown STIs was attractive for psychological as well as practical reasons.

13. I use the term latent illness to refer to an illness which remains in the body and can be controlled, but not completed cured. Such illness manifests now and then, when the person is weak or the illness is provoked in some way causing it to flare up. A latent source of illness (such as impurity, or 'germs') may accumulate in the body to a point when an illness occurs or relapses. My use of the term latent illness overlaps with, but is distinct from, asymptomatic disease. Both are invisible, but latent illness is more robust in the sense that it manifests and subsides and remains within one's body for a long time. One may be aware of a latent illness and this may influence their behaviour as well as be a source of concern.

14. This informant was rather vague about illness transformation, but his comments suggested that penile discharge (*tulo*) was a minor illness which could develop into major

illness if not treated or controlled. I use the word control because he was not sure if once you had an STI, it was ever completely cured, an opinion I have come across in other interviews as well. He further noted that if one had more contact with a woman who was dirty (*dumi*), their latent or asymptomatic illness would be more likely to manifest or relapse (*benat*). When I pressed him for more details, he voiced a second opinion which was that *tulo* might come from other sources of vague contamination. He spoke of a person developing an infection (*impeksiyon*) caused by germs (*microbyo*), a concept he had little to say about. See Tan (1996*a,b*) for a discussion of *tulo* and its treatment. In Thailand, men speak of the feelings that pus is coming out of the penis (*nong lii*), which indicates that a disease may be developing in the body, although not yet manifest. Often this condition is more a feeling of discharge than an actual discharge. Like the case of *tulo*, men feel *nong lii* is a developing condition which warrants treatment with medicines from the pharmacy, but is not yet serious enough to consult a doctor about.

15. Filipino notions of the utility of antibiotics extend beyond treating infection. On different occasions I have observed people taking antibiotics to reduce pain and prevent illness from becoming severe. I have also heard people speak of taking antibiotics when they are weak, although I have not heard anyone say that they make one stronger. I have observed similar behaviour in Thailand. On Filipino perceptions of medicines as enhancing resistance, see Tan (1996*a*).

16. Three thousand women ranging in age from 18 to 35 work in the Cebu City hospitality sector and are registered with the Cebu City social hygiene clinic. These women are required by law to have a weekly checkup, during which time they receive a Gram stain which detects Gram-positive and -negative infection as well as gonorrhoea. Every six months they receive a blood test for syphilis, hepatitis B, and AIDS.

17. Local terms for STIs were used during interviews including the term 'micro' popular among women attending the social hygiene clinic. Micro is commonly used by clinic staff to refer to a specific infection detected by a Gram stain which may or may not be symptomatic.

18. Informants interviewed were asked specific questions about what antibiotic they used to validate that they were indeed using an antibiotic and not some other medicine. Awareness about what drugs are classified as antibiotics needs to be probed as lay people often group drugs in relation to illnesses, not pharmacological properties (Tan 1996*a,b*). In the general population the term 'antibiotic' is associated with strong medicine. Experienced commercial sex workers exposed to routine STI screening and the treatment of infections were familiar with antibiotics although they sometimes mixed up antifungal vaginal tablets for antibiotics.

19. See Tan (1996*a*) for more details on bar owners encouraging commercial sex workers to use antibiotics to test negative when attending social hygiene clinic weekly checkups.

20. This is very likely a low estimate as the girls interviewed did not like to think about their live-in boyfriends as being unfaithful. There are methodological problems with the term 'boyfriend'. Boyfriend can mean a wide range of things.

21. In the survey, 124 of the 200 commercial sex workers reported that they had been told at some point that they had 'micro' by clinic staff. Twenty-nine per cent of these women attributed the cause of their infection to their boyfriends or husbands.

22. This woman suspected that her boyfriend might have been ill, not told her, and sought treatment from a private doctor. She did not confront him about this.

23. On the use of medicines to ward of STIs in Thailand, see Lyttleton (1994*a,b*), Havanon *et al.* (1992), and Podhisita and Prattaravonich (1995). Kanato (personal

correspondence) reports that many Thai men perceive red-coloured urine, a side effect of rifampicin, to be evidence of illness and impurities leaving their body. This contributes to this antibiotic's popularity as a prophylactic for STIs among men. Attendants at several chemist shops investigated during our 1997 surrogate patient study, sold men kidney cleaning and prophylactic medicines for STIs which contained medicines which changed urine colour. Women do not desire medicine which turns their urine red as this is associated with menstrual blood. Sex workers spoke of clients being afraid of contact with them if they were menstruating or had red urine. Men feared the folk illness *khi tute*, an illness which, like leprosy, leads to parts of the body shrinking and decaying. Rifampicin is rarely used by women for prophylaxis or self-treatment.

24. Kanato documented a folk theory of cumulative impurity during his fieldwork in Northeast Thailand (personal communication). I found few people who were able to elaborate on this theory, although concern about the accumulation of impurity does affect health practice. General notions of impurity (*so ka prok*) are sometimes linked to *chu' arrok*, a local term encompassing germs. It is thought that *chu' arrok* may build up in a woman's body at the time of menstruation. Gender differences appear to exist as to the origin of such impurity. Some men feel that sexual contact with any woman exposes them to impurity, while others feel that it is only exposure to unclean women which does so. Some women feel that the impurity in their body comes from contact with men who are not clean; men who 'do not even wash their penis after urination.'

25. I have encountered similar logic in the United States in 1990. Following a negative AIDS test, a gay male informant proceeded to celebrate his good fortune with unsafe sex with several partners. When I talked to him about this several days later, he replied that the test indicated to him that his 'level of exposure to the HIV virus' was low. Being fit and in good health, he felt he could afford to be a little wild. His interpretation of risk to HIV was that the more exposure to the disease you had, the more disease you accumulated and the closer you were to becoming ill yourself—a process hastened by drugs, smoking cigarettes, and drinking alcohol. On the positive side of the balance, one could eat right and exercise, thereby increasing resistance and reducing one's cumulative level of disease. The same informant viewed the taking of antioxidants (vitamins and foods) as a means of burning bad residue (insecticides, preservatives, etc.) from the body, much like the 'high octane car additive STP burns sludge from an engine.'

26. According to official reports, sexually transmitted diseases have dramatically decreased in Thailand following universal condom policy implementation in brothels, the closing down of non-registered brothels, and AIDS education programmes for men focusing on condom use when frequenting prostitutes (Hackenberg *et al.* 1994). Government sexually transmitted disease clinics report fewer patients and in some areas clinics have closed down due to low patient load. Impressions that STIs have fallen are based primarily on rates of gonorrhoea and syphilis reported by government clinics, not community-based studies. While there is little doubt that populations of men such as soldiers have much lower STI rates as a result of government programmes, it is important to bear in mind two things when assessing official reports. First, among men who suspect they have an STI, there is a tendency to frequent private, not government, clinics. Self-medication with such potent drugs as Norfloxin may also be high. Second, among groups of men who have been hit hard by Thailand's economic crises, visiting prostitutes has decreased dramatically. Staff at the government STI clinic in Khon Kaen informed me in 1997 that they saw one-third the number of commercial sex workers than they had seen 2 years previously. Many sex workers no longer came for regular checkups. Business was so bad

that they no longer felt there was a need. One woman interviewed at the clinic, resorted to self-treatment with antibiotics (for prophylaxis and cure) until her symptoms became acute. She had previously come to the clinic regularly. She blamed her present illness episode on latent disease which flared up after intercourse with her one and only customer in two months. She did not hold her customer accountable.

27. Dr. Mario Festin and I recently investigated adolescent male's knowledge of prophylactic antibiotics in the Philippines as the first stage of an intervention project funded by the International Network of Clinical Epidemiology. Data collected to date suggest that approximately 30 per cent of 170 college boys aged 16–17 interviewed in Manila had heard of the use of antibiotics to prevent STIs (Festin and Nichter 1998). The age most boys lose their virginity in the Philippines is between 16 and 18 depending on the region of the country.

28. One adolescent male interviewed in the Philippines recounted to me how he took an antibiotic two days following intercourse with a school mate because he learned through gossip) that she had sold her body to an older man to get money for her school fees. Asked if he would have taken medicine in this way had he learned that she had slept with another boy in school, he laughed and asked why? No boy he knew had ever had an STI! I followed up on his response during two focus groups. Of the ten boys attending these focus groups, all but two thought that their class mates were safe. However, when asked how many girls in their class were likely to exchange sex for money to pay school fees, etc., estimates varied between 10 and 25 per cent.

29. We also know little about women's self-treatment with antibiotics for gynaecological complaints in different cultures. Aside from self-care, does concern that vaginal discharge may negatively affect a partner's health motivate their use of medicines?

30. Some men I have interviewed undertook an HIV test before returning home of their own volition. In other cases, they were encouraged to do so upon returning home by anxious wives. In no case that I have documented has a man consciously abstained from sex or practised safe sex for three or more months as a means of getting an accurate test reading. Additional research is needed to establish whether it is becoming more acceptable for a wife to ask her husband to get a test upon returning home or whether this is an unspoken expectation. On the variety of reasons for getting an HIV test, including the expression of responsibility and the symbolic closure or commencement of a relationship, see Lupton *et al.* (1995).

31. Prophylactic medicine use to protect against STIs has been reported elsewhere, but not studied in any detail (Africa: Ajuwon 1990; Green 1992; Masango and Rakolojane 1987; Meheus *et al.* 1974; Orubuloye *et al.* 1994; Osoba 1972; Central America: Reeves and Quiroz 1987; South Asia: Awaasthi *et al.* 2000).

32. Most informants that I have interviewed viewed antibiotics as powerful medicines, but not magical talismans which could protect them from all types of disease.

33. Young (1982) and Hahn (1984) provide a critical assessment of the illness/disease/sickness distinction made in the health social science literature.

34. Being 'at risk' has assumed the status of a condition midway between health and illness. Being 'at risk' does not mean one 'has an illness', but does encourage one to assume a 'risk role' akin to a sick role in some ways.

35. Dose response curves may differ significantly for different individuals.

36. Risk is often understood comparatively. An individual or group compares their risk to a reference group or someone who represents a marker of higher risk (Weinstein 1987; Leventhal *et al.* 1987; Sobo 1995). Perceptions of relative susceptibility influence the way people respond to information about risk (Hansen *et al.* 1990).

37. The analogy of seed and soil was sometimes cited. A germ, like a seed, flourishes when soil conditions are right. This analogy has been widely cited in the medical anthropological literature associated with both illness and fertility.
38. Kanato (1994, p. 147) has also documented that in Thailand, there is a perception that HIV/AIDS becomes epidemic periodically like other epidemic diseases such as dengue and cholera. Men curtail going to commercial sex workers during times when there is a lot of publicity about AIDS.
39. This impression was validated by a series of rank-ordering exercises we conducted using pictures of different types of people (ethnic groups, etc.) ranked on the basis of their likelihood of having AIDS or STIs.
40. One Filipino commercial sex worker told me she was not worried about getting AIDS from her live-in boyfriend, although he sometimes went out with his *barkada* (group of drinking buddies) and visited other women. When I asked her why not, she stated that he did not have the language skills or confidence to make a friendship with a foreigner. Whatever disease he might bring home would be a local problem. He, on the other hand, was afraid that she might pick up a foreign disease, or leave the city with a foreigner and not support him while she was gone. Based on this concern, he demanded extra money from her whenever she had a foreign customer.

References

Abellanosa, I., and Nichter, M. (1996), 'Antibiotic prophylaxis among commercial sex workers in Cebu City, Philippines: Patterns of use and perceptions of efficacy', *Sexually Transmitted Diseases*, 23 (5): 407–12.

Ajuwon, A. J. (1990). 'Socio-cultural practices that may favor the transmission of Acquired Immunodeficiency Syndrome (AIDS) in a rural Yoruba community: Implication for health education', MPH dissertation, University of Ibadan.

Aral, S. O., Holmes, K. K., Padian, N. S., and Cates, W. Jr. (1996), 'Overview: Individual and population approaches to the epidemiology and prevention of sexually transmitted diseases and human immunodeficiency virus infection,' *Journal of Infectious Diseases*, 174 (Suppl. 2): S127–S133.

Awaasthi, S., Nichter, M., and Pande, V. K. (2000), Developing an interactive STD—Prevention program for youth: Lessons from a North Indian slum, *Studies in Family Planning* 31(2): 138–50.

Bandura, A. (1990). 'Perceived self-efficacy in the exercise of control over AIDS', *Project Evaluation and Program Planning*, 13: 9–17.

Beck, U. (1992*a*), *Risk Society. Towards a New Modernity,* translated by Mark Ritter, London: Sage.

—— (1992*b*) From industrial society to risk society: Questions of survival, social structure and ecological enlightenment, *Theory, Culture and Society*, 9: 97–123.

—— (1995), *Ecological Politics in the Age of Risk*, Cambridge: Polity Press.

—— (1996), 'Risk society and the provident State'. Translated by Martin Chalmers. In S. Lash, B. Szerszynski, and B. Wynne (eds.), *Risk, Environment, and Modernity: Toward a New Ecology*, London: Sage.

Bond, K. (1995), *Social and Sexual Networking in Urban Northern Thailand,* School of Hygiene and Public Health, Johns Hopkins University, PhD dissertation.

Boonmongkon, P., Nichter, M., Pylypa, J., and Chantaposa, K. (1998), *Understanding Women's Experience of Gynecological Problems: An Ethnographic Case Study from Northeast Thailand*, Center for Health Policy Studies: Mahidol University.

Bourdieu, P. (1990), *The Logic of Practice*, Oxford: Polity Press.

Chant, S., and McIlwaine, C. (1995), *Women of a Lesser Cost: Female Labour, Foreign Exchange and Philippine Development*, Quezon City: Ateneo de Manila University Press.

Clatts, M. C. (1995), 'Disembodied acts: On the perverse use of sexual categories in the study of high-risk behavior', in Hans ten Brummelhuis and G. Herdt (eds.), *Culture and Sexual Risk: Anthropological Perspectives on AIDS*, Amsterdam: Gordon and Breach, pp. 241–55.

de Zalduondo, B. (1991), 'Prostitution viewed cross-culturally: Toward recontextualizing sex work in AIDS intervention research', *The Journal of Sex Research*, 28 (2): 223–48.

—— and Bernard, J. M. (1995), 'Meanings and consequences of sexual-economic exchange: Gender, poverty and sexual risk behavior in urban Haiti', in R. G. Parker and J. H. Gagnon (eds.), *Conceiving Sexuality: Approaches to Sex Research in a Postmodern World*, New York: Routlegde, pp.157–80.

Douglas, M. (1985), *Risk Acceptability According to the Social Sciences*, New York: Russell Sage Foundation.

—— and Wildavsky, A. (1982), *Risk and Culture*, Berkeley: University of California Press.

Farmer, P. (1995), 'Culture, poverty, and the dynamics of HIV transmission in rural Haiti', in Hans ten Brummelhuis and G. Herdt (eds.), *Culture and Sexual Risk: Anthropological Perspectives on AIDS*, Amsterdam: Gordon and Breach, pp. 3–28.

Festin, M., and Nichter, M. (1998), 'Preventing STDs among adolescent males in Manila, Baseline project report, International Clinical Epidemiology Network, Philadelphia.

Fisher, J. D., and Fisher, W. A. (1992), 'Changing AIDS-risk behavior', *Psychological Bulletin*, 111 (3): 45–474.

Foucault, M. (1980), *The History of Sexuality Volume 1: An Introduction*, New York: Vintage Books. (1979), *Discipline and Punishment: The Birth of the Prison*, translated by Alan Sheridan, New York: Vintage Press.

Giddens, A. (1991), *Modernity and Self-Identity: Self and Society in the Late Modern Age*, Cambridge: Polity Press.

Gifford, S. M. (1986), 'The meaning of lumps: A case study of the ambiguities of risk', in C. R. James, R. Stall, and S. M. Gifford (eds.), *Anthropology and Epidemiology: Interdisciplinary Approaches to the Study of Health and Disease*, Dordrecht: D. Reidel.

Green, E. (1992), 'Sexually transmitted disease, ethnomedicine and health policy in Africa', *Social Science and Medicine*, 35 (2): 121–30.

Hackenberg, R. S., Rojanapithayakorn, W., Kunasol, P., and Sokal, D. C. (1994), 'Impact of Thailand's HIV-control programme as indicated by the decline of sexually transmitted diseases', *Lancet*, 344 (July 23): 243–5.

Hacking, I. (1990), *The Taming of Chance*, Cambridge: Cambridge University Press.

Hahn, R. (1984), 'Rethinking "illness" and "disease"', *Contributions to Asian Studies*, 18: 1–23.

Hansson, S. E. (1989), 'Dimensions of risk', *Risk Analysis*, 9 (1): 107–2.

Hansen, W. B., Hahn, G. L., and Wolkenstein, B. H. (1990), 'Perceived personal immunity: Beliefs about susceptibility to AIDS', *The Journal of Sex Research*, 27 (4): 622–8.

Havanon, N., Knodel, J., and Bennett, A. (1992), 'Sexual networking in a provincial Thai setting', AIDS Prevention Monograph Series Paper No. 1, June 1992.

—— Bennett, A., and Knodel, J. (1993), 'Sexual networking in provincial Thailand', *Studies in Family Planning*, 24 (1): 1–16.

Kanato, M. (1994), 'An ethnographic-participatory study of commercial sex workers responding to the problem of HIV/AIDS in Khon Kaen, Thailand', Ph.D. Thesis, McMaster University.

—— and Rujkarakorn, D. (1994), 'Cultural factors in sexual behavior, sexuality and sociocultural contexts of the spread of HIV in the Northeast, Thailand', Paper presented at the conference on Cultural Dimensions of AIDS Control in Thailand, Chiang Mai, Thailand.

—— M., Homchampa, P., Sinpisut, P., Damrichaimongkol, C., Muntai, S., and Srisupan, H. (1993). 'Qualitative-multicenter study on STD seeking behaviour', Manuscript, Khon Kaen University.

Kavanagh, A. M., and Broom, D. H. (1998), Embodied risk: My body, myself? *Social Science and Medicine*, 46 (3): 437–44.

Kearns, R. (1993), 'Place and health: Toward a reformed medical geography', *Professional Geographer*, 45 (2): 139–47.

Kendall, C. (1994), 'The construction of risk in AIDS control programs: Theoretical bases and popular responses', in R. G. Parker and J. H. Gagnon (eds.), *Conceiving Sexuality: Approaches to Sex Research in a Postmodern World*, New York: Routledge, pp. 249–58.

Koopman, J. S. (1994), 'The ecological effects of individual exposures and nonlinear disease dynamics in populations", *American Journal of Public Health*, 84: 836–42.

—— (1994), 'Comment: Emerging objectives and methods in epidemiology', *American Journal of Public Health*, 86 (5): 630–2.

—— and Longini, I. M. (1994), 'The ecological effects of individual exposures and nonlinear disease dynamics in populations', *American Journal of Public Health*, 84: 836–42.

Krieger, N. (1994), 'Epidemiology and the web of causation: Has anyone seen the spider?', *Social Science and Medicine*, 39: 887–903.

Lear, D. (1995), 'Sexual communication in the age of AIDS: The construction of risk and trust among young adults', *Social Science and Medicine*, 41 (9): 1311–23.

Leventhal, H., Glynn, K., and Fleming, R. (1987), 'Is the smoking decision an "informed choice"?', *Journal of the American Medical Association*, 257: 3373–6.

Lupton, D., McCarthy, S., and Chapman, S. (1995), 'Doing the right thing': The symbolic meanings and experiences of having an HIV antibody test', *Social Science and Medicine*, 41 (2): 173–180.

Lyttleton, C. (1994a), 'The love your wife disease: HIV/AIDS education and the construction of meaning in Northeast Thailand', Ph.D. Dissertation, Department of Anthropology, University of Sydney.

—— (1994b), Knowledge and meaning: The AIDS education campaign in rural Northeast Thailand, *Social Science and Medicine*, 38 (1): 135–46.

Maine, Deborah, Freedman, Lynn, Shaheed, Farida, Frautschi, Schuyler, and Akalin, Muratz (1995), 'Risks and rights: The uses of reproductive health data', *Reproductive Health Matters*, 6: 40–51.

Masango, E., and Rakolojane, M. J. (1987), 'Sexually transmitted diseases baseline survey', Mobabane Family Life Association of Swaziland.

Mathews, H. F., Lannin, D., and Mitchell, J. P. (1997), 'Coming to terms with advanced breast cancer: Black women's narratives from Eastern North Carolina', in G. Henderson, N. King, R. Strauss, S. Estroff, and L. Churchill (eds.,) *The Social Medicine Reader*, Durham: Duke University Press, pp. 43–60.

Maticka-Tyndale, E., Elkins, D., Haswell-Elkins, M., Rujkarakorn, D., Kuyyakanond, T., and Stam, K. (1997), 'Contexts and patterns of men's commercial sexual partnerships in

Northeastern Thailand: Implications for AIDS Prevention', *Social Science and Medicine*, 44 (2): 199–213.

Meheus, A., De Clercq, A., and Prat, R. (1974), 'Prevalence of gonorrhea in prostitutes in a central African town', *British Journal of Venereal Disease*, 50 (1): 50–2.

Nichter, M. (1996), 'Self-medication and STD prevention', *Sexually Transmitted Diseases*, 23 (5): 353–6.

Orubuloye, I. O., Caldwell, P., and Caldwell, J. C. (1994), 'Commercial sex workers in Nigeria in the shadow of AIDS', in I. O. Orubuloye, J. Caldwell, P. Caldwell, and G. Santow (eds.), *Sexual Networking and AIDS in Sub-Saharan Africa: Behavioural Research and Social Context*, Canberra: Australian National University Press, pp. 101–16.

Osoba, A. O. (1972), 'Epidemiology of urethritis in Ibadan', *British Journal of Venereal Disease*, 48 (2): 116–20.

Parker, R. G. (1995), 'The social and cultural construction of sexual risk, or how to have (sex) research in an epidemic', in Hans ten Brummelhuis and G. Herdt (eds.), *Culture and Sexual Risk: Anthropological Perspectives on AIDS*, Amsterdam: Gordon and Breach, pp. 257–69.

Pile, S., and Thrift, N. (eds.) (1995), *Mapping the Subject: Geographies of Cultural Transformation*, Routledge: London.

Pliskin, K. L. (1997), 'Verbal intercourse and sexual communication: Impediments to STD prevention', *Medical Anthropology Quarterly*, 11 (1): 89–109.

Podhisita, C., and Prattaravonich, U. (1995), 'Youth in contemporary Thailand: Results from the family and youth survey', Institute for Population and Social Research Publication No. 197, Mahidol University, Salaya, Nakhon Pathom, Thailand.

Ramos, R., Shain, R. N. and Johnson, L. (1995), ' "Men I mess with don't have nothing to do with AIDS": Using ethno-theory to understand sexual risk perception', *Sociological Quarterly*, 36(3): 483–504.

Ratliff, E. (1996), 'Women as "sex workers", men as "boyfriends": changing identities in Philippine go-go bars and their importance in STD/AIDS control', Paper presented at the American Anthropological Association, November 1996, San Francisco, California.

Reeves, W. C., and Quiroz, E. (1987), 'Prevalence of sexually transmitted diseases in high-risk women in the Republic of Panama", *Sexually Transmitted Diseases*, 14 (2): 69–74.

Rhodes, T. (1995), 'Theorizing and researching "risk": Notes on the social relations of risk in heroin users' lifestyles', in P. Aggleton, P. Davis, and G. Hart (eds.), *AIDS: Safety, Sexuality, and Risk*, Washington D.C.: Taylor and Francis, pp. 125–43.

Royce, R., Seno, A., Cates, W., and Cohen, M. (1997), 'Sexual transmission of HIV', *New England Journal of Medicine*, 336 (15): 1072–8.

Shiloh, S., and Saxe, L. (1989), 'Perception of risk in genetic counseling', *Psychology and Health*, 3: 45–6.

Sibthorpe, B., Fleming, D., Tesselaar, H., and Gould, J. (1991), 'Needle use and sexual practices: Differences in perception of personal risk of HIV among intravenous drug users', *The Journal of Drug Issues*, 21 (4): 699–712.

Slovic, P. (1987), 'Perception of risk', *Science*, 237(23): 280–5.

Sobo, E. J. (1993), 'Inner-city women and AIDS: The psycho-social benefits of unsafe sex', *Culture, Medicine & Psychiatry*, 17: 455–85.

—— (1995), *Choosing Unsafe Sex: AIDS-Risk Denial Among Disadvantaged Women*, Philadelphia, PA: U Penn Press.

Stall, R., Mukusick, J., and Wiley, J. (1986), 'Alcohol and drug use during sexual activity and compliance with safe sex guidelines for AIDS: The AIDS behavioral research project', *Health Education Quarterly*, 13 (4): 359–71.

Standing, H. (1992), 'AIDS: Conceptual and methodological issues in researching sexual behavior in sub-Saharan Africa', *Social Science and Medicine*, 34 (5): 475–83.

Susser, M., and Susser, E. (1996a), 'Choosing a future for epidemiology: I. Eras and paradigms', *American Journal of Public Health*, 86: 668–73.

Susser, M., and Susser, E. (1996b), 'Choosing a future for epidemiology: II. From black box to Chinese boxes and eco-epidemiology', *American Journal of Public Health*, 86: 674–7.

Tan, M. (1996), *Magaling na gamot: Pharmaceuticals and the Construction of Power and Knowledge in the Philippines*', Ph.D. Thesis, University of Amsterdam.

Tan, M. L. (1996b) 'Summary report of action research on the social and cultural context of reproductive tract infections in the Philippines', Unpublished report.

Thomas, J. C., and Thomas, K. K. (1999), 'Things ain't what they ought to be: Social forces underlying racial disparities in rates of sexually transmitted diseases in a rural North Carolina county', *Social Science and Medicine*, 49: 1075–84 .

Van Landingham, M. *et al.* (1995), Friends, Wives and Extramarital Sex in Thailand: A Qualitative Study of Peer and Spousal Influence on Thai Male Extramarital Sexual Behavior and Attitudes. Rockefeller Foundation, Institute of Population Studies, Chulalongkorn University, and Population Studies Center of the University of Michigan.

Wasserheit, J. N. (1992), 'Epidemiological synergy: Interrelationships between human immunodeficiency virus infection and other sexually transmitted diseases', *Sexually Transmitted Diseases*, 19 (2): 61–77.

Weinstein, N. D. (1987), 'Unrealistic optimism about susceptibility to health problems: Conclusions from a community-wide sample', *Journal of Behavioral Medicine*, 10: 481–500.

Winder, A. E. (1993), 'Risk assessment—Risk perception: Who Shall Decide?', *International Quarterly of Community Health Education*, 13 (4): 405–10.

Wing, S. (1994), 'Limits of epidemiology', in R. C. Wesley, and V. W. Sidel (eds.), *Medicine and Global Survival*, Vol. 1, London: BMJ Publishing, pp. 74–86.

Wynne, B. (1996), 'May the sheep safely graze? A reflexive view of the expert-lay knowledge divide', in S. Lash, B. Szerszynski, and B. Wynne (eds.), *Risk, Environment and Modernity*, Sage: Thousand Oaks, pp. 27–44.

Young, A. (1982), 'The anthropologies of illness and sickness', *Annual Review of Anthropology*, 11: 257–280.

Zwi, A. B., and Cabral, A. J. R. (1991), 'Identifying "High risk situations" for preventing AIDS', *British Medical Journal*, 303: 1527–9.

PART II

DISCOURSE, PRACTICE, AND REPRODUCTIVE CHOICES

6

Managing 'the Missing Girls' in Chinese Population Discourse

SUSAN GREENHALGH

THE MISSING GIRLS OF CHINA: A VEXED ISSUE FOR ALL

One of the most vexed issues in the post-Cairo era of international population policy[1] is that of the 'missing girls', or, less generously, 'gender violence' in China's birth control programme. A growing body of evidence has linked the one-child-per-family policy introduced in 1979 to the abandonment and infanticide of baby girls and, more recently, widespread abortion of female foetuses (Johnson 1993, 1996, 1998; Greenhalgh and Li 1995; Lavely 1997).[2] As a result of these and other gender-differentiated practices, the sex ratio at birth has been rising. Between 1982 and 1989 the number of boys born per 100 girls born rose from 107 to 114, well above the biologically normal level of 105 to 106 (Zeng et al. 1993).[3] In the early 1990s the ratio of boys to girls continued to climb, reaching 121 in 1993 and 1994 before falling to 116 in 1995 (Lavely 1997). What this means is that every year roughly a million baby girls vanish from the statistics, abandoned, killed, adopted, or aborted in utero.

The disappearance of these infant girls poses awkward problems for many groups of population specialists. The matter is troublesome for official representatives of the Chinese government because gender equality has long been a tenet of Chinese Marxism; indeed, the Chinese Constitution declares men and women equal before the law. For good political reasons, Chinese officials have never publicly acknowledged that the one-child policy might be partly responsible for the disappearance of countless thousands of infant girls. The 'missing girls problem' is also awkward for advocates of third-world population control in the international population community. China is the single greatest contributor to the decline in global population growth rates. If China's population policy were shown to lie behind the death of large numbers of baby girls, it would be difficult for fertility control enthusiasts to support it. Finally, this problem presents complications for feminist reproductive health advocates, whose rights-based population policy, embodied in the Cairo Program of Action, specifically forbids any form of violence against women and girls.[4] Because of the complicated politics surrounding abortion in the US and population control in China, and the difficulties facing Chinese citizens who might wish to criticize their government's policy, open criticism of China's policy is politically difficult, even for rights advocates outside of China who privately condemn it.[5] Caught in these uncomfortable conundrums, these groups have generally dealt with the problem of the disappeared Chinese girls by clothing it in a cloak of silence. Yet this non-stance stance carries its own problems, for it leaves them open to charges of violating their ethics or policy preferences in the service of political goals.

While those groups most centrally involved in the formation of international population policy have remained relatively reticent about the China question, several other groups have not been so reserved. Three sets of actors—journalists, human rights activists, and a small number of Washington, DC-based China demographers[6]—have been highly vocal in criticizing the Chinese programme. While these groups have played crucial roles in bringing gender violence and other problems in the Chinese programme to light, their representations of the situation are troubling in other ways.

Perhaps because the political stakes have been so high, too often the issues have been framed in oversimplified, black-and-white terms in which the complex and contradictory intertwinings of culture and power, state and society have been lost from view. At a time in which China is seen as one of the world's worst violator of human rights (cf. Bernstein 1997), political discourse in the US seems to tolerate the dissemination of 'ethnophobic' if not quite racist images in which China is portrayed as a place with a brutishly misogynist culture and a brutally uncaring state. In an op-ed piece published in mid-1996, for example, Bob Herbert, an editorialist for *The New York Times*, writes of the self-evident barbarism of Chinese culture:

China is a place where girl babies are seen to have such little value (especially in light of the brutally enforced one family per child mandate) that they often are starved, drowned, suffocated, or otherwise slain immediately after birth. (Herbert 1996)

In a report on violations of the human rights of Chinese women and girls, the New York-based group, Human Rights in China, portrays the Chinese state as all-powerful, cruel, and inhumane:

[H]arsh official implementation measures, enacted under the pressure of, and tolerated by, the state policy have . . . encouraged practices such as . . . female infanticide and the abandonment of female infants by individual parents . . . In exposing violations and the Chinese state's responsibility, we seek alternatives to . . . the inhumane, cruel and degrading methods employed in China's population control policy. (HRIC 1995, pp. 32–3)

In these journalistic and human rights discourses on China's population programme, China's problems have been fitted into long-standing American scripts on issues as contentious as individual rights, women's rights, abortion, and state intervention in private life. (The more scholarly critiques draw less heavily on these political discourses.[7]) Because these issues tap deeply rooted American values, the discourses on China tend to have strong moral overtones. The more extreme representations are judgemental in ways that are likely to be offensive to many Chinese and non-Chinese as well.

Not surprisingly, China has reacted to these accusations with hostile denials. While it sometimes acknowledges the existence of violence against women and girls, official statements describe them as isolated violations of central policy by overzealous local officials. In statements prepared for international consumption, the Chinese government has increasingly sought to counter such criticisms by emphasizing the benefits of the one-child policy for women. Both the *National Report of the PRC on Population and Development* issued at the 1994 Cairo International Conference on Population and Development, and the 'White Paper on Family Planning' distributed around the time of the 1995 Beijing International Conference on Women, include substantial sections on the benefits to women of the one-child policy. Improvements in women's political position, economic status, educational level, and status in family life are all attributed to the birth control programme (Chinese Government 1994, pp. 13–14, 26–7; Information Office n.d., pp. 13–15). Indeed, rural women, who make up the great majority, are described as 'that part of the population to benefit most from the policy of family planning' (Information Office n.d., p. 14). These official representations are troubling because some readers might take them at face value, when the connections between birth planning and changes in women's status are complex and multi-directional. At a time in which the larger climate is largely hostile to the advancement of women's status in both public and domestic domains (e.g. Honig and Hershatter 1988; Gao 1994; Woo 1994; Jacka 1997), it would be surprising if the birth planning programme had such uniformly positive effects on women's lives. Tellingly, neither of these government reports, nor the document describing the current phase of the programme, *The National Family Planning Program of China, 1995–2000* (SFPC n.d.), makes more than passing mention of the problem of the missing girls.[8]

In American political discourse, China's population control experiences have been viewed through the lenses of quintessentially Western, usually American, values. What is missing from the American and, indeed, the international discussions of the missing-girl problem is a sense of how these issues look from the Chinese perspective. How do Chinese leaders talk about these issues among themselves? Where does the question of the missing girls fit in the larger Chinese discourse on population and development? To date there has been no serious attempt to understand these problems in Chinese terms.

CHINA'S OFFICIAL DISCOURSE ON POPULATION: THE ANALYTIC TERRAIN

Using internal policy documents made available to outsiders only recently, this paper attempts to understand how the issue of gender violence against infant girls—what the Chinese call *zhongnan qingnu* (to value males and devalue females)—has been framed in internal discussions among Chinese population policy makers. How seriously has it been taken? Have China's leaders dismissed the issue as trivial, or have they made serious attempts to resolve the problem? How do the images of Chinese culture as hopelessly misogynist and the state as brutally uncaring look from inside the Chinese population policy-making establishment? Answers to these questions should be of interest both to groups who have spoken out against the policy and to groups that have not yet decided how best to treat the matter. The official Chinese discourses on population control also hold special interest for students of culture and reproduction. The Chinese materials show how population policy makers, in struggling to overcome 'traditional culture', ended up repackaging it, incorporating it into state policy, and then redeploying it in 'traditional' parts of the society. The Chinese case reveals how 'traditional culture' can travel from society to state and back to society again, in the process gaining legal weight it did not initially have.

This chapter is a small part of a larger project that explores the discourses, practices, politics, and consequences of population control in China. While much of that larger project deals with birth control practices and politics, this chapter deals only with the cognitive grids through which population issues are understood. Those familiar with my other work on the Chinese programme (especially Greenhalgh 1994; Greenhalgh and Li 1995) will know that my intention is neither to divert attention from the material and bodily consequences of the one-child policy, nor to excuse the policy on grounds that it was discursively mandated. To the contrary, it is precisely because I consider those political and corporeal issues so important that I believe a close study of the ideas underlying them is so crucial.

In this chapter I treat official Chinese understandings of population as a discourse, in the Foucauldian sense (especially Foucault 1970, 1972, 1978, 1979). For Foucault, discourse refers not to language or linguistic systems, but to relatively bounded, historically specific bodies of knowledge, or disciplines (for more, see Dreyfus and Rabinow 1982; McHoul and Grace 1997, pp. 26–56). Each discourse is connected to a set of disciplinary practices, or forms of social subjectivity and control. Discourses are important because they both enable and constrain what can be said, written, and thought about a given social object or practice (such as reproduction or birth control) in a particular time and place. The post-World War II discourse on family planning in the US, for example, enables a very different set of ideas about reproduction, rights, and gender from those permitted by the discourse on birth planning in post-1949 China.

In Foucauldian analysis, a discourse is structured, or made up of conceptual elements that fit together into a larger, coherent whole. In the Chinese population discourse, the key structural elements are constructs from the larger political discourse of post-1949 China, that is, those of Marxist, Leninist, Maoist, and, since the late 1970s, Dengist Thought. The most important constructs for this exploration are the Marxian notion of the stages of societal development, the Leninist idea of the vanguard Party, the Maoist concept of mass voluntarism, and the Dengist or reform-era command to 'start from reality'. Beneath these contemporary discourses lie the deeply rooted ideas of Confucian culture, in particular, the notion that males are superior to females.[9] These conceptual elements drawn from the larger political and cultural discourses of Chinese history are important because they shape and constrain the way population problems can be understood, by leaders and led alike. By specifying *what is thinkable*, they open up some policy and behavioural options while closing others. In this chapter I am concerned with their constraining influence on China's leaders and the population policies they devised.

The population discourse is part of a larger official discourse on sexuality that has been propagated by the party-state since 1949 (Evans 1997; for historical precedents, see Dikotter 1995). Reiterating themes in Confucian culture, this larger Communist discourse on sexuality defines love, marriage, and reproduction as matters of public rather than private concern. Sexuality is a site of political control, to be regulated in support of larger party–state projects of socio-economic development, state strengthening, and nation building. The discourse regulates individual sexuality by establishing a set of didactic distinctions between right and wrong, normal and abnormal in sexual behaviour. Because of the importance of regulating sexuality to the Chinese Communists, the proliferation of discourses on sexuality has been accompanied by the construction of political and legal institutions aimed at formally controlling sexual behaviour. In the domain of reproduction, the one-child policy period has witnessed the establishment of the State Birth Planning Commission, with related committees at every level of the administrative hierarchy; the development of formal population policy codified in numerous laws and regulations; and the formalization of the birth planning programme, with its myriad enforcement techniques aimed at keeping fertility within limits established by the state (for details on these institutional accompaniments to the discourse, see Winckler 1999). Far from being 'mere talk', then, the discourse on population is embedded in institutions, policies, and programmes that are backed by the power of party and state. The material effects of this institutionalized discourse include intended consequences—fertility decline, marriage delay, and so forth—as well as unintended effects, such as the disappearance of the baby girls.

The *official state discourse on population* that I focus on has always been the predominant, and long been the hegemonic discourse on population in China. In the early 1950s, before the state position on population had become entrenched, other discourses existed and even competed with it. Most prominent were the discourses of (Marxist) feminism, public health, and demography.[10] Although they remained below the level of political articulation, popular peasant discourses most certainly also flourished, based in the rationalities of China's familistic society and pronatalist culture. Since the mid-1950s, however, when the party began to take an active interest in population, it declared its own views the only acceptable views, forcing these other popular, scientific, and feminist discourses on population out of the political realm. In the 1980s the relaxation of state control over the media and cultural life led to a proliferation of discourses on sexuality generally (Evans 1997). Yet because of the centrality of population control to China's development effort, the state has maintained rigid control over the discourse on population. As a result, for the past 40-plus years, the official state discourse on population has been virtually the only way of thinking about China's population problems and their solutions available to officials and ordinary people alike.

Before beginning, a word on sources. The best statements of the official discourse on population are central-level documents, especially those issued by the Central Committee of the Communist Party and the State Council, directives of the State Birth Planning Commission and its organizational predecessors, and speeches on population by top leaders. Because of the extremely high priority assigned the one-child policy in China's reform programme, and the greater openness of China under the 'open-door policy', a number of key documents from the period since the historic Third Plenum of December 1978[11] have been released (or discovered through serendipity in Hong Kong bookstores). My analyses in this chapter draw on a group of ten key documents issued during the 12 years 1979–91. These documents were selected on the basis of their influence on national (and hence also local) population policy. All are documents of the Party's Central Committee and the State Council or speeches by top leaders of the Party, state, or State Birth Planning Commission. The documents analysed are listed at the end of this chapter. Although my analysis stops in 1991, policy developments since that time indicate that the formulations worked out between the late 1970s and early 1990s continue to shape policy in the late 1990s (see, for example, SFPC n.d., SFPC 1996).

Finally, a note on terminology. Although some of the materials I draw on use the term 'family planning' in connection with the Chinese birth control programme, the Chinese term, *jihua shengyu,* is appropriately translated as 'birth planning'. Birth planning differs from the Western liberal notion of family planning in that the role of the party–state (or simply 'the state') is paramount: births are planned by the state to bring the production of human beings in line with the production of material goods. Where the English term 'family planning' occurs in materials that I quote, I retain the original. Elsewhere I use the term birth planning. The reader should remember that in this chapter the two refer to the same programme and practices.

PLANNED BIRTHS: A WEIGHTY MATTER FOR NATION AND STATE

One of the most striking features of the Chinese population discourse of the late 1970s to early 1990s is the absence, except in a few selected passages, of any explicit recognition that population policy bears special significance for women and girls. This absence of gender concerns from the one-child population discourse marks a departure from earlier treatments of women in official population thought. In the 1960s and 1970s, 'raising women's status'—more specifically, enabling women to participate more fully in socialist construction through education and labour—was one of the key rationales for delaying marriage, spacing children, and lowering fertility. Although such arguments have been resurrected in statements for international consumption in the 1990s, since the late 1970s the internal discourse on population has defined birth planning as a macroeconomic issue of utmost significance to the country and the nation. Any benefits that may accrue to, or any harm that may befall, specific sectors of society, such as women or girls, are trivial matters relative to the weighty importance to the entire society.[12]

From its inception, the one-child policy has been driven by the idea that much is at stake in China's effort to bring population growth rapidly under control. Virtually all of the major documents on birth planning policy have begun by establishing the vital national goals that the policy is designed to achieve. The 1980 Open Letter to all Communist Party and Communist Youth League members, which first announced the call for one-child families to the broad masses of the Chinese people, stressed the 'four modernizations' (in agriculture, industry, science and technology, and national defence) and the health and happiness of future generations:

For the purpose of striving for limiting the total population of our country to 1,200 million by the end of this century, the State Council has already issued a call to the people of the whole country, advocating each couple to have only one child. This is an important measure which concerns the speed and the future of the four modernizations and the health and happiness of generations to come. (Open Letter 1980, p. 1)

The urgency of the task is conveyed by catastrophic scenarios in which too-rapid population growth is portrayed as jeopardizing the country's prospects for development:

This rapid population growth is confronting the whole nation with ever-increasing difficulties in food, clothing, housing, transport, education, public health and employ-ment, making it difficult to bring about a speedy change in the country's impoverished and backward state. . . . [I]f 'one couple, one child' is not widely promoted in the coming 30 or 40 years and particularly in the next 20 or 30 years, . . . [we will be facing] a grave situation in which the people's living standards can hardly be improved. (Open Letter 1980, pp. 1–2)

The one-child policy was launched at a time when rural life was still structured by socialist collectives. By 1981–2, however, the economic reforms introduced on a partial basis a few years earlier had spread throughout the country. By giving peasant families control over their land and livelihood, and by dismantling local policy enforcement structures, the rural political and economic reforms put upward pressure on the birth rate, imperiling fulfilment of population targets. Concerned about reaching those targets, in February 1982 top policy makers issued the Directive on Doing a Better Job of Family Planning Work. The Directive declares that China has only two choices: controlling population growth and bringing about national prosperity, on the one hand, and failing to control population and sinking into disaster, on the other. The clear implication is that there is only one choice, that of drastic population control:

We are faced with two possibilities: either we control the population growth strictly and effectively, make a gradual enhancement in the standards of living of the people as a whole, and expand the country's construction with each passing year; or we do not exercise strict enough control, our measures are insufficient, and we allow the population to continue to grow in large numbers, with the result that we would neither be able to improve the people's lives nor carry out economic, cultural, and national defense construction well. Our only choice is between these two alternatives; we have no other possibilities. (Directive 1982, pp. 18–19)

In September 1982 the one-child policy was designated a 'basic state policy', of fundamental importance to the country as a whole, thus beyond criticism on fundamentals. Hu Yaobang, General Secretary of the Party, made the announcement at the Twelfth Party Congress, using the opportunity to emphasize the importance of not 'relax[ing] the slightest bit':

In our country's economic and social development, the population problem has always been and will always be extremely important. To carry out family planning is a basic national policy in our country . . . An excessively rapid rate of population growth will not only affect the enhancement of per capita income, but the supply of food and housing as well; satisfying education and labor employment needs will become severe problems. Even the society's stability and security can be affected. That is why we cannot even relax the slightest bit in our family planning work. (Hu Yaobang 1982, pp. 55–6)

In the mid-1980s, after a nationwide sterilization campaign gave rise to widespread peasant backlash, the leadership relaxed the policy rules and policy enforcement for a few years, stressing issues of party-mass relations and political security instead (Document 7 1984, p. 27). In the late 1980s and early 1990s, however, facing a projected baby boom, and with only 10 years left in which to reach turn-of-the-century goals, population policy makers again grew concerned about 'excessive' population growth and its deleterious consequences. The Decision on Stepping Up Birth Planning Work, issued by the Central Committee and State Council in May 1991, articulated these concerns, adding worries about the fate of the Chinese nation to earlier concerns about the Chinese state and people:

A strict control of population growth is an important and urgent task confronting our country . . . Over the past 20 years . . . our country has achieved universally acknowledged results in controlling population growth . . . But it should be clearly noted that . . . the task of reining in population growth is quite difficult . . . The 1990s is a very critical period . . . in our country's effort to control population growth. In particular, the Eighth Five-Year Plan period [1991–5] will coincide with a baby boom which makes family planning even more urgent. If we fail to effectively control population growth, it will directly affect the realization of the strategic objective to modernize and construct our country; affect further improvement of the people's living standards and quality of the entire nation; and at the same time accelerate the depletion of natural resources and worsening of the ecology, leaving behind grave consequences to future generations. It is thus evident that family planning is a major event which is tied to whether the country's strategic objective of modernization and construction will be achieved or not; it is a major event which is tied to the rise or fall of the nation; it has reached a stage which allows for no laxity or reticence. On this we need to have a strong sense of responsibility to history and a sense of urgency of the times. (Decision 1991, p. 33)

If the need for drastic control is a matter of historic urgency that is 'tied to the rise or fall of the [Chinese] nation', it would seem obvious that concern about the fate of a small subgroup of the population, such as infant girls, is by comparison quite trivial.

SON PREFERENCE AS A FEUDAL REMNANT TO BE ERADICATED

Although most of the language in the population policy documents was ungendered, gender issues did feature in discussions of obstacles to successful policy enforcement. Gender—or, more precisely, son preference—was positioned as an unwelcome feature of 'feudal culture', the main barrier to be overcome. Thousands of years of feudal culture, it was said, had left two unhealthy legacies among the peasantry: the idea that 'many sons bring much happiness' (*duozi duofu*) and the notion that 'sons are more valuable than daughters' (*zhongnan qingnu*). These ideas, moreover, had been strengthened by the economic reforms carried out in the early 1980s. Discursively, son preference had to be labelled 'feudal' because, under socialism, men and women are by definition equal; any evidence of inequality must be a remnant of the pre-socialist past, which must be, and can be, eliminated.[13] As in general Marxist history, in the population discourse, elements of culture such as childbearing preferences were classified as feudal or socialist, old or new, backward or progressive, categories that are mutually exclusive. Feudal views on sons and daughters were attached to a backward or historically prior social group—the peasantry—rendering discursively unthinkable the possibility that gender bias might also exist among other groups, say, urban residents or even party cadres, or might also have contemporary roots, say, in state population or other policies.

The central question posed by the discourse was how to deal with these 'feudal' views so that the one-child policy could be successfully carried out. The initial answer, and the one more consistent with Marxian and Maoist world views, was that feudal culture must be eradicated, cleared away so that a new and progressive socialist culture could take hold. In the late 1970s, when the one-child policy was being formulated, 'old' ideas favouring many children and sons were seen as rooted ultimately in material problems such as parents' need for support in old age. State policies aimed at changing the pronatal and pro-male institutions of Chinese life were proposed to deal with these economic problems. In an article published in the leading Communist newspaper, *People's Daily*, in 1979, Deputy Prime Minister Chen Muhua articulates this view:

[Leaders] must also help the masses . . . to solve their actual problems. At present, although the old idea of 'among the three things that are unfilial, no posterity is the greatest' stubbornly persists among the masses (especially among the rural masses), so that they will not be satisfied until a male child is born, one has to realize that son preference continues because parents are seeking to avoid genuine problems of increased age—for example, social security, welfare benefits, and so on. Realistic measures should be adopted to gradually solve these problems. We must insist on the principle of equal pay for equal work for both sexes, implement the policy of the husband settling down with his wife's family . . . The economic factor is the one that plays the major role. When the economic problem is solved, a greater part of the problem of having more or fewer children and the problem of their sex will also be solved. (Chen Muhua 1979, p. 730)

Yet the economic viewpoint advanced in the late 1970s was short-lived. From the early 1980s on, the problem of feudal culture was seen as a strictly ideological one which would be solved through ideological exhortation of the masses and the setting of good examples by party and state cadres. These ideas were based on Maoist notions of the role of mass enthusiasm and thought change in promoting social transformation. Mao's ideas, in turn, were rooted in Lenin's notion of party-led ideological agitation as a source of political transformation. Reflecting the discourse of these masters, the Open Letter urges the 'people of New China' to overcome 'old ideas' and prods party cadres to 'take the lead' in getting rid of 'erroneous views':

Since one-child families were advocated, investigations on the sex ratio of firstborns in a number of areas have been conducted by the departments concerned with the . . . conclusion that boys were slightly more numerous than girls . . . The people of New China, particularly the young generation, must overcome the old idea of looking down upon women. If the only baby is a girl, her parents must take just as good care of her . . . Cadres who are Party members ought to take the lead in getting rid of feudal ideas. They should rid themselves of the erroneous view that the family cannot reproduce itself without giving birth to a baby boy. (Open Letter 1980, pp. 3, 4)

The Open Letter reveals an early awareness of the son preference problem among those fashioning the one-child policy. Indeed, if the Letter can be taken at face value, it suggests that the party had conducted investigations to see whether the ratio of boys to girls would rise if peasants were restricted to one child. Party researches apparently concluded that the sex ratio would not be unduly affected, for the Open Letter quite clearly takes the matter off the political agenda.

In the early 1980s, however, investigations at the grassroots level revealed that the economic reforms had exacerbated problems of fertility control by increasing peasants' desires for sons. The February 1982 Directive on Doing a Better Job draws attention to this problem and the contradictions it created for birth planning work. Note how gender preference continues to be framed as 'traditional' and 'old-fashioned', drawing attention away from the possibility that contemporary conditions might be supporting it:

The traditional, old-fashioned mentalities of 'the more sons the greater happiness' and emphasizing men over women still have both a broad and a deep impact among the masses. Since the production responsibility system was carried out in the countryside, the peasants have put forth a demand to have more children, and especially more boys. They believe that because their livelihoods seem to have improved, it does not matter much if they have a few more children; and with more children they can increase their labor power and be allotted more responsibility fields. The contradictions that are thus generated by old-fashioned ideas under new circumstances have created a special degree of difficulty for our work. (Directive 1982, p. 19)

Yet the Directive does not propose any solution to the contradiction. Instead, it insists that birth planning is entirely consistent with rural economic reform, and that cadres must 'resolutely and unwaveringly' carry out both at the same time. The key is to conduct 'long-term penetrating and insistent propaganda and education . . . , so that more and more people will come to truly understand the great significance of launching family planning' (Directive 1982, p. 20). Ideological work was to be backed by economic sanctions, where necessary (Directive 1982, p. 21).

Embedded in these notions of ideological progression toward new gender mentalities, control of population growth, and national development, however, was a hidden paradox. According to the Marxian stage-theory of human development as applied to China, by definition only peasants could manifest feudal culture, while leading cadres all exhibited socialist culture. But, in the same breath that leading population cadres instructed local cadres to 'take the lead' in getting rid of male-biased ideas and practices, they themselves offered discursive constructions that seemed to embody the devaluation of female lives and abilities that they were decrying. The Central Committee's Open Letter, in encouraging the people of 'New China' to 'overcome the old idea of looking down upon women', offers the following reason: 'When girl babies grow up, they are as good a source of labor as males and may work very well at certain jobs and even better at housework.' (Open Letter 1980, p. 3). The explicit emphasis here is not on gender inequality, but on gender difference: girls are better at housework. But inequality is built into this difference. Inasmuch as housework is not paid and lies outside the socially valued realm of 'social production', it is a less valued form of labour. Local cadres might be forgiven for hearing these words as support for their own and their constituents' views that sons are more valuable than daughters.

This passage is especially interesting for it shows how, even when China's population policy makers are trying to discourage gender discrimination, they seem unconsciously to embrace the Confucian notion of the unequal value of sons and daughters. In this way, the idea of the differential value of the genders came to be embedded in the population discourse from the time the one-child policy was introduced.[14] Once inscribed, it became very hard to erase.

Discursive reinforcement of traditional ('peasant') bias in favour of males by top ('progressive') leaders in the country occurred again and again, often in subtle ways. Increasingly, it took the form of accepting gender disparities as part of 'social reality' rather than challenging them as contradictions to socialist ideals. It is not surprising, then, that, when the first solution to the problem of feudal culture failed to alleviate it, the discursive emphasis shifted from eliminating gender-differentiated values to accommodating them.

SON PREFERENCE AS A PEASANT REALITY TO BE ACCOMMODATED

The second solution to the problem of son preference involved not eradicating, but accepting peasant views about the unequal value of females and males. The views that were accommodated, of course, were no longer construed as 'feudal'; rather, they were repositioned as part of Chinese 'reality'. Under the Dengist reform banner of 'proceeding from reality' and finding 'effective' solutions to 'actual problems', in the mid-1980s a new discourse emerged in which the only possible response to the problem of persistent patriarchal reproductive culture was to accept it and modify state policy along gendered lines.

The ground for this shift was laid in the formative years of the one-child discourse, when conditions legitimizing couples' requests to have a second child were framed as 'actual difficulties' or 'real difficulties' (Open Letter 1980, p. 4). This formulation continued to be used every time the issue of conditions for second children came up. For example, Document 7 of 1984, the first significantly to increase the number of conditions for second childbearing, referred to 'the masses who do indeed have practical difficulties that require of them to petition to have two children' (Document 7 1984, p. 33). Document 13 of 1986 indicated that '[T]he focus will be . . . the countryside . . . [where] we must adopt effective measures . . . The key . . . is to proceed from actual realities . . . [We must stress] "seeking truth through facts", and proceeding from practicality in all things . . . [Our perfected policy allows] couples that truly have difficulty complying with a single-child policy to give birth to two children' (Document 13 1986, pp. 42, 43). Although the concrete meaning of 'actual difficulties' was not specified in the official discourse of the early and mid-1980s, since the main obstacle was patriarchal feudal culture, or son preference, the implication was that the major 'difficulty' legitimizing permission for a second child was having a daughter on the first try.

The new approach was incorporated into the official population discourse in early 1988. In a speech delivered to a national conference of provincial birth planning directors, Premier Li Peng described son preference as a 'traditional concept . . . left behind by thousands of years of feudal society', a formulation that drew attention away from any contemporary sources of that preference. 'Under current conditions', Li said, without specifying those conditions, peasant couples 'will tend to want . . . a boy'. The effect of this simple construction was to naturalize son preference, to accept it as a given fact, an inevitable residue of a long history. With economic and educational development, however, things will eventually change:

[I]n the work of family planning we must overcome traditional concepts that have been left behind by thousands of years of feudal society . . . Under our country's current conditions, unless propaganda and education is [sic] promoted, the masses in the countryside will tend to want to have more children, and will hope to have a boy. This is at odds with our goals. In the advanced developed countries, with the enhancement of the economic and cultural and educational standards, . . . population does not increase . . . [I]n our larger cities and municipalities, . . . [t]he degree of difficulty of the work of family planning is no longer that great . . . Therefore, we can see that the society's and the people's cultural and educational quality and the economic conditions play a major role in this. (Li Peng 1988, pp. 65, 68–9)

What Li was suggesting is that urbanization and development would gradually take care of the problem. If that is so, then no ameliorative measures need to be adopted now.

It was thus a small step that Peng Peiyun, newly appointed Minister-in-Charge of the State Birth Planning Commission, took in May 1988 when she announced that, henceforth, having only a daughter was sufficient hardship for a peasant couple to be granted permission to have a second child. This announcement was made in a major speech delivered to the directors of the provincial birth planning commissions. That this was a sensitive subject is clear from the long discussion devoted to explaining the decision in the speech. It was evidently also a politically important subject, on which only the top leaders in the country could decide, for Peng went to great lengths to attribute everything she said to the Standing Committee of the Politburo, the innermost circle of party leaders:

[T]he Standing Committee of the Political Bureau of the Central Committee . . . pointed out . . . 'In the countryside, those among the masses that truly have difficulty complying with the one-child-per-couple policy (and this would include single-daughter households) . . . may, after permission is granted, and after an interval of several years, give birth to a second child.' (Peng Peiyun 1988, pp. 84–5)

The Standing Committee distanced itself from the view that it was condoning male bias, defining its decision instead as a 'realistic move' based on the material circumstances of low economic level of rural China and the centrality of the family as the basic unit of production. The quote from the minutes of the Standing Committee meeting continues:

In implementing this policy, we are by no means proceeding from the viewpoint of emphasizing males over females; rather, we are realistically considering that at the present moment the level of our force of production in the countryside is still relatively low, and the family remains the basic unit of production. Under such circumstances, if a peasant household has only a young girl, that household would quite possibly have real difficulties in production and in maintaining its livelihood. (Peng Peiyun 1988, p. 85)

What remained unarticulated in the Standing Committee's report was the gender division of labour in the peasant family, according to which only sons are deemed capable of performing certain crucial production tasks. The family division of labour by gender was apparently either too self-evident (because biologically based) or too unchangeable (because deeply rooted in peasant tradition) to be mentioned, let alone challenged. The effect of this silence was to naturalize the gendered division of tasks, taking it off the agenda of targets for policy intervention.

Peng went on to legitimize the decision on the 'daughter-only policy' in a variety of terms. Although she mentioned what might appear to be humanitarian considerations—preventing the drowning of babies—these concerns seem to arise from questions of China's international image. Reflecting the socialist planner's concern with reaching state population targets, and using Dengist language of efficiency and efficacy, she stressed as the major rationales for the daughter-only policy the need to make the policy more workable and the need to guarantee fulfilment of the population plan. Continuing to quote the minutes of the Standing Committee, she said:

If we permit single-daughter households in the countryside to have a second child but in a planned way, it will make our policy more workable, and help to prevent the phenomenon of people drowning babies. Our international image will be improved, and, moreover, this will also be beneficial to reducing the number of births that are beyond the limits of the plan, and to our ability to realize the target of controlling the population. (Peng Peiyun 1988, p. 85)

Finally, Peng added later in the passage, the daughter-only policy 'appeals to the people', something that was desirable because it 'improves party-mass relations', which in turn is good for policy enforcement. Throughout the speech, the emphasis was on reaching goals. Using reform language, she characterized the adoption of the daughter-only policy as 'a practical move' that will improve policy enforcement and appeal to the people.

Some comrades apparently were worried that the policy change would effectively relax the policy, producing another dreaded rise in birth rates. Minister Peng contested this view, arguing that broadening the rules would only legitimize what was already rural practice, bringing existing practice into line with official policy:

[W]ith regard to the broad expanse of the countryside, what this does is to demand that the childbirth of the masses be absorbed into the track permitted by the currently existing policy, and so, in effect, it tightens up the policy, rather than relaxing it. The fertility rate in the countryside is 2.6. For about 80 percent of the countryside, in reality, the overwhelming majority are generally giving birth to two children, with some giving birth multiple times. If we can, through arduous work, achieve a situation in which we give special consideration only to the 'single-daughter households' . . . that would be a major improvement.

Under current conditions, to allow, in the countryside, 'single-daughter households' to have a second child after an interval of several years would take care of some of the real difficulties on the part of some of the peasants; it would also be conducive to controlling the overly rapid population increase. Therefore, it is a practical move, and . . . something that can be accepted by the vast majority of the peasants. This epitomizes the state's concern and caring for the masses. (Peng Peiyun 1988, pp. 85, 87)

Peng's speech reveals the difficult dilemmas China's policy makers faced. If they insisted on retaining the one-child rule, many peasant couples would likely resort to drowning their first-born baby girls. But in allowing couples with only a girl to have another child, they reinforced older, Confucian notions about the unequal value of sons and daughters. Asked if households with only one son did not face difficulties too, she answered that their difficulties would be less serious than those of daughter-only households, reproducing in official discourse the gender bias that was evident in peasant family culture:

Although 'single-son households' can also experience difficulties, after all, the difficulty they have would be less severe than that of the 'single-daughter households'. Therefore, let us not force a comparison. (Peng Peiyun 1988, p. 87)

In stating that this move 'epitomizes the state's concern and caring for the masses' (see the previous quote), Peng seems to place infant girls outside the category of the masses into a non-category of essentially non-persons.

In this way the one-child discourse, which started out challenging male preference, ended up accepting 'peasant' views that sons are better than daughters, framing the decision in the reform language of 'proceeding from reality'. This shift in the discourse was translated into state policy (Zeng 1989), building the daughter-only policy, and thus gender inequality, into the regulations of the majority of Chinese provinces (see, for example, Greenhalgh and Li 1995). The decision to allow peasant couples with one girl to have another child probably saved the lives of baby girls, but it reinscribed their social inequality in the family and in the law.

GENDER VIOLENCE: A MATTER FOR THE CRIMINAL JUSTICE SYSTEM

The Open Letter of 1980 had defined gender violence and distorted sex ratios at birth as non-issues, removing them from the agenda of population policy makers. When these very problems appeared in the countryside a couple of years later, they were occasionally acknowledged in internal documents, but treated as secondary matters relative to the control of population growth. Equally importantly, in these documents actions such as drowning or otherwise harming infants were represented as crimes that belonged to the discursive and legal world of the criminal justice system,[15] not the birth planning bureaucracy. A rare acknowledgement of such problems can be found in a November 1982 report to the National People's Congress made by Premier Zhao Ziyang:

We must control population growth rigorously during the period of the Sixth Five-Year Plan [1981–5] . . . We must carry out persuasive education among the peasants, in order to powerfully dispel and abolish such feudal customs as emphasizing males and diminishing women, or thinking that 'the more sons, the greater the happiness'. We must emphasize the protection of female infants and the mothers who give birth to female infants. Anyone who gives birth to a girl as a single child and raises her well and educates her well even more worthy of praise, recognition, support and reward than the person who gives birth to a single male child. The entire society must join in resolute condemnation of such criminal actions as the drowning and harming of female infants; the judicial organs must extend the penalties and other sanctions of the law resolutely. (Zhao Ziyang 1982, pp. 57–8)

Yet while the crimes against infant girls were unmistakably represented as problems, beyond instructing the 'entire society . . . [to] join in resolute condemnation', and urging the judicial organs to penalize offenders, Zhao's report did not mention any concrete actions to be taken to stop the violence. To the contrary, by placing the problem within the domain of the criminal justice system, Zhao cleared the birth planning establishment of culpability, while at the same time failing to attend to serious problems of enforcement of the criminal code (HRIC 1995; Palmer 1995; Li 1996). Additionally, this statement by Zhao was made on the eve of a nationwide sterilization campaign, whose restrictive rules and heavy-handed enforcement led huge numbers of couples to engage in precisely those criminal practices Zhao was censuring. Had the leadership deemed the problem of violence against infant girls serious, it was precisely at this time that it should have specified corrective action to resolve it. Zhao's statement makes the state's priorities very clear.

In the late 1980s and early 1990s, when demographers' research provided incontrovertible evidence that the sex ratio at birth was rising rapidly, public concern about the difficulties men would face finding brides forced the issue back onto population policy makers' agenda. Although there was no mention of the problem in the birth planning documents examined, short statements by leaders of the State Birth Planning Commission occasionally admitted the existence of these gender problems, while downplaying their seriousness (e.g. Mingpao 1993). As in the early 1980s, they were referred to the criminal justice system, this time to be handled under a host of new laws formulated to bring family life within the orbit of socialist legality. New laws with articles prohibiting female infanticide, abandonment, and mistreatment included the 1980 Marriage Law, the 1991 Law for the Protection of Minors, the 1991 Adoption Law, and the 1992 Law for the Protection of the Rights and Interests of Women (Palmer 1995). Yet once again, problems of enforcement of the law—which were marked—were not addressed. And again, since there was no acknowledgement that the rising sex ratio had been fostered in part by the one-child policy, there was no apparent need to alter that policy.

CONCLUSION: AN ERASURE AND EXACERBATION OF GENDER BIAS

This reading of internal Chinese documents has shown that, despite the silence surrounding the question of the missing girls in statements for international audiences, this issue has been a difficult one for Chinese leaders, one they have grappled with time and again. However, the larger discursive grids into which the matter was fitted narrowed the range of responses China's policy makers were able to make. Once population was defined as a matter of vital national interests, concerns of the collectivity—the state, the people, future generations and, most recently, the nation—outweighed the interests of any subgroup of the population, including infant girls. Almost by definition, the problems of those subgroups—even life-and-death problems—had to be submerged and marginalized so that the primary emphasis could continue to be placed on the 'strategic significance' of the one-child policy to the 'Chinese people' as a whole.

While son preference/daughter discrimination was very much a secondary issue, contra the image of a heartless state that accorded girls no value, Chinese policy makers did address the problem and attempt to find solutions to it. Drawing on Marxian stage-theory of societal development, in the late 1970s they defined son preference as part of 'feudal culture' and proposed eradicating it through Maoist techniques of ideological education and more traditional Marxian strategies of altering the material bases of gender inequality. When the economic reforms introduced in the late 1970s and early 1980s apparently increased the preference for sons, policy makers changed tack. One response, rarely but occasionally reflected in central-level population documents, was to define gender violence as a legal problem to be handled by the criminal justice system. This move absolved the State Birth Planning Commission of responsibility while failing to solve the problem, since the thorny question of enforcement of the criminal codes was not addressed. A second and more consequential response was to reposition the problem in discursive space. Following Dengist reform discourse of 'starting from reality', policy makers redefined son preference as part of 'peasant reality'. Instead of challenging it, they sought to accommodate it and to contain its effects within a broadened state policy that allowed couples with only a daughter to have a second child. Ironically, in trying to eradicate son preference, Chinese discourse makers ended up reinforcing it, so that by the mid-1990s son preference had become embedded not only in Confucian culture, but also in Chinese Communist law. This reformulation of the issue at the political centre legitimated 'traditional' cultural bias against girls in the 'modern' discourse and laws of the reform era, with profound consequences for girls throughout the country.

For political reasons, Chinese population policy makers consistently failed to acknowledge a connection between the one-child policy and the growing numbers of missing girls. To the contrary, that connection was erased again and again by discursive constructions that positioned son preference as part of 'feudal culture' and, later, 'peasant reality'. Both formulations diverted attention from the contemporary roots of peasants' gendered practices in state population and other policies.

While feminist reproductive health advocates may prefer to see gender violence against the girl child as an issue of individual human rights that is forthrightly addressed in population policy, such an approach is not thinkable in official Chinese discourse. This examination of central-level documents helps us understand how developments in China's population programme that many Westerners see as state-supported devaluation of female lives are rendered invisible—in effect, not occurrable—because they are unsayable in the discourse. What is unsayable is then deniable in representations for international consumption.

If a fundamental change in the one-child policy is to occur, there must first be a change at the level of discourse or understandings. These changes must come from within, for any new understandings that are devised will have to be *Chinese conceptions* that build on Chinese history and political culture. Non-Chinese interested in promoting such change need to work with concerned Chinese citizens to foster new ways of framing population issues. The first step is to demonstrate that the terms within which China's population problem is now understood are in fact 'only' a discourse—*one way among many* of viewing population and its regulation. Beyond that, the task is to search for new ways of understanding China's population problems and policies that reflect the interests of all groups that make up the 'Chinese people'.

Notes

1. The International Conference on Population and Development held in Cairo in 1994 marked a major turning point in thinking on international population policy. The traditional emphasis on reducing population growth rates was downplayed in favour of a new emphasis on women's reproductive health, rights, and choice. McIntosh and Finkle (1995) and Hodgson and Watkins (1997) provide insight into the process leading up to Cairo.

2. Journalistic reports support the scholarly findings. See Yan (1983), *Beijing Review* (1989), and Kristof (1993).

3. For more on the demography of China's rising sex ratios at birth, see Johansson and Nygren (1991), Hull and Wen (1992), and Coale and Banister (1994).

4. Lucid expositions of these reproductive rights-based policies can be found in Dixon-Mueller (1993), and Correa (1994). The Program of Action of the 1994 International Conference on Population and Development is reprinted in *Population and Development Review* (1995).

5. Some of these political complexities are brought out in Crane and Finkle (1989). I thank Carmen Barroso for an illuminating discussion of these issues.

6. The most prominent are Banister (e.g. Banister 1987) and Aird (e.g. Aird 1990).

7. The more scholarly work suffers from other problems. Some of these are reviewed in Greenhalgh (1990).

8. The National Report presented at the Cairo Conference reports that: 'Like the case in some other developing countries, with a sharp decrease of birth rate, there has been a rising trend of sex ratio at births in recent years. The Government . . . attach[es] great importance to this issue and [is] taking steps to solve it . . .' (Chinese Government 1994, p. 31). The 1995 'White Paper' notes that: 'There are also problems in the quality and structure of population that should not be neglected. These problems include the high sex ratio. . .' (Information Office n.d., p. 29). The report on the current phase of the birth planning programme says that: 'Constant efforts should be made to . . . put an end to the infanticide and abandonment of girl babies' (SFPC n.d., pp. 32–3). This document goes so far as to claim that 'viewing male and female children as the same . . . [has] become an irresistible trend of the times', without, however, citing any supporting evidence (SFPC n.d., pp. 9–10). In each case, discussion of the missing girls problem falls near the end of the report, signalling its relative unimportance. None of the reports acknowledges a connection between the policy and the rising sex ratios at birth, describing the skewed sex ratio merely as a problem that needs to be addressed.

9. A useful summary of the main features of Maoist and Dengist thought, and their borrowings from Confucianism, Marxism, and Leninism, can be found in Lieberthal (1995, pp. 60–77, 128–44).

10. A brief history of the feminist discourses on population that evolved from the 1930s to the mid-1950s can be found in White (1994).
11. The Third Plenum of the Party's Eleventh Central Committee ratified the reform programme that transformed China's political economy in the 1980s. For a succinct review of these and other crucial political developments that form the backdrop to the evolution of the official discourse on population, see Lieberthal (1995).
12. Even in the 1960s and 1970s, however, the benefits promised individual women—education, occupation, and so forth—were granted so that women could better serve the larger socialist cause. At no time in the post-1949 history of the People's Republic were women treated as beneficiaries of economic, political, or legal reform in their own right (see, for example, Andors 1983; Johnson 1983; Stacey 1983).
13. On the invention of the Chinese peasantry as a 'feudal' group incapable of creative participation in China's reconstruction, see Cohen (1993).
14. Gender bias was evident in earlier population policy discourse as well; that, however, is the subject of another paper.
15. Chinese legal discourse distinguishes between criminal punishments, which apply to the most serious offences against society, and administrative sanctions, which cover everything else. In Chinese laws dealing with gender violence (which are discussed just below in the text), female abandonment and infanticide are treated either as crimes or as administrative offences, depending on the heinousness of the act. Although the Chinese would not label the regulations guiding administrative punishments 'criminal', legal specialists consider those regulations an important item of criminal legislation (Clarke and Feinerman 1995, p. 141). Similarly, one might say that the process of dealing with offences requiring administrative sanction is an important part of the criminal justice system. For more on these matters, see Clarke and Feinerman (1995).

References

Aird, J. S. (1990), *Slaughter of the Innocents: Coercive Birth Control in China*, Washington, DC: American Enterprise Institute.

Andors, P. (1983), *The Unfinished Liberation of Chinese Women, 1949–1980*, Bloomington: Indiana University Press.

Banister, J. (1987), *China's Changing Population*, Stanford: Stanford University Press.

Beijing Review (1989), 'Stop sex checks of fetuses', *Beijing Review*, 32 (28) (10–16 July): 8–9.

Bernstein, R. (1997), 'From a Chinese Prison, Thoughtful Defiance', *The New York Times*, 12 May, pp. B1, B7.

Chinese Government (1994), *National Report of the People's Republic of China on Population and Development for the International Conference on Population and Development, Cairo, 5–13 September 1994*, Beijing: n.a.

Clarke, D. C., and J. V. Feinerman (1995), 'Antagonistic contradictions: Criminal law and human rights in China', *The China Quarterly*, 141: 135–54.

Coale, A. J., and J. Banister (1994), 'Five decades of missing females in China', *Demography*, 31 (3): 459–79.

Cohen, M. L. (1993), 'Cultural and political inventions in modern China: The case of the Chinese peasant', *Daedalus*, 122 (2): 151–70.

Correa, S. (1994), *Population and Reproductive Rights: Feminist Perspectives from the South*, London: Zed.

Crane, B. B., and Finkle, J. L. (1989), 'The United States, China, and the United Nations Population Fund: Dynamics of US Policymaking', *Population and Development Review*, 15 (1): 23–59.

Dikotter, F. (1995), *Sex, Culture, and Modernity in China: Medical Science and the Construction of Sexual Identities in the Early Republican Period*, Honolulu: University of Hawaii Press.

Dixon-Mueller, R. (1993), *Population Policy and Women's Rights: Transforming Reproductive Choice*, Westport, CT: Praeger.

Dreyfus, H. L. and Rabinow, P. (1982), *Michel Foucault: Beyond Structuralism and Hermeneutics*, 2nd edition, Chicago: University of Chicago Press.

Evans, H. (1997), *Women and Sexuality in China: Dominant Discourses of Female Sexuality and Gender Since 1949*, Cambridge, UK: Polity.

Foucault, M. (1970), *The Order of Things: An Archaeology of the Human Sciences*, New York: Random House.

—— (1972), *The Archaeology of Knowledge*, New York: Harper Colophon.

—— (1978), *History of Sexuality, Vol. 1: An Introduction*, New York: Random House.

—— (1979), *Discipline and Punish: The Birth of the Prison*, New York: Random House.

Gao, X. (1994), 'China's modernization and changes in the social status of rural women', in Gilmartin *et al.* (eds.), *Engendering China: Women, Culture, and the State*, pp. 80–97 Cambridge: Harvard University Press.

Greenhalgh, S. (1990), 'The evolution of the one-child policy in Shaanxi, 1979–88', *The China Quarterly*, 122: 191–229.

—— (1994), 'Controlling births and bodies in village china', *American Ethnologist*, 21 (1): 3–30.

—— and Li, J. (1995), 'Engendering reproductive policy and practice in peasant China: For a feminist demography of reproduction', *Signs: Journal of Women in Culture and Society*, 20 (3): 601–41.

Herbert, B. (1996), 'From sweatshops to aerobics', *The New York Times*, June 24, A15.

Hodgson, D., and Watkins, S. C. (1997), 'Feminists and neo-Malthusians: Past and present alliances', *Population and Development Review*, 23 (3): 469–523.

Honig, E., and Hershatter, G. (1988), *Personal Voices: Chinese Women in the 1980's*, Stanford: Stanford University Press.

HRIC (Human Rights in China) (1995), *Caught between Tradition and the State: Violations of the Human Rights of Chinese Women. A Report with Recommendations Marking the Fourth World Conference on Women*, New York: Human Rights in China.

Hull, T. H., and Wen, X. (1992), 'Rising sex ratios at birth in China: Evidence from the 1990 population census', Paper presented at International Seminar on China's 1990 Population Census, Beijing, October 19–23.

Jacka, T. (1997), *Women's Work in Rural China: Change and Continuity in an Era of Reform*, Cambridge: Cambridge University Press.

Johansson, S., and Nygren, O. (1991), 'The missing girls of China: A new demographic account,' *Population and Development Review*, 17 (1): 35–51.

Johnson, K. A. (1983), *Women, the Family and Peasant Revolution in China*, Chicago: University of Chicago Press.

Johnson, K. (1993), 'Chinese orphanages: Saving China's abandoned girls', *Australian Journal of Chinese Affairs*, 30: 71–87.

—— (1996), 'The politics of the revival of infant abandonment in China, with special reference to hunan.' *Population and Development Review*, 22 (1): 77–98.

—— H. Banghan, and W. Liyao (1998), 'Infant abandonment and adoption in China', *Population and Development Review*, 24 (2): 469–510.

Kristof, N. D. (1993), 'Peasants of China discover new way to weed out girls', *New York Times* (July 2): 1.

Lavely, W. (1997), 'Unintended consequences of China's birth planning policy', Paper presented at Conference on Unintended Social Consequences of Chinese Economic Reform, Cambridge, MA, May 23–24.

Li Xiaorong (1996), 'License to coerce: Violence against women, state responsibility, and legal failures in China's family-planning program', *Yale Journal of Law and Feminism*, 8: 145–91.

Lieberthal, K. (1995), *Governing China: From Revolution Through Reform*, New York: Norton.

McHoul, A., and Grace, W. (1997), *A Foucault Primer: Discourse, Power and the Subject*, New York: New York University Press.

McIntosh, C. A., and Finkle, J. L. (1995), 'The Cairo conference on population and development: A new paradigm?' *Population and Development Review*, 21 (2): 223–60.

Mingpao (1993), 'Use of B Ultrasound Prohibited', JPRS (Joint Publications Research Service)-CAR-93-043: 21–22.

Palmer, M. (1995), 'The re-emergence of family law in post-Mao China: Marriage, divorce and reproduction', *The China Quarterly*, 141: 110–34.

Population and Development Review (1995), 'The Program of Action of the 1994 International Conference on Population and Development', 21 (1): 187–213; 21 (2): 437–61.

SFPC (n.d.), *The National Family Planning Program of China, 1995–2000*. Beijing: State Family Planning Commission.

SFPC (1996), 'The population situation in China: The insiders' view', Beijing: China Population Association, State Family Planning Commission, October.

Stacey, J. (1983), *Patriarchy and Socialist Revolution in China*, Berkeley: University of California Press.

White, T. (1994), 'The origins of China's birth planning policy', in Gilmartin *et al.* (eds), pp. 250–78.

Winckler, E. A. (1999), 'Re-enforcing state birth planning', in E. A. Winckler (ed.), *Transitions from Communism in China*, Boulder: Lynne Rienner.

Woo, M. Y. K. (1994), 'Chinese women workers: The delicate balance between protection and equality', in Gilmartin *et al.* (eds.), *Engendering China: Women, Culture, and the State*, pp. 279–95.

Yan Keqing, (1983), 'Problems and prospects in population planning', *China Reconstructs* (June): 11–13.

Zeng Yi (1989), 'Is the Chinese family planning program 'tightening up'?' *Population and Development Review*, 15 (2): 333–7.

—— Tu Ping, Gu Baochang, Li Bohua, and Li Yongping (1993), 'Causes and implications of the recent increase in the reported sex ratio at birth in China', *Population and Development Review*, 19 (2): 283–302.

Documents analysed

Chen, M. (1979), 'Realization of the four modernizations hinged on planned control of population growth', mimeo. Also printed in *Population and Development Review* (1979) 5 (4): 723–30. Originally published in *People's Daily*, August 11.

Open Letter (1980), 'Open letter from the central committee of the communist party of China to all members of the party and the communist youth league concerning the problem of controlling the country's population growth', in *China: Population Policy* and *Family Planning Practice*, State Family Planning Commission. Beijing: China Population Information Centre, 1983, pp. 1–4. Originally published in *People's Daily*, September 25.

Directive (1982), 'Directive of the central committee of the communist party of China and the state council of the PRC on doing a better job with family planning work' (February 9), in *Chinese Sociology and Anthropology* 24 (3) (Spring), edited by Tyrene White, pp. 17–26.

Hu Yaobang (1982), 'Carrying out family planning is a basic national policy for our country' (September 1), excerpt in *Chinese Sociology and Anthropology* 24 (3) (Spring), edited by Tyrene White, pp. 55–6.

Zhao Ziyang (1982), 'The control over the growth of the population is something to which the entire society must pay great attention' (November 30), excerpt in *Chinese Sociology and Anthropology* 24 (3) (Spring), edited by Tyrene White, pp. 57–8.

Document 7 (1984), ' "Report on the Conditions of the Work of Family Planning" of the Party Group of the State Family Planning Commission, as approved and issued by the Central Committee of the Communist Party of China' (April 13), and 'Report on the Conditions Regarding the Work of Family Planning' (March 22), in *Chinese Sociology and Anthropology* 24 (3) (Spring), edited by Tyrene White, pp. 27–30 and 31–9.

Document 13 (1986), 'Directive of the Central Committee of the Chinese Communist Party's Approval of the "Report on the Conditions of Family Planning Work during the Sixth Five-Year Plan Period and Recommendations on the Work during the Seventh Five-Year Plan' (May 9), in *Chinese Sociology and Anthropology* 24 (3) (Spring), edited by Tyrene White, pp. 41–50.

Li Peng (1988), 'Speech while receiving the Report of the National Conference of Directors of Family Planning Commissions' (January 20), in *Chinese Sociology and Anthropology* 24 (3) (Spring), edited by Tyrene White, pp. 64–70.

Peng Peiyun (1988), 'Speech at the Closing of the National Conference of Directors of Family Planning Commissions' (May 12), in *Chinese Sociology and Anthropology* 24 (3) (Spring), edited by Tyrene White, pp. 80–96.

Decision (1991) 'Decision on stepping up family planning work', in FBIS-CHI-91-119, June 20, pp. 33–5.

Note: Only English sources cited.

7

Reproductive Health Counselling in the Islamic Republic of Iran: The Role of Women Mullahs

HOMA HOODFAR

Historically, formal religious authority in Iran is dominated by men, and women's role in the mosques is primarily as an audience. However, women, at least in urban centres, have developed their own informal religious activities with much vitality. These activities are usually home-centred and frequently exclude men. Research in this field has documented that these activities are far from peripheral to Islamic belief; rather they play significant social as well as spiritual roles in the lives of women and the community (Betteridge 1980, 1983; Torab 1996).[1] In addition to religious and ethical matters, major social issues—and particularly how they relate to women and family—are frequent topics of discussion at these gatherings which represent women-centred social institutions and which, far from marginalizing women, are major channels through which women integrate themselves into the wider social and political concerns of the society (Kamalkhani 1993; Torab 1996).

Although during the Shah's regime the educated middle classes grew less interested in women's religious activities, adherence among more *sonnati* (traditional as opposed to modern and 'westernized') segments of the population remained solid, despite criticism of both educated and orthodox religious authorities (Betteridge 1980) that such activities mix religion with superstitious beliefs. However, under the Islamic regime of the last two decades, these exclusively female religious gatherings have attracted renewed public interest and greater participation as part of a general revival of Islam. More significantly, there has been a substantial reduction in the criticism and apprehension occasionally expressed by some members of the formal religious establishment towards these 'unorthodox' practices (Betteridge 1980). Nonetheless, as I will discuss, the relative silence of the formal authorities should not be perceived as unequivocal approval of these activities. In practice the religious leaders have overtly encouraged women to participate in religious activities only when these have clearly been under formal (read male) leadership.[2] Religious authorities have remained ambivalent about women-centred religious activities despite their approval and encouragement of many unorthodox male religious activities, such as the passion play staged on Ashura.[3]

Such ambivalence of course is consistent with the patriarchal world view of the clergy that resist accepting female leadership or equal worth (Hoodfar 1998; Afary 1996; Paidar 1995). This is despite the fact that a considerable number of religious leaders have tried, with some success, to broaden the role of religion in diverse aspects of Iranians' social and economic lives. Thus religious gatherings now more than ever address most political and controversial issues and try to bring together scientific and religious beliefs and activities. One prominent example is the direct and positive role religious leaders have played in promoting family planning. The Islamic regime has made effective use of concern over the population question to bring religion, science, and politics together in such a manner that the interconnectedness between these issues would not be lost on the general public (Hoodfar 1995, 1996). These campaigns have also allowed the regime to demonstrate their view that Islam as a religion is not outdated, as some modernists claim, and that indeed it is truly timeless.

To the credit of the Islamic Republic and the family planning programme, it is clear that planners are aware of women's central role in the success of the programme and have tried to reach out to them. However, while they have mobilized and encouraged male preachers to discuss family planning matters for the public and in particular for women, they have generally overlooked the women's religious gatherings and the female preachers whose historical concerns had always included family matters and health issues.[4] This has occurred despite common knowledge of the popularity of female preachers among women, and in particular among the least-privileged and more tradition-bound women. Instead the authorities have expended great efforts to create a completely new institution of female community volunteers (which has gained international recognition for its success) in order to reach less-privileged women in the urban centres and encourage public participation in the development process.

In this chapter I review the government's formal dissemination of health and contraceptive information and the unrecognized activities of women preachers in health promotion. I argue that the regime's ambivalence toward women preachers stems from the tension between their desire to mobilize women, whom they view as a local resource (Ministry of Health 1996), while concurrently controlling the gender debate and the definition of sexuality. Given the inherently decentralized nature of women's gatherings, such control would not be possible without attempting to fundamentally change the nature of these women's religious gatherings.[5] As well, they are ambivalent about encouraging popular (grassroots) institutions whose political potential may escape the regime's control. After all, they are well aware of the role these gatherings played in mobilizing women for the anti-Shah movement. Calling on women preachers, whether or not they respond positively, would increase their legitimacy in the eyes of the public, a prospect that the orthodox clergy has resisted. Nonetheless such an oversight by the clergy has not meant a lack of participation on the part of women preachers. Here, I provide a brief overview of the population programme in the context of the women's volunteer health worker initiative, the framework within which many women preachers have engaged in promoting health and family planning. The chapter then proceeds to a discussion of typical female religious gatherings and to the data collected in these gatherings between 1995 and 1997 on female preachers' presentations of family matters and family planning and health issues.[6]

HEALTH AND FAMILY PLANNING IN THE ISLAMIC REPUBLIC OF IRAN

In 1979, to the world's astonishment, Iran experienced one of the largest revolutions in modern history. Mohammed Reza Pahlavi Shah's semi-secular government was replaced by a self-proclaimed Islamic regime led by Ayatollah Ruhollah Khomeini, a conservative religious leader and long-standing opponent of the Shah and his westernization programmes. Since that time, Islam as a political and religious ideology continues to play a significant role not just in the formation of the state but also in the nation's social and political development. The regime's sceptics and critics predicted that the induction of religion into a modern system of government and development planning would have a disastrous impact, particularly for poorer segments of society and women in general. The preoccupation of the regime's leaders with the imposition of Islamic clothing on women, the control of female sexuality, and the promotion of domesticity and motherhood as the most appropriate role for women have contributed to these concerns.

A prominent field in which the regime has managed to refute critics has been the delivery of health services. Despite an American-led embargo which began in 1979, and a devastating war with Iraq between 1980 and 1988, the Islamic regime has achieved considerable success in the delivery of basic health services and education, particularly to rural areas, and in generally improving the country's infrastructure (London Economist 1997; UNICEF 1992). The development of a culturally appropriate and economically efficient rural health network remains one of the greatest success stories of the Islamic Republic. The infant mortality rate (IMR) declined from 104 in the 1970s—when the country's GNP was at its highest—to 52 in 1985, and to 25 in 1996; significantly, the difference between male and female IMR is also diminishing. Life expectancy at birth has increased from 55 years in the 1970s to 68 years in 1994 (UNICEF 1992, p. 47).

In the early days of the Islamic Republic, the government viewed family planning as an imperialist plot to reduce the number of Muslims, and dismantled a fairly successful family planning programme which had been in existence since 1967 (Aghajanian 1991). Pronatalist policies such as lowering the age of marriage, encouraging early marriage, and promoting polygamous and temporary marriages, coupled with the improvement of public health services, culminated in a very high fertility rate. The 1986 national census estimated the population at close to 50 million, and had a sobering effect on religious/political leaders who realized that the delivery of basic services to such a large and young population would be virtually impossible given the depressed economy. The failure to deliver basic services would severely affect the credibility of the 'government of the *mustazafin*' (oppressed and powerless), which had pledged to build a just Islamic society in which all would enjoy basic health care, education, and equal opportunity. Having no other options, the government introduced and carried out one of the most efficient family planning programmes in the economically developing world (Hoodfar 1995, 1996; Ladier-Fouladi 1996). In less than a decade, the population growth rate dropped from 3.4 per cent in 1986 to 1.8 per cent in 1995 and the total fertility rate fell from 5.6 to 3.3 (United Nations Demographic Yearbooks 1966–76; Iran's Centre for Statistical Information 1986–96).

This extraordinary success can be attributed to three overlapping factors: a comprehensive design and definition of the programme; the effective national consensus-building campaign; and efficient delivery services which have won a considerable degree of support from women. The campaign emphasizes that the programme's central goals are to prevent unwanted pregnancies and genetic abnormalities, allow parents to space the births of their children, treat infertility, and improve women's and children's health.

Having once opposed family planning and publicly criticized family planning as a tool of imperialism, religious authorities were conscious that they would have to explain this turn-about, and that the programme might be seen as government interference in private decisions. People had to be convinced that family planning promotes the interests of the nation, and not just those of the government. The government worked to promote understanding of the necessity for population control if Iran was to remain independent and develop both economically and socially. Otherwise, a fate such as those of the poorer nations with large populations such as Bangladesh or Nigeria would await Iranians. Iran's land and resources are limited and can only support a certain number of people, particularly if Iran is to build a strong, healthy, and educated nation. These messages, supported by clear examples and conveyed in accessible language, were repeated on radio and television and in newspapers, and above all in religious gatherings at local mosques and during the Friday prayer sermons where the political/religious leaders present their platforms.[7]

The initial concerns of religious leaders were to demonstrate, using examples from the life of the Prophet and medieval writings, that the government's vision of family planning was Islamic, and to establish that contrary to some people's assumptions, Islam has permitted family planning.[8] The government and religious scholars (*ulema*) presented the family planning programme as empowering men and women, and raising awareness of the ethical as well as social and economic implications of having many children. They warned that these apparently private decisions have collective consequences, and asked people to make a wise choice so that their children and grandchildren will be spared the fate of Draconian population restriction policies such as China's. While experts have convinced Iran's educated and elite classes of the urgency of population control, it is clearly the religious leaders using stylized sermons, vernacular speech, and religious idioms who have had the most success in popularizing the population debate and building national consensus.[9]

These campaigns were accompanied by effective health care and information about different contraceptive means, including the advantages and disadvantages of each method as well as its possible side effects. The new family planning programme as well as general health services are primarily directed at the low-income segments of the population. Since a large proportion of adults (particularly women) in these strata are illiterate and traditionally more receptive to oral and face-to-face forms of learning, service providers had to design non-conventional yet economically feasible means of transferring information and obtaining the trust of their clientele.

Ironically, this problem was more easily addressed for the rural population since the government had already put in place an extensive health network which included a small health centre or 'health house' for each village.[10] These centres were staffed by local people, usually a man and a woman, who were trained in basic health care. Their duties included providing mother and child health care, vaccinations, as well as recording births, deaths and other vital health information on all members of the village. The centre also provided the medical care services of a doctor who visited once or twice a week; in urgent cases, the health workers referred residents to the nearest hospital. Workers were instructed about contraceptive use and provided with information and supplies for the local population. During the 1990s, the government embarked on training rural traditional midwives and engaged them in promoting family planning, particularly in encouraging tubal ligations and vasectomies where couples have already had their desired number of children. Generally, the rate of success in rural areas has been significant, particularly in light of lower levels of education and the traditional desirability of large families.

The success of the health and family planning programme depended on its acceptance by these urban groups, and health outreach in less-privileged and frequently overpopulated urban neighbourhoods presented a greater challenge than in rural areas. The government has organized factory-floor classes on basic health and family planning, which are directed primarily at men, who form the majority of workers. In addition, despite having introduced laws or strengthened existing ones that render women under the control of their male folk (husbands in particular), the government has demonstrated some awareness that women exercise considerable autonomy in decisions of fertility and that the collaboration of women, more so than men, is central to the success of the family planning programme.

Given that the regime has repeatedly claimed it would utilize the nation's cultural/religious heritage to improve the standard of living and develop the country (Abrahamian 1993), one could expect that the authorities would have tried to identify existing social institutions—such as traditional women's religious gatherings—that would be effective means of outreach. However, despite the apparent compatibility of these institutions with the regime's ideology, the authorities chose a different path. They inaugurated a women's health worker programme, composed of volunteers appointed from low-income neighbourhoods to act as intermediaries between the community health centre and local women. Examining the ideological and organizational structure of this successful 'governmental non-governmental organization' is interesting and informative, but also reveals the regime's ambivalence about the public role of women and their autonomous and collective formal or informal social institutions.

VOLUNTEER WOMEN'S COMMUNITY HEALTH WORKERS ORGANIZATION

Although this extremely successful initiative is ambiguously presented as a non-governmental organization (Ministry of Health 1996), it was conceived by the ministry of health and medical education in 1991. It was launched with a pilot project of 200 women from low-income neighbourhoods in south Tehran, and by mid-1996 the programme included over 19,000 volunteers throughout Tehran and all major cities in all provinces (Ministry of Health 1996; Malek-Afzali and Askari-Nasab 1997). The organization's success has attracted funding from major international organizations such as UNICEF and the World Bank, despite initial apprehensive assessments of the project (Bulatao and Richardson 1994; UNFPA n.d.).

Community health centres, which are set up by the ministry of health, appoint women in each neighbourhood who act as intermediaries between local women and the health centre. These volunteer health workers receive basic health care training. Each volunteer covers approximately 50 households in her neighbourhood, serving as the centre's contact person and providing health information for her neighbours. Moreover, volunteers are expected to keep records of all families with young children, new births, and pregnancies, and to invite pregnant women to visit the clinic for ante- and post-natal care and vaccinations. Volunteers also monitor the health needs of their neighbourhoods and communicate them to the centre.

Female volunteers are selected during annual door-to-door fertility surveys. The surveyors are instructed to identify middle-aged women who are mothers, have some education, and appear knowledgeable and sociable. At a later date, the Organization of Volunteer Women Health Workers, housed in the local health centre, contacts them and invites them to join the organization. The volunteers then meet in weekly sessions, during which a guide familiarizes them with the concerns, principles, and organizational structures of the ministry of health. They can assume their volunteer duties after several months of training and are given a card which introduces them to their neighbours. The cards are renewed every six months.

The training includes a review about children's health, mothers and families, public health, and common diseases. Substantial emphasis is placed on family planning and contraception information. Volunteers also learn how to fill out health information cards for the households they cover and deliver them to the health centre. However, the most interesting part of these training sessions is the effort directed at making the training participatory, in contrast to the traditional (and current) system of education which relies on authority figures to provide information that students are expected to accept. The manual for training *morabis* (trainers and teachers of volunteer women) emphasizes that classes should be limited to 15 women, that groups should sit in a circle, and that everybody should participate in the discussion. Volunteers' experience and existing knowledge—traditional knowledge as well—should be acknowledged and praised. Dr. Fatahi, the author of the primary training manual (Fatahi 1375/1996), states repeatedly that the paramount goal of these sessions is to give women confidence while improving their knowledge. In other words, these training courses are also leadership training sessions, though reference to this is carefully avoided.

In fact, the training manual is a skilful adaptation of the latest discussions on teaching for empowerment, based on the experiences of marginal groups from African Americans to Latin Americans and South Asians. There are many examples in the manual of how modern 'scientific' practices can be harmful as well as helpful, as well as discussions of the many traditional practices that are not only accessible and cheap but also more effective, especially since they allow people to retain more control over their lives.[11] Thus trainers are to guide volunteers to be open-minded and respectful of traditional ways and knowledge, while finding tactful ways to warn mothers about harmful practices. Stories and role-playing exercises aim to teach volunteers to share knowledge without embarrassing the mothers. They are advised to establish good relations with neighbourhood mosques, and religious and community leaders. In addition to these training sessions, the fact that volunteer women work in their own neighbourhoods and are often from similar cultural and class backgrounds as their neighbours also facilitates the programme's success.

Besides follow-up and outreach programmes, the data that women volunteers provide are sometimes used for research purposes. As some officials have brought to my attention, the Family Planning Board is in a position to collect much more in-depth and detailed information than ever before. Many ministry of health researchers hope this will improve the quality of their research findings, leading to more effective planning and service delivery.

The volunteers are unpaid, and their only direct material reward is that they are supplied with an information kit which includes four books and a bag stamped with the ministry of health logo, and occasionally items such as a pen. They and their family members do, however, receive free treatment or priority in some health care services and they can use the new women's sports centres free of charge. Recently, a budget from the ministry of health has allowed the organization to provide free programmes and invite successful volunteers to visit important shrines in Mashhad and other locations.

Ministry of health officials frequently refer to the organization as an example of how the Islamic Republic has made room for indigenous initiatives and public participation.[12] While this is correct to some extent, it is evident that while the government welcomes the idea of public participation, they like to be firmly in control of these organizations, particularly in urban settings. For instance, authorities are apprehensive about making it possible for volunteers to meet in large groups, and to this day have not facilitated the production and circulation of a newsletter for them. An interviewee in Tehran told me it was suggested a special centre be built for the volunteers so they could come together in an independent space. Apparently the idea was immediately rejected by the authorities who feared that if 25,000 strong and committed women gathered no one would be able to control them.[13] Although this was presented to me as a somewhat humourous anecdote, it gives important insight into why the government has deliberately ignored women's religious gatherings which have operated independently, though individually, for centuries.

WOMEN'S RELIGIOUS GATHERINGS AS FORA FOR HEALTH DISCUSSION

Although the research plan did not originally encompass women's religious gatherings, these institutions play a key role in the lives of women, particularly the least privileged. These gatherings were not some residual performance of outmoded superstitious rituals, but rather dealt with pertinent family matters as well as issues of national concern. The structure and the format of these religious meetings are of several different types that can be broadly grouped into three categories: *jaleseh, rozeh zaneh,* and *sofreh.*

The jaleseh

Jaleseh is the least controversial of women's religious gatherings since it greatly resembles more orthodox formal religious practices. These meetings are periodical and are often held monthly, although some are weekly. Different women, usually regular members, volunteer to host the *jaleseh* in their homes. The hostess provides tea and soft drinks, and occasionally food is served as well. Adult men and sometimes boys as young as seven or eight are excluded from the meeting (Kamalkhani 1993; Torab 1996), warned by a triangular flag outside the house which signals the location to women and also tells men to be vigilant and not to enter the house. News of these gatherings is spread by word of mouth, although more recently notices might be placed in a local mosque, and they are open to all women whether or not they participate regularly. Usually women's religious gatherings are held in the early afternoon—allowing time for women to complete their domestic chores and serve lunch to their families—and end by late afternoon. Although many younger women participate in *jaleseh*, the core group is generally older women whose children are old enough to be left by themselves for a few hours. The number of participants varies from a dozen to sixty or as many as the available space permits, and is directly related to the popularity of the particular preacher and of the hostess.

The sessions are usually conducted by an older or middle-aged woman called *khanom-e ra'is jaleseh* (director of the *jaleseh*) who leads the Qur'an reading and devotes considerable time to interpreting the selected passages. Many of the verses she chooses relate to women, family relations, and sexuality, and the overarching assumption is that those who attend are educating themselves to become good Muslims. The secret to a preacher's popularity lies in her ability to relate religious issues to women's interests and intertwine her lessons with the complex issues of modern life and 'Islamic' ethics. In that sense, women attend these meetings with the hope of surmounting their own problems, and there is usually time to address specific questions raised by participants.

The questions are frequently issues that women feel uncomfortable discussing with men, even male religious leaders who may be known as helpful in resolving family issues,[14] and the responses given by the director provide normative statements based on interpretations of Islamic principles, regarding such topics as sex or family planning. For instance, in one session a woman said that a female relative had approached her to ask a question on her behalf. Then, somewhat hesitantly, knowing the community's disapproval of premarital sex, she said: 'My relative is 18 and engaged to be married but she is pregnant with the child of her husband-to-be. She wonders whether her child will be considered illegitimate religiously.' The preacher reflected for a moment, and answered:

It depends when the child was conceived. If it was conceived before the intention of marriage was implicitly or explicitly understood by the young couple, then the child is illegitimate. But if they always intended to get married then the child is legitimate. You see, in Islam, the intention is very important. If the man and woman were irresponsible and were just having fun, the consequences of their action are very different than if they cared for each other and in a moment of neglect and passion, they lost their minds. In these situations God is forgiving, if the sinners have really repented.

She stopped and looked at the woman and then at the crowd and then, as though she wanted to save the woman from embarrassment, said:

Although some *ulema* believe that once the couple are married, especially if it is before the birth of child, then the child is legitimate. But if you are still not happy with my explanation, I would be glad to consult with my sources further.

In another *jaleseh*, a woman asked the preacher about her own dilemma:

I have four children and I am pregnant again. I really didn't want to have even the fourth one, although once I found myself pregnant, I went ahead and had the child. But I do not really want to have this one. I do not have the physical or emotional energy to look after yet another child, nor can we financially afford it. Is it a big sin if I abort this stomach [foetus]?

The preacher looked at her with sympathy and asked if she knew about contraceptives. She replied:

Yes, I had an IUD but I had to have it removed. I was bleeding all the time and could not do my prayer or other religious duties [implying that she was unable to go to the mosque or visit shrines, nor could she respond to her husband's sexual needs]. I could not take pills every day because it gave me a backache and an upset stomach which weakened me and I could not take care of the children. They are all less than twelve years old.

The preacher asked how her husband felt about the situation. She responded, 'He did not want another child but he thinks maybe we should have this one too now that it has happened.' The preacher looked at her and replied:

I think you should go ahead and have the child. Abortion is no easy matter. Islam only allows it in very special circumstances. Abortion is not a contraceptive. Deliver your baby in a hospital and ask the doctor to close your tubes [perform a tubal ligation] right then and there, so that you do not go through this agony again.

Light-heartedly and with a smile, she added, 'We do not want another mistake. It is better to think about these matters before they happen.' And then she continued with her talk on the same topic:

Some people keep having children, and say they are gifts of God, which they are. But they forget that these little precious gifts are the most important blessing God gives us. We need to love them, and give them the best care we possibly can. Educate them and let these flowers of God reach their potential, become good Muslims and human beings (*insan-e vaghe'i*) who will help their parents and the community of Muslims (*ummeh*). Today because we Muslims didn't appreciate or do our best for our children, the *ummeh* is in disarray and is treated badly by the unjust *kuffar* (unbelievers). Just see what is happening in Bosnia. If Muslims were educated, strong, and principled, with as many Muslims in the world as we are who would dare to touch the Bosnians even if they are a minority in the heart of Europe? Who would dare to slaughter defenseless Muslim men and children and rape women in front of their fathers and brothers? Who would dishonor them and parade them in front of the television to humiliate Muslim men and Muslim women? Because Muslims don't understand the spirit of their religion but superficially follow just the rules, they have grounded themselves with poverty and ignorance. They have become easy prey and subject to the assault of non-Muslims. Beside tearing our hearts for Bosnia, we have to try to correct our mistakes and make a strong community so as not to witness these things again. . .

While these sessions deal with religious matters, they are closely related to the general discussion and politics taking place in wider society. Abortion and premarital sex are old matters, but contraception, tubal ligation, and family planning are certainly current social and political concerns in Iran. The 'ethnic cleansing' of Muslims in Bosnia is of international concern and the preacher's analysis of the situation indicates a reflective and coherent understanding. She has proposed a resolution to a very personal situation while using the opportunity to inform women of a whole set of issues at the family, national, and international levels at the same time, pointing out the wider implications of their very private decisions.

The government and the experts of the family planning boards have recognized the role of neighbourhood religious leaders, particularly in low-income districts, and invited them to cooperate with the programme and discuss the issues with their constituencies, but women preachers have never been included, despite the authority they have in the poor neighbourhoods. In fact there seems to be no interest on the part of the official religious leaders to recognize the role and existence of women preachers and their religious activities. Such ambivalence on the part of a regime that proclaims an intent to achieve prosperity and ideal society through indigenous social institutions and cultural practices cannot be coincidental, particularly since they have borrowed and customized the concept of a women's volunteer organization from other societies including China, in order to promote the health and family planning message among low-income and less-educated women. This oversight is consistent with some women preachers reporting that in the early years after the revolution they faced pressure from the mosques and other supporters of the regime who wished to curtail their religious activities.[15]

Admittedly, in many cases, the lack of connection between women's religious gatherings and the formal religious structure is the result of mutual disinterest. There is no evidence to suggest that women preachers would respond positively to a formal call to participate in promoting health and family planning. In fact generally these women cherish and try to protect their independence.[16] For instance on occasions when we had opportunities to informally converse with women preachers, I inquired about whether they held these sessions in the local mosques. One preacher said she did teach Qur'an in the mosque, but *jalesehs* are different and it is better to have them at home. Then she suggested it was because women feel freer in a women-only place, and that even though the mosque is a holy place there are still men in the vicinity of the women's quarters. Another preacher suggested that women cannot easily take young children to the mosque; another said that when *jaleseh* is held at home the house is also blessed and that is good for the host and her family. Moreover it was suggested that some women make vows to hold a given number of *jalesehs* at their home and need to fulfil these vows. An older preacher said:

These meetings are blessed because no man is supposed to hear us, but how can we avoid that in a mosque? Even if we are sitting in the women's section they may hear our voices. A mosque is a house of God, can we say no man should enter because the women have a *jaleseh*? Obviously not. No one can say that a Muslim man or woman cannot enter the mosque at anytime.

While this was presented as a justification for holding *jalesehs* in private homes, increasingly women preachers are using microphones which means their voices are heard in adjacent houses.[17] These justifications may indicate that in the present situation women preachers do not want to lose their autonomy and domain of activity to the formal religious structure. Nonetheless, as Torab (1996) has pointed out, women preachers already frequently compromise and accept patriarchal definitions and interpretations of religious matters (particularly on gender issues), in exchange for, if not recognition of their legitimacy, some room to manoeuvre. While government agencies may have recognized the importance of this institution, they have been faced with a dilemma: enlisting women preachers gives them—and their interpretations of religious doctrine in domains such as sexuality and gender-role definition—more legitimacy than formal religious authority is prepared to allow.

The rozeh zaneh

The second group of women's religious activities are *rozeh zaneh* religious meetings that are held in fulfilment of a vow or in memory of a deceased loved one, and are usually dedicated to a *Shi'ite Imam*, one of the Prophet's daughters, or one of his granddaughters. These gatherings function very much like *jaleseh*, with the difference that the preacher is usually informed of the intention (*niyat*, from the Arabic *niya*) of the *rozeh* and she tailors her sermon accordingly. While *jalesehs* tend to attract middle-aged women from the more economically secure families of the neighbourhoods, *rozehs* draw many younger women.[18] By virtue of their age and stage of the life cycle, these women are generally less comfortably settled, and their questions tend to focus on family matters, frequently family disputes, family planning, and unwanted pregnancies.

An excerpt from my field notes below describes an event which was typical of many *rozehs*.

Spring 1994: An acquaintance invited me to a *rozeh*. One large room is crowded with maybe fifty or more women of all ages in black *chadors*, a cape-like outer garment which covers the body and hair and hangs to the ankle. This occasion is a *Rozeh Imam Hassan* which the hostess is holding to fulfil a vow she made for the safe delivery of her first grandchild. Many *rozehs* are held in the Muslim lunar months of *Safar* and *Moharram*, when according to tradition women do not organize *sofrehs*.[19]

Although normally people sit on the floor in these gatherings, many participants have problems with their legs and knees and have to sit on short stools or, after asking permission from others, sit with their legs straight out in front of them. (Culturally such an act is considered improper, particularly in front of older people and especially for a religious gathering.) At the front of the room, a thin cushion is placed against the wall with a short-legged microphone on the floor in front of it, evidently intended for the woman speaker. There is much enthusiasm about her and the hostess was especially pleased to have been able to invite her because she draws the largest crowd, sometimes from distant neighbourhoods both rich and poor. This woman mullah gives Qur'an classes in her house and sometimes in the mosque, particularly during the fasting month of Ramadan. She often presides over *sofrehs* and since she is popular it is not easy to invite her, particularly on short notice. Before the mullah arrived, the hostess was saying how difficult it was to schedule this meeting since the mullah's time was all booked up. Some younger women who struck up a conversation with me said that her popularity stems from her ability to make women, regardless of their education and class, understand their mission as Muslim women toward themselves, their children, and the *ummeh*. One woman said:

As a woman, she knows women's and family problems and is sympathetic to the situation of women and always gives good advice. Not like some of the women mullahs who since the revolution come and give political speeches, and not good and critical ones at that.

They just repeat, 'Follow the government, follow the government, because if you do not you go to hell!' [The other women laughed.] But they forget that for most women with all their problems already their lives are as bad as if they lived in hell.

At this stage another woman who had been quietly listening to the conversation broke in and said, 'They forget that if we wanted one of those, we would simply turn the radio on. Why would we go through all the trouble of coming here or organizing one of these sessions in our homes?'

Finally the woman preacher arrives and women stand up to welcome her. She seems to be in her late forties; she has a serene and dignified appearance and a pleasant smile. She looks about the room and acknowledges some familiar faces, chats for a few seconds, and then starts reciting the Qur'an. This goes on for some time, then there is a prayer. And then she begins her sermon. She looks around and says:

Every time I go to a *rozeh* I see women who can't fold their legs. Others who should be in their youth look as old as a grandmother. I feel a heavy clot of sorrow in my heart and a responsibility on my shoulders to warn you about your health. My sisters and daughters, do you know that God has given you your body to service you in your life? In return, it is your religious duty to look after your body. Remember on the day of judgement in front of God and his Prophet your hand will tell you, I gave you my service. I helped you to do your work, to cook, to carry and hold your babies, and hug your dear ones. Your eyes will say I was with you, guided you daily in your pleasure and sorrow, pleased you by making you see your dear ones, and shed tears to relieve your heart from dark sorrow. I helped you to read when you decided to put effort into education and added to your *savab* (good deeds) by making you see and read the Qur'an, the words of God to brighten your life in this world and the next. Your legs will tell you, I carried you wherever you wanted to go, to the mosque, to school, to visit your loved ones, to help you to stand on your feet. Without my service you would be sedentary, your life would be more like a prison. . .

She continues:

Then they all ask, What did you do for us? How did you return our favors? Did you look after us so as we could better aid you in this world and in the after world? What can you say if you have not done your duty? If you have taken the gift of God for granted and you have disserviced your bodies? My sisters, my daughters, sin is not just gossiping about neighbors, stealing the money of the poor, and not saying your prayers. If you do not look after your health and beauty you commit a sin. If you get yourself pregnant every year when your body has barely recovered from your last pregnancy and birth you are committing a sin. Have fewer children. Space them so your body recovers from the damages and pressure of childbirth and so that you have enough energy to breastfeed your child. So that you have time to look after your body and remain healthy. Health is best gift of God. You do not believe that too many births exhaust your body? Listen to this.[20]

Then she looks around and sets her eyes on a woman who looks tired and not so young. She asks how old the woman is. The woman answers, 'I think 35 or 36.' The mullah asks how many children she has, and the woman says five. Then she sets her eyes on me, and asks me how old I am. A little embarrassed, I say more than 40 or so. Some women say, '*Mashallah*' (which means 'Whatever God wants', and is something people say when they hear good news), which indicates that they believe I look younger than my age. The mullah asks how many children I have, and I answer that it has not been my fate yet.[21] She responds, 'You look very young and healthy. *Inshallah*, God will give you what you wish.' I say, 'I have no complaints. I am happy with what God has written for me' (*be-rezay khoda razim*). Then she puts the same questions to a few more women. Without saying much, it becomes clear to everyone that there is a relationship between their youthful looks, their health, and the number of children and births they have had. Then she asks the audience how old they think she is. People say 40, 45. She replies that she is in her mid-fifties and has four children and several grandchildren.[22]

Then she continues proudly:

...but I still can work hard and can walk to Behesht-e Zahra if the need arises.[23] I do all my housework single-handedly and even help my daughters and daughters-in-law. Because I took good care of my health and everyday I praised God for having given me the good sense to appreciate my health, his gifts. My sisters, my daughters, look around you. Compare those women who look after themselves and are having fewer children with others who have many. You are the only one who is responsible for your body and beauty. Have fewer children. Take care of your health and theirs. Have you not heard that every pregnancy takes about five years from a woman's youth and beauty? You invite old age before your time if you have too many children. This is scientifically proven and all the doctors and the most learned Ayatollahs and men of God have been saying it. ...

Do not come and complain to me that Islam is unfair to women. That your husband has abandoned you with five kids and has married a younger woman. Ask yourself why he left you. Do you remember all those days that he came home? You were in your dirty clothes and uncombed hair running around the house with a bad temper because you were not well. The children were not bathed, they were dressed in dirty clothes, shouting at each other and fighting over a broken toy or something. Remember when you sat, you couldn't get up because your back and knees hurt like an old woman. Remember he saw that instead of appreciation when he came home from a day of hard work at the factory, shops, or office, hoping to rest and see the smile on your face and satisfaction on his children's faces. What a pity, no peace for him in your home. You just talk about your aches, the children's fights, and so on.

Too many births, too little care. That is what has happened when you look fifteen years older than you should. Men in this society are brought up to have expectations of their wives and if you do not deliver, they may go to other women. Not that I am justifying their actions, I just want to caution you that if you do not care for yourself, if you are not just with your body and health, why should you expect your husband to be? After all our husbands are not millionaires. They are ordinary working men who would rather pay for one family and not more. By looking after yourself and being a good mother and wife you can eliminate a lot of problems from your life.

Her talk is followed by some questions and answers, mostly about contraceptive methods. The hostess serves tea, and the *rozeh* ends. The women are satisfied with the event. After many people have left, I talk to the daughter of the hostess, who is to graduate from university shortly with a psychology degree. I tell her that while it was good to remind women to take care of themselves and give them information, I also felt bad that women were blamed for all that went wrong, for instance their bad marriages, their sicknesses, and so on. She agrees, but says, 'Remember that in sessions like this the preacher has to talk in general terms and women need to be shaken so that they will take the initiative to help themselves and stop crying and blaming others.' With a smile, she adds, 'At least this way they are helped in this world, if not in the next. It breaks my heart when I see my mother's friends in their thirties and forties all act as if they are a hundred years old.'

The sofreh

The third and most frequent type of women's religious gathering is the *sofreh*. Although there is some consensus among scholars that its origins are Zoroastrian (Jamzadeh and Mills 1986), this institution has clearly been Islamicized. *Sofrehs* are often given in honour of Islamic saints whose names they bear. Although many are given in honour of women saints, the most common one *is Sofreh* Hazrat Abbas, the young brother of Imam Hossein, who was 14 years old when he was killed while caring for the wounded at the battle of Karbala, where Imam Hossein was martyred. Women identify with him because they believe he was innocent, sensitive, and caring; they invoke his blessing to help to cure a loved one or maybe bring an honourable marriage to a daughter. Although men may sponsor *sofrehs*, they usually do it through a female relative. For instance, they may ask their wives or sisters to make a vow for them; while men pay for the expenses, they never participate in person.

There are different types of *sofreh*. Some are more popular than others among the poor because their requirements are minimal and inexpensive. For instance the *Sofreh Hazrat Roghieh* needs only some herbs, cheese, water, and a candle. Conversely, some rich women may throw an elaborate *sofreh* with fancy decorations and much food and drink. *Sofrehs* are held to fulfil a vow made to a saint during a request for help of some sort. Although they are usually held after the request has been granted, sometimes women vow to hold three *sofrehs*: two *sofrehs* before, and a third serves as insurance, promised to be given only after the request has been granted. Others may vow to give a *sofreh* every year (often for a specific period such as 10 years) in recognition of a saint's help. Another popular *sofreh* is *Bibi Seshanbeh* (Lady Tuesday) which is given on Tuesdays or sometimes the night before Tuesday. Traditionally many women have used this as a reason to have a rotating party on Tuesday afternoons, although there are usually no *sofreh* held during the Muslim lunar month of *Moharram* and *Safar*.

During a *sofreh*, the required food is prepared and placed on a clean white tablecloth (*sofreh*) with candles. No men are present. As during a *jaleseh*, a female preacher is invited and she opens the ceremony by reading a *surah* from the Qur'an, sometimes followed by a special and relevant prayer in which all women participate while facing in the direction of Mecca. After the prayer, all the women are invited to make their *nazer* and *niyat* (declare their intention, though often they do not make it public), if they have any. Then everyone wishes together that God and the saint in whose honour the *sofreh* is held will grant the wishes of Muslims and all good people.

After the prayer, the preacher gives a short sermon. Sometimes, especially among poorer segments of society, the preacher may announce that someone needs their help. For instance, at one *sofreh*, the preacher announced that a widow wished to get her daughter married, but because she had no means to buy even the most meagre trousseau she repeatedly postponed the marriage, and worried that the groom would eventually cancel the marriage. This would reflect badly on her daughter, especially because she had no father or brother to defend her honour. Some of the participants helped in whatever way they were able. One woman said she could give a set of plates. Another woman gave a set of water glasses. Some people gave money. At another *sofreh*, a woman brought prescriptions for medicine for her child. She said she could not afford to buy the expensive medicine and yet otherwise the child might die. Would the participants help her buy the medicine, either for the sake of the mother or for the sake of the child? Many people gave what they could. However this kind of request rarely happens in middle-class *sofrehs*.

The sermon is usually short and then the preacher asks if there are questions or issues that women would like to discuss. At one session, one woman said that she had four children and she did not want to have any more, although her mother-in-law objected to the use of contraceptives and had told her husband not to allow it. The young woman said that she was taking oral contraceptives anyway, and asked if she was committing a sin. The preacher said:

You already have four children. How many would satisfy your husband and mother-in-law? It is of course more desirable that the couple agree on these matters. Try to reason with your husband and mother-in-law. If they do not listen, you should approach maybe an older person they respect or go and see the *akhond* (religious authority) of your local mosque and ask him to intervene and convince your husband. If you want, you can bring your mother-in-law and I will talk to her.

She paused for a moment; then, addressing the entire audience, she continued:

Having too many children on the pretext that they are a gift of God is like going to a *sofreh* or a gathering where food is served for a religious occasion and eating so much that once you are home, you become sick and throw up. Wasting religiously blessed food is a sin by itself. Worse yet, one has also damaged one's body which many of us forget is the first essential gift of God to every person. Thus on judgement day one has to answer for two great sins.

When you have so many children that they end up to be uneducated, poor Muslims or worse—bad Muslims—it is like wasting God's greatest gift. You may be able to have ten gifts, ten flowers, from God's garden of blessings but ask yourself, can you do justice to these little angels you decided to accept from God? Take as many as you can handle the way a gift of God deserves to be treated and do not bring upon yourself more sin, as we are all responsible in front of God for our actions.

In another *sofreh* gathering, one woman hesitantly presented her dilemma:

I have three daughters and my husband and I wanted only three children, but we have no sons. Although he is sad that he has no sons, he thinks maybe I should go ahead and have a tubal ligation, but my mother and friends advise me against it. They say why would he not have a vasectomy, which he would not have because he thinks it will interfere with his health as a man [i.e. his sexuality]. I do not know what I should do.

The preacher thought for a second and said:

Daughters and sons are the same, they are both gifts of God. Remind your mother and friends that it is the Prophet's daughter who is the light of the world. Was not the Prophet always praising his daughter Fatima? If you educate a daughter and bring her up well you probably have more *savab* (good deeds) because she could then be a good mother and bring up good, ethical, and responsible children. But why don't you try an IUD or the pill for a little while, just to ascertain that your husband is serious about not wanting a son. But be careful, make sure you follow the instructions correctly. I know of one woman who got pregnant because she kept forgetting to take her pill every night. If you are forgetful, ask your doctor for an IUD, it may be safer and many women are happy with it.

Another *sofreh* was held by a woman as part of three Hazarat Roghieh *sofrehs* for the health of her 30-year-old daughter, who never recovered from the birth of her fifth child and was frequently sick and haemorrhaging, and had been hospitalized several times.

After the usual Qur'an reading and a long prayer in the midst of the mother's tears over her daughter, who was too sick to participate, the speaker gave a pleading sermon to women to look after their health, repeating that they must let go of the notion that women as mothers should put themselves last. 'If you do not eat properly and look after yourself properly, you will not be able to look after your children', she stressed.

It is your religious duty to look after your health which is the gift of God. It is a sin if you get sick as a result of your own negligence. Who is going to look after your family? As mothers not only you should look after your family, you should look after your own health. Have fewer children, do not drag your body down with frequent births. Take the pill or whatever, nowadays it is not like the old times, there are all sorts of child pills [a popular phrase for oral contraceptives, as is 'family pill'], IUDs, and whatnot. Use them and save yourselves and your families. . . By staying healthy you also service your country. It makes my heart sad to hear women talk and sometimes boast about taking this medicine and that medicine. They spend day after day going from this hospital to the next to get better medicines because they have ulcers, bad backs, bad legs, bad knees. Though they are very young they have exhausted their bodies.

Do you know that these hospitals and most of the medicine you take is financed from the *beit ol-mal* (the collective income of Muslims, meant to be spent on orphans, widows, the poor and collective needs of the community). We are not a rich country, we do not have possibilities for all. When you use the hospital and medicine, someone else has to go without. This is unfair if you could have prevented these problems with a little care about your health. If you want to be happier in this world as well as the next, take this advice to your heart. *Amin* (Amen).

CONCLUSION

A review of the Islamic Republic of Iran's family planning programme demonstrates the flexibility and sophistication of the Islamic regime in understanding and co-opting all that modernity can contribute to the regime's survival. The regime accepts the principle of public participation for the promotion of development and, specifically, family planning. However, the possibility of an organized, autonomous body with its own structure and networks spread among the less-privileged segments of the society, which they view as their principal constituency, is alarming to the religious/political leaders who jealously guard their monopoly over political power and 'ethics'. Given that control of women and gender roles have been central to the regime's Islamization ideology (Paidar 1995; Hoodfar 1998), it is that much more reluctant to encourage any autonomous women's social/political institution.

Hence when deemed necessary for the success of family planning to reach out and encourage public/women participation, the government did design, finance, and create the 'women volunteer health workers' as a non-governmental organization. With control of the organization firmly placed within Ministry of Health, and despite unprecedented levels of success and appreciation of women's positive participation, they have thus far been denied autonomy even to the extent of communicating among themselves. It is unlikely that they will be granted such freedom.

On the other hand, as the data presented above indicate, women initiate diverse strategies for challenging and overcoming their historical exclusion from the power structure and so to create social and political space for themselves. Women's religious gatherings, under the leadership of female mullahs, have, in post-revolutionary years, become a vehicle for women to reinterpret their roles in the family and society as well as participate in major social developments in the wider society.

Within this context, women preachers have become willing agents of the government's population policy in addition to promoting general health messages during their sermons. However, in contrast to the practices of male religious leaders, the women preachers' explanations of the logic of family planning are always presented from women's vantage point and only then are related to community, national, and international perspectives. Moreover, their advice and discussions aim to improve and enrich the fate of women and their families in this world and the next, a bonus which secular institutions are unable to offer their clients.

This advocacy role is, in a way, a mechanism through which they make their own role as preacher relevant and central to the lives of their audience and the wider society while at the same time perpetuating the significance of women's religious gatherings. Regardless of their intentions, women preachers legitimize the government's health and family planning policy which advocates many fewer children than traditional norms dictated. More significantly, they also implement a central concern of the Islamic regime, the reassertion of religion as a central concern with respect to all aspects of life, and not just a separate institution in the lives of individuals and society.

However, the advocacy role of women preachers has gone completely unrecognized and their roles as community religious leaders are overlooked despite the government's recognition of the importance of outreach in low-income neighbourhoods. That is because recognition of the unlisted collaboration of women preachers in this respect would not only mean a higher profile for women's religious gatherings, it would also imply a degree of legitimacy for their 'Islamic' interpretation of Islamic law, ethics and (particularly) gender roles, a domain that the religious leaders have been careful to deny to the women preachers.

Notes

1. The belief that such activities are peripheral stems from theologians' and scholars' customary study of texts rather than practices, privileging the textual voice of authority over those outside the formal structure. In fact, on many occasions formal interpretation and practices have had far less influence on the lives of the majority of people than did informal practices, particularly prior to the age of electronic mass media.
2. For instance, although the opening/expansion of the Qum theological school to women is often presented as proof of the establishment's support of women's participation in religious matters, the school is dominated by male religious authorities. Similarly, mobilizing women for political demonstrations is frequently done through the male-controlled mosque network.
3. The passion play or *ta'zieh* is a reenactment of incidents at Karbala in which the third Shi'ite Imam, the Prophet's grandchild, was killed in an ambush along with 72 of his family members and supporters on the tenth day of the month *Moharram*. This ritual enactment has become a political as well as religious institution (Antoun and Harik 1972; Hegland 1983; Thaiss 1973).
4. Many women's religious gatherings are held to fulfil a vow (*nazer*), usually asking for a saint's help in asking God to improve the health of a sick loved one. Thus concern for health has traditionally been prominent in these gatherings.
5. The major rigidity/limitation within this otherwise very flexible institution is its exclusion of men and the fact that the debates take place from women's perspectives even when not contradicting a patriarchal point of view. For the clergy to recognize these gatherings is to validate much of the discussion that takes place within them which the clergy has no control over. This is contrary to the intense desire of the clergy and the Islamic regime to control gender debates, the importance of which they are keenly aware (Hoodfar 1998).
6. The data presented here are part of a comprehensive study of women and law conducted under the auspices of the Women Living Under Muslim Laws Network. Data from

religious gatherings were collected between 1995 and 1997, based on attendance at 35 *sofreh* and *jaleseh* gatherings given by 23 different women preachers, mostly in Tehran. Only four out of the 35 meetings were strictly religious with little reference to family life or discussion of social issues. In all the other 27 meetings, issues of family and in particular health and reproductive matters were prominent aspects of the discussion or were the subject of questions that were raised for clarifications.

7. For a more detailed account, see Hoodfar (1995).

8. During this period the government sponsored research and the publication of several books on the discussion of family planning during the medieval Islamic period (very similar in content to Musallam 1983).

9. The result has been the broad acceptance of the family planning programme. Several large nationally representative surveys indicate a high rate of approval of family planning. Similarly, in our research out of 340 women who were interviewed on issues of family planning and status of women, less than 5 per cent disagreed or were not sure that family planning is good for women (Hoodfar 1996).

10. For a comprehensive description and discussion of the Iranian rural health network, see Shadpour (1994). This efficient, low-cost system was designed by doctors and health officials (such as Dr. Malek Afzali) who had completed their compulsory military service under the Shah as Health Corps members in rural areas and had first-hand experience of the problems and conditions.

11. For example, the manual compares feeding babies manufactured baby food of dubious quality with the traditional practice of breastfeeding.

12. The initiatives, however, are not as original as they claim since the principal idea is borrowed from non-Iranian public and governmental initiatives. For instance, the programme greatly resembles China's neighbourhood grandmother system as well as non-governmental Islamic health organizations such as *Pesantren* in Indonesia (Sciortino *et al.* 1996). To the government's credit, however, the plan has been well adapted to the cultural setting of urban Iran.

13. Although recent official figures describe the programme as incorporating 19,000 volunteers, officials anticipate that it will shortly reach 25,000 and this figure is used frequently.

14. This however does not mean that men do not consult women preachers. In fact once a woman preacher has made a name for herself, frequently men as well as women may consult with her (see also Torab 1996).

15. Kamalkhani (1993), who carried out her research in Shiraz during the early 1990s, reports similar findings.

16. Torab (1996) has documented some of the cases of reluctance and my data confirm her findings.

17. The popularly held idea that women should not make public speeches nor should their voices be heard by men outside their immediate family (*namahram*) has been compromised by the political ideology of post-revolutionary Iran. The Islamic Republic frequently engages and mobilizes women to participate in street demonstrations and shout slogans. Thus it is now said that if women's or, for that matter, men's voices are not 'seductive', there is no reason for avoidance. In fact this position was expressed by the late Ayatollah Mutahhari, known for his conservatism, in 1966, more than a decade before the Islamic revolution, who justified his interpretation by the fact that women were known to discuss their problems with the Prophet (Mutahhari 1988, p. 62; see also Kamalkhani 1993, p. 50).

18. It is important to note that male preachers may also be invited to this kind of gatherings. In that case the meeting tends to be much more formal and the preacher leaves after delivering his sermon. But generally women tend to prefer women preachers, which also gives them the opportunity to discuss matters of general interest.

19. *Safar* and *Moharram* are the holy months during which Shi'ites commemorate the martyrdom of the Imams Hassan and Hossein, the grandchildren of the Prophet.

20. Her sermon was taped apparently for an invitee who was too sick to come, and my host lent it to me before sending it to her.

21. I was not sure if I could say I had chosen not to have children since I thought this would alienate the other women.

22. Among *sonnati* Iranians, particularly women over 40 years old, age commands greater respect. It seems unlikely that the audience was trying to flatter the preacher by suggesting that she was young.

23. This is a famous cemetery about an hour south of Tehran, which is the burial site of many martyrs of the revolution and the war as well as Ayatollah Khomeini.

References

Abrahamian, E. (1993), *Khomeinism: Essays on the Islamic Republic*, Berkeley: University of California Press.

Afary, J. (1996), *The Iranian Constitutional Revolution 1906–1911: Grassroots Democracy and the Origins of Feminism*, New York: Columbia University Press.

Aghajanian, A. (1991), 'Population change in Iran, 1966–1986: A stalled demographic transition?' *Population and Development Review*, 17: 703–15.

Antoun, R., and Harik, I. (eds.) (1972), *Rural Politics and Social Change in the Middle East*, Bloomington: Indiana University Press.

Malek-Afzali, H., and Askari-Nasab, M. (1997), 'Cost-effectiveness of women health volunteers' project in selected PHC activities (Family Planning)', Memo, Tehran University of Medical Sciences and Health Services, Ministry of Health and Medical Education, Iran.

—— Betteridge, A. H. (1983), 'Muslim women and shrines in Shiraz', in S. J. Palmer (ed.), *Mormons and Muslims: Spiritual Foundations and Modern Manifestations*, Provo, Utah: Brigham Young University Press, pp. 218–36.

Betteridge, A. H. (1980), 'The controversial vows of urban women in Iran', in N. Falk and R. Gross (eds.), *Unspoken Worlds: Women's Religious Lives in Non-Western Cultures*, New York: Harper and Row, pp. 141–55.

Bulatao, R., and G. Richardson (1994), *Fertility and Family Planning in Iran*, New York: World Bank.

Fatahi, M. (1375/1996), *A Workshop Manual for Training Trainers of Community Health Workers*, Tehran: Ministry of Health and UNICEF. [Farsi]

Hegland, M. J. (1983), 'Two images of Hussain: Accommodation and revolution in an Iranian village', in N. Keddie (ed.), *Religion and Politics in Iran: Shi'ism from Quietism to Revolution*, New Haven: Yale University Press, pp. 218–35.

Hoodfar, H. (1995), 'State policy and gender equity in post-revolutionary Iran', in C. Makhlouf Obermeyer (ed.), *Family, Gender, and Population Policy in the Middle East*, Cairo: American University in Cairo Press.

Hoodfar, H. (1996), 'Bargaining with fundamentalism: Women and the politics of population control in Iran', *Reproductive Health Matters*, 8: 30–41.

—— (1998), 'Volunteer health workers in Iran as social activists: Can governmental non-governmental organizations be agents of democratization', Paper presented at American Anthropological Association, Philadelphia, Pennsylvania, December 1–6.

Iran's Centre for Statistical Information 1986–96.

Jamzadeh, L., and Mills, M. (1986), 'Iranian *sofreh*: From collectivity to female ritual', in C. W. Bynum, S. Harrel, and Richman (eds.), *Gender and Religion*, Boston: Beacon Press, pp. 23–65.

Kamalkhani, Z. (1993), 'Women's everyday religious discourse in Iran', in H. Afshar (ed.), *Women in the Middle East: Perceptions, Reality, and Struggles for Liberation*, London: McMillan.

Ladier-Fouladi, M. (1996), 'La Transition de la Fécondité En Iran'. *Population*, 6: 1101–28.

London Economist (1997), 'Children of the Islamic republic revolution: A survey of Iran', January 18.

Ministry of Health (1996), *Participation for Health Promotion and Development: The Case of Community Health Volunteers*, Tehran: Islamic Republic of Iran and UNICEF.

Musallam, B. F. (1983), *Sex and Society in Islam*, Cambridge: Cambridge University Press.

Mutahhari, M. (1998), *Nizam-i huquq-i zen dar Islam*, Tehran: Islamic Publishing House.

Paidar, P. (1995), *Women and the Political Process in Twentieth-Century Iran*, Cambridge: Cambridge University Press.

Sciortino, R. Natsir, L. M. and Mas'udi, M. F. (1996), 'Learning from Islam: Advocacy of reproductive rights in Indonesian *pesantren*', *Reproductive Health Matters*, 8: 86–97.

Shadpour, K. (1994), *The PHC Experience in Iran*, Tehran: UNICEF.

Thaiss, G. (1973), 'Religion and social change: The drama of Husain', Thesis, St. Louis, Missouri: Washington University.

Torab, A. (1996), 'Piety as gendered agency: A study of *jalaseh* ritual discourse in an urban neighbourhood in Iran', *Journal of the Royal Anthropological Institute*, 2: 235–52.

United Nations Children's Fund (UNICEF) (1992). *Situational Analysis of Women and Children in Islamic Republic of Iran*, Tehran: UNICEF.

United Nations Demographic Yearbooks 1966–76.

United Nations Population Fund (UNFPA) (n.d.), *Program Review and Strategy Development Report*, No. 44, Tehran: Islamic Republic of Iran.

8

Abortion in Egypt: Official Constraints and Popular Practices

DALE HUNTINGTON

INTRODUCTION

The analysis of abortion practices is complicated by the interplay of a wide range of issues that will confound a narrowly conceived review. Clearly, contraceptive practices are intimately related to abortion. In addition, societal norms, religious beliefs, and legal restrictions will influence not only women's practices but their willingness to discuss abortion with researchers. Tolerance for a degree of ambiguity is required for those seeking information on societal level indicators of abortion activity. Great sensitivity is an asset for understanding personal behaviours.

These challenges aside, one point is incontestably clear with respect to the study of abortion activity. In settings where access to abortion is restricted, many women will still resort to an unsafe practice to end an unwanted pregnancy and as a result they will have to seek emergency medical care for complications. Unsafe abortion is defined as a procedure for terminating an unwanted pregnancy either by persons lacking the necessary skills or in an environment lacking the minimal medical standards, or both (WHO 1993), and it is something that approximately 20 million women worldwide undergo each year resulting in substantial levels of morbidity and mortality (WHO 1994). Recognition of these health consequences has been a compelling fulcrum for leverage to study abortion and develop rational health care policies for managing harmful sequelae of unsafe abortion. The 1994 International Conference on Population and Development directly addressed these issues through the carefully crafted paragraph 8.25 of the *Programme of Action* that every participating government signed. Although the substance of this statement is widely known, it is worthwhile repeating part of it here.

All Governments and relevant intergovernmental and non-governmental organizations are urged to strengthen their commitment to women's health, to deal with the health impact of unsafe abortion as a major public health concern and to reduce the recourse to abortion through expanded and improved family planning services . . . In all cases, women should have access to quality services for the management of complications arising from abortion. (ICPD, 8.25)

Improvements in the treatment of an incomplete abortion centre upon the introduction of vacuum aspiration under local anaesthesia, counselling about the patient's medical condition, provision of family planning and related reproductive health care services. The development of such high-quality services for what is customarily a neglected dimension of women's health care involves changing ingrained clinical practices and attitudes. Particularly difficult is overcoming barriers to improved counselling processes.

The findings that are presented in this chapter draw upon a body of health services research conducted as part of a larger programme to improve post-abortion care in Egypt. They reveal how both physicians and women manipulate official constraints on abortion to avoid unwanted pregnancy. The few anthropological studies of abortion that have been undertaken in Egypt will be reviewed to familiarize the reader with pregnancy termination practices. The overall prevalence of abortion is characterized through a hospital-based study, with the range of medical complications being shown to substantiate the anthropological findings on abortion practices. The subjective experiences of women who have experienced an abortion are reviewed in the final section of this chapter. Their skills in negotiating the dilemmas and uncertainties will be shown to be suggestive of emergent moralities surrounding abortion in Egypt.

LEGAL AND RELIGIOUS DIMENSIONS OF ABORTION IN EGYPT

Egypt's abortion policy is usually classified as 'rather restrictive' on a worldwide scale. The Egyptian Penal Law of 1937 (still active today) contains articles that explicitly prohibit acts that cause an abortion and provides stiff penalties if the aborter is from the medical profession (Azer 1979). The same penal law also contains articles that permit women to obtain necessary medical services in life-threatening conditions. These latter articles are interpreted to legally permit abortion in the presence of serious maternal health risks.

The legal dimension of abortion is strongly moderated by religious considerations in the Arab world. There are different approaches to Islamic jurisprudence and differing positions on abortion, ranging from complete prohibition (the Hanbali school, Sunni) to complete permissibility (the Zaidi school, Shi'i) (Omran 1992). Islamic theologians in Egypt generally view the termination of a pregnancy to save a woman's life as acceptable, even beyond the 120 days that is frequently cited in the literature (IPPF 1992). Additionally, there appears to be some latitude concerning the definition of a serious maternal health risk, with consideration given by some prominent Islamic theologians in Egypt to issues such as the wantedness status of the pregnancy (if the couple was using contraception at the time of conception), the economic ability of the couple to support another child or if the pregnancy was caused by rape or incest.[1] For all schools of Islamic jurisprudence as well as the individual interpretations given by authorities, a critically important issue concerns the interpretation of when the 'ensoulment' of the foetus occurs. Prior to 'ensoulment' an abortion may be permitted, even if it is considered loathsome.

ABORTION PRACTICES IN EGYPT

Few anthropological studies of abortion in Egypt have been conducted that provide evidence on abortion practices (notably Hoodfar 1986; Ragab 1995, 1997). Evidence from these community-based anthropological studies suggests that while abortion is not an unheard of fertility regulation practice, it is neither widespread nor a frequent option for most women who have unwanted pregnancies. Ragab's work suggests that women who are on the 'borders of motherhood' (i.e. the unmarried or the grandmothers) are the most likely group to terminate an unwanted pregnancy. Societal norms in Egypt view a childbirth by a grandmother as inappropriate, while premarital childbirth is a most serious issue for both the woman and her family. In addition, women who have a young child to care for or a large family living with extreme poverty are likely to induce an abortion.

Surgical abortion is available in Egyptian private practice settings by physicians who are commonly known through informal communication networks, although the procedure will be quite expensive. Most commonly a physician will not have adequate medication in his private clinic for an abortion and will perform a procedure to initiate bleeding. The woman can then seek care at a hospital where he can complete the abortion under general anaesthesia, labelling the admission as incomplete miscarriage. This is not an uncommon practice in many settings where abortion is legally restricted, serving to obfuscate the physician's actions and the woman's intentions from official scrutiny.

Although inducing an abortion is a highly confidential and socially sensitive procedure, it is not an extremely risky act for Egyptian physicians due to the high degree of prestige and autonomy that they enjoy. As members of a medical profession that operates without peer review or institutional board oversight, an individual physician is quite capable of decreeing that a significant health risk exists to justify terminating the pregnancy. Additional support may be enlisted by obtaining religious ruling (*fatwa*) that proclaims 'ensoulment' of the foetus has not yet occurred. Access to a medical abortion will be expensive in any case and contacting a local religious authority will necessarily involve a woman's husband and a sufficient degree of personal autonomy. These characteristics are highly dependent upon a woman's social and economic class. As in other societies in the world where abortion is legally restricted, women with influence and wealth will be able to obtain a safe medical procedure while poorer women will have to use other means for terminating an unwanted pregnancy.

There does not appear to be substantial evidence of lay practitioners providing abortion services in Egypt. Rather a woman who does not seek assistance from a physician will most likely self-induce the abortion, perhaps with assistance from a pharmacist. Many of the traditional means for self-inducing an abortion reported on in other countries are also found in Egypt. For example, carrying heavy loads, physical massage, and introducing foreign objects into the uterus are reported on (Hoodfar 1986; Ragab 1995, 1997). Although several varieties of reeds or soft sticks are popularly known to be used for inducing an abortion, it appears that a shift has occurred away from mechanically inducing an abortion in favour of ingesting medications (that are easily and cheaply obtained without prescription) that will provoke a miscarriage (e.g. an overdose of hormonal contraceptives). As the availability of family planning services has increased in Egypt so too have anecdotal reports of women requesting an IUD to provoke a miscarriage. This practice is certainly possible as it is known that family planning providers do not commonly perform a pregnancy test prior to inserting an IUD.

A critically important distinction is made between deliberately inducing an abortion of a recognized pregnancy (i.e. an induced abortion) as opposed to inducing an abortion of an unrecognized pregnancy (i.e. an act akin to menstrual regulation). A combination of traditional or biomedical practices may be employed to induce bleeding, which can then be socially constructed as an early miscarriage of an unknown pregnancy that was not intentionally induced (since the pregnancy was not consciously recognized at the time a menstrual regulation or contraceptive practice was performed). The woman will be able to present at a nearby hospital or private clinic and obtain medical assistance in completing the abortion/miscarriage. Her husband and family's support will be provided (to the extent that it is available) and although there is considerable stress associated with lost pregnancies, it will be qualitatively different from the consequences of openly inducing an abortion. Societal normative restrictions on abortion are successively manipulated by the woman, although at great risk to her psychological health.

He gave me injections and told me that if what I have is a missing period it will come down, and if it is a pregnancy the fetus will be stabilized in my womb. (Huntington *et al.* 1995*a*)

To date, however, there has not been a sufficient body of ethnographic investigations into abortion practices to enable any firm conclusions regarding the range of practices related to pregnancy termination in Egypt or the extent to which official constraints are circumvented. What is known is largely deduced from the few studies described above, or induced from the presenting complications of women who seek emergency medical treatment for incomplete abortion. As will be shown in the next section, these presenting symptoms corroborate this largely anecdotal evidence of abortion practices and suggests a skilful—if not rationally explicit— manipulation of legal and religious constraints on abortion to avoid carrying to term an unwanted pregnancy.

PREVALENCE OF ABORTION IN EGYPT

The incidence of abortion in Egypt has not been adequately investigated through sample surveys.[2] The 1995 Egyptian DHS yielded a response of 2.51 per cent to a direct question about ever inducing an abortion, with an additional 25.13 per cent of ever-married women indicating a previous miscarriage (El-Zanaty *et al.* 1995). These results clearly represent an under-reporting of induced abortion in population-based surveys. The alternative of a hospital-based study was only recently conducted in a manner that overcame several constraints on collecting data from health facilities. Among the problems with hospital-based studies is that cases that receive treatment for abortion (a spontaneous miscarriage or induced abortion alike) are frequently masked under the category of 'In-Patient, OB/GYN Admission', which lumps together several other diagnostic categories.

A nationally representative study of Egyptian public sector hospitals conducted in 1996 (Huntington *et al.* 1998) used a specially developed abstract form to collect information on all post-abortion admissions during a continuous 30-day period. Results from this study (presented in Fig. 8.1, previously published in Huntington *et al.* 1998) reveal that among the 22,656 OB/GYN admissions in the study's 86 hospitals, approximately one out of every five OB/GYN patients (19 per cent) or about one out of every three obstetric admissions was admitted for treatment of an abortion. An abortion ratio of 7.95 abortions per 100 reported pregnancies for this hospitalized population is observed (these results group together spontaneous and induced abortion cases).

In order to tease apart cases which are induced from spontaneous miscarriage cases, the WHO-recommended protocol for classifying morbidity related to abortion using hospital-based survey results was applied to this study (WHO 1987).[3] The results presented in Fig. 8.1 show that only 5 per cent of the patients can be classified as 'certainly induced' and approximately one-third (35 per cent) are cases of spontaneous abortion. In between these two poles of certainty lie the

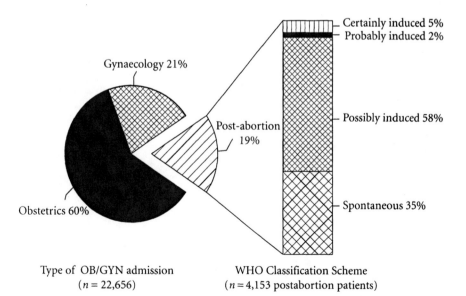

Figure 8.1. *Results of a study of Egyptian public sector hospitals conducted in 1996.*

majority of cases which are either possibly induced (58 per cent) or probably induced (2 per cent). There is a significant difference ($p < 0.0000$) in patients' mean age across the four categories of the WHO Classification Scheme. The average age of patients who are classified as 'certainly induced' is 30.41 years, 'probably induced' is 29.25 years, 'possibly induced' is 28.16 years, and 'spontaneous' is 25.68 years. Patients who certainly induced the abortion are hence more likely to be older than other categories (on the 'border of motherhood') while miscarriage patients are more likely to be younger and nulliparous.

In order to generalize this to the entire population, a standard methodology was applied to these results (Singh and Henshaw 1996). A somewhat conservative multiplier was used to represent the minimum number of abortions that do not lead to medical treatment in hospitals.[4] After removing spontaneous miscarriage patients (estimated at 35 per cent, based on the findings of Fig. 8.1 above) the total was compared to the number of births in 1994 (most recent national level information available) plus the number of abortions and miscarriages. This procedure yielded a ratio of 14.75 abortions per 100 pregnancies in Egypt, which is comparable to ratios from North Africa, Tunisia and previous research in Egypt (Table 8.1).

Post-abortion patient characteristics

Overall, the mean age of the patients is 27.43 years, the large majority ranging from 20 to 50 years ($n = 4,151$), which is younger than the general population of women of reproductive age, as characterized by the 1995 Egyptian DHS (that found slightly more than one-third are under the age of 30 compared to almost two-thirds of the post-abortion patients less than 30 years of age). This suggests that abortion activity

Table 8.1. *Number of abortions and abortion ratio by country and region**

Country	Number of abortions	Abortion ratio per 100 known pregnancies**
Egypt 1996 Case Load Study	323,950	14.75
Egypt 1987 MCH Study[1]	Unavailable	10.8
Turkey[2]	531,400	26.0
Tunisia[2]	23,300	9.8
North Africa[2]	550,000	11.4
Southern Africa[3]	240,000	16.3
Middle Africa[3]	190,000	5.1
Africa Overall[3]	3,820,000	12.9

**Source for Table 8.1*: Huntington *et al.* (1998).
**Known pregnancies are defined as all types of abortions plus live births.
[1]*Source*: CAPMAS and UNICEF (1987) includes both spontaneous and induced abortions.
[2]*Source*: Henshaw and Morrow (1990).
[3]*Source*: Singh and Henshaw (1996) (taken from a table based on multiple data sources).

in general may cluster at early borders of motherhood. The educational level of the patients is also lower than it is for women of reproductive age in general. Approximately 61 per cent of the patients do not have any formal education as compared to 43 per cent in the 1995 DHS, 24 per cent have obtained primary education, 13 per cent have obtained secondary, and 2 per cent have gone to a university ($n=4,153$) (see Table 8.2).

The patients' mean parity is lower than the general population with a relatively large proportion of the post-abortion patients being nulliparous. This suggests that a substantial number of miscarriages occur among this group as the strong familial pressure to have the first child among married women of all social classes will preclude a significant number of nulliparous married women inducing an abortion. Accordingly, approximately 37 per cent ($n=4,151$) of the patients reported a previous miscarriage. Though not shown in Table 8.2, the mean number of previous miscarriages among those patients is >1 (1.59) indicating repeat miscarriages among this group of women. There are more women who have 1–2

Table 8.2. *Post-abortion patients' characteristics**

Characteristic	1995 Egyptian DHS** ($n=14,779$)	1996 Case Load Study ($n=4,153$)
Age		
<15	—	<00.0
15–19	4.6	08.5
20–24	14.5	26.3
25–29	18.6	26.9
30–34	17.6	18.8
35–39	17.4	13.7
40–44	13.9	04.7
45+	13.4	01.1
		Mean 27.4, S.D. 6.5
Education		
No education	43.7	61.3
Primary	19.7	23.9
Secondary	13.0	12.8
University	Unavailable	2.0
Parity		
Nulliparae	9.4	16.1
1–2	28.5	37.9
3–5	39.3	36.1
6+	22.8	9.9
	Mean 3.7	Mean 2.7, S.D. 2.2

*Source for Table 8.2: Huntington *et al.* (1998).
**Note that parity estimates from the 1995 EDHS are based on currently married women while age and education estimates are based on ever-married women.

children among the post-abortion patients than the general population. This could mean that the 'borders of motherhood' concept is not only defined by age, but also by having children too closely spaced.

Family planning history among post-abortion patients

The linkages between abortion and contraceptives are complex and inextricable. Previous contraceptive use among post-abortion patients in Egypt is lower (47 per cent) than among the general population of currently married women (68 per cent, El-Zanaty *et al.* 1995). The post-abortion patients clearly either did not consider themselves at risk of becoming pregnant or are more averse than the general population to using a contraceptive method. The findings in Fig. 8.2 corroborate anthropological research that suggests some women willfully request an IUD as a means of inducing a miscarriage: slightly less than one-fifth (17 per cent) of the patients reported having used a contraceptive method at the time they became pregnant with the foetus that was just aborted.

Although there is a moderately strong intention to begin using a contraceptive method soon after discharge (approximately 42 per cent of the patients reported such an intention), it is slightly lower than the results from the 1995 Egyptian DHS that indicates 58 per cent of currently married non-users have the intention to use a family planning method some time in the future (El-Zanaty *et al.* 1995). Subjective reports from the patients themselves (presented in a later section) will clarify this lower than expected intention to use contraceptives as partially due to confusion about the post-abortion amenorrhoea period, as well as other popular belief systems regarding physical health.

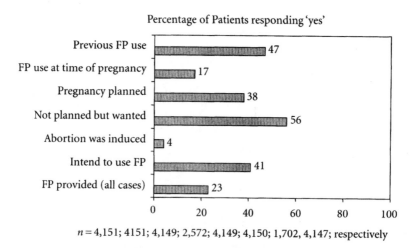

$n = 4,151; 4151; 4,149; 2,572; 4,149; 4,150; 1,702, 4,147;$ respectively

Figure 8.2. *Family planning use among post-abortion patients.*

SEVERITY OF COMPLICATIONS FROM UNSAFE
ABORTION IN EGYPT

The results from the case load study provide the first evidence of the range and severity of complications from unsafe abortion in Egypt. These findings will be shown to largely substantiate the anecdotal information concerning practices for self-inducing an abortion or menstrual regulation practices.

The mean gestational age of the pregnancies lost by patients is 10.79 weeks, ranging from 2 to 28 weeks, although the assessment of gestational age among patients with an incomplete abortion is acknowledged to be problematic.[5] A 95 per cent confidence interval reveals little variation around this mean as it ranges from 10.7 to 10.9 weeks with a large majority (86 per cent) having a gestational age of 12 weeks or less. Patients are therefore likely to have recognized the potential for the pregnancy very early in the first trimester and either performed a menstrual regulation procedure or induced an abortion (apart from miscarriage cases, obviously).

More significant in developing our understanding of abortion practices is the nature of the presenting complications. Only about 14 per cent of the patients presented with excessive blood loss while the remaining 86 per cent exhibited mild to moderate bleeding. Less than 1 per cent (0.7 per cent) of the patients were diagnosed with one or more signs of trauma due to mechanical injury and very few (4.96 per cent) patients presented with one or more signs of infection (fever, foul discharge, salpingitis, peritonitis). The infrequent cases of trauma or sepsis combined with the high proportion of patients exhibiting mild to moderate bleeding corroborate the evidence from anthropologic research that abortion practices seem to centre upon the ingesting of medications, heavy labour, or other relatively benign medical procedures to induce bleeding.

It is noted that the pattern of serious complications found in Egypt is comparable to that observed in Latin American countries with similar legal restrictions on safe abortion, although there are different levels of specific complications being reported in each region. In Latin America there were fewer cases with excessive blood loss (6.9 per cent), a comparable proportion admitting with signs of trauma (1.2 per cent) and more cases of sepsis or infection (15.7 per cent) (Singh and Wulf 1993, p. 137).

Surgical procedures and pain control medication

As will be shown in the next section a most salient issue for women who have sought treatment for an incomplete abortion is the amount of pain that they experienced and the interpersonal treatment they received by the medical staff. Findings from the case load study are investigated in an attempt to clarify the source(s) of this pain. The predominate surgical practice for treating incomplete abortions in Egypt is a dilatation and curettage (D&C) (95 per cent of the cases) under general anaesthesia (89 per cent of the cases) (Huntington *et al.* 1998), which is known to carry a two- to four-fold increased risk of mortality (Petersen *et al.* 1981) and to be associated with higher costs (Brooke *et al.* 1993) than vacuum aspiration using local anaesthesia. It is also revealing of a clinical practice that fundamentally ignores the woman by heavily sedating her. The type and timing of pain control medication are critical aspects of effective case management (Margolix *et al.* 1993). Preoperative and postoperative sedation or analgesics are customary elements in clinical protocols (Winkler *et al.* 1995) and were shown to have a positive effect on the reduction of Egyptian patient reports of pain (Huntington *et al.* 1995b). Yet less than one half of the patients (44 per cent) received these medications, either alone (33 per cent of the cases) or in combination (11 per cent) (Huntington *et al.* 1998).

The results from the case load study provide strong evidence that the treatment of incomplete abortion is a common practice in Egyptian public sector hospitals, with the case load being neither alarmingly high nor insubstantially low. The socio-demographic and medical characteristics of the patients in part substantiate the findings from anthropological research that suggests women will seek to terminate unwanted pregnancy most commonly by self-inducing a miscarriage through non-invasive procedures or relatively benign medical practices. Although the evidence is inconclusive, menstrual regulation procedures may be widespread. More certain is the antiquated nature of the surgical procedures commonly used in the treatment of the incomplete abortion and the relatively unsophisticated use of pain control medication.

SUBJECTIVE EXPERIENCE OF ABORTION

The subjective experience of women who have received treatment for an incomplete abortion is immediately suggestive of several indicators of service quality. What is more important for the subject of this chapter, however, are the insights into the social constructs women create to rationalize difficult choices made about unwanted pregnancy in a patriarchal, Islamic society. Findings from a rapidly conducted qualitative study (Huntington *et al.* 1997) that utilized the two qualitative methods in-depth with post-abortion patients and focus group discussions with nominally healthy women are drawn upon to explore this dimension of abortion in Egypt.[6]

Physical condition and recuperation

Not surprisingly, her immediate physical condition is a paramount concern for a post-abortion patient. Whether the women had spontaneously or deliberately induced the abortion, the resulting physical condition was consistently described by the patients as their bodies being in excessive disorder. This physiological state was acutely felt by these women, with the primary symptoms being extreme pain generalized throughout their bodies.

I was dying yesterday and I was dying before the operation. . . . It is very painful to go through the operation. Afterwards the pain only gets worse. I am still in pain till now.

I feel like my body is broken into pieces. I cannot sleep, I cannot sit down, and I feel severe pain with every move I make. I know it will be some time until this pain goes away. This has been the most painful experience I have ever had.

It is not altogether clear why so much pain was experienced during their medical care, particularly since general anaesthesia is most commonly used. Their pain may have been due to an absence of preoperative or postoperative sedation or analgesics, or to the presence of an underlying medical condition that was aggravated by the abortion. Other reproductive health research in Egypt has indicated the presence of untreated infections in rural women that complicated the expression of other, unrelated morbidities (Younis *et al.* 1993), which may also be a source of affliction for post-abortion patients. In any case, women reported that the back, especially the lower back, was a main source of agony. The chest/heart, stomach, and breasts were also reported as being sore or tender.

The patients' physical agony was aggravated by the shock of massive blood loss. These patients recognized that they can anticipate a protracted period of weakness due to the haemorrhaging. Physical weakness is quite a serious concern for disadvantaged Egyptian women, as they recognize their normal physical condition is already compromised due to a poor diet and heavy work load (especially in cases of rural women). A considerable burden of disease among rural Egyptian women has been investigated with alarmingly high prevalence of several morbidities shown to exist (Younis *et al.* 1993). Women's anxieties about their ability to physically recover are hence not altogether unfounded but may in fact reflect a sound understanding of their compromised health.

Our bodies are already tired and going through an abortion affects the health tremendously. The blood that a woman loses makes her weaker than she was before. It also causes anemia. As a result a woman has to rest for a long time to regain her strength . . .

Having survived the ordeal of an incomplete abortion, these patients were confronting a return to their normal lives. Because of beliefs that their bodies were profoundly disturbed by the abortion, these women strongly expressed a need to regain a natural order or balance.

During this period we say that the woman is hot as she has had an abortion. Only after forty days have passed can the woman start using contraceptives or else she will get pregnant.

A cooling-down period of 40 days was called for, similar to the post-partum period, during which they could rest and recuperate and get increased dietary supplements of protein-rich foods that are considered necessary to restore the body's order and equilibrium. The use of a contraceptive method immediately post-abortion was not viewed as advisable for several reasons. The need to regain bodily order precluded any type of tampering with bodily systems, including using an IUD. Information regarding the timing of sexual relations following an incomplete abortion is not available, nor was this issue probed in this study. The analogy of the 40-day post-partum period is relevant to the post-abortion patients, as they anticipated a period of sexual abstinence due to customs surrounding bleeding. They extended this analogy to include when the return to fertility following an abortion could be expected. Many said they thought that menstruation will probably not occur for some time after the abortion (e.g. several months).

Because a woman who has aborted does not have a newborn infant to care for, none of the patients thought it was likely that they could avail upon their families to provide the necessary support for a 40-day period (as they could, perhaps, for ensuring post-partum recuperation). In addition, the poverty of the rural women makes it highly unlikely that their families possess resources to compensate for the woman's absence from farm labour. Their immediate return to physically demanding work and child care responsibilities was most troubling to all of the patients, urban and rural alike. The uncertainty about being able to fully recover from the abortion is exacerbated by prevailing cultural values in Egypt that enhance a 'culture of silence and endurance' which women endure instead of seeking health care (Khattab 1992).

To get back to her normal condition, a woman needs a proper diet and a place to relax and rest. But how can I get that? Where I come from (a rural area) women have to work hard, and we also have to provide all what we can for our children.

In addition to the assistance with physical work, emotional support is an important dimension for achieving positive mental health. The discussions relating to emotional support following an abortion were obscured by the probability that many of the women had induced a deliberately unrecognized pregnancy and have therefore constructed their reactions to a miscarriage, with feelings of loss and grief being necessarily expressed. Occasional statements penetrate through these conflicting motives and confused emotions, and suggest that a great many post-abortion patients are chiefly concerned about their ability to physically recover and are relatively unconcerned about their own ability to resolve the contradictory emotions they feel.

Physical problems are the most important. I will still have to face some other problems, things like what people will say about me when they know that I have had an abortion. But I know that the most important thing I should concern myself about is resting for at least two months so that I can get back my original health. The only problem in doing that is there is no one to help me during that time.

Just as their expectations about being able to receive any assistance from their families with the work were quite low, many women expressed misgivings about relatives leaving them untroubled during their convalescence. There was clearly a perceived risk that either the husband or his family would dwell on issues concerning the 'ensoulment' of the foetus and place blame on the woman for having lost a living child. The patients were also worried that their in-laws would openly question their ability to conceive and carry a future pregnancy to full term. Most of the women interviewed expressed how dealing with their husbands and his family is a lasting concern following the abortion. To the extent that they are able to insulate themselves from such anxieties, the patients felt more secure about their recuperation.

[A] woman may not be extremely upset following an abortion. It is her in-laws who will be waiting for her and they will always annoy her about losing a child. The first time I had an abortion they told me that it would have been much better if the buffalo had died [than to] have the abortion. Now they will annoy me all the more, and I have to be ready for this.

Uncertainties and moral dilemmas

Marriage and children are inextricably linked in the patriarchal Egyptian society, and most young couples will not practise any contraception until the first child is born. Motherhood throughout the Arab world is highly esteemed and idealized, and Egyptian women of all social classes are driven to realize the fulfilment of this role by early childbearing and devoting considerable 'maternal investments' to their family (Georges 1996).[7] Such investments will involve making sacrifices of all kinds, as women balance the demands of child care and providing for an adequate domestic environment with limited economic resources. The stresses associated with balancing a religious morality and a morality grounded in the role of motherhood can become a crisis when an unwanted pregnancy is recognized.[8] The familial morality has prevailed for many post-abortion patients: the reason for an abortion will often be couched within the construct of sacrificing herself for the good of her family.

People will always annoy a woman who has undergone an induced abortion. They will tell her that she has done something that is like killing a soul. They will tell her that it is sinful. I know that what they say is right. But I had to sacrifice myself for the sake of my children and my husband. What else could I have done?

The contradiction expressed by this woman clearly positions her between religious beliefs and her maternal responsibilities. Negotiating within this space is fraught with dilemmas for Egyptian women, as they seek to balance moralities bound by Islam and socially negotiated moralities linked to their families. Interestingly, the increase in religious fundamentalism that has occurred in Egypt during the past several years has been influencing resolution of this conflict. Resorting to a fatalistic acceptance of the ultimate meaninglessness of their individual actions is extended to a belief that it remains in God's power to make a woman bear more children regardless of her actions, a finding which has been reported on in the anthropological context of research on infertility in Egypt with remarkable similarity (Inhorn 1994). An emerging morality on abortion is thus framed. Practices to induce an abortion do not necessarily contradict God's wishes as He is omnipotent and nothing an individual can do will counteract God's ultimate Will. They see themselves as being instruments of God's desires. In case they misinterpret His wishes their actions will be overruled by His will and be of no consequence. Cases of unsuccessful attempts to induce an abortion are cited as examples of divine intervention.

It does not work. A woman can drink onion juice or garlic juice, or she can get anything from the herbs-man. I know a woman who tried everything and they never worked. God did not wish it for her.

My mother was pregnant and wanted to have an abortion. She took seven injections and the pregnancy was not terminated. Still, the baby was alive at birth. It is all in God's hands and what He decides on will happen.

For those women who truly had a miscarriage, resorting to their faith did not lessen their anxieties about having another miscarriage. The belief that the miscarriage may have been predetermined by God was profoundly disturbing for these post-abortion patients, particularly since many of them had not yet achieved their desired family size and worried about their ability to conceive and bear children in the future.

CONCLUSIONS

This chapter began with a plea for tolerating a substantial degree of ambiguity concerning the definition of abortion practices in Egypt. Although a great deal is known, there are still substantial holes in our knowledge that is left to future research. Most apparent is the absence of a body of anthropological research on abortion practices in Egyptian communities. The few studies that have been conducted suggest that abortion is not common yet is not unheard of either. The national case load of post-abortion patients reveals a steady stream of women present in the country's hospitals for emergency treatment of incomplete abortion. This is more than would be expected for a miscarriage alone but not enough to suggest widespread practices of unsafe abortion practices. Women who are on the 'borders of motherhood', the young grandmother or child bride, or who already have one or two young children are most likely to resort to terminating a pregnancy. In addition are those women whose family obligations are too great (or whose available resources are too few) to support another child.

While surgical abortion is certainly available in Egypt, obtaining such services is highly dependent upon a woman's skills in negotiating with religious authorities and having access to relatively large sums of money. An important consideration is the distinction between inducing a recognized pregnancy and inducing menstruation when a pregnancy is possible but unconfirmed. The latter practice is most common in Egypt through a variety of self-induced actions that primarily involve ingesting medications (including hormonal contraceptive methods), having an IUD inserted or benign medical procedures to induce bleeding. The range of complications that were found through a study of post-abortion patients confirms these findings, as very few patients presented with signs of trauma or sepsis. Evidence exists to suggest that providers as well as women are skilful in manipulating official constraints on abortion, both to protect themselves and to provide a lucrative, if illicit, practice.

Physical recuperation is the paramount concern of women who were treated for an incomplete abortion, as many felt they had just emerged from a life-threatening condition (contrary to the actual complications they presented with, their lay perception of blood loss and the severity of the pain was frightening). Although these women somewhat wistfully spoke about appreciating any assistance with their daily work during the convalescence period, most commonly they acknowledged that such support was not likely. The most they could hope for was simply not to be bothered by their husbands' families about losing a pregnancy. Thus, their own emotional distress did not figure prominently during the immediate post-abortion period.

Women's skills in negotiating an emotional and intellectual space for coming to terms with abortion suggests three somewhat overlapping moralities about abortion in Egypt today. The first has to do with the role of motherhood and the sometimes extreme requirements of maternal investments (in terms of time, attention, domestic labour, etc.). Intimately bound to these investments are the sacrifices that Egyptian women make for their children and families. Providing adequate maternal investments apparently can extend to jeopardizing her individual spiritual well-being for the sake of her family. A second, somewhat emerging morality of abortion concerns the effects of the rising influence of fundamentalist beliefs in contemporary Egyptian society. By adopting a fatalistic position facile resolutions of potentially difficult conflicts are possible, as trust is put in divine will to overcome any actions a woman may take to induce an abortion. And the third, more self-determinant morality concerns aligning one's religious beliefs with a compatible school of Islamic jurisprudence so that an abortion can be done prior to 'ensoulment' of the foetus—no sacrifice is made nor recourse to divine will is taken.

These three moralities provide Egyptian women with considerable latitude to manoeuvre between opposing societal and religious forces influencing their fertility. Skilful use of easily available medications or manipulating the use of a contraceptive as an abortifacient has been shown to be used by disadvantaged women, while the more wealthy elements of society are able to obtain safe medical abortions in private facilities. More research needs to be conducted that examines the relationship between abortion and contraception in order to improve our understanding of why Egypt's largely successful family planning programme has so obviously failed to reach the population of women who most commonly present at the country's hospitals for treatment of incomplete abortion.

Notes

This chapter draws heavily upon research conducted by the author in collaboration with colleagues in the Population Council's Cairo office. Dr. Laila Nawar in particular had a pivotal role with several of the studies cited in this chapter. Dr. Nahla Abdel-Tawab and Sahar Hegazi contributed to the Case Load Study, both in its field work and reporting. The Case Load study cited in this chapter was a collaborative study conducted by the Population Council with operations managed by the Egyptian Fertility Care Society. Dr. Ezzeldin Osman Hassan and Dr. Hala Youssef's important role with this study is acknowledged. Selected findings are presented from the article 'The Postabortion Caseload in Egyptian Hospitals: A Descriptive Study' published in *International Family Planning Perspectives* Vol. 24, No. 1, March 1998. Findings from the chapter 'Women's Perceptions of Abortion in Egypt', published in *Reproductive Health Matters* Vol. 9 (May) 1997 by the author, Dr. Laila Nawar and Dalia Abdel-Hady, are drawn upon as well. Both the Case Load and Women's

Perceptions studies were funded by USAID. The contribution of these individuals and agencies to the work that is synthesized in this chapter is gratefully acknowledged and greatly appreciated. The conclusions and manner in which results from these studies are presented is the responsibility of the author only, and should not be attributed to any other researchers.

1. It is noteworthy that this issue was discussed in the Egyptian popular press prior to the ICPD in an interview given by the Grand Mufti of Egypt, Sheikh Mohammed Sayed Tantawi, August 18, 1994 edition of *Al-Ahram Weekly*.
2. The material presented in this section is drawn from previously published results in Huntington *et al.* (1998) and is reprinted with permission from *International Family Planning Perspectives*.
3. The WHO-recommended scheme depends upon a combination of medical symptoms and self-reported practices to classify the abortion as either certainly, probably, possibly induced or spontaneous. While the classification system is imperfect, it does provide a reasonably useful categorization for policy development and subsequent analyses.
4. The selection of this multiplier for representing abortion cases that do present for medical treatment is admittedly arbitrarily low, particularly compared to Latin America where a multiplier of 3–7 has been recommended. Because of the very strong religious beliefs and cultural traditions against abortion in Egypt, combined with the overall absence of severe complications (presented later in this chapter), the incidence of abortion is judged to be relatively low, with the majority of cases being incomplete self-induced abortions, or incomplete menstrual regulation practices. This suggests that the majority of cases will seek post-abortion treatment in the country's hospitals. Using larger multipliers (to estimate the number of abortions not treated in a hospital) produced abortion ratios substantially higher than WHO estimates for the region, further suggesting the appropriateness of the 1.5 multiplier used in Table 8.1 (Huntington *et al.* 1998).
5. There are two difficulties associated with calculating gestational age of incomplete abortions. The first is related to the physical fact that part of the products of conception have been lost (i.e. the abortion is incomplete). This will result in a smaller uterine size and increase the likelihood that the gestational age will be underestimated. The second difficulty concerns the definition of abortion in use by a country's governmental authority. WHO recommends 28 weeks as the upper gestational limit in defining abortion 'because it is used by most of the countries that have adopted a definition of abortion, because it complements the definition of stillbirth recommended by the WHO Expert Committee on Health Statistics, and because it corresponds to a definition given in the International classification of Diseases' (WHO 1970, pp. 6–7). Egypt does not have an officially endorsed definition of abortion. The point is relatively unimportant in the classification of post-abortion patients, however, as only 3.27 per cent of the foetal deaths had a gestational age of 20–27 weeks (source: Huntington *et al.* 1997*a*).
6. All of the citations are from in-depth interviews with post-abortion patients unless noted in brackets and much of the interpretation is abstracted from Huntington *et al.* (1997) and reprinted with the permission of *Reproductive Health Matters*.
7. The idealization of motherhood is not limited to the Arab world, as many other societies both within the Mediterranean region and elsewhere glorify women's role as mothers above all others. The discussion of abortion in Greece by Georges (1996) is relevant to this point.
8. The juxtaposition of the two moralities was identified by Michael Herzfeld (1985) in the context of Crete.

References

Azer, A. (1979), 'Law as an instrument for social change: An illustration from population policy', *Cairo Papers in Social Science,* 2 (4).

Brooke, R. J., Benson, J., Bradley, J., and Ordonez, A. R. (1993), 'Cost and resource utilization for the treatment of incomplete abortion in Kenya and Mexico', *Social Science and Medicine,* 36 (11): 1443–53.

Central Agency for Public Mobilization and Statistics (CAPMAS) and UNICEF (1987), *Maternal Health and Infant Mortality in Egypt.*

El-Zanaty, F., Hussein, E. M., Shawky, G. A., Way, A. A., and Kishor, S. (1995). 'Egyptian demographic health survey', National Population Council, Cairo, Egypt and Macro, International, Demographic and Health Surveys, Calverton Maryland, 1995.

Georges, E. (1996). 'Abortion policy and practice in Greece', *Social Science and Medicine,* 42 (4).

Henshaw, S., and Morrow, E. (1990), *Induced Abortion: A Worldwide Review, 1990 Supplement,* New York: Alan Guttmacher Institute.

Herzfeld, M. (1985), *The Poetics of Manhood: Contest and Identity in a Cretan Mountain Village,* Princeton, NJ: Princeton University Press, pp. 232–47.

Hoodfar, H. (1986), 'Child care and child survival in low-income neighborhoods of Cairo', *The Population Council West Asia and North Africa Regional Papers,* Cairo: The Population Council.

Huntington, D., Nawar, L., and Abdel-Hady, D. (1995a), 'An exploratory study of the psycho-social stress associated with abortions in Egypt', Final Report ANE OR/TA Project, The Population Council, Cairo.

—— Hassan, E. O., Toubia, N., Attallah, N., Naguib, M., and Nawar, L. (1995b), 'Improving the counseling and medical care of post abortion patients in Egypt', *Studies in Family Planning,* 26 (6) (Nov/Dec): 350–62.

—— Nawar, L., and Abdel-Hady, D. (1995), 'An exploratory study of the psycho-social stress associated with abortions in Egypt', Final Report ANE OR/TA Project, The Population Council, Cairo.

—— Nawar, L., Hassan, E. O., Youssef, H., and Abdel-Tawab, N. (1998), 'The postabortion caseload in Egyptian hospitals: A descriptive study', *International Family Planning Perspectives,* 24 (1) (March).

—— Nawar, L., and Abdel-Hady, D. (1997),'Women's perceptions of abortion in Egypt', *Reproductive Health Matters,* No. 9 (May): 101–7.

Inhorn, M. C. (1994), *Quest for Conception: Gender, Infertility and Egyptian Medical Traditions,* Philadelphia: University of Pennsylvania Press, pp. 242–5.

International Conference on Population and Development (1994), *Programme of Action,* United Nations.

International Planned Parenthood Federation (1992), 'Unsafe abortion and sexual health in the Arab world', Damascus Regional Conference, organized by IPPF and the Syrian Family Planning Association, December.

Khattab, H. A. S. (1992), G. Potter (ed.), *The Silent Endurance: Social Conditions of Women's Reproductive Health in Rural Egypt,* Cairo: UNICEF and the Population Council.

Margolix, A., Leonard, A., and Yordy, L. (1991), 'Pain control for treatment of incomplete abortion with MVA', *Advances in Abortion Care,* vol. 1, IPAS, Carroboro N.C.

Omran, A. (1992). *Family Planning and the Legacy of Islam,* New York: Routledge.

Petersen, H. B. *et al.* (1981), 'Comparative risk of death from induced abortion at 12 weeks or less gestational performed with local versus general anesthesia', *American Journal of Obstetrics and Gynecology*, 141: 763–8.

Ragab, A. R. (1995). 'Abortion decision making in an illegal context: A case study from rural Egypt', Ph.D. thesis submitted to the University of Exeter, UK.

—— Serour, G. I., Ford, N., Ankomah, A. 'Socio-cultural determinants of abortion behavior in an Egyptian community'. Unpublished manuscript.

Singh, S., and Wulf, D. 'The likelihood of induced abortion among women hospitalized for abortion complications in four Latin American countries', *International Family Planning Perspectives*, 19 (4) (December)

—— and Henshaw, S. (1996). 'The incidence of abortion: A worldwide overview focusing on methodology and on Latin America', *Seminar on Socio-Cultural and Political Aspects of Abortion from and Anthropological Perspective*, International Union for the Scientific Study of Population Trivandrum, India, March 25–28.

Judith, W., Oliveras, E., and McIntosh, N. (1995). *Postabortion Care: A Reference Manual for Improving Quality of Care*, Postabortion Care Consortium, AVSC, Int., IPPF, IPAS, JHU/CCP, JHPIEGO and Pathfinder, Int.

World Health Organization (1970), *Spontaneous and Induced Abortion*, Report of a WHO Scientific Group, WHO Geneva.

—— (1987), 'Protocol for hospital based descriptive studies of mortality, morbidity related to induced abortion', WHO Project No. 86912, Task Force on Safety and Efficacy of Fertility Regulating Methods, WHO, Geneva, revised edition of 14 August 1987.

—— (1993), 'Prevention and management of unsafe abortion, Report of a Technical Working Group', WHO, Geneva.

—— (1994), *Abortion: Tabulation of Available Data on the Frequency and Mortality of Unsafe Abortion*, 2nd edition, Geneva: WHO.

—— (1995), *Complications of Abortion: Technical and Managerial Guidelines for Prevention and Treatment*, Geneva: WHO.

Younis, N., Khattab, H., Zurayk, H., El-Mouelhy, M., Amin, M. F., and Farag, A. M. 'A community study of gynecological and related morbidities in rural Egypt', *Studies in Family Planning*, 24 (3) (May/June).

9

The Reproductive Consequences of Shifting Ethnic Identity in South Africa

CAROL E. KAUFMAN AND
DEBORAH JAMES

The importance of ethnicity to fertility behaviour, and to changes in fertility behaviour, has been supported in demographic research for some time (Goldsheider and Uhlenberg 1969; Lesthaeghe 1977; Anderson 1986). Fertility levels and contraceptive use patterns often show distinction along language groupings or religious lines. This is no less true in South Africa. Given a context in which rights and privileges were apportioned according to skin colour, variation in shape and pace of demographic change by racial group is perhaps expected, if not well documented (though see Mostert 1990; Chimere-Dan 1993). What has been almost completely ignored is the striking difference in reproductive patterns across various language groups of the African population of South Africa. The former government administered Africans in ethnic units, a policy which fostered divisiveness through differential granting of scarce resources. The relationship between reproductive outcomes and uneven access to social and economic opportunities thus appears to present a promising analytic explanation for ethnic reproductive differences in South Africa. However, socio-economic standing is not in itself a sufficient explanation; ethnicity may be as much produced as explained by differentials in education or income (Handwerker 1986). Analyses applying statistical controls generate broad indications of patterns, but they cannot of themselves evaluate the interrelationship between material conditions and ethnicity, nor the specific ways in which that relationship subsequently informs reproductive outcomes. We argue that 'ethnicity', as defined by language or religious affiliation, is a useful definition for quantifying general patterns, but the associations produced require interpretive criticism. Not all members adhere with equal conviction to practices and beliefs which may have been deemed to be representative of their ethnic group, and the set of practices and beliefs that distinguish one group from another are themselves not timeless, but are continually reshaped and redefined by members. While demographic studies generally focus on the association between an ethnic category and

Table 9.1. *Ethnic/language group and 'assigned' homeland, South Africa*

Ethnicity/ language group	Homeland
Zulu	KwaZulu
Northern Sotho/Pedi	Lebowa
Tswana	Bophuthatswana
Swazi	KaNgwane
Tsonga/Shagaan	Gazankulu
Xhosa	Transkei
	Ciskei
Ndebele	KwaNdebele
Southern Sotho	QwaQwa
Venda	Venda

reproduction, we argue that this association derives meaning from the process of ethnic identification and the cultural and historical construction of that identity.

In South Africa, the use of ethnic labels to define identity has been particularly contentious. The term 'ethnic', with its connotations of cultural rather than rigidly physical difference, made its first official appearance in South African state ideology as a substitute for 'race' (Dubow 1994, pp. 356–7), and gained wide currency during the 1960s as a justification for further subdividing the populace, already partitioned into broad racial groups, into smaller cultural/linguistic entities with separate territories or homelands (Table 9.1). Each group within the African population was thought of as having a distinctive relationship to its own culture, a relationship so unique as to render cultural mixing inappropriate (Sharp 1980, p. 3).

In response to this official view of ethnic identity, social scientists and historians with a revisionist perspective have dedicated themselves to showing that apartheid's rigid and essentialized ethnic identities—like its broader race divisions—were 'made' not 'born' in the process of establishing and maintaining the inequalities on which South Africa's capitalist and segregationist political economy was based. They showed how tribes had been transformed into fixed units, or even created, through various colonial processes, such as missionization and the indirect rule system of government (Harries 1989; Vail 1989). Further processes which encouraged the development of tribal or ethnic allegiance were related to the conditions of rapid urban and industrial development which these regions were undergoing. On the mines of the Witwatersrand, workers' stressing of tribal difference expressed their new-found identity as workers and their wish to monopolize particular employment sectors or residential enclaves (Guy and Thabane 1991, 1989a). These niches in turn became the basis for differential incorporation into the workforce, which further cemented workers' tendency to identify themselves by reference to home area or ethnic group (Marks and Rathbone 1982).

Similar processes had occurred in other African countries. But what gave ethnicity in South Africa its particular character was the homeland system of government, citizenship and land access, consolidated during the 1960s and 1970s. Prevented from moving their families into the cities by the infamous 'pass laws', workers remained committed to their rural homes and dependent on the local chiefs who would guarantee their continued security in these areas (Vail 1989, pp. 11–16). However, although these identities have been to some extent imposed by the state's rigid apartheid policies and by equally inflexible material constraints, anthropological studies show that they have also been actively constructed, and experienced in fluid terms, by African migrants and their dependants (Coplan 1987; Spiegel 1991; Webster 1991).

It is in recognition of the need to highlight such contingent and subjective reshapings of ethnicity, while at the same time exploring the usefulness of survey data which favours fixed indicators of ethnic identity such as language, that this paper combines qualitative and quantitative approaches. It aims, in so doing, to transcend some of the limitations of these types of data when used in isolation. A qualitative approach with its focus on subjective and fluid identities might fail to acknowledge the constraints imposed by official ethnic classifications. It might, as well, be thought to be too particularistic to have an impact, in turn, on official statistics about ethnic difference. Analyses based purely on survey data, on the other hand, can be criticized for an incapacity to recognize the specificities of cultural context and the need for interpretive flexibility.

In combining these two methodologies, the paper aims to make a contribution to that cross-disciplinary field of study which brings anthropologists' studies of fertility into conversation with those of demographers. While this field is by now well established, many contributions to it still tend to remain on one side or other of the qualitative/quantitative dividing line. The result is a constriction in the potential range and reach of research findings, with the nuanced results of a qualitative study being of more interest to historians and anthropologists while graphs and tables have more interest for statisticians and demographers, and more impact in the world of policy and planning.

But our paper aims to do more than simply to bridge the gap between these divergent readerships. It shows, as well, that interlocking methodologies can afford new insights which neither broad-based surveys nor local-level case studies would yield on their own. Interrogating these dovetailing sets of data, we ask: How does ethnic identification or definition vary across and within boundaries, be they geographic, political, or affiliative, and how does that variation consequently shape our interpretation of numerical description? And closely related to that question: How can an analysis of subjective ethnic experience with respect to fertility and reproduction inform demographic research, both qualitative and quantitative?

After presenting the methodological and conceptual framework guiding our research and discussing our sources, we turn to a quantitative demographic analysis to provide descriptive and multivariate assessments of reproduction by ethnic category in South Africa—estimates not previously available due to the sensitivity of both topics. To complement these assessments, we then draw on ethnographic evidence to demonstrate the malleability of ethnic identity along generational and gender lines for the particular cases of Northern Sotho- and Ndebele-speaking people, two language groups of South Africa. A combination of these data with the results of the multivariate analysis allows us to situate ethnically contrasted reproductive patterns within local understandings of society. We find that the two sets of data, combined and analysed in relation to each other, indicate the importance of successive stages in the life-course of women. These life course stages—birth, marriage, entry into the labour market—both influence reproductive outcomes and in turn become central to understandings of ethnic belonging. Ethnic identity, we find, is not merely linked to a certain type of reproductive behaviour but is actually predicated upon it.

CONCEPTUAL AND METHODOLOGICAL APPROACH

Researchers commonly set out to study designs that include qualitative and numerical data collection in order to address a particular problem. Our approach is different in that we use existing data sources, one quantitative, one qualitative, to address our research questions. Joint analysis of existing sources of data has, in this study, yielded important interdisciplinary perspectives. The use of existing data may also be a worthwhile investment as a preliminary step before initiating large, expensive primary data collection activities. The process may generate conflicting or corroborating evidence on a particular issue (thus refining the research questions), clarify the successes or failures of a given data collection technique for a region, or provide an indication of questions or topics inadequately addressed in prior studies. Sensitivity of research topics, or political or economic conditions precluding fieldwork, are other factors that may also necessitate a more creative analysis of existing data.

In the case of South Africa, the highly contentious subjects of ethnicity and family planning had received only limited research attention. In trying to help fill this vacuum, and provide insights into the relationship between ethnicity and reproduction in the late apartheid era, we found it fruitful to proceed by utilizing existing studies, investigating how these dovetailed, and analysing their points of interaction. While the approach holds obvious benefits, it is not a straightforward task. It called for a merging not only of differing methodological approaches, but also of somewhat dissimilar disciplinary perspectives. Our sets of data were collected for purposes other than an analysis of ethnicity and fertility, and had to be interrogated in particular ways to yield direct measurement of or testimony on this specific relationship.

The quantitative data come from the South African Demographic and Health Survey (SADHS), collected by the South African Human Sciences Research Council (HSRC) in 1987–9. The survey was modelled on the Macro International/USAID studies, but because of sanctions against South Africa at the time, no international financial or technical assistance was provided. The study is unique in that it surveyed almost 22,000 women from all four officially sanctioned race groups and all areas of South Africa, including the former homelands, at a time when apartheid boundaries were still entrenched; many studies frequently excluded homelands or certain race groups for political or logistical reasons. Indeed, apartheid proscriptions are reflected in the sample; the SADHS is actually a pooled set of 14 surveys, one for each of the ten homelands, and one for each race group in the 'white' area of the Republic of South Africa (RSA). All samples are stratified, random probability, and self-weighting.[1] Women aged 12–49 who were currently in a union or living with someone, had been in a union, or living with someone previously, or who had ever given birth or were currently pregnant were included in the survey.

The qualitative data come from two case studies in the former Lebowa homeland—now Northern Province—where most residents have been dependent on the labour-migrant economy. Both demonstrate the subjective and flexible nature of ethnic identification. The first study investigates ethnic boundary-maintenance between Northern Sotho (calling themselves simply Sotho) and Ndebele living in a single village.[2] It shows that the homelands were not as ethnically homogeneous as they were planned to be, and that many of the homeland residents whom the state represented as natural citizens of these areas had moved to them from their former homes on white-owned farms only a few decades before apartheid's official dissolution. The conditions under which members of both groups had lived on these farms, their time of arrival in the homeland, and the nature of their clientelist ties to the Ndebele chief when they arrived, fed into a process of mutually reinforced ethnic stereotyping, in which fertility behaviour was seen as a key marker. Sotho saw Ndebele girls as traditionalists who abandoned schooling to marry and have children, while Ndebele saw Sotho girls as modern and career-advancing (James 1985, 1987).

The second case study describes the little-understood phenomenon of ethnic identity construction among women workers in the 1970s and 1980s. These first-generation female labour migrants left home in what was then called Lebowa to work on the Witwatersrand. At first lacking any sense of group affiliation other than that which bound them to church or the male kinsmen who acted as their protectors, they later began to develop a sense of themselves as autonomous wage earners, and in the process to form strong group ties which were experienced and expressed as those between 'Sotho' people. This newly established affiliation to Sotho ways in some cases overrode these women's earlier primary affiliations to a Christian identity which had transcended ethnic particularities, and in other cases contrasted with alternative ethnic identifications, based on first language, which the women might have been expected to espouse (James 1999a,b).

Methodologically, these case studies had the small scale and localized character of most first-hand anthropological accounts. The first involved a survey of 54 households out of a village total of 487, accompanied by more thorough discussions with, and participant observation among, a smaller number of informants and families within the village. The later case study of migrant women's emergent Sotho identity encompassed a broader rural base, since the men and their female partners in the two main performance groups studied came from two different areas in the former Lebowa homeland. The study entailed intensive life-history interviewing of and discussions with individual performer/migrants, observation of and participation in performances, and group discussions about the significance of dances and lyrics with a particular focus on 14 male migrants, 20 female migrants, and 20 stay-at-home wives. The present study draws on several key insights offered by these case studies; delineating the full methodology and substantive findings is beyond the scope of this paper (see James 1985, 1987, 1990, 1999*a,b*).

The prime motivation for collaborative secondary data analysis centred on research questions about reproduction and ethnicity. The questionnaire used by the SADHS could not problematize 'ethnic' as a category since the only approximation of ethnicity it offered centred on the supposedly 'objective' feature of language and contained no reference to the subjective experiencing or construction of ethnic identity. It did, however, contain rich, detailed data on reproductive experiences from a nationally representative sample of South Africans. The ethnographic study, in contrast, had investigated fluid and unfolding ethnic identities rather than focusing explicitly on issues of fertility and reproduction. As a conceptual bridge between the two data sources, we framed our research questions broadly around ethnicity and fertility in our quantitative analysis, and using the ethnographic material, we focused on life course, family and household relationships that may be reflective of the ethnicity–fertility association in a local context.

To proceed with analysis in this conceptual frame, we first had to consider data collection dimensions and limitations, summarized in Table 9.2. For example, the multi-ethnic village of Sephaku, site of one ethnographic study, is located in the former homeland of Lebowa (now Northern Province). Since the sample design of the quantitative study includes representative samples from each homeland, the data can be used to generate estimates for the population of Lebowa without compromising sample representativeness. The survey, however, cannot be used to determine reproductive estimates for any particular village, nor for the Ndebele living within the Lebowa homeland. These populations are quite small and the SADHS does not contain a representative sample of them. However, the SADHS can provide national estimates for a particular ethnic group, in this case Sotho or Ndebele, provided the appropriate weights are applied. Conversely, the experiences of women in the ethnographic studies are not generalizable to broader populations such as Sotho speakers, or to female migrants. Still, their experiences demonstrate one way women interpret or shape their own identities, as subjectively constructed and experienced, which are closely tied with the particular timing and sequence of demographic events.

Both our sources were constrained by the level of analysis. For the SADHS, interviews were conducted with women, and no information was gathered on the existence of or accessibility to community social services, such as surrounding clinics or schools. While some evidence suggests that contextual factors are likely to be important in reproductive behaviour in South Africa (Kaufman 1998), community data are not readily available. The ethnographic work provides some insights into commonly held attitudes or preconceptions of what 'acceptable' or 'expected' behaviour is for a Sotho or an Ndebele. Several of these are linked with reproductive

Table 9.2. *Summary of design dimensions of survey and ethnographic studies*

SADHS (1987–9)	Sotho ethnographic projects (1980s)
Purpose	
Provide demographic and health data on the population of South Africa; contains rich fertility and contraceptive use information, little on ethnicity or class.	Data collected to examine the construction of a Sotho identity among migrant Sotho women. Contains detailed information on ethnicity and ethnic identity, little directly on fertility or contraceptive use.
Geography	
Nationally representative, separate analyses possible at the level of the homeland. Includes all geographic units in South Africa, including Lebowa.	Sephaku, a village in the former homeland of Lebowa, and Northern Sotho-speaking women working in Johannesburg.
Sample eligibility	
Women aged 12–49 who were currently in a union or had been, or who had children or were currently pregnant at the time of the interview.	Women of the village, purposefully chosen, and in Johannesburg, women who participated in Sotho singing groups.
Scope and type of data	
Survey data, focused on women's characteristics, their reproductive histories, contraceptive use, and child health. Includes some household information and spouse/partner information.	Genealogies, in-depth interviews, observation, and village census to gather accounts of women's experience in migration, household dynamics, and gendered patterns of education and employment.
Level of inquiry	
Interviews with individuals, though includes some household-level information. Community-level data possible through aggregation or outside data sources (e.g. census).	Interviews with individuals, observations of households and communities. Genealogies contain intergenerational information on household composition and migration patterns.
Institutional environment	
No data available on clinics or schools in or nearby a sampled cluster. No complete, reliable data available from other sources.	No systematic collection of data on resources available for the communities studied, but some observational notes.
Inference	
Generalizable to national or homeland level.	Not intended to be generalizable, but to explore in depth the gendered construction of ethnicity.
Temporal reference	
Cross-sectional data; very limited retrospective material.	Cross-sectional, but emphasized accumulated experiences over time.

outcomes, as is discussed below. However, since reproduction was not a primary focus of the original study, the institutional environment such as accessibility to schools or health clinics did not receive systematic attention. The case studies, however, benefit from a variety of data collection methods, including genealogies, in-depth interviews, and a village survey.

Finally, our respective sources of data have divergent temporal frames. The ethnographic information, though collected cross-sectionally, emphasizes accumulated experiences, expectations, and conditions in the lives of Sotho and Ndebele women. The survey data were also collected cross-sectionally, but contain almost no information on the sequence or timing of important life events such as work or education. In both cases, we make assumptions about the validity of retrospective data.

Emerging out of these divergent sources of data is the importance of different stages in the life course. Guided by this, we choose selected key life transitions, such as childbirth, marriage, and entry into work, and consider the variation across these transitions. We use quantitative information to describe numerically the variation across ethnicities, and interpretive data to deepen our understanding of the phenomena underlying those variations for Sotho- and Ndebele-speaking communities. Before focusing on specific communities, in the next section we provide a quantitative analysis of reproduction across all major ethnic groups in South Africa.

DEMOGRAPHIC ANALYSIS OF ETHNICITY AND FERTILITY IN SOUTH AFRICA, 1987–9

The scant research that exists on reproductive patterns in South Africa has focused almost exclusively upon the dramatic changes in fertility regimes and the striking differentials exhibited by race (Brown 1987; Chimere-Dan 1993, 1997). Whites at the end of apartheid had an estimated 1.9 total fertility rate, while the rate for blacks was about 4.6, but racial patterns of reproductive behaviour obscure the important differences within each category, such as the ethnic variations within the African population which this paper explores. This section uses statistical description and multivariate analyses to investigate the content of ethnic differences. It explores the extent to which social and economic characteristics of black women account for ethnic diversity in reproductive patterns, including two features of central importance to the lives of millions of black South Africans in the late 1980s: homeland residence and the labour migration system.

We use recent fertility as a dependent variable to focus our analyses.[3] Recent fertility is defined as all live births occurring to black South African women between the ages of 15 and 49 within the 5 years prior to the interview. The definition focuses on the recent past to facilitate analysis; it assumes that a woman's current circumstances (e.g. her level of education or income) have not changed substantially over the course of her fertility history during the past 5 years. Recent fertility measures have the added advantage of minimizing biases introduced through recall errors since misreporting of births or misplacing the dates of births is more likely for children born further in the past (IRD 1990). Measuring fertility in this way, however, is not without analytic costs. The number of children women are able to have over a 5-year period is, by definition, limited. In South Africa, where fertility is already at moderately low levels, the degree of variation will be modest. For example, nearly half of the sample had no children (43 per cent), and approximately 42 per cent had one. Only about 13 per cent had two children, with the small balance having had three or more children.

The central focus of this analysis, ethnicity, is operationalized in the survey data by home language. In the terms outlined above, this is problematic since it obscures the very fact of multiple, subjective or shifting identity on which the present study is focused. For many respondents, it may indicate merely the bureaucratic classification imposed by the former regime. Nonetheless, since home language was the official basis for ethnic categorization, and since state-imposed ethnicity did strengthen identity in some respects, 'home language' is likely to capture some general patterns of fertility and contraceptive use across groups. A series of dichotomous variables are coded representing each of the major African languages. Other independent variables include urban or rural residence in childhood (before the age of 12), current urban or rural residence, type of sanitation system (a proxy for wealth), and a dummy variable representing whether or not one or more of a woman's children have died. Age is coded as a series of dummy variables because of the likely non-linear relationship with contraceptive use and fertility; education is also represented by a series of dummy variables corresponding to important educational transitions in South Africa. Male migration is derived from a question on the survey about the frequency with which a woman's partner returns home. In order to allow analysis over the whole sample, including those who had never been married, a partner's absenteeism was brought into the analysis through an interaction. Women who were married and who had a partner that returned home once a month or less were coded one. All other women, those never married, or those who had partners who returned home more frequently, were coded zero. Because a partner's absenteeism is treated here as an interaction, marital status is also included in the analysis to capture the main effects in the multivariate analysis. Marital status is coded one if ever-married, zero otherwise.

Finally, three sets of geographic variables are included in the analysis. The geographic coding scheme is based on the apartheid geography of 'separate development': the euphemistically named policy which sanctioned not just racial but also ethnic separatist policies. In the Republic of South Africa—designated as a 'white' area within which segregated residential areas were set aside for whites, coloureds, and Indians—Africans were allowed to stay only under strict employment provisions, living in black townships apart from white cities. Africans not qualifying under these restrictions were technically assigned to live in one of ten ethnic homelands, supposedly according to home language. The ideology of separate development proposed that groups in each of these areas would progress and develop to the point of independence, at which time it would become its own state or country, and South Africa would relinquish governance (and citizenship rights). Four homelands, Transkei, Bophuthatswana, Venda, and Ciskei, elected for independence (the TBVC states); the other six remained self-governing territories (SGTs) so that they had some sovereign rights within their borders but remained a part of South Africa. While all homelands received substantial economic assistance from the central government, the TBVC states were in general more impoverished than the others. Thus, the first geographic variable is one indicating whether a woman is currently residing in a homeland, another set of variables indicate whether she lives in a self-governing homeland (SGT), an independent state (TBVC state), or the 'white' areas of the country, and finally a further set indicates which of the four provinces she lived in at the time of the interview.

The bivariate relationship between recent fertility and several key sample charac-teristics is summarized in Table 9.3. Recent fertility by ethnic group ranges from a low of 0.66 children for Zulus to a high of 0.90 for the Venda. The table confirms many other expected associations: rural women have more children than their urban counterparts, women who are not working have more children than those who work, and low levels of wealth, here represented by type of sanitation system, correspond to high levels of fertility. Not all associations reveal the expected pattern, however. Women with 1–3 years of formal education have the highest levels of fertility compared to women in other educational groups. Finally, the table also shows distinctive patterns in reproduction by distinguishing features of South Africa: geopolitical unit and male migration. A woman's recent fertility is higher on average if she lives in an independent TBVC homeland than if she lives in an SGT or the 'white' areas of the country. Indeed, the estimates provided for each homeland indicate a great deal of variation even within a particular 'type' of homeland. The table also shows a positive association between recent fertility and men's absence, an indicator of male migration. This at first seems counterintuitive as prolonged absence by men decreases coital frequency and the likelihood of falling pregnant. However, it could be that if women are not using contraception regularly, they are in fact more likely to become pregnant when partners do return. Anecdotal evidence also suggests that men prefer to leave their partners pregnant before they depart on a work contract since it will ensure their wives' fidelity.

The picture that materializes suggests that while markers indicating an ethnic identity appear to contribute to an explanation of reproductive behaviour, so too do many other characteristics of women. The distribution and accessibility of family planning services, or the supply environment, is also an important part of the story of reproductive experiences of black women. Under apartheid, homelands were responsible for their own health services, including family planning (South African Department of Health 1973, 1975). Representatives from the South African government's family planning programme could not enter the homelands in an official capacity unless invited to do so. Family planning services provided within the homelands, however, were poorly funded, if they existed at all (Brown 1987, p. 268; Sai *et al.* 1993). From the point of view of the central government family planning administration, fertility levels in the homelands were high and so was the demand for services. To avoid compromising 'sovereign rights' of homeland areas, the national family planning programme set up mobile clinic sites and services in

Table 9.3. *Weighted mean number of children born to black South African women within 5 years prior to the survey, by various characteristics*

Characteristics	Mean	N	Characteristics	Mean	N
Total mean # children born, prior 5 years	0.73	16,038	*Education*		
			None	0.64	2,393
			Std. 1–3	0.79	2,305
Ethnicity			Std. 4–5	0.75	3,313
Zulu	0.66	4,808	Std. 6–7	0.74	3,591
Pedi/ N. Sotho	0.73	2,015	Std. 8–9	0.73	2,852
Tsonga	0.89	738	Std. 10+	0.75	1,580
Ndebele	0.81	301			
Swazi	0.83	414	*Residence before the age of 12*		
Xhosa	0.78	3,897	Rural	0.76	10,532
S. Sotho	0.70	1,480	Urban	0.68	5,435
Tswana	0.71	1,895			
Venda	0.90	429	*Residence*		
Other	0.38	60	Rural	0.76	8,680
			Urban	0.70	7,358
Survey area					
RSA (African)	0.65	6,577	*Sanitation system*		
Cape	0.60	1,284	No toilet	0.83	2,144
Orange Free State	0.64	964	Bucket	0.73	9,512
Natal	0.70	818	Flush	0.68	4,367
Transvaal	0.67	3,510			
			Experienced death of a child		
Self-governing territories	0.75	5,495	Yes	0.90	2,368
Gazankulu	0.95	413	No	0.70	13,670
KaNgwane	0.89	291			
KwaNdebele	0.84	185	*Marital status*		
KwaZulu	0.68	2,974	Ever married	0.75	10,091
Lebowa	0.77	1,482	Never married	0.71	5,946
QwaQwa	0.83	149			
			Frequency of partner's visits home		
Independent states	0.86	3,966	Every night	0.71	5,501
Transkei	0.94	1,850	Weekends	0.72	1,216
Bophuthatswana	0.79	1,290	Once a month	0.82	1,699
Venda	0.93	792	Less often	0.31	1,372
Ciskei	0.69	759			
			Partner absenteeism/marital status		
Age			Married and partner returns home once a month or less	0.86	3,010
15–19	0.64	1,967	Otherwise	0.70	13,028
20–24	0.92	4,339			
25–29	0.88	3,586	*Work status*		
30–34	0.82	2,167	Currently not working	0.78	11,349
35–39	0.66	1,482	Currently working	0.60	4,388
40–49	0.24	2,497			

Source: 1987–9 SADHS.

Table 9.4. *Recent fertility (5 years prior to survey) of black South African women, by ethnic group and homeland residency*

Ethnic Group *(Homeland)*		Total	Residence	
			Homeland	Non-homeland
Zulu	*KwaZulu*	0.66	0.67	0.64
N. Sotho/Pedi	*Lebowa*	0.73	0.77	0.63
Tsonga	*Gazankulu*	0.89	0.96	0.77
Ndebele	*KwaNdebele*	0.80	0.87	0.75
Swazi	*KaNgwane*	0.83	0.92	0.69
Xhosa[a]		0.78		0.63
	Ciskei		0.69	
	Transkei		0.94	
S. Sotho	*QwaQwa*	0.70	0.84	0.66
Tswana	*Bophuthatswana*	0.71	0.78	0.64
Venda	*Venda*	0.90	0.93	0.74

Source: 1987–9 SADHS.
[a] Xhosa is the dominant language in both homelands of Ciskei and Transkei.

places most easily accessible to homeland women: clinics sometimes were located 'across the street' from homelands so women could walk over the border, or sometimes clinics were organized at shops frequented by black women when they travelled to the RSA (very little commercial activity transpired in homeland areas—market activity was another domain controlled under apartheid) (Stockton 1995). Homeland areas were widely believed to be underserved relative to other areas, but strategic placement of clinics may have confounded this generally held belief. Thus, to the extent that ethnicity and homelands are correlated, and to the extent that homelands systematically differ in the accessibility women had to services, fertility differentials by ethnicity may be a function of homeland services. Available data unfortunately do not allow for direct measures of family planning clinic distribution, density, or effectiveness since each homeland was responsible for its own record keeping, and few had the interest or resources to do so. However, available data on recent fertility levels for each ethnic group by homeland residency help to clarify the relationship between access to services and observed reproductive behaviours, as presented in Table 9.4. Dramatic differences in reproductive patterns across geopolitical units within ethnic groups do exist, and indicate that accessibility may have been constrained in homeland areas. However, outside or inside homelands, the relative rankings of groups do not vary substantially. That is, while most groups living outside of homeland areas have lower fertility than their homeland counterparts, the relative levels across groups change very little.[4]

The homeland differentials suggest that many characteristics are likely to have an important relationship with ethnicity and reproductive outcomes which must be investigated using multivariate analysis techniques. Again, statistical analyses cannot examine the possibly mutually reinforcing relationship between ethnicity

Table 9.5. *OLS regression analysis of recent fertility (prior 5 years) for black South African women*

	M1			M2			M3		
	Coeff.	Std. Err.	t	Coeff.	Std. Err.	t	Coeff.	Std. Err.	t
Urban residence before age 12	−0.08	0.01	−5.77	−0.07	0.02	−4.16	−0.05	0.02	−3.04
Ethnicity (ref. = Zulu)									
Pedi/N. Sotho	0.06	0.02	2.76	0.08	0.02	3.29	0.02	0.02	0.75
Tsonga	0.24	0.03	7.70	0.22	0.03	7.55	0.14	0.03	4.96
Ndebele	0.16	0.04	4.39	0.18	0.04	5.08	0.14	0.04	3.98
Swazi	0.23	0.03	7.17	0.23	0.03	7.50	0.15	0.03	5.22
Xhosa	0.11	0.03	4.21	0.13	0.03	5.06	0.04	0.03	1.60
S. Sotho	0.10	0.03	3.83	0.10	0.03	3.89	0.05	0.02	2.10
Tswana	0.07	0.03	2.48	0.08	0.03	2.91	0.01	0.03	0.35
Venda	0.22	0.04	6.17	0.22	0.03	6.54	0.08	0.04	1.99
Age (ref. = 20–24)									
15–19				−0.29	0.02	−15.89	−0.26	0.02	−14.04
25–29				−0.03	0.02	−1.43	−0.06	0.02	−3.19
30–34				−0.10	0.02	−4.78	−0.15	0.02	−7.30
35–39				−0.27	0.03	−10.43	−0.33	0.03	−12.83
40–49				−0.73	0.02	−37.20	−0.81	0.02	−39.78
Education (ref. = none)									
Std 1–3				0.06	0.02	2.87	0.06	0.02	2.77
Std 4–5				−0.02	0.02	−0.79	−0.02	0.02	−1.15
Std 6–7				−0.02	0.02	−1.18	−0.03	0.02	−1.41
Std 8–9				−0.11	0.02	−4.77	−0.10	0.02	−4.71
Std 10+				−0.15	0.03	−5.72	−0.15	0.03	−5.92
Current residence is urban				−0.02	0.02	−1.00	0.00	0.02	0.21
Toilet facilities (ref. = flush)									
Bucket system				0.01	0.02	0.72	−0.03	0.02	−1.24
No toilet				0.08	0.03	2.81	0.04	0.03	1.31
Survey area type (ref. = RSA, non-homeland areas)									
Self-governing territories							0.10	0.02	4.82
Independent states							0.18	0.03	6.68
Partner absenteeism/Marital status (interaction)									
Ever married							0.15	0.02	9.54
Ever married/Partner returns once a month or less							0.07	0.02	4.62
Constant	0.70	0.02	41.70	0.91	0.03	27.46	0.80	0.03	23.57
N	16,027			16,012			16,010		
Adjusted R^2	0.012			0.113			0.128		

Source: 1987–89 SADHS.

and material conditions; yet, they can describe distinctive socio-economic patterns across groups, thereby providing a foundation for localized interpretive analysis.

MULTIVARIATE ANALYSIS

Recent fertility experience is analytically estimated by ordinary least-squares regressions techniques. It is assumed to approximate an interval variable, and ordinary linear regression modelling is used to evaluate the effects of selected independent variables on the dependent variable. The data are obtained from the 1987–9 SADHS study which used a complex sampling design. Using the statistical package STATA, Huber corrections to standard errors were used in analysis to adjust for the cluster design of the study (Guilkey 1992).

Table 9.5 shows the results of the multivariate regressions for recent fertility for black women in South Africa. The table shows three models. The first considers only early childhood residence and ethnicity. The second includes demographic and socio-economic controls, and the third includes controls for the political geography of the country and male migration.[5] Model one indicates that growing up in an urban setting was negatively related to recent fertility, an association that held when other controls are added. All ethnic groups were significantly more likely to have more children than Zulu speakers. The effects were particularly strong for the Tsonga, Swazi, and Venda. All of these groups had about 10.2 children more than Zulus over the course of 5 years, after controlling for childhood residence. Model two shows that even after controlling for age and socio-economic controls, ethnic categories remained important, though the effects were diminished. It is not until the third model, when controls for homelands and male migration were introduced, that the effects of ethnicity on recent fertility decreased notably. Indeed, once these controls were added, some language groups—the Tswana, Xhosa, and Northern Sotho—were no longer statistically different from the Zulu. The effects of the homeland controls indicated that the type of homeland played a role: women living in homelands had more children over the previous 5 years than black women in the 'white' RSA, but the effect was greater for women in the independent states[6] than for those in homelands which had not chosen independence. Including homeland variables also provides some controls, albeit imperfect ones, for variations in access to services across these areas. That is, the homeland variables pick up effects of these areas, including differences in service provision, as evidenced by the diminished effects of ethnicity once these variables are introduced. Finally, the male absentee variable was significant and positive, as was the main effect of marriage. Net of other influences, women who have partners that return home once a month or less had more children than others, in spite of presumably lowered coital frequency and reduced exposure to conception.

The multivariate results in general uphold the patterns presented in the bivariate analysis, but show that even after controlling for individual characteristics, ethnicity still has an important relationship to reproduction. The amount of variation

Table 9.6. *Estimated number of children born (prior 5 years) to black South African women, by ethnicity*

Ethnicity	Estimated recent fertility
Zulu	0.72 (ref.)
Pedi/N. Sotho	0.74
Tsonga	0.86***
Ndebele	0.87***
Swazi	0.88***
Xhosa	0.77
S. Sotho	0.78*
Tswana	0.73
Venda	0.80*

Source: 1987–9 SADHS.
*$p<0.05$. **$p<0.01$. ***$p<0.001$.

explained by the models, not quite 13 per cent in the final model, is at the low end of the range of *r*-squared values for reduced-form regression-type models used to examine fertility in other sub-Saharan African settings (Beegle 1999, personal communication). The low value is perhaps not too surprising given the complexity of South African society, though clearly the figure suggests that we need to understand more about the influences shaping reproductive dynamics in the country. The particular contribution of the ethnicity variables to explaining fertility differentials also is not great (about 10 per cent of the explained variation). However, as demonstrated in Table 9.6, estimates of recent fertility vary considerably by ethnicity. That is, controlling for other influences, the effects of ethnicity produce a range of fertility estimates varying from 0.725 for Zulu up to 0.879 for Swazi.

What the multivariate analysis has shown is that the relationship between ethnicity and reproduction cannot be explained solely by socio-economic differences, or differences that might arise from the political strictures of the apartheid economy, such as residence in a homeland or participation in the male labour migration system. It has also suggested that particular relationships of reproduction to social or economic factors may be in part subsumed in the categories used as markers of ethnicity in this analysis. In the next section we examine this broad relationship between ethnicity and reproduction in the light of the qualitative evidence from the case studies.

ANALYSIS: REPRODUCTION AND ETHNIC IDENTITY

The many dimensions of ethnic identity cannot be fully captured in a numeric survey even though these other dimensions may be extremely important in explaining variations in reproductive behaviour across ethnic groups. The quantitative assessment presented patterns of reproductive behaviour by ethnic group and showed the role socio-economic factors played in that relationship; even after controlling for socio-economic status, 'ethnicity' remained a salient category of analysis. In this section, we turn to the ethnographic material to examine the fluidity and experience of ethnic identification, and then show how these two types of data might be wedded to shed light on the relationship of reproduction to ethnicity.

Qualitative data from the two case studies make it clear that ethnic identity, rather than being static in character, develops processually in relation to gendered subjects who are linked to family or household groups in particular ways, and whose view of their own trajectories as bearers of children is closely linked to these family relationships. Inherent in the stereotypes which Sotho and Ndebele sustain of themselves and of each other, in the first case study, are assumptions about the individual and family life course which a person in each of these groups normally follows. Similarly, the wage-earning women's developing sense of themselves as Sotho, in the second case study, contains emerging ideas about the size and shape of the appropriate Sotho family and how it evolves through time. Although the initial findings of these two studies contain no numerical details about fertility specifically, we can use the survey data to show how subjective dimensions of ethnicity, revealed through the case studies, were represented (or not) in the numeric estimates of reproduction or of family-building events surrounding fertility.

THE LIFE COURSE

While the term 'life course' is often used as an analytical concept, we employ it here mainly to illuminate the folk perspectives of self-defined ethnic subjects. In the case of the Sotho and Ndebele living in the single village, members of each group had reciprocally reinforced expectations of the sequence of events in the typical life course of the other. There is a set of processes by which a woman growing up comes to view herself as, for example, a Sotho person, and acquires in the process an associated set of attitudes and behaviours concerning fertility and reproduction. Her ethnic socialization proceeds through learning various customary forms of behaviour and attitudes about womanhood from her mother and from senior women at initiation. But it also owes much to her experiencing of the visible and continually stressed contrast between herself and her Ndebele counterparts, and especially between the reproductive destinies which each is thought to be ordained to fulfil. The stereotypical image of a Sotho woman has her completing her education and setting her sights on a career in teaching or nursing; young Ndebele girls, in contrast, are depicted as leaving school prema-turely in order to attend initiation, working for a few years as a domestic servant in Pretoria, and thereafter starting a family. When a Sotho girl does become a mother, this is expected to occur within the small and compact nuclear family which accords with the image of modernity and Christianity, in contrast to the rambling extended family of the Ndebele with its presumed roots in paganism (James 1990).

Table 9.7. *Number of children born to Sotho and Ndebele within prior 5 years of survey (weighted)*

Age	Sotho	Ndebele
15–19	0.56	0.80
20–24	0.84	0.99
25–29	0.90	0.90
30–34	0.86	0.82
35–39	0.78	0.81
40–49	0.31	0.32
Total	0.73	0.80

Source: 1987–9 SADHS.

Table 9.8. *Per cent of Sotho and Ndebele women currently using contraceptives, by age (weighted)*

Age	Sotho	Ndebele
15–19	26.35	45.42
20–24	39.32	41.40
25–29	37.20	54.56
30–34	34.94	49.60
35–39	29.74	36.16
40–49	19.72	23.62
Total	32.42	42.42

Source: 1987–9 SADHS.

In fact the survey data indicate that Sotho women have fewer children than Ndebele women at most age groups (Table 9.7). The peak of childbearing for Sotho women occurs later than for Ndebele women, consistent with the stereotype of Sotho women staying in school longer and planning smaller families around employment. Interestingly, Sotho maintained lower levels of recent fertility, but also had substantially lower levels of contraceptive use (Table 9.8). This apparent anomaly underscores the real or perceived expectation of the stereotype; even in the absence of contraception, Sotho have lower recent fertility. The results may be rooted in unequal access to resources—Ndebele may have greater access to family planning services than Sotho, accounting for higher levels of use, though this does not address Sotho's higher recent fertility level. The higher levels of use by Ndebele may also be related to the ways in which prior experiences on white farms have shaped their attitudes towards state-run programmes. Ndebele, having lived for several generations on white farms as indentured labourers, developed a close relationship, albeit an unequal one, with Afrikaner farmers, which may have increased their acceptance of state-backed policies. On a more local level, the family planning programme used farmers'

Table 9.9. *Recent fertility (prior 5 years) of Sotho and Ndebele women by frequency of partner's visits home (weighted)*

Partner returns home	Sotho	Ndebele
Every night	0.69	0.82
Weekends	0.77	0.87
Once a month	0.83	0.76
Less often	0.79	N/a

Source: 1987–9 SADHS.

wives to administer contraceptive services to farm workers, which may have proved to be an effective means of promoting acceptance of family planning methods among the Ndebele.

The type of sexual unions formed by women from each group may also partially explain this difference. For example, if Sotho women are more likely to have partners absent for long periods of time, the risk of becoming pregnant, and the need for using contraceptives, may be lower. The in-depth interviews show that the absence of partners is common to both groups of women. Many Sotho and Ndebele women rear children in the virtual absence of men: Sotho women within the context of their matrilocal natal families characterized by uterine links, and Ndebele women within the families they had married into, which were structured along orthodox patrilineal lines (James 1985). The survey data show that Sotho women are, in fact, somewhat more likely to have partners absent than the Ndebele (58 per cent of women in a union had partners that did not return home every night, as opposed to 46 per cent for Ndebele women). However, the absence of men for Sotho is generally positively associated with recent fertility; that association does not appear to hold for the Ndebele, and suggests that the type of migration and its consequences for reproduction differ by group (Table 9.9). In short, the family-building strategies employed by women from both these groups function within the context of high levels of male migration. The consequences for fertility and contraceptive use nonetheless are quite dissimilar. Can this dissimilarity be understood within folk concepts of an appropriate life course? How do concrete conditions—for example, the prolonged absence of partners—shape the definition of 'appropriate'?

These questions cannot be answered directly with our data. However, if we consider once again the contrasting family types, we can see how the typical 'ethnic' life course, underpinned by material circumstances, influences fertility patterns. In the next section we analyse the survey data focusing on the life-course expectations of work and education, but now informed by evidence from the case studies. First, we examine the patterns of work as experienced by different age groups for the samples of Sotho and Ndebele women, each within their respective homelands (Table 9.10).

Table 9.10. *Proportion currently working by age group for Sotho and Ndebele women (in homelands)*

Age	Sotho (Lebowa)	Ndebele (KwaNdebele)
15–19	0.04	0.02
20–24	0.10	0.16
25–29	0.25	0.21
30–34	0.29	0.20
35–39	0.18	0.17
40–49	0.19	0.15
Total	0.17	0.16

Source: 1987–9 SADHS.

Overall, the figures for Ndebele and Sotho support the general pattern for homeland women mentioned in the 'Conceptual and methodological approach' earlier: most depend on male wage earners rather than doing wage work themselves. The table shows a pattern which ties in quite neatly with the expected Ndebele life course. Work for Ndebele women reaches its peak—0.20—in the 25–29 age group, after which it drops gradually to 0.14 for those in the 40–49 bracket. It is considered appropriate for an Ndebele woman to return home from her stint in domestic service towards the end of her twenties, to rely on her husband's (and later, son's) earnings, and begin to manage the household economy. The pattern of work for Sotho women, in contrast, peaks later (in the 30–34 age group) and does not dip so markedly in the 40–49 age group. This pattern is also congruous with cultural expectations. For Sotho women, the low level of employment at early ages may reflect her entry into childbearing soon after she completes her education, and for those who were not supported by male wages, entrance into the labour market in later years.

What these survey data cannot show is the relationship between childbearing, rearing, and family type. The case study findings revealed that Sotho women who are forced by circumstance to work have their children cared for in their absence mostly by female consanguineal relatives (often their mothers) within their own natal families, while the Ndebele women who work for the short space of time dictated by the ethnic life course, or who are constrained by material need to work for a longer period, almost invariably leave their children in the care of female affines—usually their mothers-in-law—within the families into which they had married. Family relationships, then, are directly related to women's ability to seek and maintain employment; these relationships ensure that children will be properly cared for in their mothers' absence. What we cannot systematically evaluate here is how the differing female relationships, through marriage or through natal kin, might have had an impact on both a woman's propensity to work and her desire to limit or space the number of children she had.

Table 9.11. *Completed years of formal schooling by age group for Sotho and Ndebele women (in homelands)*

Age	Sotho (Lebowa)	Ndebele (KwaNdebele)
15–19	6.98	6.08
20–24	7.21	5.58
25–29	6.49	4.77
30–34	5.24	2.31
35–39	3.58	1.66
40–49	2.88	0.64
Total	5.77	3.51

Source: 1987–9 SADHS.

Evidence from the case studies indicates that work for these two groups of women is closely tied to their educational experiences. We present this association using the survey data in tabular form (Table 9.11).

The breakdown of education patterns by age group also revealed contrasts. In the case of both groups, younger cohorts achieve a higher level of education than their older counterparts. Within that general pattern, however, Sotho women at every age level have more years of education than Ndebele women, particularly in the 35–49 age group. This again corresponds with the expected life course, and is partly explained by differential access to schooling while both groups were living on the white farms. Although schooling in this context was universally restricted, there were schools in neighbouring reserve or mission areas to which young Sotho women were more likely than their Ndebele counterparts to be granted access. Ndebele, thought of as quintessentially traditionalist by missionaries and farmers alike, were not offered such opportunities (Delius 1989a).

MARRIAGE AND FAMILY RELATIONSHIPS

These differing preconceptions of the life course include a set of ideas about the sequence of work, education, and the timing of marriage: marriage is, not surprisingly, the event around which these other activities appear to be organized. Despite its apparent centrality as a moment in the expected life course of a woman, however, the ethnographic studies suggest that defining marriage as a relationship between two individuals is too limiting. Marriage is not necessarily the defining feature in influencing reproductive outcomes, since there are other relationships in the household—either in the absence of or alongside marriage—which play a crucial role. We can see from the Sotho/Ndebele village case study, for example, that it is not marriage alone which influences contraception, the timing and spacing of pregnancies, and the subsequent rearing and socializing of children, but rather the broader sets of relationships to which a woman is committed by marriage or its absence.

Bearing this in mind, it is clear that the survey question on marital status is not in itself sufficient to understand the familial context of decisions on childbearing and rearing. It distinguishes only between women who have never lived in any conjugal union and those—whether presently married, informally conjoined, widowed or divorced—who have done so. A different section of the survey asks whether female respondents living with men were doing so in the home of parents or other relatives, but fails to specify whether these were natal or affinal relatives: a detail which, from the Sotho/Ndebele village case, can be seen to be important. If we move on to the migrant-labourer women from the second case study, we find evidence to corroborate a suggestion made by the findings of the first: that what is more crucial than the existence of a conjugal union in shaping families' reproductive patterns is a household's capacity, through a wage earner of whatever sex, to earn a stable income. (Correlating remarkably with information from other regions in South Africa, this case study shows that the key partnerships in which Sotho wage-earning women are involved for the purposes of maintaining their rural homes and rearing children are with their mothers (Izzard 1985; Preston-Whyte 1978) and/or their brothers (Niehaus 1994), rather than those relatively ephemeral ones which they sustain with the fathers of the children.) For the women in this case study, as for many of the Sotho women in the first case study, the effective family unit which decides on issues such as appropriate family size and other fertility-related issues (Lockwood 1996) is natal rather than conjugal in shape and structure.

WAGE EARNING

There is normally an association made between employment and constraints on reproductive behaviour, since pregnancy and childbirth often jeopardize a woman's position at the workplace. For an African woman in a wage-earning position in pre-1990s South Africa, there have been no guarantees that she would be able to return to the same employment should she fall pregnant. This association is borne out by the survey data, which indicates that recent fertility for Sotho women in employment was 0.58 while that for women not working was 0.77. Findings on contraceptive use paralleled these, with 45 per cent of employed Sotho women using contraception while only 29 per cent of those not working did so.

The informal sphere of domestic service in which women in the second case study are employed, however, does allow for somewhat more reproductive flexibility than this picture suggests. Each one of them had children during the course of her career as a domestic worker, and employed specific strategies to diminish the risk of job loss when she did so. One of these was to return to the homeland for a short period of leave and thereafter to leave the baby with her mother; another was to ask her sister or another female relative to act as a substitute domestic servant during the period of the child's infancy and later to return the job; and a third was to give up her job altogether, but then rely on the connections already established by a female relative or friend in order to secure a new position on favourable terms, rather than starting over on the bottom rung of the domestic service 'ladder'. Considerations of work and fertility were thus not mutually exclusive, but accommodated each other within the life course of these migrant women. Whatever constraints might have been placed on fertility by employment were counterbalanced by the imperative to bear and raise children. This imperative, far from being contingent upon involvement in a long-term conjugal relationship and thus signalling dependency upon a man and the second-class ethnic status which is often assumed to accompany this, was essential in the process through which these women came to conceive of themselves as autonomous and self-motivated ethnic subjects (James 1999*b*).

The suggestion that a Sotho identity arises, not as an inevitable result of home language or region, but out of the individual effort of women occupying specific contexts in the urban wage-labour market, raises interesting questions which are not answered by the survey data. The case study shows that when women developed a notion of themselves as Sotho people, one of the bases for the construction of this identity, in addition to a notion of a shared geographical place of origin or 'home', was a particular way of relating to one's family: a unit whose initial definition specified a woman's siblings and parents but later expanded to include her children. The corpus of Sotho law and custom prescribes that a younger son should support his parents when they grow old, and that an older son should eventually assume general responsibility for the broader family. Although sons playing such roles within families are assessed in terms of their approximation to Sotho behaviour, a failure to act as expected would not endanger their ethnic status. For the women in this study, to characterize their wage-earning and supportive roles using the same ethnic adjective required a definitive switch and the active pursuit of an identity rather than its passive acceptance. Being Sotho, as an achieved rather than an ascribed or inborn status, was thus within the reach of even those women who, within the ethnically and linguistically diverse northern Lebowa region, originally spoke a home language other than Sesotho. The transformation of these women into Sotho people was achieved more through socialization within their urban-based singing group than through parental teaching and/or initiation in childhood. The group's members even appointed themselves to initiate a Setswana-speaking novice in her adulthood, prior to her marrying a Sotho man (James 1999*a*). It is in this characterization of Sotho as an achieved status, linked to roles played within the family, that we see considerations of ethnicity and reproductive behaviour dovetailing most precisely. Ethnic or cultural identity, therefore, is not merely linked to a certain type of family and reproductive behaviour but is actually predicated upon it.

ETHNICITY AND ACCESSIBILITY TO FAMILY PLANNING SERVICES

We conclude this section with a note on the relationship between ethnicity and access to clinics and services. As explained earlier in the paper, ethnicity and geography are highly correlated. To the extent that there is a difference in the supply of family planning or health services across areas—particularly homeland areas—of South Africa, there may be a commensurate relationship between ethnicity and reproductive outcomes. The limitations on the data do not allow us to test for this possibility and thus we cannot exclude this as a potentially confounding variable explaining the relationship between ethnicity and fertility. However, two important points emerge from the analysis. First, even though a particular geographic area may have had limited access to family planning and other health services, the evidence brought forth in this analysis suggests that ethnicity, or rather ethnic identity, may still play an important role in the timing and sequence of life events, including reproduction. Following this point, achieving the appropriate timing may be closely related to how that ethnic identity had been constructed—in this case by women. For example, just as earning wages in the modern sector was considered a way to achieve good Sotho womanhood, so too these women may also have concluded that appropriate timing of fertility, also constituting a part of 'Sotho-ness', would be best facilitated by the use of modern contraceptives. In short, while the question of obtaining appropriate contraceptives to achieve fertility goals no doubt was a considerable obstacle for many women, our analysis suggests that ethnicity nonetheless was an important factor shaping both the fertility goals and the means for achieving them.

CONCLUSION

South African reproductive patterns, as expected, vary by ethnicity. Using statistical methods, we estimated the patterns of reproduction by ethnicity and showed how socio-economic factors contributed to the variation. We have argued in this paper, however, that the relationship between ethnicity and reproduction cannot be fully understood by 'controlling' for other factors. In part, covariates used in analyses may constitute the fabric of ethnicity. In part, a categorical definition of ethnicity required for statistical analyses excludes other integral dimensions such as the malleability of ethnicity, or the strength of ethnic identification. The case studies provide evidence supporting these caveats. They show that some aspects of ethnic identification are underpinned by socio-economic factors: Sotho/Ndebele stereo-types reflect historically grounded material differences, for example, and migrant women's pride in Sotho identity is founded upon their status as wage earners for their families. What this indicates is that ethnic differences are not primordial or automatic in nature, but are linked to changing social and material circumstances. Such circumstances alone cannot, however, comprehensively account for the subjective dimensions of ethnic identity and the ways in which it is culturally experienced.

Ethnic identities are subjective, and the ways in which they form and unfold over time, as well as people's own interpretations of these trajectories, carry important implications for reproductive behaviour. Using both quantitative and ethnographic data, we have examined two language/ethnic groups within South Africa—Northern Sotho and Ndebele. The ethnographic data yielded insights into the subjective and culturally constructed nature of ethnic identity and suggest that there is an ethnically specific expectation of the pattern of events within a woman's life, including marriage, work, education, and fertility. We also considered the ways in which these patterns are supported by the survey data. Each group sustains firmly held beliefs about itself and the other, and the actual levels of fertility reflect those stereotypes. Life-course events such as education, duration of schooling, the extent and type of labour force participation for women, and marriage varied markedly by ethnic group. Once the survey data had alerted us to the broad associations between each of these events and ethnic affiliation, the ethnographic evidence indicated that its discrete categories required further refinement. Each association between life events and reproductive behaviours is set within a broader context of familial associations which in turn affects the ongoing process of ethnic identification. For example, while the strong negative association between women's labour force participation and fertility is upheld by the quantitative data, the ethnographic evidence demonstrates how working women are able to mobilize family and other relationships to ensure continued employment after the birth of a child. The compatibility of work and fertility as specified by a given ethnic life course is thus made possible through these broader relationships.

The paper also has implications for theorizing ethnicity–fertility relationships in a broader context: relationships assuming heightened demographic importance with the emergence of strong ethnic and religious movements in many parts of the world (Amin *et al.* 1996; Anderson and Silver 1995; Lutz *et al.* 1994; Aghajanian 1991). In particular, research in other parts of sub-Saharan Africa suggests that a reification of tradition is often promoted by African men attempting to sustain or reassert their positions in the household, in part through high levels of fertility, and that the assertion or resurgence into daily life of ethnic primordialism is likely to result in female subordination, associated with a decline in women's autonomy and a subsequent increase in fertility (Wilson 1982; MacGaffey 1986). However, local definitions of what it means to be a member of a particular group in fact may, as shown here, come to include many 'modern' dimensions, highlighting female autonomy and solidarity rather than privileging patriarchal and pronatalist beliefs. Our analysis indicates how women have reshaped their own versions of ethnic identities, which enable them more effectively to pursue strategies of independence. By balancing the imperative to earn a wage as well as bear and rear children, they are able to influence the formation of their families.

Bringing together divergent sources of data has provided a number of insights not attainable through independent analysis. The process has not been without its limitations, but these have been instructive in identifying further research questions and design strategies. For example, this study has suggested that men's migration plays a decisive role in reproductive outcomes, perhaps not in terms of a conjugal bond, but because of the ways in which women cope with the absence or lack of partners, through wage-earning activities or by establishing households on the basis of sibling or parental relationships. The study has also shown how the construction of ethnic identities by women is often closely tied to reproduction, yet these identities can be reshaped to accommodate changing circumstances. If one were to conduct research, for example, focused on the way in which teens interpret their own identities with respect to adolescent pregnancy, or on the way in which women understand the advent of HIV/AIDs—of increasing significance in the 'new' South Africa—in their homes and communities, these links between reproduction and ethnic, or indeed other, subjective forms of identification could provide specific insights into appropriate programme formation and intervention design for particular reproductive issues. Understanding the way in which the enforced and objective dimensions interact with the subjective and fluid dimensions of ethnic identification should be—and can become—central to policy and programme formation.

Notes

The contributions of the Centre for Science Development, South Africa, are hereby acknowledged. Opinions expressed are those of the authors alone.

1. The sampling methodology followed for each of the 14 samples is documented and critically assessed in Kaufman (1997). The evaluation of field reports, sampling notes, and from the data themselves indicate that although some dimensions of the study were carried out in a less than ideal manner, overall, it adhered to recognized survey methodological principles. The data produce distributions and tendencies which resemble those in the USAID/Macro DHS samples for other countries in the region, and no systematic bias of sampling across the surveys was detected.

2. The official terms used to describe the Sotho language and culture of the former Lebowa were 'Pedi' or 'Northern Sotho' and are the labels used in the nationally based tables in this paper. However, most people speaking the language and espousing the cultural ways of life which are thought of as accompanying it, call it simply 'Sesotho' (the noun) or use the adjective 'Sotho' to qualify. This usage does not distinguish it from the 'Southern Sotho' spoken in the small independent country of Lesotho and the former homeland of Qwaqwa, and adjacent regions, but since the ethnographic material here refers only to Lebowa we will retain the folk usage.

3. We also consider current use of modern contraception. The results of those analyses are not reported here, but are analogous to the findings for recent fertility.

4. The case of the Xhosa in Table 9.4 deserves special mention. The Xhosa are supposed to be of the same ethnic group, but live in two different homelands. The Ciskei benefited from a government that was in favour of family planning and worked closely with the national family planning programme. The Transkei had a government particularly hostile to family planning. The marked differences in reproductive patterns across the two homelands are no doubt reflective of the difference in political will. In fact, it is likely that although linguistically the Xhosa are homogeneous, Xhosa living in each homeland area have quite distinct identities—a construction of identity transpiring over time and imbued with apartheid policies. Unfortunately, for the Xhosas not living in a homeland, no information about their geographic origins is provided in the data to explore these relationships further.

5. Homeland areas are highly homogeneous with respect to language, and discerning the effects of the homeland (as an indicator for the structural conditions found there) from

the effects of ethnicity (representing particular practices or beliefs of a dominant group of a homeland) is methodologically and conceptually complex. In multivariate analyses, ethnicity variables and variables representing each of the homelands cannot be included in the same model because of the substantial overlap of effects. In this analysis, we control only for the type of homeland, self-governing territory or independent state.

6. Provincial controls did not produce significant results in any model of recent fertility, indicating minimal variation in black recent fertility in the 'white' RSA. The results of these models are not shown here.

References

Aghajanian, A. (1991), 'Population change in Iran, 1966–86: A stalled demographic transition?', *Population Development Review*, 17: 703–15.

Amin, S., Diamond, I., and Steele, F. (1996). 'Contraception and religious practice in Bangladesh.' Research Division Working Paper No. 83. New York: The Population Council.

Anderson, B. (1986), 'Regional and cultural factors in the decline of marital fertility in Western Europe', in A. J. Coale and S. C. Watkins (eds.), *The Decline of Fertility in Europe*, Princeton: Princeton University Press.

Anderson, B. A., and Silver, B. (1995), 'Population redistribution and the ethnic balance in Transcaucasia', Research Report No. 95-330, University of Michigan, Ann Arbor: Population Studies Center.

Beegle, K. (1999), Personal communication in reference to table containing adjusted and unadjusted *R*-squared values for fertility equations. DHS data, sub-Saharan African countries.

Brown, B. B. (1987), 'Facing the "Black Peril": The politics of population control in South Africa', *Journal of Southern African Studies*, 13: 256–73.

Chimere-Dan, O. (1993), 'Racial patterns of fertility decline in South Africa', in International Population Conference, Montreal 1993, 24 August–1 September, Vol. 1. Liége: International Union for the Scientific Study of Population.

—— (1997), 'Recent fertility patterns and population policy in South Africa', *Development Southern Africa* 14 (1): 1–20.

Coplan, D. (1987), 'Eloquent knowledge: Lesotho migrants' songs and the anthropology of experience', *American Ethnologist*, 14: 413–33.

Delius, P. (1989a), 'The Ndzundza Ndebele: Indenture and the making of ethnic identity', in P. Bonner, I. Hofmeyr, D. James, and T. Lodge (eds.), *Holding Their Ground: Class, Locality and Culture in 19th and 20th Century South Africa*, Johannesburg: Ravan Press and Wits University Press.

Delius, P. (1989b), 'Sebatakgomo: Migrant Organisation, the ANC and the Sekhukhuneland Revolt', *Journal of Southern African Studies*, 15: 581–615.

Dubow, S. (1994), 'Ethnic euphemisms and racial echoes', *Journal of Southern African Studies*, 20: 355–70.

Goldscheider, C., and Uhlenberg, P. H. (1969), 'Minority-group Status and Fertility', *American Journal of Sociology*, 74: 361–72.

Goodkind, D. (1995), 'The significance of demographic triviality: Minority status and zodiacal fertility timing among chinese malaysians', *Population Studies*, 49: 45–55.

Guilkey, D. K. (1992), 'Community effects in demographic and health survey data', Working Paper, Columbia, MD: IRD/Macro.

Guy, J., and Thabane, M. (1991), 'Basotho miners, ethnicity and workers' strategies', in I. Brandell (ed.), *Workers in Third-World Industrialization*, London: Macmillan.

Handwerker, W. P. (ed.) (1986), *Culture and Reproduction: An Anthropological Critique of Demographic Transition Theory*, Boulder: Westview Press.

Harries, P. (1989), 'Exclusion, classification and internal colonialism: The emergence of ethnicity among the Tsonga-speakers of South Africa', in L. Vail (ed.), *The Creation of Tribalism in Southern Africa*, London: James Currey.

Institute for Resource Development (IRD) (1990), An Assessment of DHS-I Data Quality, DHS methodological reports 1 and 2, Columbia, MD: Institute for Resource Development/Macro Systems, Inc.

Izzard, W. (1985), 'Migrants and mothers: Case-studies from Botswana', *Journal of Southern African Studies*, 11: 258–80.

James, D. (1985), 'Family and household in a Lebowa village', *African Studies*, 44 (2): 159–87.

—— (1987), 'Kinship and land in an inter-ethnic community', Unpublished MA dissertation, Department of Social Anthropology, University of the Witwatersrand, Johannesburg.

—— (1990), 'A question of ethnicity. Ndzundza Ndebele in a Lebowa village', *Journal of Southern African Studies*, 16 (1): 33–54.

—— (1999a), 'Bagagešu/those of my home: migrancy, gender and ethnicity in the Northern Province, South Africa', *American Ethnologist*, 26 (1): 69–88.

—— (1999b), *Songs of the Women Migrants: Performance and Identity in South Africa*, Edinburgh: International Africa Institute and Edinburgh University Press.

Kaufman, C. E. (1997), '1987–89 South African Demographic and Health Survey: Methodology and data quality', Research Report No. 97-395, University of Michigan, Ann Arbor: Population Studies Center.

—— (1998), 'Contraceptive use in South Africa under apartheid', *Demography*, 35 (4): 421–34.

Lesthaeghe, R. J. (1977), *The Decline of Belgian Fertility, 1800–1970*, Princeton: Princeton University Press.

Lockwood, M. (1996), 'Institutional and cultural determinants of demand for reproductive health services in sub-Saharan Africa'. Unpublished paper.

Lutz, W., Scherbov, S., and Volkov, A., (eds.) (1994), *Demographic Trends and Patterns in the Soviet Union before 1991*, New York: Routledge.

MacGaffey, J. (1986), 'Women and class formation in a dependent economy: Kisangani Entrepreneurs', in C. Robertson and I. Berger (eds.), *Women and Class in Africa*, New York: Africana Publishing Company.

Marks, S., and Rathbone, R. (1982), 'Introduction', in S. Marks and R. Rathbone (eds.), *Industrialisation and Social Change in South Africa*, London: Longman.

Mostert, W. P. (1990), 'Recent trends in fertility in South Africa', in W. P. Mostert and J. M. Lötter (eds.), *South Africa's Demographic Future*, Pretoria: Human Sciences Research Council.

Niehaus, I. (1994), 'Disharmonious spouses and harmonious siblings: Conceptualizing household formation among urban residents in Qwaqwa, South Africa', *African Studies*, 53 (1): 115–56.

Preston-Whyte, E. (1978), 'Families without marriage: A Zulu case study', in J. Argyle and E. Preston-Whyte (eds.), *Social System and Tradition in Southern Africa: Essays in Honour of Eileen Krige*, Cape Town: Oxford University Press.

Sai, F., Rees, H., and McGarry, S. (1993), 'Reproductive Health and Family Planning Consultancy Report: National Review and Recommendations (Final Report)', Commission of the European Communities.

220 *Carol E. Kaufman and Deborah James*

Sharp, J. (1980), 'Can We Study Ethnicity? A Critique of Fields of Study in South African Anthropology', *Social Dynamics* 6 (1): 1–16.

Spiegel, A. D. (1991), 'Polygyny as myth: Understanding extramarital relations in Lesotho', in A. D. Spiegel, and P. A. McAllister (eds.), *Tradition and Transition in Southern Africa: Festschrift for Philip and Iona Mayer*, Vol. 50, *African Studies* Special Fiftieth Anniversary.

South African Demographic and Health Survey (SADHS), Annual Reports, various years (1968–1993), Pretoria: Government Printers.

Stockton, N. (1995), Chief Executive Director, Women's Bureau of South Africa, Former Director of South African Family Planning Services. Interview with first author, Pretoria, October 24, 27.

Vail, L. (1989), 'Introduction: Ethnicity in Southern African history', in L. Vail (ed.), *The Creation of Tribalism in Southern Africa*, London: James Currey.

Webster, D. (1991), 'Abafazi bathonga bafihlakala: Ethnicity and gender in a Kwazulu border community', in A. D. Spiegel and P. A. McAllister (eds.), *Tradition and Transition in Southern Africa: Festschrift for Philip and Iona Mayer*, Vol. 50, *African Studies* Special Fiftieth Anniversary.

Wilson, F. R. (1982), 'Reinventing the past and circumscribing the future: Authenticité and the negative image of women's work in Zaire', in E. G. Bay (ed.), *Women and Work in Africa*, Boulder: Westview Press.

10

Critical Perspectives: The Feminist Critique of Medicine, Medicalization, and the Making of Breast Implant Policy

NORA JACOBSON

The breast implant story is of interest in its own right, but it is important because of what it illustrates about broader issues of women's health policy making. In this section I use two critical perspectives—the feminist critique of medicine and medicalization—to examine the history of US policy toward breast implants. I focus on several tensions that emerge in the breast implant story: abuse and neglect, coercion and collaboration, autonomous choice and action that is always circumscribed by a social context.

THE FEMINIST CRITIQUE OF MEDICINE: MEDICALIZATION AS ABUSE

Among the contributions of the second wave of the feminist movement was a technique called consciousness raising, a practice through which women sought to see the effect of patriarchy in their own lives. The goal of consciousness raising was to politicize the quotidian events and interactions that every woman thought only she had experienced (a goal made explicit in the slogan of the women's movement—the personal is political). What was most familiar often was scrutinized most closely: women examined (literally and figuratively) their own bodies and, in their roles as patients and care-givers, their interactions with the medical system.

When the feminist critique of medicine took shape in the early 1970s, it reflected this process of politicizing the personal. Women's stories of unpleasant or horrific treatment by doctors and medical institutions were understood in the context of patriarchy, a system in which women were subordinated to male power. A sociological study of the women's health movement characterized the central tenet of the critique this way: 'the very organization of the health care system reflects and perpetuates the social ideology of women as sex objects and reproductive organs' (Ruzek 1978, p. 11). The critique explained many levels of experience: middle-class women's anger at being patronized by their physicians; the paucity of female medical practitioners; the overprescription of psychotropic medication for women; the high rates of caesarean section among poor women of colour; and the revelations about the dangers of contraceptives like the Dalkon Shield and the pill. All could be understood as forms of oppression and misogynistic abuse.

This early feminist critique identified the medicalization of women's experience as part of this pattern of abuse. Medicalization is the 'process whereby more and more of everyday life has come under medical domination, influence and supervision' (Zola quoted in Conrad 1992, p. 209). Medicalization theory examines the processes and implications of this shift of responsibility. One conceptualization of medicalization focuses on its use in the social construction of deviance: behaviour which historically has been considered deviant—for example, alcoholism or children's misbehaviour—increasingly has been reconceptualized as sickness and construed under the tenets of the biomedical paradigm (Conrad and Schneider 1992). A second strand of medicalization theory—the version extant in the feminist critique of medicine—argues that medicalization also serves to create medical problems out of what before had been normal human experiences—for example, childbirth and overweight (Reissman 1983) and impotence (Tiefer 1986).

Medicalization operates on three levels: the conceptual, the institutional, and the interactional:

> On the conceptual level a medical vocabulary (or model) is used to 'order' or define the problem at hand . . . . On the institutional level, organizations may adopt a medical approach to treating a particular problem in which the organization specializes . . . . On the interactional level . . . . [m]edicalization occurs . . . as part of doctor–patient interaction, when a physician defines a problem as medical (i.e., gives a medical diagnosis) or treats a 'social' problem with a medical form of treatment. (Conrad 1992, p. 210)

Conrad and Schneider (1992) propose a general model for the process of medicalization. It begins with 'prospecting'. At some point speculation about the possible medical/biological basis of a behaviour or phenomenon begins to appear in medical journals or is raised at professional meetings. In the next stage, medical and non-medical interests engage in claims making about the behaviour or phenomenon. Conrad and Schneider note the dual meaning of 'claim': a claim may be an assertion as to the reality of a situation, or a marker designating ownership. The medical right to ownership of the behaviour is secured in the next stage—legitimization—when official recognition is granted to the medical definition. Finally, the medical designation is institutionalized, codified in law and bureaucratic regulation.

Alternative models of medicalization look at agency. Catherine Kohler Riessman (1983) re-theorizes medicalization as an 'interactional', or collaborative, process. Writing about the medicalization of several women's health issues, Riessman finds the explanation for its success in such areas as childbirth and PMS in the shared interests of physicians and affluent women. She argues that 'physicians seek to medicalize experience because of their specific beliefs and economic interests . . . .Women collaborate . . . because of their own needs and motives, which in turn grow out of the class-specific nature of their subordination.' (Riessman 1983, p. 191).

One effect of medicalizing a deviant behaviour is to shift the societal response from punishment or condemnation to treatment. Viewed positively, such a response is likely to be more humane than when a behaviour is criminalized. More pessimistically, however, the general effect of medicalization is to increase social control over individuals and to make physicians and other medical personnel the agents of this control. Such expansion results in a decontextualization of social problems, and individuals lose the ability to understand and to solve these problems (Illich 1976; Riessman 1983; Conrad and Schneider 1992).

In the feminist analysis of abuse through medicalization, the remedy was an assertion of self-determination. The goal of the women's health movement was to demystify medicine and increase women's autonomy in their dealings with the medical system—to stop them being passive 'patients' and make them informed 'consumers' who could choose from amongst a range of options, including self-help (a strategy exemplified by the *Our Bodies, Ourselves* series produced by the Boston Women's Health Book Collective). By rejecting medical definitions and treatments, women established control over their own lives and bodies. At the same time, they challenged these medical definitions, asking, for example, whether a housewife's complaints of dissatisfaction and vague physical symptoms constituted a disease (to be treated with psychotropic medication) or were a sign of the constraining nature of her life. Knowledge and autonomous action became forms of resistance, strategies for reducing patriarchal control (Ruzek 1978).

THE FEMINIST CRITIQUE OF MEDICINE: NEGLECT OF WOMEN'S HEALTH

In the 1980s, however, the form of the feminist critique began to change. Women were well represented in the medical profession and had attained positions of influence in other important institutions in society. Self-help groups had evolved into powerful political lobbies. While academic feminists, heavily influenced by the work of Foucault, continued to focus on issues of power in the medical system, mainstream, activist feminists shifted their emphasis. The effort to turn women from patients to consumers had the side effect of making medicine a commodity (Kay 1994). The right to health, which earlier had been understood as a right to be free of medical abuse (to be healthy *in spite of* organized medicine), was transformed: increasingly, it was understood as a right to research on and high-tech intervention for ailments particular to women. The abuse critique had become a critique of neglect.

This critique was more sophisticated than the earlier critique of abuse. Instead of blaming inchoate 'patriarchy' and turning all women into potential victims, it examined the processes of sexism in medicine: how sex and gender biases affected researchers' choice of problems to study, as well as their variables and measurement instruments. Its central tenet was a methodological criticism: that women's health had been ignored—but for women's reproductive health—because women had been assumed to be just like men (Rosser 1994; Dan *et al.* 1994). The exemplar of this argument was not the Dalkon Shield, but the realization that advances like the aspirin-a-day advice were based only on studies of men.

From the beginning, this critique worked within the system. It called not for a strategic demedicalization of women's health, but for a place for women and women's health in the medical establishment. The outcome was not *Our Bodies, Ourselves*, but proposals for a new women's health specialty, offices of women's health in all of the divisions of the US government dealing with health and health research, and legislation mandating the allocation of funds for women's health research (Sechzer *et al.* 1994).

What was lost is subtle. The abuse critique, strident as it was, suggested a real and deep examination of the role of medicine in women's lives—an examination that, in its activist roots, promised real change. It questioned the ways in which women were turning to medicine to heal what were largely social problems. It challenged inequities based on race and income. It prompted questions about power. The idea of autonomy was proposed largely as a corrective to abuses of power and was understood to be grounded in collective analysis and action. In contrast, the neglect critique has focused on the issue of parity. In seeking to equalize attention to (and financing of) women's and men's health, it has been diverted from any deep questioning of medicine as a cultural institution. While the neglect critique has been successful at collective action, it has done so under a definition of autonomy—the 'right to choose'—that discounts any challenge to the socially constructed and value-laden nature of illness and disease.

For example, in the US a recent women's health policy issue has been the phenomenon of 'drive through' deliveries, or the effort by managed care organizations to reduce hospital stays after uncomplicated childbirth to a day (24 hours) or less. Once publicized, the phenomenon aroused general indignation. The policy response was a series of State laws and a Federal law to forbid this practice and mandate longer minimum stays. The policy endorses a medicalized view of childbirth and avoids broader questions about motherhood and the medical system: isn't the problem really a lack of social support for the mother, not where she spends her 24th through 48th hours post-partum? Shouldn't policy makers be directing their efforts at reforming a profit-driven health care system? There is little political will to confront questions that might threaten the status quo.

SILICONE BREAST IMPLANTS: ABUSE OR NEGLECT?

Breasts are an obsession, signifiers of cultural ideals about femininity (Yalom 1997). In the history of breast implants we see a link between these cultural conceptions of femininity and the role played in women's lives by medicine as a social institution. We may read that history as either one of abuse or as one of neglect.

Many feminist authors have used the traditional—coercion—model of medicalization to explain the cultural phenomena of cosmetic surgery and breast implants. Arguing that plastic surgery is an intervention justified by the medicalization of appearance, these authors trace how variation in the size and shape of the female body has been characterized as cosmetic imperfection, and then as a medical problem (Spitzack 1988; Morgan 1991; Dull and West 1991; Balsamo 1993; Sprague Zones 1992; Coco 1994). This approach construes cosmetic surgery as a phenomenon of power, a mode of gender normalization, and is heavily influenced by the Foucauldian concept of 'discipline' (Foucault 1977). It argues against the possibility of women making truly autonomous choices for cosmetic surgery. Rather, these 'choices' are to be viewed as false consciousness, as instances of coercion.

An alternative feminist perspective, however, rejects this formulation. Best exemplified in the work of Kathy Davis (1995), this approach, like Riessman's model of collaboration, looks for the ways in which women's interests are served by the medicalization of appearance. In so doing, it grants them the opportunity for real agency. Davis argues that cosmetic surgery serves as a currency of cultural and psychological negotiation, as an 'intervention in identity'. For the individual woman, cosmetic surgery 'can open up the possibility to renegotiate her relationship to her body and construct a different sense of self. In this way it intervenes in the disempowering tension of Western feminine embodiment—the entrapment of objectification.' (Davis 1995, p. 113).

There is a coercive version of the history of breast implants, as well as a collaborative one. Having a nascent technology—sponge implants—plastic surgeons set out to increase the legitimacy of their work (and expand the market for their services) by promoting implants as the treatment for several newly discovered 'diseases' of the body and mind: 'hypomastia', 'post-mastectomy syndrome', and 'fibrocystic breast disease'. Each of these 'diseases' was grounded in actual physical conditions, but the meanings of these conditions were fluid, open to culturally constructed negotiation. The language of justification for surgery featured the creation of a psychological need for the devices. Thus, plastic surgeons could be said to be treating disease, rather than catering to vanity. Insurance companies and national health plans would pick up at least some of the charges. Women's reliance on the medical profession would grow.

Alternatively, one can read this history as one of answered demand. Women endured psychological suffering because of anomalies of appearance (suffering caused, as Riessman would argue, by the 'class-specific nature of their subordination'): their clothes did not fit, they were always self-conscious, they felt less than feminine. Some went to extremes, mutilating their bodies with unsafe injections and bizarre surgeries. 'Crying need'—in an interview near the end of his life, W. John Pangman, one of the originators of sponge implants, cited a 'crying need' for implants as the impetus for his early work—met technological ingenuity. Plastic surgeons responded to the suffering by developing implants, then obliged demand by improving them. Many women were happier, more contented with their bodies.

In promoting implants, plastic surgeons were providing education, a public service for women wishing their own 'interventions in identity'.

A recent policy development helps to illustrate the collaboration model. Legislation introduced in Congress in 1997 attempted to establish a 'right' to reconstructive breast surgery after mastectomy for women covered by health insurance by characterizing the procedure as medically necessary for reasons of self-esteem. While this may be the apotheosis of the medicalization of appearance—the codification stage described by Conrad and Schneider (1992)—and plastic surgeons have been actively promoting it, politicians have been responsive because the bill also has strong support from the politically powerful breast cancer lobby. If the bill succeeds, it will be because of this group; policy makers may be cynical about the motives of the plastic surgeons, but they are loathe to do anything that may be interpreted as being indifferent to women's health, and many women are vocal that this is what they want.

In the FDA controversy, the critique of abuse and the critique of neglect were represented by two highly visible groups of women with implants. The 'silicone victims' were women claiming to have been harmed by their implants. Their claims were of abuse, how the lies of doctors and manufacturers had caused their suffering. The 'implant advocates' were, by and large, pleased with their implants. While some may have experienced what they characterized as 'minor problems', they either attributed them to aging or found them an acceptable trade-off for having implants. While these women sometimes expressed concern about the lack of formal testing of implants, their central argument was that access to implants should not be restricted. To do so, they asserted, would be to ignore a specific women's health need and to constrain an adult woman's autonomy, her 'right to choose' implants, for whatever reason.

Although safety was the most visible issue in the controversy over the FDA's regulation of breast implants, the conceptualization of the need for implants was equally important. Because the FDA's decision-making calculus included a weighing of risk and benefit, the agency's understanding of the need for implants—and the devices' ability to satisfy that need—were highly relevant. In its policy determination, the FDA showed the influence of the neglect critique and an acceptance of a medicalized need for implants. There was little challenge to the reality of the 'diseases' for which implants were the treatment. By declining to press the question of women's motivations for seeking implants, the panel, quite self-consciously, endorsed the view that women were agents in the choice. Indeed, each FDA panel found that there was a 'public health need' for the devices. Ultimately, the FDA's policy toward implants—their requirement that manufacturers conduct strictly controlled clinical trials—legitimized the existence of these diseases. In focusing its ruling on the performance of further studies, the FDA implicitly endorsed the view that the problem with implants was one of neglect, and that the important questions about implants were those that could be answered by clinical trials. It declined to question the personal politics of the need for implants.

IMPLICATIONS FOR THE STUDY OF REPRODUCTIVE
HEALTH IN DEVELOPING COUNTRIES

As I have explored, the feminist critique of medicine argues for the abuse or neglect of women by the medical system. The abuser or neglecter is patriarchy—in the earlier critique—or systemic gender bias—in the more recent version. One might also, however, argue for a parallel metaphor: the West as abusive and neglectful in its relationships with the less developed nations. The West dumps technology or products that have been deemed unsafe for use at home. Similarly, the West dumps the biomedical model, a model that is often incongruent with local illness concepts. (Much qualitative health research in developing countries is devoted to understanding these local beliefs so as to find ways in which to make biomedical ideas more palatable to the 'locals'.) The West funds research to study what it deems problems, at times ignoring the indigenous population's own definitions of those, or other, problems. In addition, the West often medicalizes what are, at root, social problems (Hartmann 1993).

A second aspect of the breast implant story with relevance for reproductive health research is the tension it reveals between choice and coercion in women's decisions about what to do with their bodies. The defenders of breast implants realized early on that their best strategy for keeping the devices available was to frame the controversy as a battle between intrusive, patronizing government and a woman's 'right to choose'—a phrase meant to resonate with the language of the abortion rights movement—implants. The rhetoric of rights made any serious discussion of women's motivations for wanting implants impossible. Attempts to raise the question of motivation were quickly foiled by accusations of being morally judgemental and patronizing. Thus, the issue of need remained unexamined. While deeply felt, this need was still socially constructed: a cultural conception of the nature of beauty and femininity; a medical 'diagnosis' of physical variation as disease. But does that imply that women should not have been allowed to make a decision to get implants?

Women (all of us) are, both literally and figuratively, socially constructed. The language of choice fails to consider the power that social ideals have over an individual. To speak of autonomous choice at times seems almost disingenuous. I would here draw a parallel between breast implants and practices like female genital mutilation and the deployment of prenatal testing for the purposes of sex selection, used in some developing countries and roundly condemned by most outsiders. Should we view women who 'choose' these practices as autonomous decision makers or victims of coercion? What are the implications—political and practical—of either construction? Can we reject the practice and still accept the individual's 'right' to choose it? These are hard questions and I can do no more than raise them.

A final implication is methodological. I would like to end with a plea for recognition of the utility of historical research within the study of health and illness. As I intimated earlier, this kind of analysis amounts to an ethnography of the powerful. As with the behaviour of individuals, policy does not emerge in a vacuum. The knowledge and ideas that inform it have a social and historical context (Skocpol and Rueschemeyer 1996). We can begin to understand this context, and thus the decisions that are situated in it, when we immerse ourselves in the past.

References

Balsamo, A. (1993), 'On the cutting edge: Cosmetic surgery and the technological production of the gendered body', *Camera Obscura*, 28: 207–37.

Coco, L. (1994), 'Silicone breast implants in America: A choice of the "Official Breast?", *Kroeber Anthropological Society Papers*, 77: 103–32.

Conrad, P., and Schneider, J. W. (1992), *Deviance and Medicalization: From Badness to Sickness*, Philadelphia: Temple University Press.

—— (1992), 'Medicalization and social control', *Annual Review of Sociology*, 94: 209–32.

Dan, A. J., Jonikas, J. A., and Ford, Z. L. (1994), 'Epilogue: An invitation', in Dan, Jonikas, and Ford (eds.), *Reframing Women's Health: Multidisciplinary Research and Practice*, Thousand Oaks, California: Sage Publications.

Davis, K. (1995), *Reshaping the Female Body: The Dilemma of Cosmetic Surgery*, New York: Routledge.

Dull, D., and West, C. (1991), 'Accounting for cosmetic surgery: The accomplishment of gender', *Social Problems*, 38 (1): 54–70.

Foucault, M. (1977), *Discipline and Punish: The Birth of the Prison*, translated by Alan Sheridan, New York: Pantheon Books.

Food and Drug Administration (1982), 'General and plastic surgery devices: General provisions and classifications of 54 devices', *Federal Register*, 47 (12).

Hartmann, B. (1993), 'The impact of population control policies on health policy in Bangladesh', in M. Turshen and B. Holcomb (eds.), *Women's Lives and Public Policy: The International Experience*, Westport, Connecticut: Greenwood Press.

Illich, I. (1976), *Medical Nemesis: The Expropriation of Health*, New York: Pantheon Books.

'Is the FDA Protecting Patients from the Dangers of Silicone Breast Implants?' Hearing Before the Human Resources and Intergovernmental Relations Subcommittee of the Committee on Government Operations. House of Representatives 101st Cong. 2nd sess., December 18, 1990, Washington, DC: US Printing Office.

Kay, B. J. (1994), 'The commodification of women's health: The new women's health centers', in N. F. McKenzie (ed.), *Beyond Crisis: Confronting Health Care in the United States*, New York: Meridian.

Morgan, K. P. (1991), 'Women and the knife: Cosmetic surgery and the colonization of women's bodies', *Hypatia*, 6 (3): 25–53.

Riessman, C. K. (1983), 'Women and medicalization: A new perspective', *Social Policy*, 14: 3–18.

Rosser, S. V. (1994), 'Gender bias in clinical research: The difference it makes', in A. J. Dan, J. A. Jonikas, and Z. L. Ford (eds.), *Reframing Women's Health: Multidisciplinary Research and Practice*, Thousand Oaks, California: Sage Publications.

Ruzek, S. B. (1978), *The Women's Health Movement: Feminist Alternatives to Medical Control*, New York: Praeger Publishers.

Sechzer, J. A., Griffin, A., and Pfafflin, S. M. (eds.) (1994), *Forging a Women's Health Agenda: Policy Issues for the 1990s*, New York: New York Academy of Sciences.

Skocpol, T., and Rueschemeyer, D. (1996), 'Introduction', in Rueschemeyer and Skocpol (eds.), *States, Social Knowledge, and the Origins of Modern Social Policies*, Princeton, New Jersey: Princeton University Press.

Spitzack, C. (1988), 'The confession mirror: Plastic images for surgery', *Canadian Journal of Political and Social Theory*, XII (1–2): 38–50.

Tiefer, L. (1986), 'In pursuit of the perfect penis', *American Behavioral Scientist*, 29 (5): 579–99.

Yalom, M. (1997), *A History of the Breast*, New York: Knopf.

Zones, J. S. (1992), 'The political and social context of silicone breast implant use in the United States', *Journal of Long-Term Effects of Medical Implants*, 1 (3): 225–41.

PART III

CULTURE, REPRODUCTION, AND RIGHTS

11

Two Cultural Approaches for Understanding the Reproductive Health Consequences of Marital Violence in an Indian Area of Mexico

SOLEDAD GONZÁLEZ MONTES

VIOLENCE AGAINST WOMEN, A SOCIAL PROBLEM WITH CONSEQUENCES FOR REPRODUCTIVE HEALTH

In 1993 the United Nations' World Health Organization produced a broad definition of violence against women as: 'Any act based on gender, that results or can result in physical, sexual or psychological damage, or suffering to the woman, including coercion or arbitrary deprivation of liberty, occurring in private or public life.' Research done during the last two decades has shown the marital relationship to be the most frequent—but certainly not the only—context in which violence against women occurs. It has dismissed the notion that conjugal violence is the result of individual pathology, stressing its socio-cultural basis, bringing to light the way gender identities and relations are shared by familial and societal contexts where male control and authority are asserted in the family and society at large (Counts et al.).[1] While physical forms of violence exerted against wives are the most obvious and can have immediate health consequences, such as bodily injuries or— in the case of pregnant women—miscarriages and low-birth-weight babies (Newberger et al. 1992; Gielen et al. 1994), recent research is exploring the possible long-term effects of both physical and psychological/emotional violence upon the mental and physical health of women (Dixon-Mueller 1993; Heise et al. 1994, 1995).

In Mexico, organizations working with women on various issues find that one of the problems women consistently report is the violence husbands exert against them. Research examining the prevalence of different forms of violence against women is still scarce, but available surveys indicate a high prevalence: A random-sample survey in the State of Jalisco found that 57 per cent of 427 women from the city of Guadalajara, and 44 per cent of 1,163 women from a rural area, had suffered some form of violence, mostly from their husbands (Ramírez and Uribe-Vázquez 1993). In the northern city of Monterrey, out of a total of 1,064 ever-married women aged 15 or older, 46 per cent reported having suffered some form of spousal violence and almost one-third of these had suffered intense forms of abuse (Granados *et al.* 1997). A survey of 110 pregnant women who delivered at the public hospital of Cuernavaca city found that 33.5 per cent had suffered violence during pregnancy. These women had three times more complications during delivery than the non-battered women, and four times greater risk of having babies with low birth weight (Valdez and Sanín 1996).

The demand for services to help women who experience violence in a conjugal relation has risen in recent years, and a growing number of non-governmental organizations now specialize in providing legal, medical, and psychological support to battered and raped women. Together with the broader women's movement in Mexico they have been relatively successful in obtaining some changes in the legal system, including the creation in several large cities of government-sponsored agencies which specialize in dealing with cases of sexual abuse and battery (Riquer *et al.* 1996). Some of these organizations are now beginning to promote the involvement of the public health system since: 'The health care system is well placed to identify and refer victims of violence. It is the only public institution likely to interact with all women at some point in their lives—as they seek contraception, give birth, or seek care for their children . . .' (Heise *et al.* 1994, pp. 33–4).

A first step to initiate programmes which could respond to violence against women could be based on health providers identifying and registering cases of violence against their female patients. This would mean a recognition of the problem and would set in place a mechanism for generating the information essential to measure prevalence and consequences. For women it means acknowledging an important source of distress, with relevance for many aspects of their health and well-being. But what are the difficulties in attempting to involve health care providers? Are doctors aware of ongoing violence? Do they consider it a health risk for women, and, if so, in what ways? How do they see their own role in dealing with violence? What are their usual procedures when confronted with such cases?

These questions served as the point of departure for a project carried out in rural, semi-rural, and urban contexts, with the goal of designing policy interventions sensitive to contextual conditions.[2] Since Mexico has a large Indian population (over 12 million, which is more than 10 per cent of the total population), with specific characteristics, it was deemed important to include a case study of a predominantly Indian region. Cuetzalan, the area selected to carry out this research, has a variety of practitioners, belonging to two cultural approaches to health: traditional Indian medicine and biomedicine. In addition, Cuetzalan shares the living conditions prevailing in most of Mexico's Indian regions, and includes a network of institutions and individuals willing to collaborate with the project.[3] It was therefore well suited for a comparison of practitioners' outlook on health and for understanding the way in which the conditions of the medical encounter in an interethnic situation influence the perceptions and responses of health care providers/healers to the violence suffered by their female clients.

THE RESEARCH PROBLEM, THE SETTING, AND PROCEDURE

How do health practitioners—in our case, doctors, healers, and midwives—perceive the various forms of violence suffered by their female patients, and their connections with reproductive health? The general question that guided my research is of the nature of perception: how experience is processed, what are the constraints on what is seen, and how the cultural construction of 'reality' can make invisible empirical evidence such as physical signs of violence. These are not only epistemological but also eminently cultural questions, and, as such, they require that we consider both traditional medicine and biomedicine as cultural systems that define which ailments are recognized and addressed (Kleinman 1980; Good 1994). The notions that practitioners have concerning these issues derive from their previous training, and in the case of the public health system, also from public policies that set guidelines for action. Health policies, in turn, are based on a complex political interplay of social forces, and are legitimized by culturally specific explanatory and theoretical models of health and illness.

These models have a direct bearing upon what health practitioners 'see' or perceive in their daily encounter with the afflictions of patients and which areas they consider legitimate for intervention. This becomes apparent when comparing the approaches of biomedicine and traditional medicine to life events, the emotional distress they may produce, and their consequences on health in general and reproductive health in particular. Whereas biomedicine establishes body, mind, and life events as separate fields for professional practice, the folk etiologies of rural Mexico recognize the role of emotional distress in triggering a variety of illnesses and dysfunctions, which traditional health care providers have to address (Finkler 1985).

Another significant element in this analysis is the therapeutic relationship since the social distance between practitioner and patient, including the conditions of the medical encounter, can favour or limit knowledge of patients who have suffered violence. In an ethnically stratified context, the ethnic origin of practitioners has a bearing on how much they are able to 'see', what they think about the violence that their clients experience, and what they are able to do about it.

Most of the research was conducted in the largest hospital of the municipality of Cuetzalan, created in 1978 by the National Indian Bureau (NIB) to offer free first level attention to an open population, the majority of which is Indian. This hospital is unusual because it has an area devoted to traditional medicine, run by an organization established at the beginning of 1991 under the auspices of the Bureau. This pilot project was intended to give official recognition to traditional medicine as an important health resource, placing it under the control of the Bureau's authorities. The Maseualpajti Organization (Maseualpajti meaning 'Peasant/Indian Medicine' in Nahuat) had 65 members in 1994, almost all of them Indian. They represent only a fraction of the traditional medicine practitioners in the region. Women are the majority (48 out of 65), because of the large number of midwives (32) in the organization. The other recognized specialists are bone-setters and healers, but often these distinctions are not valid because the same person (if female) can perform the three types of activities, or at least two (midwifery and healing). Members give consultation at the hospital twice a week, or at home, charging a small fee, and keep records of their practice.

I carried out semi-structured, open-ended interviews with the six doctors (four female, two male) that worked at the NIB Hospital during 1994–5, as well as with three women who are well-known midwives and five healers (two female, three male), who belong to the Maseualpajti Organization. The interviews were held in Spanish, since that is the only language spoken by the doctors, and because the majority of the traditional practitioners are bilingual.

All health providers were asked about physical violence in the form of hitting, battery and sexual coercion exerted by husbands, and whether they thought that other forms of violence, such as verbal abuse and menaces, could have consequences for contraception, pregnancy, delivery, lactation, and post-partum care.

Another important part of the research was the examination of medical records, since an important form of intervention in the future would be to change the way records are taken so that they include the detection of violence. According to Warshaw (1989, p. 511), 'the standard medical descriptive format shapes physicians' ability to see'; yet my hypothesis was that they see more than they register. Clinical records were therefore carefully checked to compare what doctors write in their patients' files with their perceptions, thoughts, and experiences about violence as reported when they are interviewed.

The records of the traditional practitioners produced valuable statistical information about types of ailments treated, by sex and age, which helped put their perceptions in perspective. Observation of healing sessions permitted a further understanding of the therapeutic encounter, as well as the meaning of the data registered, and their connection with cases of violence.

An anthropological approach was followed throughout the study, specially aimed at situating violence in the context of social relations shaped by gender, ethnicity and at understanding the cultural meanings that underlie therapeutic practices. For this reason the next section introduces the reader to the meaning and incidence of violence against women in the region under study. It is based on interviews with women and judicial authorities carried out by a team composed of five members.[4]

VIOLENCE AGAINST WOMEN IN AN INDIAN AREA OF MEXICO

The municipality of Cuetzalan is located in the northern corner of the State of Puebla, in a rainy tropical mountain region—a five-hour drive from Mexico City.

According to the 1990 Census, it has a total population of almost 36,000 inhabitants, of which 84 per cent were registered as Nahuat-speaking Indians, distributed among several dozen hamlets with less than 2,000 inhabitants each. Most of the public services are concentrated in the town Cuetzalan (head of municipality), including the NIB Hospital where this study took place. The majority of the non-Indian population (called 'people of reason', as opposed to the Indian 'naturales'), who comprise the regional power elite, are also located in Cuetzalan. This is a coffee-producing region, where the majority of the population (both male and female) work on small family plots and/or as day labourers. Temporary male migration to the capital and the United States increased rapidly after the 1989 drop in the price of coffee, and has continued ever since. Many women contribute to the family budget by selling the handicrafts they produce.

As is characteristic of other Indian regions in Mexico, Cuetzalan is an area of extreme poverty, which has 'pre-transitional' epidemiological and demographic indicators. It has the typical pattern of extremely high infant and high adult mortality, due to preventable causes, and birth rates have not gone down significantly. The most frequent causes of death are directly associated with poverty. According to the Civil Register, malnutrition, anaemia, respiratory diseases, and intestinal infections account for 40 per cent of all the deaths which occurred in 1994. Whereas national infant mortality rates were 34.8 per thousand births in 1990 (Fernández Ham 1993), in Cuetzalan they were 90.1.[5]

Under regional conditions of extremely low incomes, many men can barely sustain the role of providers for the family and many times fail. Male alcoholism is an endemic problem which, together with violent deaths (homicides and accidents), takes a high toll on men in their productive ages; half of Cuetzalan men that died between ages 20 and 49 in 1994 died as a consequence of homicide or accident. As is true in the rest of the country, men are the main victims of their own violence, most of it occurring in public places.[6] Violence against women is more widespread as a daily and domestic event whose consequences are not immediately fatal.

Although our purpose was not to measure the prevalence of the different forms of violence exercised against women, or their intensity, we thought it was important to have a general idea of women's experience of violence in their lives. For this purpose we conducted semi-structured interviews with 50 women aged 18 or older.[7] Only 2 had not lived with a man; of the other 48 ever-married, 24 declared not having been beaten at all, 5 would not speak about the subject, and the remaining 19 recognized they were beaten in a previous relationship or in their present relationship. In a context in which there is the widespread belief that 'wives should keep their husbands' secrets', one out of four women in union at the time of the interview reported they were recurrently beaten by their husbands.

The overall picture derived from these interviews is that the use of physical force is considered legitimate by Cuetzalan men and women if it is wielded by figures of authority, such as parents, husbands, and teachers, provided that they apply it for the purpose of disciplining their subordinates, and as a punishment for those who do not comply with obligations or the respect due to such figures. On marrying, the authority of the father over his daughter is transferred to the husband, who has the obligation to protect her as a father would, and the right to punish her if she does not fulfil her duties. The husband is entitled to control his wife's services, movements, and sexuality; beating her is justified as 'a corrective' if she does not prepare his food in time, does not ask his permission before going out of the house, or gives him 'reasons' to suspect she is unfaithful to him. As one woman put it:

I think that if the wife is guilty, the husband has the right to hit her. If I have done something wrong, let him beat me; even if I'm killed, if I'm guilty, nobody should defend me. But if I haven't done something wrong, I have a right to be defended.

But even if women accept the discourse that the use of physical force is a prerogative of their husbands as heads of the household, it is hard to find one that will admit to having given her husband reasons to resort to violence. Women consider their husbands' jealousy, alcohol consumption, and womanizing to be the more frequent immediate 'causes' of their aggressive behaviour against them. In this sense, their husbands' violence is seen by the women more than anything else as one of the 'bad habits' inherent to men, almost a normal element in the relationship between husband and wife, yet one to which they never get completely used to, since it is a constant source of fear, worry, anger, sadness—emotions which, according to the cultural notions prevalent in the Mexican countryside, usually have a negative impact on health (Finkler 1985).

Together with the idea that a person should not be punished if innocent ('without a reason'), there is also the notion of excessive violent behaviour, which is clearly recognized when the physical punishment is too intense and causes injuries that require the intervention of healers or doctors, or that leave the person incapacitated for work (having to stay in bed, with broken bones, etc.). The idea of excess, of going beyond the limits of legitimacy, can be applied to parents who 'correct' their children's faults 'too energetically', or to husbands who beat their wives too brutally or too often. These situations are deemed to justify a recourse to an external intervention.

In Cuetzalan the discourse on the rights of the husband over his wife is rarely challenged, but this does not mean that the use of force by the husband is accepted passively. On the contrary, a significant number of women undertake various courses of action, which include asking for the intervention of well-respected relatives or even reporting the husband's maltreatment to the local authorities. Considering that culture legitimates the right of husbands to exercise physical force on their wives and that authorities are male and prone to favour the husbands' versions, it is quite impressive that out of the 19 women interviewed who recognized being abused by their partners, 7 had gone to the local authorities to lodge a complaint. Some did this right after the first beating while others only after a long time of enduring domestic violence (Martínez and Mejía 1997).

HEALTH PRACTITIONERS AND THEIR RELATIONSHIP TO
FEMALE CLIENTS IN A BICULTURAL CONTEXT

In Cuetzalan two medical systems operate side by side, each one with its own perspective on health and sickness, and with its own therapeutic theories,[8] procedures, and remedies. The explanatory models of illness that both sets of practitioners apply, partially account for their ability to establish connections between violence and health. But another most important element is the relationship that health care providers/healers have with their clients, which has a direct bearing upon the number of cases of violence that are brought to their attention.

As is the case in many other rural and Indian areas of Mexico (Zolla *et al.* 1988), traditional medicine is very important in the daily life of Cuetzalan's population. Healers, midwives, and bone-setters are numerous and deal not only with the so-called culture-bound syndromes,[9] but also with most of the same respiratory, dermatological, gastrointestinal, gynaecological, bone, and muscular problems treated by biomedicine. Despite these similarities, the diagnostic methods and therapies applied by traditional healers are very different from those utilized by doctors since healers combine technical procedures not usually employed by doctors (such as the use of herbs, massage, chiropractics), with rituals and prayers.

Indian patients arrive at the NIB Hospital from their villages and hamlets to consult its doctors and healers, especially on weekly market days. They use both medical systems in a complementary or alternative fashion, according to how they evaluate the type of health problem they have, its acuteness, the efficacy of the treatment given to them by one or the other, or the costs involved. There is a constant moving from one system to the other, according to a very pragmatic criterion: if one type of practitioner does not work, try the other, whenever possible.

Because midwives and healers live in the same villages as their patients, speak the same language, and share the same living conditions, they know of many more cases of violence suffered by their clients, and in more detail, than doctors. This is also due to another important difference in the therapeutic encounter: Indian women go to the midwives and female healers unaccompanied, whereas they routinely go to the doctor with their husbands and/or mothers-in-law, who act as intermediaries and translators between doctor and patient.

Doctors do not speak the Indian language, and more Indian men are bilingual (Nahuat/Spanish) than women; but this is not the only reason why husbands 'take' their wives to the doctor. A wife is under her husband's responsibility and protection, both of which he can delegate to his own mother; further, the medical encounter is a situation which is seen as requiring that husbands exercise their authority and control over their wives.

The doctors report that the presence of husbands or mothers-in-law influences the explanations given by women for visible bruises and injuries, or for reproductive mishaps such as premature labour. In response to doctors' questions, the women always attribute bruises to accidents (which are not entirely out of the question in the type of environment where they live) and premature labour to having lifted heavy objects or having exerted themselves by excessive efforts when walking or washing. Doctors are well aware that many women are concealing the fact that these problems are caused by their husbands' maltreatment. They find that the women's fear of retaliation from their partners is a strong obstacle for them 'to get to the truth'; nonetheless, two doctors said that with adequate questioning, they could (and sometimes do) find out what really happened. None mentioned worrying about the possibility of intruding on their patients' privacy, as they are used to making recommendations about family planning. They see their Indian patients as particularly in need of such guidance, since most of them are illiterate or poorly educated, and feel it is their duty to 'look after their patients' well-being'.

PRACTITIONERS' PERCEPTIONS OF CONNECTIONS BETWEEN VIOLENCE AGAINST WOMEN AND THEIR REPRODUCTIVE HEALTH

Contraception, pregnancy, and violence

Since 1974 the Mexican State abandoned its pronatalist demographic policy and incorporated family planning programmes into the public health system. As part of the national campaign in favour of family planning, the health sector developed specific programmes to train midwives to improve their skills—especially to detect problematic pregnancies to be referred to hospitals—and also to promote the use of government-subsidized contraceptives (Parra 1991).

As the State has extended public health services through a network of local clinics, the number of births attended by midwives has diminished rapidly at the national level. But in Indian areas, where there are few or no services and the population lives in disperse hamlets, government services are not easily accessible, and midwives still play a vital role, not only in attending births, but also in providing prenatal and post-partum care, as well as family planning services.[10]

In Cuetzalan, both midwives and doctors are aware that there are obstacles to the use of contraception, as husbands usually expect and want their wives to be periodically pregnant. Since midwives are responsible for providing most of the family planning methods available and are closer to their clients, those interviewed reported more cases than doctors of women who had suffered violence because they did not bear children. They pointed out that barren women are called 'mules' and are held responsible for the couple's infertility, usually suffering recurrent maltreatment, even if there is no certainty as to where the problem lies.

All the midwives involved in family planning give details of clients who had suffered beatings by husbands enraged by their wives' actions in using contraception. This is why providers routinely advised their clients to hide any evidence of contraception from husbands opposed to its use. When their clients have had 'many children' and feel they cannot support any more, they recommend sterilization, which is done at the NIB Hospital by a team of surgeons that visits periodically.

Undoubtedly, high infant mortality, the need for the labour contribution of a large family to agricultural production, the absence of social security for old age, as well as other psychological factors, contribute to the high value of childbearing. But interviews with women and midwives indicate that women would prefer to have fewer children. As happens in other regions of the world,[11] fear of violence from husbands—in conjunction with the above-mentioned factors—is an important reason for low contraceptive coverage in Cuetzalan. Whereas family planning has been quite successful at the national level, Cuetzalan has not followed the national downward trend of birth rates: according to Census data, the average number of children per woman aged 45–49 (those that have completed their reproductive cycle) was 5 in 1970, 5.2 in 1980, and 5.1 in 1990, which is more than double the national average (INEGI 1991).

Nonetheless, childbearing is not devoid of ambiguity on the part of husbands since, as midwives and women pointed out, an increase of violence is a common occurrence during pregnancy, in some cases provoking miscarriages, premature labour, or the birth of stillborns.

Pregnancy is also the time in the life of women during which doctors are most aware of violence taking place; this is a time when doctors are most worried about husbands' violence and are more emotionally involved with their patients. One possible interpretation is that they feel directly responsible for the protection of 'the product', as they routinely call the baby, and its successful outcome. It is in connection with pregnancy that doctors tend to report many cases of marital violence.

Five of the six doctors at the NIB Hospital had detected at least one case of a female patient that had been beaten during the month preceding the interview.[12] All but one of these cases were pregnant women who arrived with transvaginal bleeding and were at risk of premature labour, having suffered injuries so bad that it was impossible for doctors not to identify them as the cause of the problem. But upon checking patients' files for that month, I found that although the descriptions of the women's immediate health conditions were complete, there was no mention whatsoever of violence, except in one case where the pregnant woman had been injured by her husband with what was described as a 'steel weapon'.

Sexual coercion and reproductive health

One of the questions I wanted to explore was whether doctors, midwives, and healers believe that women can be sexually coerced, and if so, how and with what consequences for reproductive health. It was in this area that I found more similarities between doctors, midwives, and healers, with midwives being able to give many detailed examples, derived not only from their patients' but also from their own personal experience.

Two of the female doctors interviewed began their approach to this subject by talking about adolescent pregnancies, some of which they suspected were the result of rape: 'Sometimes it is incest, committed by a father or a step-father, or sometimes it is a boyfriend who deceived and forced the girl. We know because she doesn't come accompanied by her husband and she doesn't want the baby, she wants to give the baby away [for adoption]. . . . We have had several cases of this type. . . .' But no further information could be obtained from the registers or the other doctors.

Concerning coercion in marriage, all the practitioners interviewed were aware that the principle that controls a married woman's sexuality in the Cuetzalan context is that she is obliged to satisfy her husband's desires whenever required, as part of her wifely duties. The way interviewees speak about marital sex gives an insight into their conceptions about expected roles among couples. In Cuetzalan, as in other regions of the country, the term 'service' is used to refer to all the activities undertaken by women in their role as wives, including intercourse. The expression 'he occupies his wife' is also used to mean that the husband has sex with her. The first concept underlines the subordinate role of the wife, whereas the second reveals the active and dominant role expected of the husband.

If a woman does not consider that she has a right to 'negotiate' when to have intercourse, then she will accept it without opposing resistance; under these circumstances, it would seem misleading to speak of outright coercion or marital rape. But even if in sexual matters wives are guided by the principle of the conjugal obligation due the husband, some women report that there are certain circumstances which provoked their disgust with having sex with their husbands: when the husband arrived home drunk; when the wife knew he had been with another woman; he had mistreated her previously; or when she thought having sex might be negative for her health. In these cases, intercourse was perceived as forced.

There are several situations related to reproductive health where practitioners clearly recognized that marital sex can be coercive for women:

1. Midwives and most of the doctors (but not all) consider that intercourse can be risky for the mother and the foetus during the first three months of the pregnancy, and during the last month or two, since it can trigger labour prematurely. Two midwives thought that the foetus might suffer damage or might get into a position that makes birth difficult.
2. After birth, midwives and doctors recommend abstinence during a variable period (usually two months in the case of midwives, 40 days in the case of doctors) to avoid the risk of haemorrhages or infections and to guarantee the recovery of the mother.
3. Doctors recommend abstinence during the time a woman is being treated for conditions affecting her reproductive and urinary tract, usually due to an infection.
4. Midwives and healers recommend abstinence during menstruation, on account of the belief that it may be dangerous for the health of both partners. In the case of the male, they think that he can develop an inflammation of his sexual organs and a very strong skin reaction. In the case of the wife, since she is considered to be vulnerable during her period, she can suffer an infection or a bad attack of the disease known as *aires*, which in its most intense version can provoke embolism.

Given that midwives provide most of the pre- and post-natal care for Indian women, following closely the progress of their patients, they know very well when husbands 'respect' their clients and when they do not. They are the ones responsible for trying to solve the health problems that arise when the man 'uses' or 'occupies' his wife in spite of recommendations to the contrary. Midwives are the ones that refer most cases of husbands who do not 'respect' their wives by obliging them to have sexual relations.

On the other hand, doctors said that they do give recommendations concerning 'when it is convenient or inconvenient to have sexual relations', but that their indications are not followed, 'because men do as they please and there is nothing we can do about it, even if we wanted to'.

Since 1997 the Mexican national legislation recognizes rape in marriage as a crime, but it will undoubtedly take time and effort to dismiss the widespread notion that the rape of a woman qualifies as such *only* if she was a virgin. We found that this idea is shared not only by the general population of Cuetzalan, but also by the judicial authorities at the local levels. The usual practice in the countryside is that only the rape of a virgin that results in pregnancy merits judicial action in the form of reparation by covering the expenses of the birth (Martínez and Mejía 1997).

Mind/body and violence

When doctors were asked about the possible consequences of domestic violence for health beyond immediate injuries, they did not mention other ways in which the physical body, and specifically reproductive health, might be affected (aside from those mentioned in the previous sections). They did refer, however, to psychological and behavioural effects, especially on children who witness maltreatment of the mother by the father. When giving consultations they have observed that these children remain 'introverted, shy, afraid'. In addition, doctors noted that violence can provoke 'depression, apathy, and traumas', both in children and their mothers.

But these are seen as problems outside the organic sphere and, therefore, not part of the field in which physicians are prepared and entitled to intervene. To those physicians, the bridge between the organic and the psychological spheres belongs to the domain of psychiatry.

Healers and midwives are able to establish more connections between violence and health than doctors because of the importance given by traditional medicine to the notion that intense emotional alterations can negatively affect health by provoking the loss of the person's integral equilibrium, thus debilitating the individual. This in turn may contribute (immediately or with a retarded effect) to the development of some form of disease. Given this expected chain of events, strong emotional reactions are considered to require appropriate and immediate treatment.

Maintaining equilibrium and restoring it when it is lost are the basic therapeutic aims of traditional medicine. At the risk of simplifying a complex notion, equilibrium can be conceived as consisting of multiple facets: it is internal to the body; it has to do with the relation between the body and the other parts which constitute the person (including the 'spirit' or 'shadow'); it has to do with the relation between the person and the natural/supernatural environment; and between the person and the social environment (Zolla *et al.* 1988; Signorini 1989). This notion is, of course, in strong contrast to the biomedical practices that are hegemonic in Mexico, which are built on a model of identifying the microbial agents that cause disease, and destroying them through the actions of antibiotics.

According to the midwives and healers interviewed, emotional reactions can be released not only by violence inflicted on a person's body, but also by the threat of violence, or having witnessed violent acts. If any of these produces a strong impression on the person, she has a good chance of falling ill. This idea is related to another central notion of Indian medicine: stimuli do not act on all people in the same manner; each individual responds to stimuli according to the particular 'set of characteristics or qualities which defines him or her physically and spiritually, and which it is possible to perceive in the person's reaction to circumstances such as reproduction, work, resistance to sickness, the gift of leadership, and so forth' (Zolla *et al.* 1988, p. 84). This notion highlights the role that individual constitution, often called 'the nature' of the person, plays in that person's health.

The main categories for classifying an individual's nature by traditional medicine are whether they are 'strong' or 'weak', based on how resistant they are to sickness. Parallel categories include 'tranquil' (not easily upset by circumstances) or 'angry' (quick-tempered, irritable, and prone to vexation and tantrums). Strongness/weakness is related to gender; by cultural definition, the 'nature' of women is weaker than that of men. The second set of distinctions involves strictly individual constitutional or personality traits, but it is also influenced by gender. Hence, women are more prone than men to react with emotional intensity, but among women there are those with more propensity to be emotionally intense.

The principles just outlined operate in the interpretations that Indian people (or those who do not identify as Indian but who have roots in that cultural tradition) make of the process of health and sickness. They are used to explain why females get sick and consult health care providers more frequently than males—a perception that coincides with the information provided by the records of the Maseualpajti Organization: in 1994, almost 70 per cent of the 1,645 patients who consulted healers were female.

Healers and midwives link suffering or witnessing violence to two illnesses that are among the most common in the region: fright and bile, both of which can become so severe as to produce death if not treated in a timely manner.

Fright or soul/spirit-loss is among the more studied culture-bound syndromes, found in various forms throughout Middle and Andean America and other regions of the world (Rubel *et al.* 1984; Zolla *et al.* 1988; Logan 1992). Different lines of inquiry and interpretation of these illnesses have been followed by researchers, but their gender implications have not been studied, nor their consequences for reproductive health. Their links to violence have been occasionally mentioned (Bolton 1981; Finkler 1985; Logan 1993), but have also not been explored systematically.

Fright is the most frequent reason for consulting members of the Maseualpajti Organization, accounting for one-third of the total patients registered in 1994. The distribution of this disease according to sex and age is very interesting. The Organization records show that 76 per cent of the total number of patients treated for fright were women; one-third of the patients were 1–9 years old, with no notable differences between the sexes. From 10 years on, as children grow older, the difference between the sexes increases, with a continual drop in the number of males treated for fright. From 20 years on, 70 per cent of the patients are women.

As in other regions of the country, the people of Cuetzalan think that if fright is not treated adequately, it can develop into various maladies and grave complications (Zolla *et al.* 1988). Midwives and healers believe that it can affect reproductive health directly, since in a pregnant woman fright can provoke abortion or the threat of abortion, or hinder the normal development of the baby, which is consequently born 'thin', underweight, and sickly, eventually leading to its death. The immediate cause of death might be an infection, but the mother's fright during pregnancy is held to be the underlying cause, the initial trigger of the disequilibrium. In addition the mother can have difficulties at the time of the birth, because she feels a general exhaustion or weakness resulting from fright.

Another common sickness attributed to emotional reactions is bile. With bile there is no intervention of supernatural agents as in fright. Instead, the problem is the 'bilious nature' of the person, her disposition to worry, get angry or frustrated, which eventually affects her body. The women, healers, and midwives we interviewed agreed that bile is the consequence of conflicts in social relations. Particularly daily tensions can lead a constitutionally prone individual to get sick with bile. In this respect bile is different from fright because it is cumulative, and a person can have a delayed reaction to repeatedly stressful situations. As a midwife put it, 'All those vexations keep accumulating, until the time comes when the bile breaks loose throughout the stomach.'

Bile is an even more 'feminine' ailment than fright. The general perception that 'men almost don't make bile' coincides with information from the Maseualpajti records: 85 per cent of the patients treated for bile in 1994 were female, with almost none younger than 15 years old. The majority (66 per cent) were in the reproductive age range (15–49).

According to both male and female interviewees, 'making bile' during pregnancy can have the same effect on the foetus as fright: it becomes undernourished, weak, and sickly. In a breastfeeding woman, milk production can diminish or even disappear because of strong anger and vexation. Further, these emotions can transform the quality of the milk so that it 'turns bad', provoking diarrhoea and vomiting in the baby, 'as if it had been poisoned'. Moreover, a baby breastfed immediately after an intense emotional alteration of the mother can get so sick that it may die. Whenever under stressful conditions, the lactating mother should drink an infusion made of the appropriate herbs, in order to make sure the negative emotion 'goes away'.

PRACTITIONERS' RESPONSES WHEN CONFRONTED WITH CASES OF VIOLENCE AGAINST THEIR FEMALE PATIENTS

Since traditional medicine acknowledges that suffering or witnessing violence, as well as the threat of it, can have a negative impact on health, it responds by treating the resulting symptoms which usually have a recurrent pattern. Once the diagnosis of the disease is made, healers and midwives apply various therapeutic procedures to restore health. Some are of a symbolic nature (ritual prayers and offerings), while others are physical, such as massage and herbal preparations to be drunk, eaten, or administered as suppositories or in baths.

When confronted with cases of patients badly injured or who suffer other health consequences in addition to violence, there is little that traditional practitioners or doctors do beyond treating the immediate injuries, symptoms, and dysfunctions. Some recommendations are made to husbands, especially regarding the care of their pregnant and post-partum wives, but not much more. The majority of midwives and healers believe that they have to 'act as priests do: keep secrets' to prevent further violence, including the possibility of reprisals from angry husbands.

But not all follow this generalized course of action. A midwife and a female healer said that on several occasions they had reprimanded their clients' husbands for their behaviour. These included a husband who coerced his wife into sex after beating her and, more frequently, husbands who wanted to have sex soon after delivery. During the year before the interview took place, the midwife—a very enterprising person, an organizer in her community—had even accompanied two of her patients to lodge complaints with the local judicial authorities.

None of the doctors reported having done anything similar. They write certificates of injury or rape only upon demand from the authorities, who require the certificates for the purpose of applying sanctions proportional to the gravity of the injuries (according to doctors' estimation of the number of days these take to heal). The limited written references to violence that I was able to find were contained in these certificates.[13] In the clinical files doctors record information concerning violence only when it involves injuries provoked by the use of 'a weapon': cutting instruments (machetes, knives, etc.) or firearms.

Considering that violence against women is such a widespread practice, the paucity of any form of written record of violence is remarkable, even more so when the interviews prove that doctors are aware of much more than they write down in the clinical record.

After enquiring into what is registered and why, it is clear doctors only feel compelled by legal reasons, not by health considerations, to note the experience of violence in the clinical file of a patient. They are motivated not by the gravity of the injury, the possible health hazards it causes, or by the prevention of that hazard in the future, but by whether the incident involves an action that could be defined as criminal and thus prosecuted.

Why is it that doctors write down with great precision and as a routine procedure data concerning the female patients' reproductive cycle and conditions—age at menarche, number of births, last date of menses, and so on—as well as other relevant health information, but do not make any references to violence, which is a relatively frequent event in the lives of their patients? There is obviously no single answer to this question, but doctors' main worry seems to be to follow the 'correct' procedures, according to the medical model they were taught. And their training did not include references to domestic violence as a possible risk for reproductive health in general or during pregnancy in particular, so they abide by biomedical norms of clinical encounters: make a correct diagnosis and give a prescription of medicines. This is all they record in clinical files.

CONCLUSIONS

Violence exerted against women in its various forms has not been elaborated as a health problem by traditional medicine or biomedicine, even if its practitioners recognize that it is something they are frequently confronted with when treating female clients. As there are no common guidelines, the responses to the cases that come to their attention remain highly individual. The interviews conducted demonstrate that there is considerable diversity of attitudes and responses among providers of both medical systems when cases are brought to their attention. Yet when comparing their performance, we can discover certain general trends, which can be attributed to the differences in the basic principles that guide each system's approach to health and illness.

Given the basic concepts of Indian medicine, its practitioners are able to perceive and acknowledge more links between suffering and witnessing violence and health, and reproductive health in particular, than doctors. Moreover, even the threat of violence is recognized as having significant consequences for health.

The dichotomy between the mind and body does not exist in the etiological model held by native healers and their clients. This permits healers to treat emotional responses to violence that according to this system of thought provokes a chain of illness, as shown in the cases of fright and bile. Both are examples of ailments that cannot be classified as belonging to the mental or the physical realms, which are conceived as being inseparable. Fright and bile are the most frequent causes for consultation of healers among women, in many cases related to suffering physical abuse or being threatened by it. Moreover, both healers and their clients recognize several links between fright, bile, and reproductive outcomes.

The possibility of receiving treatment along these lines seems to be a valuable health resource for women, since it gives recognition to their ailments and provides therapeutic support in terms they can understand and accept. Midwives' and healers' interventions do not confront directly, at least not in most cases, the established social order or the source of violence, which could be of importance in prevention. They do however provide a response to the immediate health consequences of violence, as well as some relief and emotional support. This probably contributes to explaining how Cuetzalan women cope with harsh living conditions, where violence is a recurrent phenomenon.

On the other hand doctors' theoretical framework and training often do not permit them to elaborate a discourse on the connections between violence against women and their reproductive health. Nonetheless, they are able to identify violence as a problem, as well as some of its consequences for health. While connections are rarely made explicit in the discourse, they do emerge when doctors are asked on specific topics such as pregnancy, post-partum care, and sexual coercion.

Doctors' views of what constitutes their area of professional competence hinders them from considering violence against their female patients as a problem of their concern. They see it as a social problem with mostly psychological consequences. They have not received training to deal with the problem, and are afraid of going beyond their field of competence. Fear is often a factor in doctors' decisions to not involve themselves in the violence suffered by their female patients; they do not know exactly how to deal with it, worry about following the officially established procedures, and are especially afraid of becoming entangled with the judicial authorities. The lack of guidelines and minimal information provided during training leave practitioners with a sense of vulnerability.

It is important to note that studies done in the United States have found that one of the main obstacles to doctors' intervention in domestic violence is their fear of intruding in the personal lives of their patients.[14] None of the NIB Hospital doctors expressed such a fear, possibly because in Cuetzalan, as in the rest of Mexico, doctors are used to constantly bringing up intimate subjects, such as birth control. Birth control is a good example of the importance of public policy in shaping what is considered a matter of public or private concern, or a legitimate area of state intervention. Contraception, as well as domestic violence, is concerned with very private aspects of married life. Yet, it has become a priority for government and the national health system. As such it has gained legitimacy as a topic to be pursued by doctors with their patients. As a result, both doctors and government-trained midwives have clear notions on what contraceptive and reproductive behaviours are negative or positive for the general well-being of the family. They not only feel entitled but are explicitly encouraged to give recommendations about those behaviours to their clients, in accordance with the official model.[15]

Currently in Mexico, no policy interventions concerned with violence against women have been attempted by the public health system. The subject has not been incorporated in the academic medical curricula, nor have practising doctors or midwives in the public sector been trained about domestic violence. Government institutions periodically offer continuing education courses on a wide variety of topics, and eventually these could include information on violence and its consequences for health.

The research carried out in Cuetzalan indicates that there would not be major obstacles from doctors, midwives, and healers to the introduction of basic information about the problem of violence and the risks it poses to women. Moreover, many of the health care providers we interviewed mentioned they would welcome guidelines concerning the detection, registration, and referral of cases, including information on the limits of their intervention. The latter should certainly include ethical and practical considerations about the patients' and the practitioners' safety.

Ultimately, the possibility of introducing a new role for health providers in ameliorating domestic violence has to be conceived of in a wider perspective. In the event that the demand of services increased as a result of referrals from the public health system, it would be necessary to ensure that regional institutions have sufficient capacity to provide adequate support to abused women. Undoubtedly, to be truly effective, interventions in the health sector would require the development of other specialized services in the region.

Notes

1. For discussions of worldwide distribution and socio-cultural explanations of gender violence, see Counts *et al.* (1992).
2. The Project for the Study of Domestic Violence and Reproductive Health is coordinated by Irma Saucedo as one of the activities of the Reproductive Health and Society Program of El Colegio de México. Our part of the project was able to begin earlier than the rest thanks to the financial support granted by the Asociación Mexicana de Estudios de la Población.
3. I gratefully acknowledge the collaboration given by the Cooperative of Artisan Indian Women, the Organization of Traditional Medicine, the Human Rights Organization of Tzinacapan, Carlos Zolla (researcher at the National Indian Bureau), and the Director of the NIB Hospital, all of whom helped to open doors for us in Cuetzalan.
4. The research team under my direction was composed of three anthropologists (María Eugenia D'Aubeterre, Pilar Alberti, and myself), a social psychologist (Beatríz Martínez), and a sociologist (Susana Mejía). The last two have worked for many years as counsellors for the Cooperative of Artisan Indian Women of Cuetzalan, which facilitated interviews with its members and transcription from a Workshop on Domestic Violence which it held in 1993.
5. Our estimate derives from the Civil Register's information on deaths for 1994 and the information of the National Indian Bureau's Hospital of births attended that year in its facilities, and in the communities (by the organized midwives). Undoubtedly there is an under-registration of both types of birth.
6. General violence has reached epidemic proportions in Mexico, taking a very heavy demographic toll, notably among men (de Keijzer 1996). Mortality differentials by sex have increased for ages 15–44: male deaths exceeded female deaths by 25 per cent in 1940, and by 80 per cent in 1980, the main cause being the tremendous weight of violent deaths for males (Camposortega 1992, pp. 371–2). A study which compares violent deaths in 31 countries finds Mexico to be in the first place, with 45 homicides per 100,000 men, a figure which doubles the United States rate (Goldsmith and Crinkel 1993).
7. Twelve middle-aged women belonging to the Cooperative of Artisan Indian Women volunteered to be interviewed at their homes, at their convenience. The fact that they knew the interviewer previously helped establish a degree of trust in the encounters. The other interviews were undertaken with 38 women of various ages, who were waiting to consult the doctors at the hospital of the National Indian Bureau. We were given permission to ask who wanted to talk with us, and the interviews were conducted in spaces where privacy was granted. All the women were bilingual except two, and the interviews were held in Spanish. In the case of the two women who only spoke Nahuat, their daughters translated.

8. The Indian population has a body of more or less coherent and recurrent explanations for health and sickness that are not expressed in abstract terms, but that can be found to underlie various interpretations of experience. It is in this sense that I speak of a 'theory'. It should be pointed out that some concepts and remedies of academic medicine are incorporated in traditional medicine, after they are reinterpreted through the filter of those theories.

9. Ailments that are not recognized and treated by biomedicine are usually called 'culture-bound syndromes' by the specialized literature, although recent critiques argue that all medical approaches, including biomedicine, are culture bound (Hahn 1995). In other words, each tradition of medical knowledge culturally constructs sickness as an ensemble of symptoms, causes, and processes, with internal coherence in terms of the categories and conceptions meaningful to those who share the same cultural system.

10. In Cuetzalan, more than 40 per cent of all births recorded by midwives and doctors at the NIB Hospital were delivered by Maseualpajti midwives in 1994. This figure is higher in practice because of high under-registration on the part of midwives. It should also be taken into account that the population covered by midwives is totally Indian, whereas around 40 per cent of the population served by the hospital that year was non-Indian.

11. Fear of violent reprisal, desertion, or accusations of infidelity are important obstacles to women's access to health and family planning services, as shown in studies from Peru and Kenya. In other cases, women avoid discussing condom use with their partners as a method of preventing STI and AIDS, out of fear of a violent reaction (Heise *et al.* 1995).

12. According to NIB Hospital records, during 1994 doctors tended a total of 350 deliveries, an average of 29 per month.

13. Certificates of injuries are kept at the NIB Hospital's small Social Work office. There I found a total of 48 certificates of injury for the period January–December 1994. Of these, 32 dealt with attacks between men, one was an attack of one woman to another, and 15 corresponded to males attacking females. Of the latter, one certificate recorded the rape of two girls, aged 11 and 16; seven corresponded to husbands who had beaten their wives, two of which were pregnant; five women did not want to declare who the aggressor was; and one certificate registered the injury of a girl by a boy.

14. In the United States there have been several attempts to introduce the subject of violence against women in health services, but there are relatively few studies analysing the difficulties encountered (see, for example, Kurz 1987; Warshaw 1989; Sugg and Inui 1992; Cohen *et al.* 1997).

15. The official discourse on birth control states that small families live better, using the slogan 'have less children to be able to give them more'. Poverty is seen as a demographic problem, and contraceptive measures are promoted using health arguments, stressing that the optimal ages for childbearing are above 20 and below 35, and that pregnancies should be spaced. This discourse has adopted the reproductive health idiom in recent years, as the National Family Planning Board changed its name to the Reproductive Health Board.

References

Bolton, R. (1981), 'Susto, hostility, and hypoglycemia', *Ethnology*, 20: 261–76.

Camposortega, S. (1992), *Análisis demográfico de la mortalidad en México, 1940–1980*, Mexico: El Colegio de México.

Cohen, S. *et al.* (1997), 'Barriers to physician identification and treatment of family violence: Lessons from five communities', *Academic Medicine Supplement*, 70 (1): 19–25.

Counts, D. *et al.* (1992), *Sanctions and Sanctuary: Cultural Perspectives on the Beating of Wives*, Boulder: Westview Press.

de Keijzer, B. (1995), 'La salud y la muerte de los hombres', in M. A. Núñez (ed.), *Estudios de género en Michoacán: Lo masculino y lo femenino en perspectiva*, Morelia.

Dixon-Mueller, R. (1993), 'The sexuality connection in reproductive health', *Studies in Family Planning*, 24 (5): 269–82.

Fernández Ham, P. (1993), 'La mortalidad infantil en la población indígena', *Demos*, 12–13.

Finkler, K. (1985), 'Symptomatic differences between the sexes in rural Mexico', *Culture, Medicine and Psychiatry*, 9: 27–57.

Gielen, A. C. *et al.* (1994), 'Interperson conflict and physical violence during the childbearing year', *Social Science and Medicine*, 39 (6): 781–7.

Goldsmith, J., and Crinkel, J. (1993), 'Mortalidad de los jóvenes adultos: comparaciones internacionales', *Salud Pública de México*, 35 (2).

Good, B. (1994), *Medicine, Rationality, and Experience: An Anthropological Perspective*, Cambridge: Cambridge University Press.

Granados, M. *et al.* (1997). *Salud Reproductiva y Violencia Contra la Mujer (El caso de la Zona Metropolitana de Monterrey)*, Monterrey: Asociación Mexicana de Estudios de la Población.

Hahn, R. (1995), *Sickness and Healing: An Anthropological Perspective*, New Haven and London: Yale University Press.

Heise, L. *et al.* (1994), *Violence against Women: The Hidden Health Burden*, Washington, DC: The World Bank.

—— *et al.* (1995), *Sexual Coercion and Reproductive Health: A Focus on Research*, New York: The Population Council.

Instituto Nacional de Estadística, Geografía e Informática (INEGI) (1991), *XI Censo General de Población y Vivienda 1990*, Vol. I (Puebla), Aguascalientes, Mexico.

Kleinman, A. (1980), *Patients and Healers in the Context of Culture: An Exploration of the Borderland between Anthropology, Medicine and Psychiatry*, Berkeley: University of California Press.

Kurz, D. (1987), 'Emergency department responses to battered women: resistance to medicalization', *Social Problems*, 34 (1): 69–81.

Logan, M. (1993), 'New lines of inquiry on the illness of susto', *Medical Anthropology*, 15 (2): 190–200.

Martínez, B., and Mejía, S. (1997). *Ideología y práctica en delitos cometidos contra mujeres: El sistema judicial y la violencia en una región indígena de Puebla*, Mexico: Colegio de Posgraduados, Campus Puebla.

Newberger, E. *et al.* (1992), 'Abuse of pregnant women and adverse birth outcome', *JAMA*, 267 (17): 2370–2.

Parra, P. (1991), 'La mujer rural, las comadronas y el sistema mexicano de salud', *Estudios Demográficos y Urbanos*, 6 (1): 69–88.

Ramírez, J. C., and Uribe-Vázquez, G. (1993), 'Mujer y violencia: un hecho cotidiano', *Salud Pública de México*, 35 (2): 148–60.

Riquer, F. *et al.* (1996), 'Agresión y violencia contra el género femenino: un asunto de salud pública', in A. Langer and K. Tolbert (eds.), *Mujer: Sexualidad y Salud Reproductiva en México*, Mexico: The Population Council and Edamex.

Rubel, A. J. (1964), 'The epidemiology of a folk illness: susto in Hispanic America', *Ethnology*, 3: 268–83.

Signorini, I. (1989), *Los tres ejes de la vida. Almas, cuerpo, enfermedad entre los Nahuas de la Sierra de Xalapa*, Xalapa, Mexico: Universidad Veracruzana.

Sugg, N. K., and Inui, T. (1992), 'The response of basic care doctors to domestic violence', *JAMA*, 267: 3157–60.

Valdez, R., and Sanín, L. H. (1996). 'La violencia doméstica durante el embarazo y su relación con el peso al nacer', *Salud Pública de México*, 38 (5): 352–62.

Warshaw, C. (1989), 'Limitations of the medical model in the care of battered women', *Gender and Society*, 3 (4): 506–17.

Zolla, C. *et al.* (1988), *Medicina tradicional y enfermedad*, Mexico: Centro Interamericano de Estudios de Seguridad Social (CIESS).

12

Eliminating Stigmatization: Application of the New Genetics in Japan[1]

MARGARET LOCK

INTRODUCTION

Mapping the human genome has been likened to the Holy Grail of biology; one scientist declared in the mid-1980s that the Human Genome Project was the ultimate response to the commandment 'Know thyself' (Bishop and Waldholz 1990). While certain members of the scientific community have been actively opposed to the genome project, in large part because it consumes a vast amount of resources that would otherwise be used for other kinds of research, many scientists have been very vocal about the benefits that society will receive by completing this project. Daniel Koshland, until recently the editor of *Science*, states, for example, that withholding support from the Human Genome Project is to incur 'the immorality of omission—the failure to apply a great new technology to aid the poor, the infirm, and the underprivileged' (1989). Robert Plomin, in supporting the project, notes that, 'Just fifteen years ago, the idea of genetic influence on complex human behavior was anathema to many behavioral scientists. Now, however, the role of inheritance in behaviour has become widely accepted, even for sensitive domains as IQ.' (1990).

The historian of science, Edward Yoxen, points out that we are currently witnessing a conceptual shift that has not been present in the language of geneticists prior to the advent of molecular genetics. While the contribution of genetics to the incidence of disease has been recognized throughout this century, it has only been in the past two decades that the notion of 'genetic disease' has come to dominate discourse such that other contributory factors are obscured from view (Yoxen 1984). Fox Keller (1992) argues that it was this shift in discourse that made the Human Genome Project both reasonable and desirable in the minds of many involved researchers. In mapping the Human Genome the objective is to create a baseline norm, but it is one that will correspond to the genome of no living individual such that we will all, in effect, become deviants from the norm (Lewontin 1992). Moreover, with this map in hand, the belief is that we will then rapidly move into an era in which we will be able to 'guarantee all human beings an individual and natural right, the right to health' (Fox Keller 1992, p. 295). Fox Keller cites a report put out by the Office of Technology Assessment in the United States in which it is argued that genetic information will be used 'to ensure that . . . each individual has at least a modicum of normal genes' (1988).

Although the term eugenics is never used by advocates of the new genetics, it is quite evident that the idea of improving the quality of the gene pool is in the air, although, as Fox Keller and others have pointed out, the language used is no longer one that focuses on social policy, the good of the species, or even the collective gene pool (1992, p. 295). We are now in an era dominated by the idea of individual choice in connection with decision making relating to health and illness. Genetic information will furnish the indispensable knowledge that individuals need in order to realize their inalienable right to health. One major disadvantage with this utopian type of talk to date, aside from the fact that it is blatantly reductionistic and often wildly inaccurate, is that as yet we do not have a single therapeutic technique available to manipulate the genetic constitution of individuals, although this technology is rapidly moving into the experimental stage. Moreover, we have definitive diagnostic capabilities for only a small number of relatively uncomplicated (although usually devastating) genetic diseases, and for no 'behavioural traits'.

Techniques for intervening in the procreation of children in unprecedented ways have rapidly become routinized in the latter part of this century. As with so many biomedical technologies, these techniques were developed and put at once into practice, to be followed by a hasty post hoc consideration of moral issues that are inevitably involved. Feminists have been bitterly divided as to whether reproductive technologies and the new genetics have the potential to free women from the constraints imposed by biology, or whether, on the other hand, these techniques will permit yet more invasive control by those in positions of power over women (see Bethke Elshtain (1989) for a summary of this debate). Much of this discussion has taken place in the abstract, however, with attention being paid overwhelmingly to questions of autonomy and agency. Surprisingly few studies make the subjective accounts of women, their partners, friends, families, and communities the starting point from which observations are made about how autonomy, agency, and other concepts central to bioethics are implicated in daily life in Europe and North America.

Without the desire of 'consumers' to cooperate with reproductive technologies, these innovations would have remained confined to the research laboratory, and it is conceivably possible that the full range of the new genetics will never become accessible to the public at large. It is already clear that not all women are willing to avail themselves of new reproductive technologies, even when labelled as infertile or 'at risk' for carrying a foetus with a major genetic disorder (Beeson and Doksum, 2001). That there are those who apparently resist technological intervention suggests that competing ideologies and practices, contradictions, and inconsistencies must be at work in the popular domain. It is at the 'intersection of discourses' (Yanagisako and Delaney 1995), particularly when decisions have to be made with grave consequences for the lives of involved individuals and their families, that we can gain some valuable insights about the medicalization and manipulation of reproduction, and the reception of these practices among the public. Governments and certain members of the medical establishment may, for utilitarian reasons, encourage the use of genetic testing in association with in vitro fertilization to promote, through 'informed choice', the selective elimination of offspring who are likely to become a 'financial burden' to society. However, unless these utilitarian reasons coincide rather closely with individual and family wishes about desirable children, this subtle neoeugenics will not be successful.

This chapter focuses on the situation in Japan, a technologically sophisticated society, one with a comprehensive socialized health care system where health care costs remain low compared with all other complex societies (Campbell and Ikegami 1998). Fidelity to equality in access to health care services is of fundamental concern to the Japanese government, as is the promotion of preventive medicine, although highly invasive therapeutic technologies tend to be implemented cautiously, if at all (Ikegami 1989). Throughout much of this century the Japanese population has increasingly been monitored through the systematic implementation of state-wide programmes dedicated to the promotion of the health of all citizens. For their part, on the whole, Japanese have cooperated with these programmes, in part due to a strong, centuries-old set of practices fundamental to East Asian medicine that requires individuals and families to take responsibility for the condition of their own bodies. Explicitly included in this monitoring from the outset has been reproduction, notably the creation of healthy families of the desired size. One aspect of this emphasis on the 'ideal', normative family has been a stigmatization of those children labelled as 'unfit' in one way or another (Miyaji and Lock 1994). Given this situation, one might predict that Japanese women and their partners would avail themselves very willingly of the new reproductive technologies, and especially of the new genetics as they become more widely available. This paper will show that the issue is more complex than simply one of compliance with or ambivalence about new technologies, and argue that in addition to considering questions of power, knowledge, and agency, so deeply implicated in the medicalization of reproduction, the effects of culture must also be recognized.

CULTURES OF MEDICALIZATION

Medicalization of reproduction exhibits a coalescence of the two poles of biopower articulated by Foucault. At one pole, the human body, usually the female body, is made into an object for the enactment of technologies of control—a site to be manipulated. Women (and their partners) who subject themselves to such manipulation do so, it is assumed, because they have been 'disciplined' into an ideology in which individual reproduction is considered both a 'natural' outcome of a committed relationship and essential to a fulfilled life. At the other pole, where the control of populations is located, political concern about reproductive outcomes ensures that medicalization is neither simply a personal nor a medical matter (although it is almost always billed this way in clinical settings). There is evidence of explicit coercion, for example, in connection with the new genetics where insurance companies have refused to insure infants born to women who underwent genetic testing but who refused to have an abortion despite the detection of a 'faulty' gene in the foetus they were carrying (Caulfield and Feasby, 1998). However, most of the coercion that has taken place in connection with the new genetics has been largely indirect, the product of unexamined value systems, as when, for example, genetic counsellors unconsciously guide certain women towards an abortion after a foetal abnormality has been detected[2] (Rapp 1988).

Although Foucault acknowledged the heterogeneity of the social order, and the importance of the micro-politics of power relations, little attention was given by him to body praxis as it is enacted by those whom power objectifies. Foucault insisted that individuals are not wholly determined by those in powerful positions; nevertheless, his attention was initially focused largely on the mechanisms of repression enacted by those in power, although he modified this position considerably towards the end of his life. Responses of individuals to new technologies and to medicalization are neither simply those of compliance nor of resistance; indeed they need not be responses at all. Rather, there is abundant evidence of pragmatism on the part of many women and their partners (Lock and Kaufert 1998); a pragmatism that although it is confined by social circumstances, nevertheless is often initiated and orchestrated by individuals and those around them, rather than being the effects of repression. Furthermore, in many instances the expectations of medical practitioners and the desires of their patients and clients converge to such an extent that a search for resistance is entirely misleading.

The body is obviously a site where power is enacted and negotiated, as Foucault argued. Foucault's concept of governmentality conceived towards the end of his career can be understood, as Petersen has argued, as 'a contact point between technologies of the self (self-subjection) and technologies of domination (societal regulation). It allows one to recognize the agency of subjects without recourse to the notion of a fully autonomous subject' (1997, p. 203), and a concern with health care on the part of individuals has ensured that they have begun to formulate the 'needs and imperatives' that will constitute in their estimation a healthy life as the basis of political counter-demands (Gordon 1991, p. 5). Analyses of bodily praxis must, however, range beyond the clinic, and further beyond the perceived interests of both governments and individuals. Bodily praxis must be contextualized in specific histories and social contexts. Although Foucault obviously recognized the importance of contextualization and of the transformation of discourse through time with respect to modernization in Europe, and even though he is specific that contemporary medical knowledge can make no privileged truth claims, he was unable to predict what is now reasonably well recognized, namely that globally we live with many culturally informed biomedicines (Lock and Gordon 1988; Lindenbaum and Lock 1993). Medicine and its associated technologies are put to practice everywhere in a conceptual space, one inevitably shaped by non-discursive formations, by the 'thick tissue' of the 'background of intelligibility' (Dreyfus and Rabinow 1982, p. 58), by, in other words, culture.

One must read across cultural domains in any given setting in order to produce a contextualized analysis of reproductive behaviour. Hence, in addition to prevalent ideas about gender relations, individual autonomy, and reproduction in Japan, I will also consider briefly the recent history and transformation of family relations, attitudes towards children and their worth, attitudes towards technology and the 'mastery' of nature, and struggles with cultural identity, particularly as it is debated with respect to the alterity of 'the West'. This is the social milieu within which the government, medical professionals, and individual women, their partners and families, create knowledge and make judgements about reproductive behaviour. Of course, in a complex society such as contemporary Japan, this knowledge, although it often remains tacit, is open to dispute and transformation once made explicit in certain arenas, and it is widespread popular knowledge about what supposedly takes place in 'Western' societies that functions within Japan as a major stimulation for self-reflection about reproductive technologies and practices.

My focus of attention is on accounts in connection with reproductive technologies and the new genetics given to me by women of reproductive age living in Tokyo.[3] Their responses reveal the ways in which culturally informed ideas about kinship and the social and moral order shape discourse about reproductive technologies and the new genetics, discourse that influences but does not wholly determine the application of these technologies in Japan.[4] It is evident that despite widespread lip-service to the 'Western' notions of individual rights and choice, the extended family continues to play a major role in connection with reproduction, both as a normalized moral agent—an internalized hegemonic force—and also literally through direct intervention on the part of potential grandparents into the activities of their children of reproductive age.

It takes little imagination to realize that the burden of decision making, for the immediate future at least, which falls on women of reproductive age, their partners and, in the case of Japan, frequently on the extended family, is to do with abortion. If techniques are developed and standardized such that gene therapy that subverts certain specific diseases can be institutionalized, then abortion may be avoided. However, women considered to be 'at risk' for bearing diseased children will nevertheless have to undergo IVF (in vitro fertilization), a procedure that is by no means without a health risk, and has low success rates with respect to completed pregnancies, ranging on average between 15 and 25 per cent depending upon the clinic. An additional stage must be added to the usual IVF procedures when gene therapy is involved, namely that the resultant fertilized embryos, up to ten or more if the procedure goes well, are examined for their genetic endowment prior to implantation into the uterus. Only those embryos which do not exhibit a full complement of genes for the one or more specific diseases of concern to the future parents would be implanted. All women who go through IVF are inevitably placed in a position where the chance of multiple births is greatly increased and, more often than not, unwanted 'inferior' embryos are either disposed of or stored for possible use in the future. The Japanese women whom I interviewed were, with very few exceptions, not cognizant of these outcomes associated with IVF, and interviews I have conducted in North America reveal a similar lack of knowledge among women of reproductive age.

PROTECTING THE FAMILY FROM NATURE'S MISTAKES

Yamada-san (let us call her) has two boys under the age of two and a half, the eldest of whom, Kenji, unmistakably has Down's syndrome. She lives in a rather spacious house, by Tokyo standards, with her husband, parents-in-law, unmarried brother-in-law, and her mother-in-law's mother. The young Yamada couple occupy two rooms on the second floor where all the activities of their daily life take place, except for the relatively rare occasions when the entire family engages in some activity together. Yamada-san's husband was out at work when I visited their home at her invitation, proffered when I met her at a routine clinic visit in connection with Kenji's health. Yamada-san sat and talked to me in the confined space which serves as both kitchen and living room. An enormous television set, the sound turned down as we talked, dominated the scene, but it failed for the most part to distract the youngsters as intended, who worked very hard at capturing their mother's attention, using the entire gamut of tactics available to children with an as yet limited verbal capacity. Twenty-eight at the time of her first pregnancy, Yamada-san had been assured that everything was 'normal', and she experienced a relatively easy and uneventful birth, although the baby was rather small, and was kept in hospital for a couple of weeks. It was only four or five months later that, together with her husband, she was informed that Kenji had Down's syndrome. Yamada-san insists that she did not suspect that anything was wrong prior to hearing the doctor's diagnosis, but in retrospect she believes that the medical staff were aware of the problem soon after the birth. Yamada-san and her husband debated as to who should be told about the diagnosis. After consulting with their doctor, who agreed with them that nobody other than themselves need know, they decided not to tell even members of their extended family, who to this day apparently are unaware of any major difficulty. The family has been told only that Kenji is a little slow in developing, and that is all.

The interpretation given by the ten or more Japanese acquaintances to whom I have talked about this case, is that Yamada-san's brother-in-law can expect great difficulty in securing a marriage partner if it is publicly known that there is Down's syndrome 'in the family'. Furthermore, it is too painful for the older generation to have to directly confront such 'shameful' knowledge, namely that there are 'poor' genes in their lineage. (The assumption that this condition is inherited is, of course, mistaken. The chromosomal abnormality which results in Down's syndrome occurs in utero.) It is agreed that in all probability the grandparents have surmised what is wrong with their grandchild. However, that which is not verbalized does not exist, even if visual evidence works to the contrary.

Not all Japanese families would, of course, deal with the situation in similar fashion, but this particular family is living out a dominant ideology of long standing (equally evident in many other societies), namely that it is understandable that no one would want to marry into a family where there is clear evidence of genetic disability (even if it is not clearly an inheritable disability), or madness in the progeny. Hence the affected child and his mother must be isolated, hidden, lied about, in order that the family as a unit can be protected. Before the war a child like Kenji may well have been kept as a virtual prisoner in the house. Today many institutions in Japanese society—support groups, the medical world, the school system—provide some assistance; nevertheless behind the closed doors of the family residence, women are often confined with their offending children to an inconspicuous corner. If they are to procure help, then they must reach out secretively, as does Yamada-san, to obtain whatever community support she can find.

My reading of why Yamada-san asked me to come and visit the family is that she wishes her plight to be known and talked about, no doubt in order that others might become more aware of the constraints on women in her situation. Yamada-san did not hesitate for a moment to undergo amniocentesis during her second pregnancy, and she would have had an abortion if an anomaly had been detected. She states that she could not possibly have cared for two children with Down's syndrome given the circumstances in which she finds herself. However, Yamada-san does not believe that one should use technology to create the 'perfect' baby, nor would she have submitted herself to amniocentesis if it had been offered to her during her first pregnancy. Although she could not manage two affected infants, Yamada-san has reacted to the birth of her child as do many women in her position. Her experience has made her fully alert to the prejudice inherent in Japanese society towards those citizens labelled as 'deficient'. She loves and is devoted to her child, and her prime response is to protect him from stigma; nevertheless, Yamada-san occasionally detects feelings of ambivalence in herself, since she admits that at times she longs for Kenji to be 'normal'. This is in spite of the fact that their current doctor has encouraged the Yamadas to think of Kenji not as abnormal or diseased, but simply as having a particular body constitution—a body 'type'—similar to someone with an allergic predisposition or a tendency to put on weight. Yamada-san remains conflicted about the abortion of foetuses in which an 'abnormality' is detected, not because she is against abortion or testing in principle, but because she fears (as do many people around the globe concerned about the rights of the disabled) that there will be a backlash against children such as her son, so that even the limited progress made to date in Japan to integrate such children fully into society will be undone, and the prejudice they often experience will continue unchallenged.

Yamada-san's case gives us a glimpse into the pressure placed on Japanese women with respect to reproduction, pressure which one would predict might drive them to cooperate willingly with the medicalization of their bodies. Pregnancy and childbirth are not the affair of an individual, or even in most cases that of a couple. In Japan they remain, as was the case historically, the intimate concern of the extended family, even when the family no longer resides under one roof (Miyaji and Lock 1994). The extended family should be protected at all costs and the 'standing of the family' (*iegara*) must be maintained. Although public campaigns and media exposure have worked to reduce the stigma associated with disability of all kinds, people with psychiatric diagnoses, for example, are still abandoned by their relatives in institutions at times, as are babies born with deformities, or unwanted infants. Although many of the physically impaired are more publicly visible than formerly, others pass their lives secreted away from public view. Concern about genetic anomalies has also meant that those people exposed to atomic bomb radiation, together with their offspring, have found it exceedingly difficult to get married, except among themselves. The Japanese are not alone, of course, in this kind of response to sick and marginalized people.

Yamada-san and her husband, like virtually all Japanese except the very old, understand simple Mendelian inheritance. They are cognizant of what so many people fail to recognize, even when primed about genetics in general, namely that Down's syndrome is not transmitted from one generation to another through the inheritance of mutated genes, but is the result of a mutation in a mother's genes during her lifetime. Perhaps because he is sensitive to this, Yamada-san's husband has suggested that Kenji's problem may have resulted from something his wife did during pregnancy. Such an attitude is common in Japan, and stems in part from an awareness shared by most educated people that the genotype by no means determines phenotypic expression. Yamada-san has gone over her memories of the nine months before the birth of her son, for she too is fearful that her behaviour may have influenced the fate of her child. Genetic explanations, although apparently providing rational accounts about the way in which certain diseases are beyond human control, do not necessarily rule out multicausality in the minds of those seeking answers as to why their particular infant is afflicted. Nor do they necessarily relieve the family, especially the mother, of moral responsibility. This is particularly so in societies, such as Japan, which have never been enamoured with explanations grounded in biological determinism.

THE STIGMA OF DIFFERENCE

The mother of a 4-year-old girl with neurofibromatosis has had a very different experience to that of Yamada-san, in that, in her estimation, her husband and the four grandparents have been fully engaged in doing all they can to help the child. The grandparents have actively encouraged this couple to get the best medical help that can be obtained (all of which is available under the socialized health care system), and to make their daughter's life as happy as possible. While being interviewed, Doi-san made it clear that she wishes a genetic test had been available at the time she became pregnant.[5] Although she is very impressed by the mothers she meets at the genetics clinic and how, in her words, they are 'doing their best for their children', she also believes that she may well have chosen to undergo an abortion if she had known about the suffering and prejudice her daughter would have to face. Her child is stigmatized by her peers because she has numerous brown pigmented blotches all over her face and body that are impossible to hide. Doi-san is concerned not so much about future serious illness that may be in store for her daughter, but about the discrimination both she and her daughter experience in public places. Parents of children in the kindergarten that Doi's daughter attends have told their children not to play with her, and several mothers communicated to Doi-san that they were concerned about infection. Doi-san believes that the values of Japanese society discriminate against her daughter, and is adamant that until public attitudes change, children who have visible signs of illness or deformity, and their parents, will never be at ease living in Japan. As we will see, it is this concern about the stigmatization of children who are visibly different that is one of the strongest forces driving Japanese attitudes about the utility of genetic testing and screening.

NATURE AS MODEL FOR THE PLANNED FAMILY

Recent anthropological research into social change and the reproductive patterns of populations shows indisputably that there is no simple transition from pre-modern 'natural fertility', that is, a situation where fertility is apparently little controlled, to a modern situation, one where family size is planned. Handwerker (1986) argues that a fertility transition reflects a cultural transformation. Greenhalgh (1990, 1995) insists that inquiry into fertility patterns must be understood as multi-levelled, that is, as 'explicitly historical and attentive to political and economic as well as social and cultural forces' (1995, p. 13). Further, she argues that attention should be paid to the specific location and agency of subjects in the context of their everyday lives, which are in turn part of larger macro-variables—national, regional, and global. Bledsoe points out that it is inappropriate to limit investigation to prenatal practices of fertility control. Practices such as infanticide, fosterage, and adoption must be added into the picture (1990). One of my objectives in this paper is to show how, despite massive economic and organizational changes in Japan, there does not appear to have been a radical break in attitudes towards the reasons for control of fertility. Further, although techniques for control of family size have changed, if both pre- and post-natal behaviours are taken into consideration, then these continuities become increasingly apparent. The present findings are exploratory, and need further systematic examination.

It is widely agreed that the dominant gender ideology in Japan today is one in which women are expected to enter into marriage and to produce two children, preferably one of each sex, for whose health and well-being the mother is held primarily responsible. It is also recognized by a good number of Japanese cultural commentators that this is a post-war ideology, a hardening of more flexible pre-war conceptions about women's roles in the family (Wakita and Hanley 1994–5). Until well into this century, the majority of Japanese women were valued above all for their economic contribution to the household. If no offspring were forthcoming from a marriage, or if the children were unable for whatever reason to carry on the family business, then a suitable substitute could be adopted quite easily into the extended family, either as a child or as an adult (Backnick 1983; Lebra 1993 (see Bledsoe (1990) for similar practices in Africa)). Prior to the World War II economic pragmatism was the rule and, if blood ties (*chi no tsunagari*) were not effective in keeping the household competitive, then kin-related or even non-kin adoptees would do as substitutes. Of course, fertility was of concern; women were described at times as a 'borrowed womb', or a 'household utensil' or 'tool' until the end of the nineteenth century, and those who did not produce children within a year or little more after marriage were labelled as 'stone women'. But rather than fertility itself, it was the quality of the offspring that was of prime concern. Women could on occasion be sent back to their natal families if they failed to conceive; nevertheless in many households, their physical labour and management skills were equally, if not more, important. After the Meiji Restoration of 1867, women were also valued highly as educators of their children, particularly in connection with morals, community and national objectives. Motherhood and the raising of healthy, intelligent children rather than fertility was invested with prestige, so much so, that Japanese feminists have described the Meiji government literature designed to invest worth in mothering as *boseiron* (treatises on motherhood) (Mitsuda 1985).

The planned family was a key concept used by the Japanese state founded at the Meiji Restoration of 1867, but it has been argued that something akin to family planning has a history which commenced long before the nineteenth century (Hanley 1985). La Fleur notes the evidence that infanticide was practised from at least medieval times in Japan. Nevertheless, by 1725, the population had swelled to approximately 30 million and Edo, at one million, was the most densely populated city in the world at that time, followed closely by Osaka and Kyoto. There is reliable historical evidence, however, from both temple and government records which shows that from the mid-eighteenth century, for at least 100 years, population growth levelled off, in strong contrast to China and Korea (La Fleur 1992).

Malthus's thesis was that a reduction in the growth of a population could be attributed only to famine, war, or epidemics, since the majority of individuals would not exert control over their own reproductive behaviour. La Fleur creates a more sophisticated argument. He suggests that in Japan, in areas ravished by poverty and food shortage, high infant mortality existed, probably exacerbated by the practice of infanticide. However, in central Honshñ, where, in the eighteenth century, there was considerable prosperity, reduction in family size can be largely attributed to human volition. The explicit objective was to create small, healthy, and economically productive families. It is of note that official government policy of the time strongly encouraged population growth, since the shogunate wished to increase its income through taxation based on the number of individuals in family units. Despite government edicts about increasing family size, sufficient people chose to enhance the quality of their family life by exerting control over unwanted pregnancies and births, producing an effect on the size of the entire population. Although abortion and infanticide were common practices, apparently no sex-selected disposal of newborn babies took place (LaFleur 1992).

Recently, Cornell has produced an argument more finely tuned than that of La Fleur in which, using the methods of comparative microanalysis on fertility and mortality rates, she concludes that deliberate fertility control through infanticide was not as systematic or as carefully planned on a long-term basis as the idea of the 'planned family' might suggest. She concludes that the most important factors that contributed to a low fertility rate in early modern Japan were the cultural practices of prolonged lactation and out-migration of married men in order to work. She notes in addition that considerable variation existed among villages, variation that can only be accounted for through the use of carefully nuanced contextual analyses. Furthermore, Cornell argues that infant mortality rates from infectious disease, although they fluctuated, remained high during this period, and therefore families could not feel secure until a child had matured, a situation that it seems reasonable to assume would not encourage infanticide practices.

Cornell insists, however, that multiple components were at work, and she does not deny that people made active choices in connection with reproduction. The data show that in the village of Yokouchi, for example, over a 200-year period from 1671 to 1871, in each of 100 households, five children survived to age one. All of these households experienced one death of an infant before age one from disease or other causes and, in addition, it appears that, in one in every three of those households, one infant was deliberately killed. These findings suggest to Cornell that short-term choices were being made about family size, and infanticide was one form of fertility control which was made use of by a good number of people (Cornell 1996). It is highly likely that deformed or obviously impaired infants would be among those who were killed.

The term for infanticide, *mabiki*, is a euphemism whose prime referent is to rice cultivation, and specifically to the culling of seedlings. It was well established among Japanese farmers of the time that thinning of seedlings, particularly the weaker ones, would yield the best crop, and an analogy was explicitly made to the cultivation of human families. Perhaps the continual likening of social arrangements to the natural order in connection with virtually all social life, basic to philosophic thinking of the time, encouraged use of the term *mabiki* in connection with the manipulation of human life. Infanticide was relatively easily justified as a 'natural' but necessary human intrusion into reproduction, and was performed in spite of government policy to the contrary. This reconstruction of the historical record tells us nothing, of course, about the suffering of those people directly involved in such practices; the fact that infanticide was likened to the cultivation of crops and was carried out, usually by midwives, for the 'benefit' of the family should not be read as an indication that there was little or no individual remorse.

From the Meiji Restoration on, systematic planning of the population was nationally orchestrated, and a self-conscious attempt to encourage 'human development' was part of this programme (Garon 1993) in which planned families played a central role. Although abortion was tacitly accepted prior to the Meiji Restoration, after 1880, it was assumed that economic growth could not be sustained without population growth, and abortion was made a criminal act. By the late nineteenth century virtually all women received some schooling. Less emphasis was placed on the Confucian edicts of chastity, obedience, patience, and devotion—the essentials of 'good wives and wise mothers'—and women were now educated more broadly with a focus on moral education and hygiene. According to government tracts of the time, the masses were to be educated to rationalize their lives in the name of progress; Japan had to 'catch up' with the West, and the 'habits' of the people must therefore be reformed through 'moral suasion' (*kyìka*) (Garon 1993). Family units were explicitly likened to the family of the Emperor, conflating the macrocosm of the nation state with the microcosm of the family. Families, like the state, were in theory to be harmonious units in which, with the exception of certain ritual occasions, individual desire was suppressed for the sake of social and moral order.

The Taisho era of 1912 to 1926 saw the routinization of a systematic collection of vital statistics, and public health interventions were set in place throughout the country. Despite the continuing widespread belief that *mabiki* was beneficial to society—that it was, in effect, a humanely instituted means of perfecting Darwinian natural selection—efforts were made to eliminate this practice, and to reduce the infant mortality rate. At the time, public concern was evident, because it was thought that encouraging the survival of every baby would simply increase the presence of 'weak' people in society (Miyaji and Lock 1994). By 1940, when human bodies were in great demand for military service, those couples who raised more than ten healthy children were given awards, a policy not unlike those of Europe and North America of the time. Although a high birth rate was actively encouraged, at the same time, shortly before Germany introduced a similar ruling, the abortion law was amended and renamed the National Eugenic Law. Abortion was now legally permitted for eugenic and medical reasons, which meant in practice that those women designated as unfit to be mothers would forcibly undergo abortions. Many Japanese women remain aware of these wartime policies, and a lingering resentment is evident at any effort on the part of contemporary Japanese governments to intrude into reproductive matters (see below).

INDIVIDUAL DESIRE AS A THREAT TO THE NATURAL ORDER

The formal extended family, the *ie*, with its national obligations and patriarchal power base, was officially abolished as a result of post-war reforms. Sixty per cent of Japanese people now live in a nuclear family. However, in addition to those 40 per cent officially designated as extended households, many people spend much of their lives in a loosely affiliated vertically extended family where elderly relatives live close by, and a sense of obligation and familial ties remain strong (Lock 1993). Although usually described as a secular society, the ancestors central to the *ie*, and keepers of moral order, continue to play a visible role in Japanese life today (Smith ms). However, most women are quick to point out that rather than the entire patriarchal lineage, as was formerly the case, it is simply in memory of the deceased parents and grandparents of their spouse that rituals are performed today. In addition, a good number venerate the memory of their own parents, even though women no longer officially belong to their natal lineage once married. These ritual activities, usually described simply as part of daily life and not as religious belief, testify to the importance of family continuity, and to the hold past generations have over the living.

Although there is evidence that many people actively uphold extended family ideals, albeit in modified form, a dominant ideology exists that the values commonly associated with nuclear households have swept through Japan. Because these values are associated with individualism and private, rather than communal or national, interests, they cause the government considerable discomfort (Lock 1993).

The production and socialization of two healthy children is today expected to fully occupy women, together with the care and nurturance of husbands and elderly relatives. Despite the fact that nearly 70 per cent of Japanese women are currently in the labour force (most designated as part-time workers and with no security, but nevertheless working full time at low wages), the 'professional' housewife is assumed by virtually everyone to be representative of contemporary Japanese women. Those numerous women who work, almost without exception, also manage the household and raise their children virtually single handedly. Under these conditions, a child with a disability places an enormous burden on the mother, particularly so because institutionalized social support is minimal. Since a woman's financial contribution to the household is often assumed to be simply for luxury items (quite erroneously in the majority of cases), the expectation is that, should a child need special attention, a mother will relinquish her job to provide this service. Because women are also made fully responsible for the care of dependent parents-in-law, the combination of economic deprivation together with the physical burden of family care and nursing duties can easily become insupportable.

Due to continuing gender discrimination in the workforce, life in a nuclear family provides relatively little opportunity to foster individualism and independence among women, even though the government fears that this is indeed the case. Current family law, despite its proclaimed concern about equality and dignity, adds further restrictions to female independence (Toshitani 1994). Nevertheless, the rhetoric about family life in Japan, influenced by what is thought to be 'modern' and 'Western' ideals, has shifted markedly in the past 20 years to one of individual rights and choice, and independence for young couples. Nevertheless, implicit in this 'modern' discourse remains the assumption that all women will 'naturally' embrace the tasks of reproduction, together with the nurturing of family members.

Until as recently as 10 years ago, 98 per cent of Japanese women married. Today this number has dropped to 88 per cent, and the divorce rate is increasing, but remains low, at 1.45 per thousand, much lower than in North America. Until very recently, virtually all women married in their mid-twenties and produced the required two children within a very narrow time span of the ensuing 5 or 6 years. Families were usually completed in size when the mother was aged 34 or younger. Women who remained unmarried at 25 were described as *urenoki* (unsold merchandise) or *tì ga tatsu* (overripe fruit); nevertheless, the average age of marriage has in the past few years increased to 27, but the basic pattern remains in place. Virtually all children are born to married couples (99 per cent of women who gave birth in 1992 were married or in committed common law arrangements, a figure which has been stable for three decades), and the majority of women stop working once pregnant for the first time (many of them are in effect forced to leave their place of employment since it is believed that women cannot work effectively with young children in the household). Desired birth spacing and family comple- tion is accomplished by a combination of contraception (the condom is the preferred technique) and abortion. As is well known, abortion plays a major role in current family planning in Japan, although in recent years, with more effective use of contraception, the numbers have decreased so that figures are now lower than in America, this in spite of the fact that the pill remains unavailable for contraceptive purposes (Lock 1993, 1996).

The Eugenic Protection Law of 1948, designed to pave the way for relatively easy legal abortion in order to control population size and quality, remains in place today with a few modifications. Japanese feminists continue to be concerned that the legality of abortion was decreed from above by those in power as a national policy, rather than being the result of activism on the part of women (Hara 1996). In theory most abortions are carried out because of economic hardship and, although abortion among young unmarried women is on the increase, the majority are performed on women who have completed their planned family of two children.

Screening for unusual, sometimes devastating, genetic diseases has been covered by the Japanese health care system for several decades. This screening programme was institutionalized because geneticists claim that consanguinous marriage has been rather high compared to other countries, with the result that certain inherited diseases are present in the population, some of which appear to be unique to Japan (Ohkura and Kimura 1989). However, very few women indeed test positive, because such diseases are extremely rare. None of the malaria-related haemoglo- binopathies, such as sickle-cell anaemia, are present in Japan, and Down's syn- drome is relatively unusual (this disease is associated with pregnancies in women aged 35 and over, and few Japanese become pregnant once past their early thirties (although the case study above was an exception)). Given this situation, there has been little pressure to institutionalize genetic counselling services, and abortion carried out as the result of genetic testing is still rather unusual in Japan.

Abortion for the purposes of sex selection is officially discouraged, with the sole exception of eliminating those very few male foetuses with major sex-linked malformations. However, everyone knows the technique is available at several major hospitals, and that if a woman insists, particularly if she hands a suitably valued gift over to the physician, she can have an abortion solely on the basis of the sex of the foetus. It is usually claimed that today in Japan it is male foetuses that will be eliminated because couples want to ensure that they have a girl to look after them in their old age (this is also borne out by adoption practices in which girl babies under 1 year are preferred, although in general adoption is unusual today (Goodman ms)). There is, however, no reason for concern at present that the sex ratio of the Japanese population could be skewed through the application of sex- selected abortions.

Although the adoption of children has been widely accepted in the past in Japan, this practice was usually carried out with the pragmatic purpose of making an extended family economically viable, where none or very few offspring were born. Surrogate mothers were made extensive use of until the end of the last century, particularly among the samurai class (Shimazu 1994). Concubines were most often household servants whose male children could be officially adopted, written into the family registry, and sometimes treated as equals to biologically related children, while their birth mothers retained the status of servants. Children were rarely adopted as babies, however, because their 'potential' as economic contributors to the household had first to be established. Alternatively, 'spare' children of relatives would be adopted once their 'worth' was clear (Lebra 1993). Another common form of adoption was to marry a young man into a family which had only produced girls. The man would be required to take on the name of his wife's family and work for them, thus continuing both the family business and its name.

In contrast to the 'controlled' selection of concubines as surrogates, and child or youth adoptees for utilitarian purposes, insemination by donor and contract surrogacy with a stranger raises moral concerns and anxieties in contemporary Japan. Principal among them are two: If only one parent (in particular the mother) is the biological parent, then it is usually assumed that such a family will not be 'harmonious'. People are explicit that a non-biological parent (especially a father) is unlikely to find himself able to love and care appropriately for a child created through semen donation (Shirai 1992); moreover there is a chance that he may not officially acknowledge (*ninchi*) the child, which will then have a diminished status as a citizen. Secondly, there is concern because the donor is anonymous and one cannot, in effect, 'control' the 'quality' of the outcome, as one could in the past by waiting until the child had shown its potential. Goodman notes a similar reservation about adoption, and cites a Japanese adage: '*doko no uma no hone ka wakaranai*' (you can't tell from which horse the bone comes) (ms). A few Japanese families seek out Japanese Americans as surrogate mothers (if necessary, Chinese Americans are acceptable as substitutes), but this is reported in the media as desperate and unsuitable behaviour, in which the financial transaction adds a considerable burden to an already distasteful act.

Almost every woman whom I interviewed, often without being asked, expressed surprise and a certain repugnance at what they understand to be a common desire among 'Western' women to adopt 'foreign' babies, especially when the external features of the child are different from those of the parents. Even though exotic facial features have a certain fascination, there is, evidently, an overriding concern about both the appropriateness of physical features and the human 'qualities' of an adopted child for successful integration into Japanese society. Offspring in which 'difference' is clearly apparent, whether it be that of 'race', disability, or behaviour, will, it is assumed, encounter discrimination such as that experienced by Doi-san and her daughter. Accounts of discrimination perpetrated against returnee Japanese children raised abroad reveal that such a concern is justified (Goodman 1990).

REPRODUCTIVE PRAXIS AND THE OTHER

Women are bombarded daily with advice and stories about how to create and produce healthy families in Japan, but much of this information is explicitly 'Western' in origin. Women's responses to the politics of reproductive technologies, and their attitudes about the 'correct' family, should be interpreted in light of this conflicted discourse about self and Other, Japan and the West, tradition and modernity, and technology and the natural. A distinct ambivalence on the part of a good number of women, including many vocal feminists, can be detected about whether what happens in the 'West' can or should be taken as a model for Japan. This ambivalence is present in the responses of the majority of women interviewed, and ensures that no simple hankering after freedom from the acknowledged constraints of Japanese society, nor a desire to emulate the West, emerges in the attitudes of women when discussing reproductive technologies and genetic testing.

To summarize thus far, throughout the history of the planned family in Japan, women and their partners have at times actively resisted government intrusion into their sexual activities; at other times they have apparently cooperated. It is not as yet clear how much resistance, if any, took place during the war years, when women were explicitly made into 'mothers of the war effort', but, as the interview data to be discussed below suggest, there is a somewhat mixed reception today in connection with the dominant ideology of reproducing the 'correct' family. Many women of all ages are sensorious about past government intrusions into what is now thought of as their private family life (a concept which barely existed in pre-war years). The majority have some awareness of the government and military propaganda broadcast in connection with reproduction during the war years, and resent it. It is not surprising that the rhetoric of today's government, to produce more children, is greeted with a mixture of cynicism and outright dismissal. By contrast, although there is some dissent, the majority of women appear to participate with little hesitation in a dominant ideology, also fostered by the government, with respect to the production of a healthy, 'normal' family, in which a married woman is made responsible for the birth and raising of productive Japanese citizens.

It is not government communications which directly affect the ideas and behaviour of women, however, but tacit knowledge, shared by the majority, about what kind of human relations and family arrangements are best for the creation and raising of children who will 'fit' successfully into society. Whereas in the past the potential economic contribution of children was of overriding importance, today there is room for sentiments such as individual happiness, pleasure, and even untrammelled desire on the part of parents in connection with their offspring. However, these aspirations remain contained within the structure of the conventional family, and should not in the long run disrupt the dominant social and moral order.

Until the recent past it was customary to investigate potential marriage partners in connection with their character and health. Such inquiries covered not only 'inherited' diseases, including 'mental' illness, but also tuberculosis and cancer.

Today these investigations are not as intensive as used to be the case, but continue to take place, particularly in connection with those marriages arranged by the extended family. A large number of middle-aged and older people remain uncomfortable about so-called 'love marriages' for which in theory individuals may freely choose their partners—it is thought that a match created out of the capricious fancy of sexual attraction is unlikely to weather the stresses of full participation in Japanese society. Just as it is acceptable to have the making of a marriage overseen (even if discreetly), it is also thought by many, both young couples and the older generation alike, to be a sensible move to make use of technology where necessary in order to create the next generation as desired. Of particular concern is the health and well-being of unborn children, since it is widely believed that any child which 'sticks out' is likely to lead an unhappy and unfulfilled life due to the stigma and prejudice present in Japanese society. Given this environment, technologically assisted reproduction of a healthy child is an attractive option for many, but any wish to resort to technology is frequently countered by another widely shared belief, namely that intrusive technologies are unnatural, contrary to Japanese custom, and dangerous to both individuals and society.

PLANNED FAMILIES AND THE LANGUAGE OF INDIVIDUAL RIGHTS

No nostalgia was apparent for the formal extended family of the past in the interviews, at least not with respect to its hegemony over female reproduction. Several women stated explicitly that a woman's body should not be used 'like a tool' in the service of the family, as had been the experience of many of the mothers of the women interviewed (Lock 1993). However, none of the 50 women, whose ages range from 19 to 44, are unequivocally opposed to technological interventions into reproduction. Without exception they find the use of contraceptives acceptable, and all but one are unopposed to abortion. Most respondents agreed that abortion among young unmarried women is a sign of irresponsible behaviour on their part (the male contribution to pregnancies is almost always ignored in this type of discussion (see also Hardacre 1997)). However, within marriage, when used to keep the family at the desired size of two children (usually determined it is claimed, as in the past, by family economics), abortion is considered to be a sad event, but an unavoidable outcome of 'human nature'. One woman stated explicitly that if the government gave more assistance for child support then there would be fewer abortions (see also Shirai 1989). Like every other woman interviewed, she believes strongly that children should be actively desired, and that there should be sufficient resources for nurturance and education through to completion of the university level.

Several women stated that it is unfair to bring children into the world who cannot be given a good chance in life; nevertheless, more than half the women regard abortion as 'a kind of murder' because they accept that human life commences at conception. Half of the women have made use of, or would (if the occasion arose) make use of, a ritualized ceremony designed to placate the soul of an aborted foetus (*mizuko kñyo*) (see also Hardacre 1997). Having an abortion clearly causes distress for numerous women who undergo this procedure, but it is important to note that there are no anti-abortion campaigns in Japan, and the institutional climate in which abortions take place is entirely free from moral retribution.

Women comply willingly with technologies which in their view are non-invasive. Ultrasound, for example, is given routinely three or four times during each pregnancy and up to seven or eight times at certain hospitals ensuring, women report, that they feel 'safe'. The interviews revealed that women often regard pregnancy as a dangerous time. It was clear that the possibility of giving birth to a baby with an 'abnormality' creates considerable anxiety, and that women feel personally implicated, as did Yamada-san, if a child is born who is less than perfect. Even the remote chance of a neonate having 'minor' aberrations such as six fingers or toes was frequently cited as a reason for undergoing repeated ultrasound examinations and cooperating with medical interventions.

The majority of women are cautious about all types of reproductive technologies deemed as invasive; nevertheless there is a widely shared sentiment that if nature can be perfected through technology, then there is nothing inherently wrong with its use. (Shirai (1992) found that infertile women feel more strongly about this than do others.) Even when reminded that powerful chemical stimulation is involved in all technologies used in connection with infertility, any fear of iatrogenesis is outweighed, it seems, by a desire to have children. This is a paradoxical response given that the pill is rejected by women themselves on grounds of iatrogenesis; nevertheless, 46 people responded that if a woman really desired a child, then IVF is acceptable. However, most of these same women went on to add that they themselves hoped that they could avoid such an unpleasant dilemma (although several of them were visiting the gynaecologist at the time of the interview because of a fear that they were unable to conceive). There was agreement that technology should be available as a service for judicious use in times of distress. Those few interviewees completely opposed to IVF stated explicitly that women and their families should be educated into realizing that life can be fulfilled in many ways, and that childbearing should not be the unquestioned goal of every woman.

Although IVF is acceptable to most, the thought of its use by unmarried or gay couples makes most Japanese women uncomfortable, although lesbian couples are regarded more favourably. Once again, nurturance of the child in a legally recognized family, and society's negative reaction to any child not raised appropriately, is uppermost in people's minds when they give these responses. Artificial insemination by donor (AID) and surrogate motherhood are considered acceptable by only five women, who agreed that if someone believes her life to be completely without meaning unless she has a child to care for, then she should make use of technological assistance. However, the majority are very concerned that a child conceived by these means would not be loved or cared for adequately; most believe strongly that biological and social parenting should coincide, and that if they do not, then the child may suffer. Tsuge (1993) has found that Japanese gynaecologists hold similar opinions.

All but six women are opposed to adoption, and among those six only one would adopt a child of foreign parentage. Nearly everyone agreed that today 'blood ties' are important and, in effect, going outside the family is 'risky', biologically speaking. Women also suggested that an adopted child might not be cared for as would a genetically related offspring. However, several women stated that if their husbands wanted to adopt a child then they would acquiesce. Adoption is explicitly associated by most women with the patriarchal extended family and even with concubinage, and so is shunned. Nearly half of the women were clear that, if IVF failed (as they well know is often the case), they would rather not have a child at all than adopt one. Once again, the well-being of the child was stated as a concern, since without exception everyone agreed that children who are 'different' have a hard time growing up in Japan.

Resort to the artifice of technology to achieve the planned family, one where the biological and social parentage coincides, is better, it seems, than transgressing categories of self and Other, Japanese and foreigner, even though by so doing one could avoid the 'unnatural' use of invasive medical technologies. Under the circumstances it is perhaps not so surprising that, despite the exceptional invasiveness of the procedure, for more than half the women interviewed, an artificially induced post-menopausal pregnancy would be acceptable, if this was the only means by which a woman could achieve the family size she desired.

Given that the economic unit of the *ie*—the formal extended family—is no longer recognized, a planned family deliberately created with economic purposes primarily in mind has fallen into disrepute and 'smells' of the old patriarchal order. Nevertheless, the planned family remains a dominant ideology in contemporary Japan, but is one composed of two children, in which biological and social parentage coincide, where the health and welfare of the children rather than the family as a whole is uppermost in people's minds. When necessary, it is acceptable to use technology, whatever the involved risks, to achieve this laudable desire.

Resort to IVF and other reproductive technologies is usually couched in the language of individual rights—the rights of a woman to have a healthy child, but further questioning reveals that this rhetoric is quite superficial. All the women interviewed consult with their husbands about reproductive decisions, and the majority indicate that husbands usually have the final word in most families. Despite the fact that everyone agreed that discussions about reproduction are no longer appropriate or necessary among the extended family, two young pregnant women whom I interviewed had been brought to the clinic by their mothers-in-law for genetic testing. It was quite evident, in spite of the doctor's efforts to keep the older women out of the clinical encounter, that it would be they who would make decisions on behalf of the younger women, both of whom had received very little education by Japanese standards.

In my previous work I have come across cases where women were forcefully urged to have abortions at the insistence of their mothers-in-law, on the grounds that the older woman would not act as a baby minder as was anticipated, given the family circumstances, by the younger couple (Lock 1993). The ideal today is one of freedom from the extended family, but reality does not always bear this out, particularly when grandparents form part of the household. Sometimes, as in the case of the Yamada family, secrets may have to be kept, causing severe limitations on aspirations for independence.

REPRODUCING THE PAST

It has been argued that Japanese women are becoming increasingly autonomous (Iwao 1993), but I want to suggest that at the same time the majority participate fully in what has been described as a 'community-based family type' where the principles of authority and equality are both recognized (Todd 1985). Thus, even if residence is that of a nuclear family, individual rights and liberty do not necessarily take priority over extended family interests. On the contrary, fulfilling community and extended family values tends to take precedence over individual desire. Communities and families often expect to influence reproductive decisions made by young couples, and explicitly censure what are deemed as inappropriate behaviours. Japanese feminists are concerned that these values drive women towards an uncritical acceptance of reproductive technologies, and increasingly to genetic testing, for the sake of the family, even when individual women may themselves be opposed to their use (Aoki and Marumoto 1992). At the same time, many Japanese women, feminist or not, are equally critical of an unfettered individualism that they associate with America.

The responses of women in this study reveal the tension inherent in the rhetoric of individualism and freedom on the one hand, and an unavoidable immersion in and obligation towards the family on the other hand which brings considerable satisfaction for most women (particularly when contrasted with media images of the violence and hedonism of the West). At the present time, this tension veers towards resolution in favour of the collectivity, but a striving for increased autonomy on the part of women may well be on the increase. Thus far, however, reproductive behaviour in which a known biological heritage is cultivated through careful planning and socialization to create, as far as is possible, desired and healthy children who will 'fit' with society, remains rock-like at the centre of the collectivity, giving it a remarkable stability. Thus, rationalized through the fostering of happiness, health, and the well-being of children, the two poles of biopower tend to coalesce, concealing in the name of governmentality contradictions and tensions between the public and private domains, individuals and the collectivity. This rigorous normalization of the planned family means that a heavy price is paid by those women and children who are socially marginalized, in terms of acceptance as full members of Japanese society. This is the case whether they be single women; women who are unable to bear children, whether it is they or their husbands who are infertile; or children who are perceived to be disadvantaged in any way (Goodman ms; Miyaji and Lock 1994; Shimazu 1994).

Perhaps because a good number of Japanese women are aware that they form the Other as seen from the West, many are sensitive these days to cultural imperialisms arising not only from within but also outside of Japan (as are other women beyond the Euro/American axis when they reflect upon their respective societies). This situation helps to make some women exceedingly alert to the complexities and contradictions in the praxis of reproductive technologies. With this in mind, one eminent research group in Japan composed largely of feminist social scientists has called for a re-examination of the idea that technological developments of all kinds possess uncontested 'virtue' (Ochanomizu Jōshidaigaku Seimei Rinri Kenkyūkai 1992). At the same time, this same group extends a sympathetic understanding to those women who choose to use technology to bring nature onside with respect to individual aspirations and familial demands.

Japanese women are in a position to, and for the most part do, fully resist any obvious intrusion on the part of government into their reproductive lives. They remain much more ambivalent, however, about questioning medical authority. Many women are equally ambivalent or actually unable to resist authority exerted directly over their fertility by husbands or close family members who are senior to them. However, other women who participated in this study reported that they live in largely satisfying, cooperative family environments, whether that of a nuclear or an extended household, where they believe that their opinions and interests are given due consideration. Whether the use of reproductive technologies is instigated primarily by individual women in their own interest, or by willing participation in familial objectives, or because individuals are coerced by family members or health care professionals, if the resultant children (when the technologies are successful) do not conform to widely held societal values about appropriate kinship and 'blood' relationships, their existence may well be judged as disruptive to the moral order. At present, the Japanese government can turn a blind eye to a small amount of sex-selected pregnancies, and a few babies produced through artificial insemination by donor or by means of surrogacy, provided that these behaviours are not openly institutionalized, even though such practices contradict the dominant moral order. The government can apparently rest assured that the vast majority of Japanese citizens do not support such practices. At the same time the state can actively support those technological practices used to reproduce the ideal, healthy family. Such support is indirect, and mediated through the medicalization of reproduction supplemented by ready, universal access to abortion. The systematic institutionalization of genetic testing and screening programmes will soon form a centrepiece of maternal health care in Japan, and the Ministry of Health and Welfare has recently picked genetic therapy as a state-of-the-art medical technology to be financially supported and widely promoted in the coming years. Those who speak up for the rights of the disabled are the only obvious dissenters thus far to the hegemony of the perfect family, the roots of which have a long heritage in Japan.

Notes

1. Portions of this chapter have previously been published under the title 'Perfecting Society: Reproductive Technologies, Genetic Testing, and the Planned Family in Japan', in M. Lock and P. Kaufert (eds.), *Pragmatic Women and Body Politics*, 1998, Cambridge: Cambridge University Press.
2. Detection of an abnormality of the most common autosomal recessive type such as sickle-cell anaemia, for example, while it reveals that the child will have the disease, cannot predict severity which may range from very mild to severe.
3. This research was conducted in 1994 with 50 women attending gynaecological and genetic counselling clinics in Tokyo. The women were aged between 19 and 44 years and all but two had received at least a high school education. Fifteen gynaecologists, a planned parenthood executive, and four Japanese sociologists and anthropologists working on related research were also interviewed.
4. The majority of women interviewed had not made use of the new reproductive technologies, aside from routine exposure to ultrasound. Thus, their views do not necessarily reflect what they would actually do, nor what is actually happening in practice, but rather convey how culturally informed expectations and knowledge influence the discourse about reproductive technologies.
5. A test is now available for neurofibromatosis, but is not routinely used for all pregnant women.

References

Aoki, Y., and Marumoto, Y. (1992), *Watashi rashisa de uma, umanai* (Being Myself: To Give Birth or Not), Tokyo: Nôsan Gyoson Bunka Kyôkai.
Bachnik, J. (1983), 'Recruitment Strategies for Household Succession: Rethinking Japanese Household Organization', *Man* (n. s.) 18: 160–82.
Beeson, D., and Doksum, T. (2001), 'Family values and resistance to genetic testing', in B. Hoffmaster (ed.), *Bioethics in Social Context*. Philadelphia: Temple University Press.
Bethke Elshtain, J. (1989), 'Technology as destiny', *The Progressive*, 53 (June): 19–23.
Bishop, J., and Waldholz, M. (1990), *Genome: The Story of the Most Astonishing Scientific Adventure of Our Time—The Attempt to Map All the Genes in the Human Body*, New York, NY: Simon and Schuster.
Bledsoe, C. (1990), 'The politics of children: fosterage and the social management of fertility among the Mende of Sierra Leone', in W. P. Handwerker (ed.), *Births and Power: Social Change and the Politics of Reproduction*, Boulder: Westview Press, pp. 81–100.
Campbell, J. C., and Ikegami, N. (1998), *The Art of Balance in Health Policy: Maintaining Japan's Low-cost, Egalitarian System*, Cambridge: Cambridge University Press.
Caulfield, T. and Feasby, C. (1998), 'The commercialization of human genetics in Canada: An overview of policy and legal issues', in B. M. Knoppers (ed.), *Social-Ethical Issues in Human Genetics*. Cowansville, Québec: Les Editions Yvon Blais, pp. 337–99.
Cornell, L. (1996), 'Infanticide in early modern Japan? Demography, culture and population growth', *Journal of Asian Studies*, 55: 22–50.
Dreyfus, H. L., and Paul, R. (1982), *Michel Foucault: Beyond Structuralism and Hermeneutics*, 2nd edition, Chicago: The University of Chicago Press.

Fox Keller, E. (1992), 'Nature, nurture and the human genome project', in D. J. Kevles and L. Hood (eds.), *The Code of Codes: Scientific and Social Issues in the Human Genome Project*, Cambridge: Harvard University Press, pp. 281–99.

Garon, S. (1993), 'Women's groups and the Japanese state: Contending approaches to political integration, 1890–1945', *Journal of Japanese Studies*, 19: 5–41.

Goodman, R. (1990), 'Deconstructing an anthropological text: A 'moving' account of returnee school children in contemporary Japan', in E. Ben-Ari, B. Moeran, and J. Valentine (eds.), *Unwrapping Japan*, Honolulu: University of Hawaii Press, pp. 163–87.

Goodman, R. (ms), ' "You don't know from which horse the bone came": Adoption and fostering in Japan'.

Gordon, C. (1991), 'Governmental Rationality: An Introduction', in G. Buchell, C. Gordon, and P. Miller (eds.), *The Foucault Effect: Studies in Governmentality*, Chicago: University of Chicago Press, pp. 1–52.

Greenhalgh, S. (1990), 'Toward a Political Economy of Fertility: Anthropological Contributions', *Population and Development Review*, 16: 85–106.

Greenhalgh, S. (ed.) (1995), *Situating Fertility: Anthropology and Demographic Inquiry*, Cambridge: Cambridge University Press.

Handwerker, W. P. (1986), 'Culture and reproduction: Exploring micro/macro linkages', in W. P. Handwerker (ed.), *Culture and Reproduction: An Anthropological Critique of Demographic Transition Theory*, Boulder: Westview Press, pp. 1–28.

Hanley, S. (1985), 'Family and fertility in four Tokugawa villages', in S. B. Hanley and A. P. Wolf (eds.), *Family and Population in East Asian History*, Stanford: Stanford University Press, pp. 196–228.

Hara, H. (1996), 'Translating the English term 'reproductive health-rights' into Japanese: Images of women and mothers in Japan's social policy today', *Proceedings of the 1996 Asian Women's Conference 'The Rise of Feminist Consciousness Against the Asian Patriarchy'*, Ewha Women's University, Asian Center for Women's Studies, Korea.

Hardacre, H. (1997), *Marketing the Menacing Fetus in Japan*, Berkeley: University of California Press.

Ikegami, N. (1989), 'Best medical practice: The case of Japan', *International Journal of Health Planning and Management*, 4: 239–54.

Iwao, S. (1993), *The Japanese Woman: Traditional Image and Changing Reality*, New York: The Free Press.

Koshland, D. (1989), 'Sequences and consequences of the human genome', *Science*, 146: 189.

La Fleur, W. (1992), *Liquid Life: Abortion and Buddhism in Japan*, New Jersey: Princeton University Press.

Lebra, T. (1993), *Above the Clouds: Status Culture of the Modern Japanese Nobility*, Berkeley: University of California Press.

Lewontin, R. C. (1992), 'The Dream of the Human Genome', *The New York Review of Book*, 49: 31–42.

Lindenbaum, S. and Lock, M. (1993), *Knowledge, Power and Practice: The Anthropology of Medicine and Everyday Life*, Berkeley: University of California Press.

Lock, M. (1993), *Encounters with Aging: Mythologies of Menopause in Japan and North America*, Berkeley: University of California Press.

—— (1996), 'Keeping the pressure off the Japanese health care system: The contribution of middle aged women', in J. Campbell and N. Ikegami (eds.), *Containing Health Care Costs in Japan*, Michigan University Press, pp. 207–25.

Lock, M. and Gordon, D. (1988), *Biomedicine Examined*, Dordrecht: Kluwer Academic Publishers.

——, and Kaufert, P. (eds.) (1998), *Pragmatic Women and Body Politics*, Cambridge: Cambridge University Press.

Mitsuda, K. (1985), 'Kindaiteki boseikan no juyô to kenkei: Kyôiku suru hahaoya kara ryôsai kenbo e' (The importance and transformation of the condition of modern motherhood: From education mother to good wife and wise mother)', in H. Wakita (ed.), *Bosei o tou* (What is Motherhood?), Kyoto: Jinbunshoin, pp. 100–29.

Miyaji, N., and Lock, M. (1994), 'Social and historical aspects of maternal and child health in Japan,' *Deadalus*, 123 (4): 87–112.

Ochanomizu Jōshidaigaku Seimei Rinri Kenkyūkai (1992), *Funin to yureru onna tachi: seishoku gijûtsu no genzai to jôsei no seishokuken* (Infertility and Women's Agony: The Current Situation in Connection with Reproductive Technologies and Women's Rights), Tokyo: Gakuyô shobô.

Office of Technology Assessment US Congress (1988), *Mapping our Genes*, Washington, DC: Government Printing Office.

Ohkura, K., and Kimura, R. (1989), 'Ethics and medical genetics in Japan', in D. C. Wertz and J. C. Fletcher (eds.), *Ethics and Human Genetics: A Cross-cultural Perspective*, Berlin: Springer-Verlag, pp. 294–316.

Petersen, A. (1997), 'Risk, Governance and the New Public Health', in A. Petersen and R. Bunton (eds.), *Foucault, Health and Medicine*, London: Routledge, pp. 189–206.

Plomin, R. (1990), 'The role of inheritance in behaviour', *Science*, 248 (April 13): 187.

Rapp, R. (1988), 'Chromosomes and communication: The discourse of medical science', *Medical Anthropology Quarterly* (n.s.) 2 (2): 143–57.

Shimazu, Y. (1994), 'Unmarried Mothers and their Children in Japan', *US-Japan Women's Journal*, 6: 83–110.

Shirai, Y. (1989), 'Japanese women's attitudes toward selective abortion: A pilot study in Aichi prefecture', *Studies in Humanities*, No. 23, Shinshu University, Faculty of Arts.

—— (1992), 'Japanese attitudes towards assisted procreation', *The Journal of Law, Medicine and Ethics*, 21: 43–52.

Smith, R. (ms), 'The ancestors: From veneration to memorialism', Paper presented to the Council on East Asian Studies, Yale University.

Todd, E. (1985), *The Explanation of Ideology: Family Structures and Social Systems*, Oxford: Basil Blackwell.

Toshitani, N. (1994), 'The reform of Japanese family law and changes in the family system', *U.S.–Japan Women's Journal*, 6: 66–82.

Tsuge, A. (1993), 'The situation of restriction for infertility treatment and gynecologists' stance towards the new reproductive technologies in Japan' (Nihon ni okeru 'funin chiryô' gijutsu no kisei jokyô to sanfujinkai no taido), *Japan Journal for Science, Technology and Society*, 2: 51–74.

Wakita, H., and Hanley, S. (eds.) (1994–5), *Kindai to Gendai Nihon to Josei*, Tokyo: University of Tokyo Press.

Yanagisako, S., and Delaney, C. (1995), *Naturalizing Power: Essays in Feminist Cultural Analysis*, New York: Routledge.

Yoxen, E. (1984), 'Constructing genetic diseases', in T. Duster and K. Garett (eds.), *Cultural Perspectives on Biological Knowledge*, Norwood, New Jersey: Ablex.

13

Re-theorizing Reproductive Health and Rights in the Light of Feminist Cross-cultural Research[1]

ROSALIND P. PETCHESKY

INTRODUCTION

By now, as the wealth of analyses presented in this volume attests, it should not be necessary to defend either qualitative methods or cross-cultural comparisons in the field of population studies.[2] Due largely to the influence on both policy and theory of women's health movements around the globe in the 1980s and 1990s (Garcia-Moreno and Claro 1994; Petchesky 1997), the mainstream discourse of the field has shifted in a number of new directions:

(1) (at least in rhetoric if not in practice) toward a broadened definition of 'reproductive health and rights'—as embodied in the 1994 International Conference on Population and Development (ICPD) Programme of Action and the 1995 Fourth World Conference on Women's (Beijing) Platform for Action[3]—replacing the older emphasis on population reduction targets (Corrêa 1994; Germain and Kyte 1995; Petchesky 1995);

(2) toward a critical consciousness about traditional ways of implementing population policies and family planning programmes;

(3) toward an emphasis on 'user perspectives' in developing standards for monitoring the quality of such programmes (Bruce 1990; Sai 1995; Sen 1995); and in turn

(4) toward a growing recognition of the need for in-depth qualitative and comparative data to determine just what those perspectives might be, how they vary across diverse cultural and country settings, and how they may differ from the assumptions and goals of clinicians, provider agencies, and policy makers.

What I will here characterize as feminist approaches to qualitative research on reproductive health/rights issues must be distinguished from the old Knowledge, Attitudes and Practices studies or other instrumental uses of qualitative methods such as those used in the 'social marketing' of family planning programmes. The two approaches are similar in that both seek knowledge not for its own sake but to inform programmatic action. But, while the latter are often geared toward assessing individual attitudes and cultural patterns regarding fertility in order to market existing services more effectively and to reduce population growth, feminist research on attitudes and values is aimed more at understanding gender relations, power, and women's own sense of their circumstances in order to transform existing policies and services and make them more responsive to women's self-defined needs. In the domain of reproductive health and fertility, this means using qualitative research methods to uncover the gender dimensions of reproductive health negotiations—between women and their partners or kin, between patients and providers, and between individual women as decision makers and dominant cultural norms or religious authorities. It also means, ultimately, harnessing research to the aim of women's empowerment, or what Batliwala defines as 'the process of challenging existing power relations and of gaining greater control over the sources of power' (1994).

By emphasizing the perspectives and empowerment of women, I do not mean to suggest that a gender-sensitive approach to research on reproductive health should ignore the perceptions of men (the 'other half' of the reproductive equation). Prodded by the urgency of finding preventive solutions to the global epidemic and rising heterosexual transmission of HIV/AIDS and other STIs, researchers in reproductive health have become increasingly aware of sexuality as a critical domain of social inquiry. A plethora of studies looking at male–female interactions and men's (especially young men's) awareness, or lack of awareness, of reproductive and sexual health issues and responsibilities are beginning to contribute much-needed insight into the process of heterosexual negotiations from the standpoint of health as well as fertility outcomes (see Becker 1996; Ezeh 1993; Gogna and Ramos 2000; Lloyd 1993; Mundigo 1995; Orubuloye 1995; Orubuloye *et al.* 1992; Paiva 2000; Ray *et al.* 1996; Weiss *et al.* 1996; de Zalduondo and Bernard 1995). At the same time, recognizing the necessity of 'bringing men in' and enhancing male responsibility should not imply seeing the position of women and men as 'equal' or the same in reproductive and sexual decision making. In most societies and communities, men still have disproportionate power, and women disproportionate burdens, with regard to both the social consequences and the enabling conditions (the 'sources of power') for making such decisions freely. It follows that the ethical values and practical strategies of women and men concerning reproductive and sexual behaviour will often differ or even conflict, and that researchers must chart these differences in order to deconstruct the myth of the couple or the family as a harmonious unit (Berer 1996; Helzner 1996; Sen 1984).

While acknowledging the importance of learning more about what men think and do, in this chapter I shall focus on qualitative cross-cultural research that seeks to illuminate 'women's voices' in reproductive and sexual decision making. Focusing specifically on testimonies gathered by the International Reproductive Rights Research Action Group (IRRRAG) in the course of a collaborative ethnographic field study conducted in 1993–6, my purpose is to scrutinize both the value and the limitations of such research from the standpoint of women's empowerment.

In brief, I will argue that the project of disclosing women's own perspectives, in their own voices, on their rights and entitlements to reproductive and sexual self-determination serves a number of useful functions. First, it allows us to see women, including poor and marginalized women, as not merely victims but also as active agents of their reproductive and sexual lives, able to act and make claims on their own behalf. Second, in-depth qualitative studies often yield more accurate data regarding people's deeply held values and motives than we can access from large-scale surveys, especially with regard to very sensitive or controversial issues where what people say and what they do diverge. Third, such studies shed light on conflicts between genders and generations within the same communities and households and on women's strategies for negotiating reproductive and sexual power differences. Finally, qualitative, ethnographic research methods can be empowering in themselves, to the extent they open up a space for previously silenced women to speak about their suffering and gain affirmation of their efforts—often secret, dangerous, and subversive—to abate it.

Yet, while ethnographic research on reproductive and sexual health and rights may help to defeat the illusion of women's powerlessness, it also must take into account the overall context of women's economic and cultural subordination. The aspirations of poor women are necessarily focused on coping with everyday realities and often take as given the social constraints that limit their power. In order to go beyond the level of witness or testimony, we have to look at the larger social and structural context—of which our respondents themselves may be unaware—that narrows not only the space in which they can act but the possibilities and rights they can imagine. Research that illuminates the ethical claims and resilience motivating women's reproductive decisions cannot by itself offer us an analytical framework for thinking about how to transform existing conditions in a way that enhances gender equality and obviates the need for accommodation and subterfuge—the tactics of the oppressed. The real challenge for researchers is how to re-link these two levels of inquiry.

THE IRRRAG COUNTRY STUDIES: RESEARCH METHODS AND CONCEPTUAL FRAMEWORK

The following remarks summarize a much larger study conducted over 5 years by IRRRAG researchers and published elsewhere; this attempt to synthesize the methods and findings of such a complex cross-cultural project can hardly do justice to its richness and diversity (see Petchesky and Judd 1998). IRRRAG is a consortium of seven country-based research teams made up of social scientists, health providers, and women's movement activists for which my staff and I at Hunter College of the City University of New York served as international coordination from its formation in 1992 through the summer of 1998.[4] Assisted enormously in integrating our work through the ability to hold semi-annual international meetings of team representatives and to participate as a group in the Cairo and Beijing NGO forums, IRRRAG developed a collective process, a common conceptual framework, and a roughly common research methodology that allowed for local variations (see below). Throughout, we attempted to balance attentiveness to local specificity with the development of a shared analysis and set of themes. Indeed, maintaining this balance presents one of the most difficult challenges to cross-country team research, insofar as the very process of working collaboratively over time and formulating questions and analytical insights together may serve to flatten the differences such research is attempting to illuminate and thus to bias the overall findings in favour of common patterns. Yet we continue to believe that the value of such a collaborative process outweighs the risks since the commonalities it yields are valid, important for international policies affecting reproductive and sexual rights as human rights, and too frequently ignored. And country team members continually reminded one another and the international coordination team of ways in which the situation or outlook of women in their countries differed from any presumed norm.

Our purpose was to investigate the perceptions, values, and strategies of grass-roots women—that is, women from non-elite, predominantly low-income sectors, both urban and rural—concerning decisions about reproduction and sexuality, in order to bring such women's voices into national and international policy debates. Although our research agenda was broad, involving many interrelated questions, one above all interested us: How do women across diverse countries, cultures, ethnic and religious groups and age/life cycle cohorts arrive at and negotiate a sense of entitlement with regard to their reproductive and sexual health and well-being? In what life circumstances and through what terms, codes and strategies do they (or do they not) begin to assert claims to decision-making authority over their reproductive and sexual bodies? We were interested not only in how and when such claims arise within the so-called 'private' arenas of family and sexual relations but also in their resonance within more 'public' domains—those of the clinic, the church, temple or mosque, and the community; in other words, the local gatekeepers of women's reproductive and sexual behaviour. Moreover, we were concerned to reflect a broad diversity of perspectives within each country, including those of age/stage in the life cycle, ethnicity, religion, marital status and parity, region, urban and rural location, and occupation. While by no means an accurate profile of national populations of women in our seven countries, our research communities nonetheless captured an interesting range of backgrounds in regard to these diverse characteristics (see Table 13.1). For example, informants in Malaysia included ethnic Malays, Chinese, and Indians; those in Egypt included both Muslims and Copts; those in the United States included urban Latina immigrants, rural African-American women, and unionized municipal workers in New York City; those in Brazil included agricultural workers in the Northeast, domestic workers in Rio de Janeiro, and housewives in São Paulo; and those in Mexico, Nigeria and the Philippines included a cross-section of the main geographical regions in the country.

Over a period of nearly 2 years (1993–4), our researchers used a variety of group and individual, in-depth interviewing techniques to conduct interviews among hundreds of women and (in two countries) some men, from 32 distinct communities in Brazil, Egypt, Malaysia, Mexico, Nigeria, the Philippines, and the United

Table 13.1. *Profile of IRRRAG respondents*

Respondents	Brazil[a]	Egypt[b]	Malaysia	Mexico[a]	Nigeria[a]	Philippines[a]	US
Number	182[c]	130	71	141	354	334[c]	130
Individual	45	12	71	29	72	28	32
Group	104	130	0	141	354	39	101
Included men	Yes	Yes	No	No	No	No	No
Urban (%)	59	79	38	44	35	36	73
Rural (%)	41	21	62	56	65	64	27
Married or cohabitating (%)	58	63	68	61	53[d]	93	42
Never married (%)	31	35	24	25	28	0	40[e]
Divorced, widowed, or separated (%)	11	2	8	14	19	7	13
Employed (%)	84	61	68	64	65	71	84
Unemployed[f] (%)	16	39	32	36	35	29	16
Age (%)							
Under 21	13	36	19	0	25	3	11
21–44	46	61	62	86	49	39	65
45+	41	3	19	14	26	57	24

[a] Percentages include only individual interview respondents.
[b] Percentages include women respondents only.
[c] Includes some respondents to the questionnaire only (not interviewed).
[d] Of these, 33 per cent were polygamous.
[e] Includes welfare (public assistance) clients with undeclared partners.
[f] Includes students and retirees as well as housewives.

States (see Table 13.1). As Table 13.1 indicates, some teams used a combination of group and individual interviews while others relied primarily or entirely on individual interviews, using either semi-structured questionnaires or life-history methods. In addition, some teams supplemented these methods with others, such as role-playing or dramatization, demographic questionnaires, and interviews among 'key informants' in the community. In keeping with the primarily subjective focus of our inquiry on women's own understandings of their reproductive and sexual entitlements, we agreed that a qualitative, ethnographic approach was the most suitable to our purposes. But all teams substantiated the interviews with statistical and secondary data on the economic, social, cultural, legal and health status of women both nationally and in the research communities and attempted to integrate this macro-data into their analysis of the local findings. In the case of the Philippines, in-depth interviews with a small sample of mother–daughter pairs was supplemented by a larger validation survey conducted in the three original research communities as well as four additional ones. During 1995–6 we analysed the data and each team wrote its country report; in 1997–8 we developed our common and comparative findings and edited the book *Negotiating Reproductive Rights*.

It should be noted that the skewed distribution of our respondents in regard to a number of variables presented in Table 13.1 resulted from deliberate strategies for selecting respondent communities in the context of resource and time constraints on the research teams. None of the participants involved in our project at either the national or the international level were ever paid full-time salaries to do the work of IRRRAG; all were carrying out other jobs and organizational commitments while simultaneously conducting fieldwork, data analysis, administration, writing, and related implementation activities for IRRRAG. This necessarily meant that the work would extend over a longer period of time but also that we would be unable to reside in the research communities for months or years, in the manner of conventional ethnography, to conduct the fieldwork. At the same time, we were convinced that good qualitative research depends less on weighting sample sizes to reflect national demographic patterns than on establishing bonds of trust and openness with the communities where the research is to be conducted.[5] Toward this end, country teams were encouraged to select groups of respondents based on their affiliation with community, labour or health groups or their residence in neighbourhoods with which our researchers or their organizations or allies had some previous connection, thus providing a basis of familiarity and trust. A by-product of this strategy is, for example, the over-representation of urban respondents in Egypt and their under-representation in Malaysia; the absence or under-representation of very young women in Mexico and the Philippines and the over-representation of older women in Brazil; and the possible over-representation of wage-earning women in all seven countries.

These methods of selecting respondents for the IRRRAG research created another tension in our research strategies—between the aims of yielding qualitative data that are robust and vivid expressions of grassroots women's voices, on the one hand, and assuring that the data are unbiased and relatively generalizable, on the other. A clear example is the decision—especially important in the Brazil, Mexico, and United States studies—to seek out women who were affiliated with organizations. Since such women are more likely than 'unorganized' women to have had previous contact with women's groups or feminist ideas, the 'finding' that they have a stronger sense of entitlement to reproductive and sexual rights may be an artefact of the research design.

Yet the skewed distributions of our study populations tell important stories in themselves. For one thing, it is well known that national data invariably undercount women as participants in the labour force due to their prevalence among informal or casual workers. The high proportion among our respondents of women (especially married women with children) who are working for income, either outside or within the home, may be a truer picture of poor women's relation to paid work than official data give. More importantly, as we observed in our research in nearly every country and local site, acquiring economic resources of their own—sometimes informally, through home-based work, or on the sly—is a crucial strategy for married or partnered women raising children. Not only does it help keep their families alive but it often provides them with the dignity and self-respect to assert their will in reproductive and sexual matters—for example, to insist on contraception or to resist spousal abuse.

The skewed age distributions in Mexico and Brazil (and to some extent in Nigeria and the Philippines) tell another story, one that sheds a different light on the selection of group-affiliated respondents. In both these countries, women's participation in popular (community, labour, church) organizations has been a major formative influence on civil society in recent years and potentially an important variable shaping their reproductive consciousness. This important contextual reality led the Mexico and Brazil teams to emphasize organizational membership and community activism in selecting their respondents. What they did not anticipate was that this research strategy would necessarily mean over-representing older women. Here too a potentially 'biased' research design helped to illuminate certain conditions, more prevalent in some political landscapes than others, that may enhance women's sense of reproductive and sexual entitlement. Group membership, IRRRAG's research found, leads to an identity outside the home that cultivates an awareness of self necessary for the articulation of personal claims. Most often, however, such awareness develops later rather than earlier in life, after children are grown, when women have a little time and space to become active group members.

Among the women we interviewed, the self as claimant was almost never static or isolated, as in the classical liberal model of individualism. Rather, it emerged from a social context of norms, responsibilities, and relationships that continually shift over the course of a woman's life. As it emerged in IRRRAG's conceptual framework, the verb 'negotiate' implies a conscious transaction or strategizing which may be non-verbal and implicit and which nearly always takes place against a background of gender-differentiated power. The Philippines team contributed the sharpest articulation of this process in defining the concept of 'negotiated entitlement'. Associating 'sense of entitlement' with the Filipino term *sana*, or 'aspirations and expectations', the Philippines analysis emphasizes the multilayered, 'relational or situational' dimensions of entitlement as it intersects with family and sexual dynamics, socio-economic conditions, availability of medical and family planning services, and a woman's place in the life cycle:

From childhood up until a woman marries, she may have more aspirations for herself. After entering into marriage, her aspirations are directed toward her family, especially children, or the aspirations for self are projected onto the children. The fulfillment of a woman's aspiration is a product of the interaction of what the woman says she wants and needs, on the one hand, and what she believes her family and society can realistically give her, as well as what she actually does for herself, on the other. It can be said, therefore, that the pursuit of entitlement is always under negotiation. Negotiation takes place within the woman herself—typically between competing demands or values—and between herself and the external world, with the family as the first layer. (Fabros 1995)

Within IRRRAG's conceptual framework, not only the concept of self but the very concept of 'reproduction' had to be problematized. Our initial decision to concentrate the study on just two aspects of reproductive health, contraception and childbearing, turned out to be inconsistent with both the broader goals of the project and the kinds of qualitative, open-ended methodologies we had chosen. The aim to contextualize women's reproductive decisions and see them in all their situational complexity led all the teams to investigate a much wider range of issues. Moreover, in both group discussions and individual interviews, the respondents themselves did not conveniently adhere to such discrete topics as contraception but rather disclosed a matrix of interrelated issues and themes that interwove fertility, sexuality, economics, gender and kin relations, work, and child care. In fact, this outcome confirmed the observation of several country teams early in the project that the experience of biological reproduction, from the standpoint of women engaged in it, is always intimately interwoven with the tasks and obligations of social reproduction. More than biological events, women experience the bearing and care of children as forms of social labour done for others and demanding considerable organization, energy, and travail. Further, we realized that the 'reproductive career' is not only socially determined and enmeshed for women with wage labour, child care, household maintenance, and community roles; it is also highly gender specific and lifelong, spanning a woman's entire life cycle and not only her so-called reproductive years. Indeed, it may well be, as our research findings in most of the countries suggest, that it is only after a woman has navigated through motherhood that she begins to develop a clear sense of reproductive entitlement. But this trajectory surely reflects a particular set of historical conditions and social constraints, those characteristic of male-dominant cultures.

SELECTED FINDINGS OF THE IRRRAG PROJECT[6]

While the concept of 'sense of entitlement' is meant to signify women's consciousness of their rights or authority to make decisions, IRRRAG's conceptual framework developed what we called the accommodation–resistance nexus to indicate how that sense gets manifested at the level of behaviour and speech. Initially we assumed a rather simplistic bipolar model in which accommodation meant passively complying or submitting to dominant or traditional norms while resistance meant actively opposing those norms, standing up for oneself and asserting one's will. As our fieldwork progressed, however, we found that the two extremes of outright resistance on the one hand and passive compliance on the other were much rarer than the kinds of complex, subtle reproductive and sexual strategies most of our respondents actually deployed in everyday life in order both to achieve some autonomy and to keep peace within the family and community.

In a few cases we were able to identify clear, overt markers of resistance: for example, when a woman's non-conformist behaviour is publicly visible and vocal (as opposed to clandestine or veiled in subterfuge); when she shows obvious willingness to risk likely punishment or disapproval (running away to be with her boyfriend for the weekend); and above all when she articulates an ideology that justifies her action or belief in terms of right, justice, or fairness (as opposed to feeling she had no choice). But most of the time our respondents' transgressive actions or speech were submerged in layers of ambiguity and contradiction in which, frequently, professions of necessity and fairness coexist with confessions of guilt or sin. (The paradigm case is that of women who characterize their abortions as 'wrong' or '*haram*' yet clearly believe they are justified in the eyes of God.) There is remarkable fluidity here: an action that is accommodative in one context may be oppositional in another; an action that appears 'resistant' may be in conflict with the woman's own moral judgement about it (as in the abortion example); or, in a more complicated twist, she herself may see no contradiction in both acting in defiance of a particular norm and speaking with deference to it.

What we learned in the course of our research is that most of the women we interviewed, across all the differences of culture, region, religion, age, and economic circumstance, engage in a very complex process of negotiation to carve out small areas where they can exercise control over their reproductive and sexual lives. They uneasily try to balance conflicting values (traditional and modern, religious and secular), and they adopt a range of strategies including subterfuge, subversion, or trading off some bodily rights in order to secure others. In fact, accommodative manoeuvres, we discovered, were more often calculating and tactical—what we came to call 'strategic accommodations'—than simply compliant; they are a way of getting one's needs met while avoiding direct confrontation. For example, some wives among the Philippines respondents would typically accommodate their husbands' desire for sex, contrary to their own wishes, in order to derive certain other benefits they considered more valuable, such as help with domestic chores or the deflection of conflict in the home. This kind of trade-off was also evident among Egyptian respondents who insisted they were glad they had endured the traditional wedding night defloration ritual (*baladi dokhla*), despite experiencing it as humiliating and painful, because it purchased them a certification of chastity and thus greater freedom and mobility outside the home.

Thus we found that the low-income rural and urban women we interviewed construct a kind of rational calculus, or political economy of the body, in their reproductive and sexual negotiations. Often they choose to go along with traditional practices or expectations they find demeaning, even ones that blatantly violate their own sense of bodily integrity or well-being, in order to gain other advantages under existing domestic and community power relations in which their manoeuvrability and their resources are clearly limited. Fitting neither the image of victims nor that of staunch feminist warriors, they do express a sense of reproductive and sexual entitlement, but on some issues more sharply than others and in a context mined with obstacles—from husbands, parents, doctors and other clinic staff, religious authorities, and the state. Within this general overview, we culled several more specific findings that reveal some common patterns as well as certain differences across the diverse country settings:

1. Women respondents in all seven countries aspire to control their own fertility, childbearing and contraceptive use, even though they do not always succeed. Often, however, this sense of entitlement is acted upon without the knowledge of husbands or partners, and secrecy results from fear of domestic violence or conflicts.

Respondents in all our countries surely know about various methods of fertility control, either traditional or modern or both, and most have access to them one way or another. However, in all countries except the US and Malaysia, the majority use methods to stop rather than to space or postpone childbearing, and a depressing number are thwarted in their brave attempts by uncooperative or belligerent husbands. We heard story after story of husbands who threw away pills, refused to sign consent forms for sterilization, or demanded that the woman produce a son. One rural woman from Northeast Brazil told how her husband 'used to snoop in her things' until eventually he found her pills hidden in a suitcase: '. . . he took the pills, put them in water, dissolved them and buried them, saying, "If I see these pills again you will pay me." Now, "pay me" means he will beat me.' (Diniz *et al.* 1998). The result of such male belligerence is most often women's subterfuge—hiding, pretending, lying outright; getting some man off the street to sign the sterilization consent form; getting an illegal abortion and pretending it was a miscarriage.

In Egypt, our women respondents' employment of such ruses was developed to a fine art, and telling their husbands about their use of contraception or abortion, much less subscribing to any kind of 'male involvement', would seem to be the furthest thing from their minds (Seif El Dawla *et al.* 1998). This is in striking contrast to the findings of a recent study, based on data from the 1988 Egypt Demographic and Health Survey, that confirms the more familiar view regarding the cultural preference of Egyptians for joint (husband–wife) decision making in matters of fertility (Govindasamy and Malhotra 1996). And it reinforces the argument made above that small-scale qualitative studies may yield information that goes deeper than the repetition of cultural norms one tends to hear in responses to survey questions. In the Philippines, the most frequent contraceptive our informants used was simply to avoid sex[7] (Fabros *et al.* 1998). Yet the intent and sense of entitlement to exert control over their childbearing was clear in such cases, even when existing power relations made it difficult to realize or was permeated, as it was in nearly all our country settings, by the hovering cloud of domestic violence.

  2. The primary justification women use for this sense of reproductive entitlement is motherhood: that they (not husbands or partners) suffer the greatest burdens, pains and responsibilities of pregnancy, childbearing and childrearing and therefore have earned the right to make decisions in these arenas.

Consistently women invoked their responsibility for children as ethical grounds for making decisions to abort, use contraception, or take over where children were concerned. Over and over again we heard the words 'pain', 'suffering', 'burdens', as though the pain they have gone through in motherhood represents a kind of currency they have had to pay out of their bodies to earn reproductive authority. This kind of bodily accounting may be the counterpart to the 'spiritual accounting' the anthropologist Ruth Behar says 'is a constant theme in Mexican women's popular discourse': 'one pays for everything in this world' (Behar 1993, pp. 289, 356). Marta, a 40-year-old Yaqui widow from Sonora, Mexico, tells how she resists her violent husband's attempts to beat the children. When he asks why she defies him and takes them under her skirt, she replies:

Because it hurts, . . .because I paid the price for them, because they were born from me, from me they were born and it hurts if someone hits them. Look at you, you can leave this house any time and who is going to stay suffering with this child? Isn't it going to be me? (Ortiz Ortega *et al.* 1998)

And Lai Yin, a rural Chinese mother of four from Malaysia, says insistently:

I am the one to make the decisions where family planning is concerned. . . . After I decide, then I tell him that we should not have so many children or that we should not space them so closely . . . because caring for them is difficult. Child rearing is not by him. . . When he comes home, . . . he only plays with them, he does not take care of them. Getting up in the middle of the night to give them milk, taking them to the doctor when they are ill—all this is my responsibility. He does not suffer, the suffering is all done by me.[8] (Raj *et al.* 1998)

But notice that Lai Yin's sense of reproductive entitlement, like that of so many other women we interviewed, is set in the context of economic hardship and survival (too little food to go around, lack of child care); not, 'this is what I want, what I need for myself or what would give me pleasure'. This is an illustration of the interconnected, socially situated self mentioned earlier, as well as the tendency of women we interviewed to feel more comfortable justifying 'resistant' reproductive decisions in terms of the family's economic survival rather than their own personal needs, much less their 'right to control over their bodies'.

   3. *Religion plays a relatively minor role in determining not only women's behaviour with regard to fertility control but their ethical reasons. Even in very religious societies (Egypt and the Philippines), they often imagine a forgiving God who understands their need to have an abortion, use contraception, or refuse unwanted sex with husbands.*

   To our surprise and great interest, a practical morality, based on women's bodily suffering and social responsibility for children, took precedence most of the time over religious belief and the teachings of the church or Islamic authorities. The Catholic Church in the Philippines would no doubt be alarmed to know poor women are saying, as our respondents there did, 'Religion is different from health'; '[birth control] is not the business of the church'; 'it's not the church that will go hungry and experience poverty' (Fabros *et al.* 1998). Likewise, listen to Soheir, a working mother in urban Cairo:

I had an abortion once. . . . I never told anybody that I did it to myself, not even my husband. He is a religious man. I was afraid of God's punishment, but at the same time I wonder, does God accept the agony of the whole family if I have to stop working [to breastfeed another baby]? (Seif El Dawla *et al.* 1998)

Soheir's question exemplifies the mosaic of values and the situational ethics that characterize many women's consciousness about reproductive decisions. Echoing almost word for word the Filipina and Brazilian women we interviewed,[9] she is saying 'God will forgive me because He understands my situation', and thus asserting her reproductive entitlement through the invention of a benevolent deity. But, like them too, she is doing so on the basis of harsh economic conditions she did not create that constrain her on all sides; and, in addition, she is accommodating to traditional norms of modesty in Egyptian culture that make breastfeeding on the job unthinkable. This is not to deny that women in our studies—especially in the Philippines, Nigeria, and the United States—were greatly influenced, in their consciousness as well as their practical ability to realize their reproductive aspirations, by religious teachings and the power of institutionalized religion over public policies and services. Nonetheless, we found even religious women tacitly negotiating with their religion, as they did with their husbands; they did not let religion govern either their behaviour or their ethical reasons with regard to fertility control.

4. In most settings, women's empowerment to express a sense of entitlement with regard to reproductive and sexual decisions was significantly enhanced by having earnings of their own, working outside the home, or in some cases belonging to community groups or unions; but the latter cases are specific to certain local and political conditions.

On the one hand, we could say that Soheir's wage-earning job reflects the economic squeeze on poor families, but it also authorizes if not empowers her to make reproductive decisions. In all seven of our countries we found that the great majority of women—across age groups but particularly those under 50—sought to work outside the home or, when husbands objected, surreptitiously to obtain part-time or home-based jobs. Such outside-the-home identities functioned as minimal enabling conditions to give women not only additional income but a little more dignity, self-respect, and space to decide and act about reproductive and sexual matters. This is by no means to say that simply having some income of their own or belonging to an organization 'liberates' women, especially under conditions of increasing marginalization and job insecurity; but it does give them a social context in which to understand their situation and the possibility of seeing themselves as active persons in their own right; it makes the self more than just a body. Natalia, a Zapotec Indian and single mother from rural Oaxaca in Mexico, tells what belonging to a local health organization has meant for her:

. . . now the people in town see me differently. It's not like before. Before, I was nobody, so to speak. Not now, nowadays everybody says, 'let's go to her, she knows', or they come and consult me about their problems and ask, 'what do you recommend about contraceptives?' or 'what shall I do about this problem?', and so on. . . . (Ortiz Ortega *et al.* 1998)

And nearly the same words were expressed by women in Brazil and some sites in the United States.

At the same time, this finding points to a major difference among the countries with regard to the circumstances that generate expressions of entitlement to self-determination in reproductive and sexual health as well as the scope of such expressions. As suggested earlier, political conditions in Brazil and Mexico are such that participation in popular, grassroots organizations—for women as well as men—has been linked with an activist form of appropriating citizenship through mobilization in social movements. In Egypt and Malaysia, however, most women are not 'organized' in any formal ways but derive their identities primarily from kin groups and residential, or sometimes religious or ethnic, communities;[10] while in Nigeria, the Philippines, and the United States, a complex mixture of these two situations exists. IRRRAG's findings suggest (although this requires further research) that there is a difference of magnitude between the kind of entitlement both expressed and reinforced by women's income-earning activities and that associated with their participation in popular organizations (especially those, like health groups, with some kind of feminist presence). Affirming Natalia's statement, the IRRRAG Philippines team found that women in their research sites who joined organizations did so primarily 'to learn something new' (to make up for poor education) and enhance their own growth, to 'have somewhere to escape to', and to expand their relations outside the family; and only secondarily 'to be able to help the family'.[11] In other words, while working and earning income may empower women to make their own decisions about reproductive issues, activism in organizations may take them another step to form an identity as citizens and active claimants, not only within the household but *vis-à-vis* the state.

5. *In most settings, particularly in Brazil, Egypt, Mexico, and the United States, respondents repeatedly complained about the poor quality, inaccessibility and high cost of health services and especially about the demeaning and inhumane treatment they received from health providers. Insensitive treatment undermines trust in methods and services.*

If grassroots organizations and independent earnings help to empower women, the health systems and services in our seven countries—all inadequate for and insensitive to poor women—certainly do not. Where health and family planning services are utterly inaccessible and unaffordable, as in Nigeria, women do not generally complain but utilize local healers, midwives, or traditional methods for childbirth or abortion; this is 'how things are'. Yet often—particularly in Egypt, the Philippines, and rural Malay communities in Malaysia (where public services are available)—the use of traditional methods seems to be a conscious choice based on inaccessibility of services, unpleasant and untreated side effects from medical methods, discomfort with being examined by male gynaecologists, or having been dismissed or demeaned by health professionals (cf. Khattab 1992; Morsy 1993; Thaddeus and Maine 1990; Younis *et al.* 1993).

The accounts from Brazil and Mexico of abusive treatment are truly hair-raising and confirm numerous reports of rampant female sterilization abuse in Mexico and punitive treatment of Brazilian women who seek follow-up treatment for complications from illegal abortion (Diniz *et al.* 1998; Ortiz Ortega *et al.* 1998). In Egypt, the Philippines, and rural Malaysia, women do not protest outwardly against such abuses but simply 'vote with their feet', refusing to go back to the clinic or hospital even if this jeopardizes their own health. But stories of abuse by reproductive health providers did not just come from the global South. Several rural African–American women in our research had been given the long-acting contraceptive Norplant. When they tried to have the implants removed because of side effects, local clinic personnel told them their complaints of continuous bleeding, weight loss, and palpitations were 'inconveniences', not 'medical problems', therefore not warranting removal under Medicaid unless they paid $300 to reimburse the state (Forte and Judd 1998). And this was not privatized medicine (yet) and not a 'third world' story.

Yet, while inadequate services seem to be the reality for nearly all our study populations, these inadequacies clearly have a more adverse impact on some groups of women than others. Simply a glance at differences in maternal mortality ratios, total fertility rates, and contraceptive utilization rates among our seven countries offers the most glaring evidence that both inaccessibility and poor quality of services are graver problems in some settings than others (see Table 13.2). Although women in all our research sites aspired to control their own fertility (finding #1

Table 13.2. *IRRRAG countries, some vital indicators*

Respondents	Nigeria	Philippines	Brazil	Egypt	Mexico	Malaysia	US
Maternal mortality ratio, 1990[a]	1,000	280	220	174	110	80	12
Total fertility rate, 1990–5	6.4	3.9	2.5	4.1 (3.6)[d]	3.2	3.6	2.1
Infant mortality rate, 1990–5[b]	96	43	57	57 (72.9)[d]	35	14 (11.6)[d]	8[e]
Contraceptive use, modern method, 1990 (%)[c]	4	25	57	44	45	31	69
Contraceptive use, any method, 1990 (%)[c]	6	40	66	45	53	48	74
Births with trained attendant, 1986–90 (%)	45	53	73	47	45	92	99
GNP per capita, 1993 (US$)	300	850	2,930	660	3,610	3,140	24,740
Public expenditures on health, 1990 (% of GDP)	1.2	1.0	2.8	1.0	1.6	1.3	5.3

[a] Per 100,000 live births.

[b] Per 1,000 live births.

[c] For married couples only.

[d] Egyptian Demographic and Health Survey and Malaysian Ministry of Health figures, where these differ from UN data on maternal mortality.

[e] For New York City, where immigrants and people of colour make up a disproportionate part of the population relative to the national population profile, the infant mortality rate is 25 per 1,000 live births.

Sources: UNDP, *Human Development Report* (1996); WHO and UNICEF, *Revised 1990 Estimates of Maternal Mortality* (April 1996).

above), some—especially in Nigeria, Egypt, and the Philippines—did so with considerably less success (Osakue and Martin Hilber 1998; Seif El Dawla *et al.* 1998; Fabros *et al.* 1998). Moreover, our qualitative data and other studies reflect the price women pay in unnecessary morbidity and physical suffering due to inadequate and dismissive care (Khattab 1992; Fabros *et al.* 1998; Germain *et al.* 1992; Diniz *et al.* 1998; Younis *et al.* 1993). We are convinced from IRRRAG's field data that problems of access—perhaps above all insensitive or abusive providers—more than lack of education are responsible for these adverse outcomes, including low contraceptive utilization rates.[12]

Table 13.2 points to just a few of the contextual factors, and their variations across our seven countries, that deny women the necessary enabling conditions to realize their reproductive and sexual rights (Corrêa and Petchesky 1994). Taking maternal mortality ratios as the principal indicator, it becomes evident that some of the correlations are not simply a matter of poverty and scarcity—although economic crises burden all the study populations, including immigrant women and poor women of colour in the United States. In the Philippines, where maternal mortality remains quite high relative to other developing countries and is no doubt correlated with the extremely low rates of contraceptive use; where public expenditure on health, both absolutely and relative to military expenditure, remains quite low; and where GNP per capita was one-third that of Brazil in 1993, infant mortality was nonetheless significantly better than that in Brazil and the percentage of births administered by trained attendants slightly higher. Does this suggest that, even within conditions of scarce resources, political will (influenced no doubt by the Catholic Church) may direct revenues and programmatic efforts in favour of infant health but not that of mothers? In Brazil, where public expenditure on health is twice as high as any of the seven countries except the United States, maternal mortality remains exceedingly high despite high rates of contraceptive use. To a large extent this is related to very poor conditions in obstetrical services and extremely high rates of illegal, unsafe abortion in Brazil, notwithstanding increased allocations to the health sector generally; again, women's health receives low political and budgetary priority (Diniz *et al.* 1998; Berquó *et al.* 1995; Singh and Sedgh 1997). This contrasts significantly with Malaysia, where, despite lower rates of contraceptive use, the quality and accessibility of maternal health services is much higher and the maternal mortality ratio, consequently, nearly one-third that in Brazil. (Note: both obstetrical services and access to safe abortion, under limited conditions and in urban areas, have improved in Brazil since the IRRRAG research was conducted, thanks to advocacy efforts by the women's health movement.)

6. Most respondents express little entitlement to sexual pleasure, either to have it or to show need for it. This is in contrast to their strong and frequently articulated sense of entitlement not to be subjected to violence from husbands or unwanted sex.

The protests so many women in Brazil, Mexico, Egypt, and the United States registered to clinical abuse were fully matched by their resistance to spousal abuse and violence (often forthright) and their tactics to avoid unwanted sex (more likely to be subversive or indirect). Frequent reports of domestic violence, especially during pregnancy, came from respondents in nearly all our research settings (cf. Heise 1995; Heise *et al.* 1995). We heard numerous stories of women in Mexico and the Philippines who confronted their violent, alcoholic husbands with knives, who fought back or left their husbands when the abuse became too much (similar stories occurred in Malaysia, Egypt, and Brazil). Moreover, respondents in Egypt and the Philippines revealed very inventive tactics for avoiding unwanted sex (pretending the baby was crying, feigning having their menstrual period or illness, etc.), even when they professed to believe in the husband's right to sexual satisfaction on demand (Seif El Dawla *et al.* 1998; Fabros *et al.* 1998). The critical ele-ment reinforcing the women's sense of entitlement in these cases was their confidence in their ability to support themselves financially or the support of parents or mothers-in-law.

Yet, when it comes to asserting their right to sexual pleasure and satisfaction, only a small handful of the women in all our research sites found their voice. A few surely did, and these, interestingly, tended to be older women who were beyond childbearing and rearing. Post-menopausal women in rural Northern Nigeria, for example, insisted: 'We are not too old to have sex, and why should we give up anything? Menopause is not an illness, and, after all, older men still have sex [so why shouldn't we?]' (Osakue and Martin Hilber 1998). And agricultural workers in their forties from Northeast Brazil affirmed that the claim to sexual rights is not just a Western bourgeois or urban feminist idea. One said, '. . . she doesn't need to ask for any permission; it's her own body and she does whatever she wishes with it.' And another:

. . . it's a matter of choice. If someone feels better with a man, she should keep to him . . . if I like a woman, it's my business. I've got to think of myself, not of what others may say. . . . Everyone has the right to choose what is right for herself. (Diniz *et al.* 1998)

We found that mothers often expressed aspirations for their daughters that they would not claim for themselves, especially in regard to education, later marriage, fewer children, and sexual self-determination. In urban settings, this change may reflect a new awareness born of the HIV/AIDS epidemic. One mother in São Paulo, casting aside traditional virginity norms and inverting the old 'good girl' dictum, urged her daughter, '. . . obey your mother and be a good girl. Even if you have sex, do it carefully; use a condom.' Many of the young unmarried women asserted their entitlement to much more information about sex than their mothers had been given, and many mothers concurred. But only one young woman—a 19-year-old in Northern Nigeria—said proudly, 'Whenever I feel like sleeping with my boyfriend, I go to him.' (Osakue and Martin Hilber 1998). And only one—a working urban Malay woman in her twenties—said unapologetically, in a society where heterosexual marriage is the absolute norm, 'I never worry about not getting married because I feel I can survive on my own . . . without a man.' (Raj *et al.* 1998). A trade union woman from New York summed up her sexual experience in terms that spoke for many others, not only those of her generation and culture:

So you had to make a decision: Do you want to be a good girl or a bad girl? If you were a bad girl, your name was posted, and everybody knew you were a bad girl. . . . So I decided to be a good girl. Made everybody happy. I got married, had five pregnancies and four babies. Did I want to get married? Did I want to have babies? No! But that was the thing to do. I've been married 31 years. You learn over the years to make changes and adjustments, and that's what I've done. In the beginning of marriage, he wanted sex every moment of the day. I dreaded it. I didn't want it, didn't like it. After you heard all these years that it is taboo, you don't do it, and it wasn't something you talked about as a pleasurable thing. I think it took years before I was able to relax myself where I could just enjoy sex. (Forte and Judd 1998)

CONCLUSION

Over and over again, the IRRRAG research findings paint a picture of tremendous resilience and courage; women who not only cope patiently with meagre resources and intransigent cultural and social barriers to their reproductive and sexual freedom but who defy the tradition of female passivity—manoeuvring around, subverting, bending, or sometimes directly challenging those barriers. Most of our respondents in all seven countries showed a clear sense of entitlement to make their own decisions in many areas of reproductive and sexual life: marriage (when and to whom), fertility (number and timing of children), contraception, avoidance of domestic violence and unwanted sex, child care, and work (whether and when to work outside the home or seek economic resources of their own). While resenting the lack of male responsibility for safe contraception and children's care, they also at the present moment seem to prefer relying on their own resources and control of things rather than trusting in the cooperation of men.[13] In this regard, they are clearly willing to go to great lengths—often risking their health—to maintain secrecy, safety and self-determination and thereby evade domestic violence, marital discord, public shame, or clinical abuse. These strategies of subterfuge, trade-off, and accommodation remind us that grassroots women express or act on their sense of entitlement almost always in a context of domination, subordination, and limited power and resources. In such a context, having a sense of entitlement may be very distant from the ability to act on it effectively.

The capacity to realize her sense of entitlement will depend on a complex interaction among a woman's beliefs and consciousness, her domestic and cultural environment, and the material circumstances in which she finds herself. It is perpetually under negotiation. Surely one of the most striking aspects of IRRRAG's findings across all the diverse countries and cultures is the extent to which women's sense of reproductive and sexual entitlement is mediated through motherhood and apt to vary over the life cycle. Having children becomes both a passage and a source of authority, after which women feel more entitled to speak their own mind, assert their views and needs regarding contraception or sterilization, fend off male violence and abuse, seek sources of personal satisfaction outside the home, or relax enough to 'just enjoy sex'. It is significant, however, that many of the women in our research who became active in community organizations or unions did so only after their children were grown (or old enough to take care of themselves or each other).

Thus motherhood as a basis of entitlement means that women's reproductive and sexual self-determination is postponed until later in life. Moreover, this maternal ethic comes freighted with other costs, such as the further stigmatization of childlessness for women and the extension of the gender-biased 'reproductive career', since activist and working women still depend on older daughters or grandmothers to replace their reproductive labour in the home.

This suggests that strategic accommodations and trade-offs not only signify conditions of oppression; they also help to perpetuate those conditions, and they exact a price. When a woman refuses to return for follow-up visits to a hospital or clinic because her complaints have been dismissed or condemned and her language, ethnicity, or customs treated with contempt, she reclaims her dignity; but she also exposes herself to additional risks of infection, unwanted pregnancy, unsafe abortion, and thus reproductive morbidity and mortality.[14] When a woman resorts to unsafe traditional practices that damage her bodily integrity (or her daughter's) in order to purchase greater mobility and respect, she not only compromises her health and sexual pleasure but also buttresses a cultural context where notions of shame and honour turn on female virginity (Corrêa 1994). When a woman argues, 'I am the one who should decide because I am the one who bears the pains and responsibilities of motherhood', she is definitely asserting a (consequentialist) ethical claim on behalf of her own entitlement as reproductive decision maker. However, her position falls short of demanding that others concerned with the well-being of children—state-sponsored child care agencies, husbands, or partners—share those responsibilities. In other words, she is still taking for granted the 'naturalness' of traditional gender divisions and defining motherhood as the core of who she is.

In sum, qualitative ethnographic studies can tell us a lot about how and in what ethical terms women make decisions about fertility and sexuality within the social and economic constraints that surround them. But 'women's voices' in themselves do not usually address the larger structural conditions that govern their everyday strategies and make the very terms in which those strategies are invented deeply unjust. They do not tell us how to transform the conditions that minimize 'choices'.[15] To understand, for example, why so many women in most of IRRRAG's focal countries participate routinely in the 'clandestine epidemic' of unsafe abortion (Paxman *et al.* 1993), we would need to take into account a range of factors that the women themselves assume are unfair, oppressive, but just part of life: angry husbands who threaten reprisals and violence, poverty, job and food shortages, state laws and punitive religious codes opposing safe legal abortion, and the unavailability of reproductive technologies except ones that pose, or are perceived to pose, unacceptable hazards or side effects. For research to go beyond revelation, to become socially transformative, we need to connect women's testimonies and their just claims—either expressed or implied through the daily negotiations of reproductive and sexual conflict—to the larger socio-economic and cultural contexts that often remain muted in their own words. From this double perspective we can mobilize stronger, more grounded actions to change policies and transform societies.

Notes

1. This paper and whatever useful insights it contains would not have been possible without the hard work and dedication of all the IRRRAG (International Reproductive Rights Research Action Group) country teams and the gracious respondents in the research communities.

2. Just a few examples of important and influential recent studies either advocating or utilizing qualitative methods to illuminate population issues regarding reproductive health include Greenhalgh (1995), Weiss *et al.* (1996), Khattab (1992), Mita and Simmons (1995), Obermeyer (1992), Schuler and Hashemi (1994), Schuler *et al.* (1994), Schuler (1995), Simmons (1996), Younis *et al.* (1993), and Zurayk *et al.* (1995).

3. The Beijing Platform for Action of 1995 incorporates the language of the ICPD Programme of Action, Art. 7(2), in its definition of 'reproductive rights': '. . . reproductive rights embrace certain human rights that are already recognized in national laws, international human rights documents and other consensus documents. These rights rest on the recognition of the basic right of all couples and individuals to decide freely and responsibly the number, spacing and timing of their children and to have the information and means to do so, and the right to attain the highest standard of sexual and reproductive health. It also includes their right to make decisions concerning reproduction free of discrimination, coercion and violence, as expressed in human rights documents.' (para. 95).

4. In late 1998, administration of the IRRRAG project was moved to ARROW (Asian-Pacific Research and Resource Centre for Women) in Kuala Lumpur, under the direction of Rashidah Abdullah. The first 5 years of IRRRAG's work were supported primarily by the Ford and MacArthur Foundations, with additional funding from the Dutch and Norwegian Foreign Ministries, the Moriah Fund, the Rockefeller Foundation, UNFPA regional offices in Brazil and the Philippines, the World Bank, and World Vision. For a fuller explanation of IRRRAG's origins, conceptual framework, and methods, see Petchesky and Judd (1998) chapter 1.

5. We were encouraged in this and other methodological protocols by our team of excellent research consultants, most of whom are professional anthropologists. They included Dr. Iris Lopez (City College of New York), Dr. Sylvia Marcos (Mexico), Dr. Carla Makhlouf Obermeyer (Harvard University), Dr. Tola Olu Pearce (University of Missouri), Dr. Rayna Rapp (New School for Social Research, New York), Dr. T. K. Sundari Ravindran (India), Dr. Beth Richie (Hunter College, New York), and Dr. Joanna Gould Stuart (New York University).

6. The following sections are adapted from Petchesky (1998).

7. In large part, this pattern may be a legacy, not so much of religious belief (see below), but of the Church-influenced policies of the Corey Aquino regime, when government-sponsored family planning programmes in the Philippines tended to emphasize 'natural family planning' to the exclusion of other methods.

8. Lai Yin was one of the very few respondents in our entire study who made any explicit reference to spacing of children.

9. Poor rural women of the Brazilian Northeast draw on a long-standing history of popular opposition to Catholic Church teaching when they commonly regard their first-trimester abortions as 'trading with God'. Liberation theology, deeply entrenched among the poor in Brazil, provides them with an alternative vision—that of a merciful, kind deity who helps women through hard times—to justify their transgression of the clergy's moral views (Diniz *et al.* 1998; Ribeiro 1994). We are not aware, however, of such a

tradition among either poor Catholic women in the Philippines or poor Muslim women in Egypt, and our researchers were fascinated to find this common theme across such different cultures.

10. An exception to this pattern existed among IRRRAG's women respondents in the Boulaq section of Cairo. These women were unusually assertive about their reproductive rights and, probably not coincidentally, were also unusual in having been organized by a local development NGO.

11. These quotations are from the follow-up validation survey conducted by the Philippines team, cited above.

12. Lack of knowledge or information itself is often attributable to poor, demeaning or inaccessible services, as was clearly evident from IRRRAG's study in Egypt. There, a comprehensive network of government-funded maternal and child health services exists, including in rural areas; yet the vast majority of women utilizing the pill obtain it from pharmacies and are unable to read or understand the package instructions, while many of the women in our study find available services very alienating and simply avoid them. See Seif El Dawla *et al.* (1998) and Trottier *et al.* (1994).

13. In 1998–9, five of the IRRRAG teams began to conduct a follow-up study in the previous research communities to investigate more fully what women want and expect from men with regard to their responsibility for reproductive and sexual decision making; and, in turn, what are the desires and expectations of men in these communities. This new research was conducted under the coordination of ARROW in Malaysia and with support from UNFPA, SIDA and the World Bank.

14. According to recent estimates, unsafe induced abortion accounts for one-third of all maternal deaths and '800,000 hospitalizations annually' in Latin America, and abortion rates have been rising most rapidly in Brazil, especially in the Northeast (Singh and Sedgh 1997). In Egypt, where reliable hospital data on complications are less available, it is nonetheless well known that 'the country's hospitals . . . receive a steady stream of emergency postabortion cases' (Huntington *et al.* 1995).

15. Thanks to Mercy Fabros and Iris Lopez for discussions that helped to clarify this point.

References

Batliwala, S. (1994), 'The meaning of women's empowerment: New concepts from action,' in G. Sen, A. Germain, and L. Chen (eds.),' *Population Policies Reconsidered: Health, Empowerment and Rights*, Cambridge: Harvard University Press.

Becker, S. (1996), 'Couples and reproductive health: A review of couple studies', *Studies in Family Planning*, 27 (6) (Nov/Dec).

Behar, R. (1993), *Translated Woman: Crossing the Border with Esperanza's Story*, Boston: Beacon Press.

Berer, M. (1996) 'Men', *Reproductive Health Matters*, Vol. 7, Special Issue on 'Men' (May).

Berquó, E., Araújo, M. J. O., and Sorrentino, S. (1995), *Fecundidade, Saúde Reprodutiva e Pobrezana en América Latina*, Vol. 1, O Caso Brasileiro, Cebrap/Nepo-Unicamp, São Paulo.

Bruce, J. (1990), 'Fundamental elements of the quality of care: A simple framework', *Studies in Family Planning*, 21 (2) (Mar/Apr).

Corrêa, S. (1994), *Population and Reproductive Rights: Feminist Perspectives from the South*, London: Zed Books.

Corrêa, S., and Petchesky, R. (1994), 'Reproductive and sexual rights: A feminist perspective', in G. Sen, A. Germain, and L. Chen (eds.), *Population Policies Reconsidered*, Cambridge: Harvard University Press.

Diniz, S. G., de Mello e Souza, C. and Portella, A. P. (1998), ' "Not like our mothers": Reproductive choice and the emergence of citizenship among Brazilian rural workers, domestic workers and urban housewives', in R. Petchesky and K. Judd (eds.), *Negotiating Reproductive Rights*, Chap. 2, London: Zed Books and New York: St. Martin's Press.

Ezeh, A. C. (1993), 'The influence of spouses over each other's contraceptive attitudes in Ghana', *Studies in Family Planning*, 24 (3) (May/June).

Fabros, M. with Guia-Padilla, M. T. (1995), 'Negotiated entitlement in reproductive decision-making: Toward a definition of reproductive rights among grassroots women in the Philippines', Report of Philippines IRRRAG team (unpublished).

—— et al. (1998), 'From *Sanas* to *Dapat*: negotiating entitlement in reproductive decision-making in the Philippines', in R. Petchesky and K. Judd (eds.), *Negotiating Reproductive Rights*, Chap. 7, London: Zed Books, and New York: St. Martin's Press.

Forte, D. J., and Judd, K. (1998), 'The south within the north: Reproductive choices in three US communities', in R. Petchesky and K. Judd (eds.), *Negotiating Reproductive Rights*, Chap. 8, London: Zed Books, and New York: St. Martin's Press.

Garcia-Morena, C., and Claro, A. (1994), 'Challenges from the women's health movement: Women's rights versus population control', in G. Sen, A. Germain, and L. Chen (eds.), *Population Policies Reconsidered*, Cambridge: Harvard University Press.

Germain, A., and Kyte, R. (1995) *The Cairo Consensus: The Right Agenda for the Right Time*, New York: International Women's Health Coalition.

—— et al. (eds.) (1992) *Reproductive Tract Infections: Global Impact and Priorities for Women's Reproductive Health*, New York: Plenum Press.

Gogna, M., and Ramos, S. (2000), 'Lay beliefs, gender and sexuality: Unacknowledged risks for sexually transmitted diseases', in R. G. Parker, R. M. Barbosa, and P. Aggleton (eds.), *Framing the Sexual Subject*, Berkeley: University of California.

Govindasamy, P., and Malhotra, A. (1996), 'Women's position and family planning in Egypt', *Studies in Family Planning*, 27 (6) (Nov/Dec).

Greenhalgh, S. (1995), *Situating Fertility: Anthropology and Demographic Inquiry*, New York: Cambridge University Press.

Heise, L. (1995), 'Violence, sexuality and women's lives', in R. G. Parker and J. H. Gagnon (eds.), *Conceiving Sexuality*, New York and London: Routledge.

—— Moore, K., and Toubia, N. (1995), *Sexual Coercion and Reproductive Health: A Focus on Research*, New York: Population Council.

Helzner, J. F. (1996), 'Men's involvement in family planning', *Reproductive Health Matters*, Vol. 7 (May).

Huntington, D. et al. (1995), 'Improving the medical care and counseling of postabortion patients in Egypt', *Studies in Family Planning*, 26 (6) (Nov/Dec).

Khattab, H. (1992), *The Silent Endurance: Social Conditions of Women's Reproductive Health in Egypt*, Cairo: UNICEF.

Lloyd, C. (1993), 'Family and gender issues for population policy', Research Division Working Papers No. 48. The Population Council, New York.

Mita, R., and Simmons, R. (1995), 'Diffusion of the culture of contraception: Effects on young women in rural Bangladesh', *Studies in Family Planning*, 26 (1) (Jan/Feb).

Morsy, S. (1993), *Gender, Sickness, and Healing in Rural Egypt*, Boulder: Westview Press.

Mundigo, A. I. (1995), *Men's Roles, Sexuality, and Reproductive Health*, International Lecture Series on Population Issues, John D. & Catherine T. MacArthur Foundation, Chicago.

Obermeyer, C. M. (1992), 'Islam, women and politics: The demography of Arab countries', *Population and Development Review*, 18 (1) (March).

Ortiz Ortega, A., Amuchástegui, A., and Rivas, M. (1998), ' "Because they were born from me': Negotiating women's rights in Mexico', in R. Petchesky and K. Judd (eds.), *Negotiating Reproductive Rights*, Chap. 5, London: Zed Books, and New York: St. Martin's Press.

Orubuloye, I. O. (1995), 'Patterns of sexual behaviour of high risk populations and the implications for STDs and HIV/AIDS transmission in Nigeria', in R. G. Parker and J. H. Gagnon (eds.), *Conceiving Sexuality*, New York and London: Routledge.

—— *et al.* (1992), 'Sexual networking and the risk of AIDS in Southwest Nigeria', in T. Dyson (ed.), *Sexual Behaviour and Networking: Anthropological and Socio-cultural Studies on the Transmission of HIV*, Belgium: Editions Derouauz-Ordina, Liège.

Osakue, G., and Martin Hilber, A. (1998), 'Women's sexuality and fertility in Nigeria: Breaking the culture of silence', in R. Petchesky and K. Judd (eds.), *Negotiating Reproductive Rights*, Chap. 6, London: Zed Books, and New York: St. Martin's Press.

Paiva, V. (2000), 'Fostering the sexual subject: Gender and class in the sexual scene', in R. G. Parker, R. M. Barbosa, and P. Aggleton (eds.), *Framing the Sexual Subject*, Berkeley: University of California Press.

Paxman, J. M. *et al.* (1993), 'The clandestine epidemic: The practice of unsafe abortion in Latin America', *Studies in Family Planning*, 24 (4) (July/Aug).

Petchesky, R. P. (1995), 'From population control to reproductive rights: Feminist fault lines', *Reproductive Health Matters*, Vol. 6 (Nov).

—— (1997), 'Spiraling discourses of reproductive rights', in J. Tronto, K. Cohen, and K. Jones (eds.), *Women Transforming Politics*, New York: New York University Press.

—— (1998), 'Introduction' (Chap. 1) and 'Cross-country Comparisons and Political Visions' (Chap. 9) in R. Petchesky and K. Judd (eds.), *Negotiating Reproductive Rights*, London: Zed Books, and New York: St. Martin's Press.

—— Judd, K. (eds.) (1998), *Negotiating Reproductive Rights: Women's Perspectives Across Countries and Cultures*, London: Zed Books, and New York: St. Martin's Press.

Raj, R., Chee, H. L., and Shuib, R. (1998), 'Between modernization and patriarchal revivalism: Reproductive negotiations among women in peninsular Malaysia', in R. Petchesky and K. Judd (eds.), *Negotiating Reproductive Rights*, Chap. 3, London: Zed Books, and New York: St. Martin's Press.

Ray, S., Gumbo, N., and Mbizvo, M. (1996), 'Local voices: What some Harare men say about preparation for sex', *Reproductive Health Matters*, Vol. 7, Special Issue on 'Men' (May).

Ribeiro, L. (1994), 'Anticoncepção e Comunidades Eclesiais de Base', in A. O. Costa and T. Amado (eds.), Fundação Carlos Chagas, São Paulo: Alternativas Escassas: Saúde, Sexualidade e Reprodução na América Latina.

Sai, F. T. (1995), *Putting People First.* International Lecture Series on Population Issues, John, D., and Catherine, T. MacArthur Foundation, Chicago.

Schuler, S. R., and Hashemi, S. M. (1994), 'Credits, women's empowerment, and contraceptive use in rural Bangladesh', *Studies in Family Planning*, 25 (2) (Mar/Apr).

—— Choque, M. E., and Rance, S. (1994), 'Misinformation, mistrust, and mistreatment: Family planning among Bolivian market women', *Studies in Family Planning*, 25 (4) (July/Aug).

Schuler, S. R., Hashemi, S. M., and Jenkins, A. H. (1995), 'Bangladesh's family planning success story: A gender perspective', *International Family Planning Perspectives*, 21 (4) (Dec).

Seif El Dawla, A., Abdel Hadi, A., and Abdel Wahab, N. (1998), ' "Women's wit over men's": Trade-offs and strategic accommodations in Egyptian women's reproductive lives', in R. Petchesky and K. Judd (eds.), Chap. 3, *Negotiating Reproductive Rights*, London: Zed Books, and New York: St. Martin's Press.

Sen, A. (1984), *Resources, Values and Development*, Cambridge: Harvard University Press.

—— (1995) *Population Policy: Authoritarianism versus Cooperation*. International Lecture Series on Population Issues, John D. and Catherine T. MacArthur Foundation, Chicago.

Simmons, R. (1996), 'Women's lives in transition: A qualitative analysis of the fertility decline in Bangladesh', *Studies in Family Planning*, 27 (5) (Sept/Oct).

Singh, S., and Sedgh, G., (1997), 'The relationship of abortion to trends in contraception and fertility in Brazil, Colombia and Mexico', *International Family Planning Perspectives*, 23 (1) (March).

Thaddeus, S., and Maine, D. (1990), *Too Far to Walk: Maternal Mortality in Context*, New York: Center for Population and Family Health, Columbia University.

Trottier, D. A. *et al.* (1994), 'User characteristics and oral contraceptive compliance in Egypt', *Studies in Family Planning*, 25 (5) (Sept/Oct).

Weiss, E., Whelan, D., and Gupta, G. R. (1996), *Vulnerability and Opportunity: Adolescents and HIV/AIDS in the Developing World*, Washington, DC: International Center for Research on Women (ICRW).

Younis, N. *et al.* (1993), 'A community study of gynecological and related morbidities in rural Egypt', *Studies in Family Planning*, 24 (3) (May/June).

de Zalduondo, B., and Bernard, J. M. (1995), 'Meanings and consequences of sexual-economic exchange: Gender, poverty and sexual risk behaviour in urban Haiti', in R. G. Parker and J. H. Gagnon (eds.), *Conceiving Sexuality*, New York and London: Routledge.

Zurayk, H. *et al.* (1995), 'Comparing women's reports with medical diagnoses of reproductive morbidity conditions in rural Egypt', *Studies in Family Planning*, 26 (1) (Jan/Feb).

14

Culturalism as Ideology[1]

DIDIER FASSIN

The anthropologist is often asked to speak about 'culture'.[2] It is generally thought that such is his fate, as part of the attributions of his discipline, just as the sociologist is expected to study 'society', thus following a long scientific tradition, from Franz Boas to George Foster by way of Malinowski. But the culture he is expected to describe is particular: it corresponds to what is believed not to be yet known, to what is in some way at a cultural distance. In other words, he is called upon when his anthropological knowledge is deemed to be irreplaceable. He is therefore supposed, with the support of ethnographic research and conceptual tools, to provide insight into far-away societies that are often referred to as traditional, or into segments of his own society that are in some way distinct from its dominant values, whether those segments be the poor, deviants, or immigrants.[3] The culture of which he draws the portrait is thus defined by its difference. It is the *culture of the Other insofar as it is different.*

This observation has two practical consequences. First, the anthropologist is rarely asked to study the cultural world to which he belongs, or when he is, he is usually asked to address what is *exotic* in it. He is not generally questioned about the beliefs of political leaders or development professionals or medical doctors, who conceive their own representations and practices in terms of their own knowledge. Secondly, when he is called upon to understand the worlds of other peoples, he is only expected to be interested in defining what is *unique* about them. There is generally no wish for him to make pronouncements on the universal or even the trivial, because it is understood by those who call on his services that his domain is that of absolute difference. It happens that the anthropologist gives in to these conditions, either because he shares these generally held views of culture—and is not this naïve conception of othernessness sometimes the catalyst of an anthropological vocation?—or because he finds it to his advantage to have the specificity of his field and the uniqueness of his contributions recognized—could it not be said that this is in part the basis of his legitimacy? The history of applied anthropology reminds us that anthropologists are no strangers to the construction of this conception of culture, which also serves to justify their presence among decision makers.

This widely held conception is particularly apparent in development institutions and health services. When the anthropologist is called upon as part of an agronomic or epidemiological study, it is often to find the right formulations that define, through the use of surveys, the cultural determinants of a particular population's agricultural or health practices. And when he is asked to participate in an irrigation project or a vaccination programme, he is generally expected to explain a failure or difficulties in terms of cultural resistance.[4] The *symbolic output* of his work is that much greater for his employers if it reveals local peculiarities that are likely to explain the problems encountered by development or health authorities in the course of their operations. Bringing to light cultural representations and practices, if at all possible traditional ones, confirms the layman's intuition, reinforcing the preconceived notions of the programme organizers and securing the position of the anthropologist employed.

The more the issues studied are related to an individual's private life or to collectively held secrets, the more the role of the anthropologist is considered essential in unveiling cultural practices. Such is the case in reproduction and sexuality. First, for the development of family planning policies, and later, for AIDS campaigns, anthropological expertise has been summoned especially within the framework of so-called KABP (knowledge–attitudes–beliefs–practices) or RAP (rapid assessment procedures) studies, and less frequently in classical ethnographic work. Setting aside the methodological problems involved in the study of subjects who do not readily lend themselves to responding to questionnaires under time constraints, we can still examine the way in which cultural facts are treated.[5] In these studies, culture appears as a *substantiated* reality, in other words with an existence of its own, separated from the social world, homogeneous throughout a particular group—it is the very soil in which society plants its roots. Thus isolated, it can take the form of 'cultural variables' which will be given precise labels in the questionnaires.[6] It can also differentiate itself through 'cultural obstacles' which contribute to the assessment of a particular programme. Its value becomes *explanatory* in the analysis of human behaviour which thereby appears overdetermined by culture.[7] Most remarkably, because of its definition in terms of difference, it would seem culture only exists for those at the receiving end of a programme, and their culture only exists in the form of ancestral behaviours. There is thus little room for the study of the culture of those who manage or implement the programme, or for the analysis of widespread modern practices in so-called traditional societies.

In this chapter I address these *practical* applications of culture, and the manner in which development and health professionals, as well as scientists—demographers, epidemiologists or sometimes even anthropologists—introduce culture in the construction of their studies and their policies. I will therefore not examine conceptions and scientific definitions of culture, even though, as we will see, a detour through these theoretical reflections can also provide certain keys to understanding. Culturalism, as is meant here, is commonsense knowledge, implicitly or explicitly applied, when describing the behaviour of others or when justifying actions that are intended for them. Inverting the title of a famous article by Clifford Geertz (1973), I am considering culturalism as ideology, and *not* culturalism as theory, with reference to the Culture and Personality movement.[8] More than a sociology of knowledge, I propose a political anthropology of common understanding. It is nevertheless obvious that this common understanding also concerns those who produce scientific statements on culture. Science cannot be exempt from the critical analysis of culturalistic presuppositions[9] that underlie some of its works and some of its assertations.

But how can we characterize this ideology such as it appears in both discourse and practice in development and health issues? My proposal is to refer to cultural-ism as the *intellectual figure* that reduces culture to mere essence and that makes culture an ultimate interpretation of human behaviour. Culturalism can thus be defined by a combination of a process of *reification of culture*, rendered concrete by objects (traits, variables, behaviours), which can be isolated from a given social reality, and a process of *cultural overdetermination* which takes the form of explanations (factors, obstacles, resistance) that stand out among all possibilities. Speaking of operations and processes shows that we are dealing with intellectual patterns that are at work in various, banal situations. It is in this *commonly applied reasoning*, as can be seen in programmes of reproductive health, that culturalism as we define it can be observed. To demonstrate this fact, I will make use of two case studies, one in Ecuador, on maternal mortality among Indian populations, and the other in France, on pregnancy among HIV-positive African women.

CULTURE IN QUESTION

At the Nairobi Conference in 1987, international institutions, foremost among which were the World Health Organization and the World Bank, decided to make the reduction of maternal mortality a global priority. The problem had been seemingly ignored by public health authorities, prompting the editorialist of a major British medical journal to ask: Where is the M in MCH? The health of mothers was seen to be of serious concern on two fronts. First, the risk of dying from the complica-tions of a pregnancy or an abortion or after giving birth reached alarming levels. In some places, where high mortality rates were combined with high fertility indices, the rate was as high as one woman in ten. Secondly, the differences in mortality rates among mothers between different countries and between social categories within a given country exceeded a ratio of one to a hundred, which made it the most unequal indicator in all public health statistics. Furthermore, effective measures to reduce these rates and disparities seemed reasonably attainable by facilitating access to maternity wards, improving the quality of care, and increasing the use of family planning methods. Backed by international declarations and matching financial support, numerous governments, following the guidelines of the conference, implemented programmes promoting 'safe motherhood'.

Beginning in 1988, guided by a new Minister of Health and the National Director of Health, a woman, Ecuador became one of the leaders of this policy in Latin America. Maternal mortality rates were among the highest on the continent, principally related to deaths that occurred during delivery. It was decided that they could be reduced through better coverage of prenatal care (to identify and monitor pregnancies thought to be at risk) and obstetrical care (to treat possible complications during delivery). Following an important survey carried out across the country, a team of physicians and anthropologists concluded that the low rates of prenatal consultations and births under medical supervision to which the high mortality rates were attributed were due to 'an essentially cultural obstacle'.[10] As the population was primarily composed of rural Indian women, the authors blamed 'not only the level of education, but also more fundamentally a symbolic world differing from that of the formal cultural system around which the institutional health care is organized'. Thus to explain the reluctance of women to go to maternities, they evoked 'cultural aspects relating to their sense of modesty' and referring to certain acts performed before giving birth, they spoke of 'ritual behaviors'. This interpretation, which satisfied the international backers as well as the national health officials, consequently led to the orientation of later research into the incriminated traditional practices and the development of health education programmes for the stigmatized Indian women.

What was the true nature of this cultural rejection described by the social scientists and denounced by the decision makers? If we resist the fascination of the exotic—which in this case was obviously as difficult for the anthropologists as it was for the physicians—it becomes apparent that the reality was elsewhere, as was revealed by a study in two provinces with a large proportion of Indian inhabitants, Chimborazo and Cotopaxi.[11] When she wants to go to a health service to receive medical care, the pregnant Indian woman is confronted by a series of obstacles that are evidently more material than cultural in nature. These obstacles are clearly even more daunting for a woman in labour or whose delivery is complicated. In the Quecha communities in the Andes, located mostly at an altitude of 2,500–3,000 m, given the distances, the routes of communication and the means of transport, it can take several hours, sometimes a full day, on foot, on horseback or, when the roads allow and vehicles are available, by truck or bus, to reach the first medical centre and often even longer to reach the closest maternity. Furthermore, in the course of this journey, her finances suffer, first because of the trip itself, especially if she has to pay for the service of a car or if she is accompanied on her trip, and secondly because of the health care itself—even though public services are supposedly free, delivery, medication and possible complementary tests add up to substantial expense: total expenditures can thus represent a month's salary for a *peón*, i.e. an agricultural worker. It is easy to understand that a woman and her relatives usually think twice before undertaking such an adventure, in which other difficulties are yet to come.

Indeed, beyond these material issues, the reluctance of the Indian women to go to the maternities also stems from the conditions under which care is dispensed in these centres. Health care structures are in fact places where symbolic violence of ethnic relationships are expressed, a violence that is perceived even more intensely because it deals with the body, and a particularly vulnerable body in this situation. Doctors, nurses, and other health workers are almost exclusively white or *mestizos*. Dealing with a peasant Indian woman, they reproduce a position of power which has its origins in a long history of domination. Responding to the respectful second person 'usted' of the patient, the health care professional uses the familiar 'tu' or 'vos'—humility and fear on one side, confronted with superiority and disdain on the other. One of the racial stereotypes of the Indians is their lack of personal hygiene, which the hospital personnel perpetuate in words and in acts. The Indians' clothes are sealed in bags as if they were contaminated and it is not rare that the only immediate attention that a woman receives upon arrival is a foot bath so that she does not soil their sheets. The body is treated with no respect, as if it was a tainted or impure object. Laid out undressed in plain view, and sometimes roughly transported from one place to another, the women recall these experiences as the most painful memories of the maternities, all the more humiliating since they do not even undress in front of their husbands, and traditionally give birth squatting and fully clothed.

One particularity of Ecuadorean obstetrics is that four out of every ten women have a caesarean, a proportion that is approximately three times higher than in most neighbouring countries. This rate is not, as some have suggested, the consequence of a peculiarity in the anatomy of the Indian women, but rather is due to two very simply identified reasons. In the private sector, a caesarean birth is much more lucrative than a natural birth, and the study proved that profit determined this choice when the customer could afford it. In the public system, where this element is not taken into consideration because the fees charged are lower than the actual cost and obstetricians do not stand to gain financially from such practices, the interviews revealed that the guiding factor is the physician's own convenience, who wants to avoid any risks if the patient has had a previous caesarean and also states a desire to shorten labour whenever possible. This increase in the number of caesareans is particularly feared by the Indian women because it is widely believed that a woman who has had the operation is no longer capable of procreation or work. There are cases of women who have been repudiated by their husbands after a caesarean, and who, on their return from the maternity, have been forced to return to their parents. Obviously this contributes to the concerns that the perspective of giving birth in a medical centre incites.

Of course there could be culturalistic interpretations, as the authors of the Ecuadorean report assert, to explain the modesty of these women who refuse to adapt to the conditions of a medically supervised delivery or their reluctance to undergo caesareans to which they attribute effects that are the result of imaginary constructs. And indeed it could be alleged that Indian culture is an obstacle to the benefits of modern medicine. But drawing that conclusion would doubtless be somewhat hasty. First of all, it seems difficult to suppose that preserving a certain degree of modesty at the hospital, expecting humane treatment and preferring less aggressive techniques can in any way be construed as culturally specific: would a European or North American woman not have the same expectations? This is most obviously a case of *banal universality of attitudes* and the notion, often used in public health, of cultural acceptability has barely any relevance in this context. Furthermore, we cannot label as irrational the Indian women's beliefs concerning the consequences of caesareans on their productive and reproductive functions. Their harsh working conditions make resuming their daily activities extremely painful, especially since the period of complete rest, traditionally 40 days, is often reduced today to just two or three weeks because of their economic needs. As for their fears concerning the possibilities of other pregnancies after a caesarean, they are substantiated by the fact that, until very recently, it was common to practise tubal ligation in the course of the operation without informing them. This was done to avoid risks in further pregnancies, it was explained. The beliefs of the women are therefore *socially and historically founded* rather than culturally determined.

Questioning the culturalistic discourse of the social sciences and public health as applied to these Indian women does not however exclude all consideration of the pertinence of cultural factors in the explanation of their behaviour in regards to reproduction. Of course these Andean women have their own representations of conception and pregnancy, they apply traditional practices in contraception and reproduction, and they enlist the services of *parteras*, *curanderos*, and more commonly female relatives: mother, mother-in-law, elder sister. Thus methods that are supposed to facilitate delivery are used, like the drinking of potions made with plants that have tranquillizing qualities, or the use of techniques like the *mantear*, which involves vigorously shaking the body of the woman in labour in a blanket. These representations, practices, and actions cannot however be considered as exclusive of, or even—as some studies more focused on creating consensus con-clude—as complementing modern methods. In reality, it is a question of distinct paradigms: seeking the advice of an older woman does not in any way exclude the possibility of going to a prenatal clinic, but it cannot be portrayed as a complement, either. On the contrary, everything goes to show that the women, even those who live in particularly underprivileged conditions, will readily accept—on the basis of a complex relation built on attraction and domination—the benefits of modern medicine, if it is dispensed with a minimum of humanity and efficiency. Though the Andean culture is very much alive, it cannot be considered as intrinsically opposed to the use of health services. It is in the accessibility of the maternities and the way they are run, in the attitudes and behaviours of the care-givers that the principal obstacles to the Indian women's recourse to preventive and therapeutic care are to be found. In incriminating culture as certain health authorities willingly do, sometimes supported by anthropological data, they are in fact blaming the victims while masking their own responsibility in the matter.

What lessons can be learned from this brief case study? There are at least two. The first point is that *the culturalistic explanation can always more easily take precedence over others when examining a different society*. This is true not only because it can reinforce widely held presuppositions, but also because it provides gratification to the one who produces the explanation, thus ensuring his own legitimacy. In speaking of traditional practices, by invoking the symbolic order and generally making good use of culture, the anthropologist unites the layman's expectations and scientific discourse, thus fulfilling the demands of society on anthropology. On the contrary, revealing geographical constraints and economic factors, speaking of poor treatment and medical failures, and more generally exposing mere trivial realities, do not respond to a 'need for the cultural' and in some way are a 'waste' of the anthropologist's skills. The second point is that *culturalistic interpretation always leads to consider the target populations as the cause of the difficulties encountered in implementing actions.* If the task of the anthropologist is to describe a culture and to show how it constitutes an obstacle to a successful programme, it can only be supposed that the pertinent explanation can be found among those who are the object of the action, not those who instigate it. Implicitly, this means questioning the target group while refusing to examine the responsibility of the agents who create and run the programmes.

A culturalistic reading when *applied* to development or health projects is therefore doubly deceptive. By overdetermining the role of cultural factors, it sweeps aside any socio-economic or socio-political explanations of the phenomena examined. By limiting its field of study to the populations it helps to alienate, it avoids any critical analysis of the programmes provided or of those who create and implement them. The culturalistic option thus has clear ethical and political implications that can now be discussed in a second example.

THE VIOLENCE OF CULTURALISM

There is no need to cross oceans to discover cultural difference. Anyone in his own society can encounter it daily. For the natives, nationals and those who make up the dominant group of a given country, immigrant and foreign minorities constitute the most easily identifiable categories of otherness.[12] However, difference can be expressed in a number of varied, sometimes less apparent, ways, but still subject to a culturalistic reading, as is the case of the poor, youth, or drug-users.

In France, populations from sub-Saharan Africa, while fewer in number than immigrants from other European countries and the Maghreb, are particularly visible not only because of obvious differences in physical appearance and dress, but also due to the effects of policies that resulted in segregation, creating concentrations in a few cities, generally in the Paris region, where they are housed either in overcrowded workers' hostels, or in unrenovated quarters where they live in poorly maintained lodgings. More recently, groups of African origin have been in the public eye because of various demonstrations, with churches being occupied and hunger strikes held, drawing the attention of French opinion to the fact that large proportions of these groups are in fact in France illegally.[13] This presence of sub-Saharan Africans takes on particular significance in light of the historic ties between the former colonial power and the subcontinent. Over the last few years, we have seen reminders of this past, both in terms of development and immigration. For all these reasons, Africans seem to provide, in the collective imagination of the French, a perfect example of otherness, the basis of projections of exoticism, as well as of racism.

The AIDS epidemic has proved particularly revealing. The existence of cases of infection among immigrants from Africa has, as we know, led to the designation of an 'African AIDS', according to the words of a French specialist. This label, adopted with almost no criticism by international scientific circles, was based on epidemiological characteristics observed on the African continent as well as among immigrants living in Europe, linking the high rates of HIV-seroprevalence and the nearly identical levels of contamination in both sexes. To explain this singular fact, the culturalistic course was immediately adopted, along two general lines. On the one hand, dangerous ritual practices were sought and singled out, from scarification to circumcision. On the other hand, unsafe sexual behaviour was identified, and labelled as promiscuity. Later, this interpretation allowed for an explanation of the difficulties in controlling the epidemic: if safer behaviour was not adopted and if condoms were not widely used, the reasons were of course cultural.[14] Culture was thus blamed twice over: as the essential 'factor' in the spread of the disease and the principal 'obstacle' in its prevention.

This approach to AIDS in Africa is evidently not without repercussions in the way in which AIDS among African immigrants is addressed elsewhere in the world. In France, where they have been particularly hard hit by the epidemic, the tensions between culturalistic prejudices that are widely held and universalistic principles which form the republican ideal can be observed in the discrepancy between words and actions. On one side, official policy is not to mention AIDS among Africans, not to publish data referring to it, not to develop specific programmes, and not to adopt any specific behaviour. On the other, everything points to a de facto differentiation: in statistics on the disease, Africans appear as a group at risk (notably, the antecedent of a 'sexual relation with an African partner' is sufficient to classify the patient in a separate epidemiological category); in the area of prevention, associations receive public grants to finance programmes in immigrant workers' hostels (thus contributing to spectacular growth in the market of 'cultural mediation'); and on the subject of health care, observation and interviews reveal that medical practices were noticeably different for these patients (while epidemiological reports show that they encounter difficulties in obtaining access to diagnosis and treatment). The universalism advocated as a fundamental value of the Republic is in fact tolerant of this incongruous development of discriminatory discourses and practices, pleading respect of different cultures as its excuse.

Confronted with the issue of pregnancy among HIV-positive women, this ambiguous ideology finds particularly favourable ground. The risk of vertical transmission of the virus—from mother to child during pregnancy, during delivery, or through breastfeeding—led doctors to strongly advise HIV-positive women against becoming pregnant. Under these conditions, the announcement of a pregnancy is perceived as a personal failure and is often met with explicit reprobation. This reaction is particularly frequent among female African patients: a recent study carried out in the Paris region showed a rate of HIV infection that was four times higher among African women than among French women. The attitudes of physicians, who feel they are to a certain extent implicated by this situation, have slowly evolved. In the first years of the epidemic, they openly encouraged termination and the women were sometimes forced into an abortion. In recent years, under the combined effects of a more accurate evaluation of the actual probabilities of contamination, the discovery of treatments that reduce this risk, and a development in attitudes that led to a greater respect of the wishes of the patient, medical doctors have more often left the choice to the women without additional outside pressure. However, the discovery of the pregnancy of an HIV-positive woman remains on the whole, for social and health care professionals, a disturbing factor that attracts commentary, sometimes condemnation and always perplexity. How can one explain that a patient who knows she is HIV-positive becomes pregnant, despite the risks involved for her unborn child? Why would a women who discovers that she is HIV-positive during medical tests early in her pregnancy want to carry her child for the full term, despite the danger of transmission? If attitudes today are more liberal, they still carry moral judgements, but above all anthropological interrogations.

The demand for analysis is forthcoming because, for the medical staff, the African women seemed to represent a greater presence for them, both objectively and subjectively. That this behaviour that they judged to be difficult to understand concerned patients from other cultural horizons led them to attribute that fact to their difference. Faced with this demand, the offer of culturalism was quick to respond, in the form of clinical studies and mediations. Thus the principal French centre for ethnopsychiatry launched a research programme with a team of celebrated Parisian paediatricians to prove the interest of an ethnopsychiatric approach in the medical care of mothers and children infected with HIV. Reporting on their experience, the members of the group explained that they wanted to 'articulate the medical thinking of western care-givers and the traditional thought of migrant patients without seeking hypothetical universal values'. The first conclusions of their work supported their initial postulates since the mothers 'easily organized the history of their life and their disease based on traditional thoughts', 'readily accepted our system of care so long as it does not require them to abandon the basic protection provided by witchcraft'; thus, 'if prevention campaigns proved ineffective, it is because most of the messages ignore the logic of witchcraft and are opposed to it '.[15] In the ethno-psychiatric practice, which is presented in France as 'the instrument which allows migrants to express themselves in a language which conforms to their culture', not only on the subject of the body and disease, but increasingly also on the subjects of justice and education, all interpretations of behaviours are based on seeking 'traditional' representations and practices, and on the return of the immigrants to their origins and the inequalities of their cultures. It is in this context that HIV-positive women must also explain their pregnancies. The study reveals, however, experiences that are far more complex and elaborate, the identification of which escapes the simplistic analysis of the 'ethno-clinical mediators'.[16] It unveils the symbolic violence that culturalism exercises over those about whom it claims to reveal the truth. This violence takes four forms.

First of all, culturalism denies the Other the *universality of his aspirations*. On the subject of African women, the culturalists feign surprise at the singular importance that motherhood has in their eyes. The recognition of their femininity is allegedly expressed by the possibility of producing descendants and the notion that a woman without a child is not a complete woman. The desire to have a child appears as a cultural factor that is an obstacle for the African women's understanding of the risk of contamination. Isolated by their supposed particularities, they are inevitably considered in the light of what makes them different. On closer inspection, however, it is surprising that this desire is considered unique and not universal: is there a human society in which there are women who do not have this desire? Where are femininity and motherhood not associated? It would after all be rather paradoxical if in a world where medically assisted procreation has pushed biological reproduction to its limits, valuing reproduction could be considered a sign of otherness. The African women express their desire for children through their pregnancy, granted. But are French women any different? Rather than being some 'hypothetical value', as ethno-psychiatrists claim, the universal still has, anthropologically speaking, a certain *raison d'être*.

At the same time, culturalism denies the Other his *right to differences*. The plural here is essential. When it is a question of interpreting attitudes or behaviours of African women in the area of reproduction, sexuality, and prevention, they are, explicitly or implicitly, thought of in the singular. The African woman, it is said, exists only as a mother. She thinks of the body in traditional categories. She adapts poorly to the constraints of modern AIDS treatments. The alleged cultural singularity is reflected by a grammatical singular. The ethnological convention that consists of generalizing from the narrative of one informer, thinking that others speak with one voice, essentializing the Dogons or the Bambaras, is in some way generalized to all others. In making 'the African woman' an entity and a subject, priority is given to a cultural essence over concrete lives. However, observation shows that behind a seemingly homogeneous appearance, there exists a diversity of representations, practices and strategies for dealing with pregnancy and disease. For example, if the majority of the women harbour the hope of having children, all African women do not make the same decisions concerning their pregnancy. The studies reveal different, sometimes contradictory, attitudes. Whereas some women, fully aware of the risks, accept the possibility of giving birth to an infected child, others abandon their plans as being too dangerous, and others still put it off to some very hypothetical later date. Likewise, if some do have recourse to mysticism and ritual practices in combating the disease, others fully embrace modern medicine, all too happy to escape the constraints of tradition and the obligations of family and religion, while many do combine both. Hence the disappointment of a young ethno-psychologist who was surprised not to have uncovered, as she had been taught by her instructors, the slightest trace of stories of witchcraft among all the African women she had met—tradition is not what it used to be! In fact, the singular does not exist and the unity of the Other is never more than a product of the imagination of the Same.

Next, culturalism denies the Other the *recognition of his rationale*. Thus, in the analysis of their pregnancies, the discussion turns to irrational behaviour. Because medical logic dictates that no risk that might infect the child should be taken, any reaction that does not adhere to the norm is labelled as irrational. The judgement is a common one, and is also passed on third world populations whenever practices that do not follow expected patterns have to be interpreted. Yet here too, studies conducted among African women who have chosen to have a child despite the risks they run reveal reasonings that are undeniably coherent in their logic. In fact, many clearly express the calculations that support their decision. Having been informed of the odds of giving birth to an infected child by physicians, by the media, and even by word-of-mouth, they make their decision to have a child once they are fully aware of the facts. If one pregnancy in five ends in contamination, it is a reality that is all in all not that different from what they have always lived with and, optimistically, they hope to be among the four that go well. Far from being fatalistic, they deploy all the methods possible to reduce the risk of infection. Some plan their pregnancies around their treatment, waiting until 'their T4 cells are up', and most accept the constraints of antiretroviral treatments, to which they attribute the power of 'making their viral load disappear'. They adopt the language of doctors, which does not prevent them from seeking through religion and tradition additional guarantees against misfortune. Be that as it may, prayer or even ritual sacrifice cannot be interpreted as being irrational. On the contrary, they are reminders of the complexity of the physical and mental processes used by one and all to avoid misfortune. Of course, all behaviour regarding pregnancies cannot be reduced to calculations of probability. Emotions, passions, contingencies, and the inexplicable all play a role in these decisions. But is this irrationality specific to African women? Irrationality certainly cannot be cultural simply because it is a fact of the Other.

Lastly, and perhaps most importantly, culturalism denies the Other his *social conditions*. Reducing African women or any other category to otherness and treating them only in terms of culture amounts to taking them out of the context of the other dimensions of their lives in society. When an explanation is sought for behaviour that is deemed not to conform to expectations—the pregnancy of an HIV-positive woman, a doctor's appointment not kept, erratically followed treatment, forgetting to use a condom—culturalism provides easy answers. Listening to these women describe their everyday existence, and observing their way of life, we discover that reality is elsewhere. The precarity of their situations—socially, economically, and legally—is often a stronger, more immediate determinant of their behaviour than their supposed beliefs. A number of African women, who entered France on ordinary tourist visas, and others who arrived illegally, in order to join their husbands who were already living in France, have been excluded of the administrative procedures that allow members of the same family to be reunited: since the mid-1980s, the immigration laws no longer allow retroactive changes in their legal status. They are therefore left without any possibility of entering the official job market and with none of the social benefits available to foreigners. Consequently, in many cases they find themselves subject to various forms of domination by their spouses or exploitation by their employers. Often, their daily existence is entirely devoted to developing tactics to leave their homes without attracting the attention of their entourage while avoiding police controls, obtaining resources either in cash or in kind, through undeclared employment or through the assistance of associations, running from one institution to another to collect a document or secure a service, and attempting to avoid undesired and unprotected sexual relations. Thus, what is perceived and understood about the reasons for their behaviour in the office of a physician or an association is far from the real world these women live in. If the social and health workers cannot be criticized for their lack of awareness of these realities, we can on the other hand wonder about the ease with which cultural interpretation allows them to brush aside socio-economic and socio-political conditions of foreigners and immigrants in contemporary society.

From this four-fold denigration results a *violence of a political nature*, as Hannah Arendt (1995) defines it when she puts politics down to 'one fact: human plurality', which in turn leads to the treatment 'of the community and the reciprocity of different beings'. By negating in the Other that which is both universal and diverse, rational and subjective, material and symbolic, and overall considering the Other exclusively in the singular, culturalism refuses the Other access to the status of political being, which by definition is plural. The otherness of culturalistic ideology is therefore both without any possible community, because the Same and the Other appear in two definitively separate worlds, and without any imaginable reciprocity, since the division between the Same and the Other is necessarily asymmetrical. Attempts must now be made to remedy this neglect of politics without going to the other extreme which would result in abandoning all cultural interpretation. We cannot without impunity throw the baby that is culture out with the bathwater that is culturalism.

CULTURE WITHOUT CULTURALISM

'How does one represent other cultures? Is the notion of a distinct culture (or race, or religion, or civilization) a useful one?' asks Edward Saïd (1978, p. 325) in a work in which he attempts to prove that Orientalism is a Western construct of the Other. Such are the questions that must now be asked: What culture is being considered? And what uses are there for it? These questions are not asked hypothetically but for their practical implications. In development projects, in public health policy, in family planning programmes, what are our thoughts on culture and why should we call upon it? Or, taking a more directive tack: *how should we, when working with individuals and groups, make use of culture?* In other words, is there a way of treating culture in a non-culturalistic manner?

The two case studies presented here and the conclusions that are drawn from them provide an unambiguous answer to the question. It is by *politicizing culture* that we can give it back its meaning and its effectiveness. If we adopt Arendt's perspective, a *political reading of the cultural* appears simultaneously as a contradiction and a remedy to the ideological interpretation of culturalism. Recognition of the plurality of different beings (Andean Indians, Africans, immigrants) supposes the rejection of reducing the Other—who is in fact multiple, diverse, impossible to express as the singular of a culture—to mere essence. Furthermore, the recognition of the community and of reciprocity implies considering difference in a historically constructed and determined context. Cultural studies cannot take the Other as an object independent of the Same. The practical implications of this double recognition are great. In the case of the Ecuadorean women, as in the example of the

African immigrants, a political reading of culture leads to a double reorientation in research and in action.

First, the study of culture is indissociable from the analysis of its determinants, in other words the *structural conditions* which underlie it. The attitude of the Andean women who prefer to give birth at home using traditional techniques can only be interpreted if these practices are viewed in the context of the material reality of their existence, in particular their isolation and poverty that limit the possibilities of obtaining preventive care and treatment. If they give birth at home, it is first and foremost because they cannot do otherwise. The behaviour of African women who have unprotected sexual relations and become pregnant when they know of their HIV-positive status only takes on meaning when seen in the light of their experience of immigration, and particularly their precarious legal and economic situation that reinforces the inequality of gender. If they do not follow the norms of prevention, of which they are aware, it is because the space that is given them in French society marginalizes and weakens them.

Secondly, the study of the Other is indissociable from the analysis of its relation to the Same, the object being to define a *social figuration* that includes the processual interactions between the culture of the care-givers and the 'care-receivers', between the development specialists and those 'to be developed'. The reticence of Indian women to go to maternities to give birth cannot be understood if the social representations and practices of the 'white' and 'mestizo' professionals, inherited from the relations of domination and discrimination from colonial and post-colonial times, are not examined. What we describe as 'Andean culture' is not isolated in a moment in time, but rather exists in the course of history in which it develops continuously in relation to 'white' and 'mestiza' cultures. The delay often observed before African women seek medical care for their pregnancy must be analysed taking into consideration the criticism they face, the fact that some women have been practically forced by physicians to have abortions, and that other illegal immigrants have been turned in by hospital administrations when they went to give birth. Here again, the 'cultural obstacles' are built on the interaction of these women and the health system.

From these two observations, we can define two simple methodological precepts to be applied by those who call on anthropologists. First, culture should never be analysed without regard for the conditions in which it is produced and reproduced. Secondly, populations should always be examined in the way they interact with institutions and the representatives they deal with. These principles clearly converge with Fredrik Barth's recommendation (1989) for 'the analysis of culture in complex societies': 'In a world where reality is culturally constituted, we must seek to show how the shapes of culture are socially generated.' Approaching culture from this perspective which is both structural and figurational[17] of course has the effect of transforming the action undertaken: instead of alienating populations while claiming to educate them, we set the objectives of transforming the social structures that underlie the so-called 'cultural constraints' and modifying institutional systems and professional practices that determine the 'cultural factors' of inadequate use of health services. This idea is to a certain degree reflected in the evolution among international institutions from the rhetoric of maternal health to the rhetoric of reproductive health.

But a political reading of culture should perhaps go further, also asking questions about *political uses of culture* in public programmes in general, and in women's health programmes in particular. It cannot suffice simply to answer Edward Saïd's question: What culture are we talking about? We also have to ask a second question: What can talking about culture do for us? An explanation based on culture is never neutral, nor is it univocal. Culturalism as ideology is an obstruction on three different levels. First of all, it often speaks of things it does not name: questioning the culture of the Other, identifying specific cultural traits among Indian women, taking an interest in cultural obstacles to the integration of African women immigrants—'It's not their fault, it's their culture', we are told—is often nothing more than providing cultural dressing to prejudices with a marked racist connotation.[18] Then, it speaks of culture while remaining silent on social inequalities and political violence. Accounting for problems in development and health care through cultural traits, supposed archaisms and alleged resistance, is eluding the analysis of relations of domination, exploitation and discrimination that far more than cultural realities restrict opportunities for transforming behaviour.[19] And lastly, culturalism as ideology addresses the culture of others to vindicate those who manipulate that culture. By focusing attention on populations whose beliefs run against the benefits of medicine and whose behaviour is contrary to the principles of prevention, it avoids all observations on the concrete conditions in which they are handled by hospital services or health care programmes.[20] To counter these ideological uses of culture by those who have an interest in maintaining this triple regime of obstruction, we could suggest the following provocative principle of analysis: culture is, until proven otherwise, the last explanation that should be retained to explain difficulties encountered in programmes of development and health care. It is the last for the reasons discussed at length here. It is last also for practical reasons because it is doubtless more effective in the long run to act on the social causes, and in the short term to modify health policy than to claim to be able to transform beliefs and behaviours.

Culturalistic prejudice is too socially conditioned for us to think that it could disappear under the mere influence of anthropological rationale. But we can hope that anthropologists will not reinforce this prejudice, and even that they will be critical of it, as Michael Herzfeld (1992) recommends: 'Basically anthropology consists of analyzing prejudice—that of others as well as our own.' In doing so, anthropologists are not abandoning the analysis of culture,[21] but are shifting it from the realm of ideology to the domain of politics.

Notes

1. Translation by Vincent Vichit-Vadakan reviewed by the author.
2. The passive form adopted here, purposefully undefined, refers in fact to any social agents who share a common representation of anthropology, sometimes explicitly claimed by

anthropologists themselves. This representation is especially frequent in development and health institutions, as will be extensively illustrated here.

3. While cultural, and indeed culturalistic, anthropology has taken for its principal object of study foreign populations, whether geographically distant (Melanesian) or not (Amerindian), in general, throughout the social sciences, a cultural approach, and again sometimes a culturalist one, has developed around dominated groups, isolating 'the culture of poverty', the 'culture of deviance', 'the culture of immigrants' or 'working class culture', without always avoiding their presentation as only 'dominated cultures' (Grignon and Passeron 1989).

4. Examples of these cultural readings of development and health care are innumerable and have been the object of critical analysis, by anthropologists in the field of development (Olivier de Sardan 1995) as well as in health issues (Gruénais 1992). Countering this use of culture, some have turned the problem around, examining the culture of development agents (Augé 1972; Hobart 1993) and medical doctors (Good 1994; Pouchelle 1995).

5. In the study of AIDS, in particular, several reports have demonstrated the methodological problems created by this type of approach and by extension the implications in terms of accuracy of the results (Caraël 1995; Vidal 1995; Giraud 1997). We have also attempted to show how a culturalistic treatment of the epidemic, with its racist undertones, has had serious consequences, not only scientifically but politically (Dozon and Fassin 1989).

6. See, for example, a recent Canadian study on 'Ethnocultural Predictors of Postpartum Infant Care Behaviours' in an immigrant population in which the 'ethnocultural characteristics' are examined through the use of a 'scale of acculturation composed of twelve items' and a 'scale of ethnic identity composed of fifteen items'. It is remarkable that this report, very detailed in its cultural aspects, gives absolutely no indication of the socioeconomic conditions of the women surveyed (Edwards and Boivin 1997).

7. On this subject, among many articles on the same theme, refer to the recent Ghanaian study entitled: 'Cultural Factors Constraining the Introduction of Family Planning among the Kassena-Nankana of Northern Ghana'. The authors, searching for the 'reasons why women in a rural, Sahelian community are reluctant to adopt family planning even when convenient services are made readily available', uncover three 'cultural constraints': 'First, women opting to practice contraception must do so at considerable risk of social ostracism or family conflict. Second, few women view personal decisions about contraception as theirs to make. Third, although children are highly valued for a variety of economic, social and cultural reasons, mortality risks remain extremely high.' After closer examination, it becomes apparent that these so-called 'cultural' constraints are in fact the reflection of social relations of domination between the sexes and of particularly difficult material living conditions (Adongo *et al.* 1997).

8. Speaking of culturalism as an 'ideology' supposes that we explain what is meant by this term. Philosophical, sociological, and anthropological writing on ideology abounds (Ricoeur 1996). I will not in this article discuss it further, but I would like to give some indication of the perspective adopted here. While not underestimating its functions of dissimulating reality, as analysed by Marx, and of legitimating domination, as demonstrated by Weber, here I will adopt an anthropological point of view, which consists of defining ideology as the cultural system through which relations of power are expressed (Geertz 1973; Augé 1975).

9. The task of deconstructing culturalistic presuppositions of anthropologists themselves when they speak of culture was undertaken by James Clifford in his systematic and radical revisiting of classical learned texts, from Margaret Mead to Edward Saïd (1978).

10. The study, commissioned by the Ministry of Public Health and backed by the Pan-American Health Organization, aimed to explain the high levels of mortality among mothers and the low rate of use of maternities (Pino *et al.* 1990).

11. This study, carried out between 1989 and 1991 by the French Institute for Andean Studies (IFEA) and the French Institute of Health and Medical Research (INSERM), examined the living and health conditions of the women. Stemming from a classically ethnographic approach based on participatory observation and non-directive interviews, the rural part of the study was carried out in two villages in the Ecuadorian Andes and in the surrounding Indian communities (Fassin and Defossez 1992).

12. The notion of 'immigrant culture' with its avatars in terms of 'acculturation' appeared in France in the 1970s, when the social context imperceptibly shifted from temporary immigration for reasons of employment to permanent immigration implying a reflection on the processes of integration and the maintaining of specificities related to one's origin (Schnapper 1986).

13. In this so-called 'sans-papiers' (illegal immigrants) movement that largely fuelled the public debate on immigration in 1996 and 1997, the sub-Saharan Africans were always in the forefront, even if the problem more generally concerned all foreigners (Fassin *et al.* 1997).

14. On the construction of 'African AIDS' and more particularly on the role of anthropologists, I will take the liberty of referring to a recent text (Fassin 1998). Beyond the theoretical issues, this ideological choice has had significant consequences in the way that the battle against the epidemic developed in Africa both in the selection of means that were implemented as in the indignation with which they were greeted on the continent (Packard and Epstein 1991).

15. In conclusion, the authors 'suggest for African patients a triple combination therapy: medication + prayer groups + calling on the village healer'. This exoticized presentation of the disease, its treatment, and prevention allows them to further suggest as an overall remedy to the psychological pathology of the patients the establishment of 'community-based ghettos', assembling patients in accordance with their ethnic origin (Nathan 1996).

16. The analysis that follows is supported by a study that was conducted from 1996 to 1998 in the Paris region among men and women of African origin, through a contract with the Fondation pour la recherche médicale (Foundation for Medical Research), parts of which have already been published (Fassin and Ricard 1996).

17. For Norbert Elias, the structural and configurational approaches proposed here are complementary: 'What we designate as "structures" when we consider people as societies are "configurations" when we consider them as individuals.' (Elias 1994.)

18. Of course, culturalism as an anthropological theory should not be confused with racism, because on the contrary it was initially conceived, by Herkovitz among others, as a scientific arm against discriminatory discourse against blacks in the United States (Jackson 1986). It is the practical ideology as it is defined in this text that often tends to function as a watered-down, politically acceptable form of racism (Donald and Rattansi 1992).

19. In a special issue of the Revue Tiers Monde on the theme 'Culture and Development', the question was asked thus: 'We can wonder if the accent that is placed on the "cultural" today is not used—sometimes—to hide major economic and social problems in the name of an ideology of unanimity: in discussion of identity, do differences in social class, ethnicity, sex, urban or rural localization, etc. disappear?' (Lê Thành Khôi 1984). Likewise, it has been shown that the focalization of the debate on multiculturalism, in the United States as

well as in France, prevents the observation of problems of discrimination: 'Perhaps it would be better to speak of minorities rather than culture, substituting the lexicon of discrimination for the vocabulary of multiculturalism.' (E. Fassin 1997.)

20. This avoidance is present in the very premiss of the analysis that opposes the 'knowledge' of medicine and the 'beliefs' of populations (Pelto and Pelto 1997).

21. As an illustration taken from anthropological work on disadvantaged groups, we can consider the evolution from a culturalistic approach defined as 'the culture of poverty' (Lewis 1965) to a social reading of the point of view of 'the culture of the poor' (Hoggart 1970).

References

Adongo, P. B., Phillips, J. F., Kajihara, B. *et al.* (1997), 'Cultural factors constraining the introduction of family planning among the Kassena-Nankana of Northern Ghana', *Social Science and Medicine*, 45 (12): 1789–1804.

Arendt, H. (1995), *Qu'est-ce que la politique?* Paris: Seuil.

Augé, M. (1972), 'Sous-développement et développement: Terrain d'étude et objets d'action en Afrique francophone', *Africa*, 42 (2), 205–16.

—— (1975), *Théorie des pouvoirs et idéologie. Etude de cas en Côte d'Ivoire*, Paris: Hermann.

Barth, F. (1989), 'The analysis of culture in complex societies', *Ethnos*, 54 (3–4): 121–42.

Caraël, M. (1995), 'Bilan des enquêtes CAP menées en Afrique: Forces et faiblesses', in J. P. Dozon and L. Vidal (eds.), *Les sciences sociales face au sida, Cas africains autour de l'exemple ivoirien*, Paris: ORSTOM Editions, pp. 25–33.

Clifford, J. (1988) *The Predicament of Culture. Twentieth Century Ethnography, Literature, and Art*, Cambridge: Harvard University Press.

Donald, J., and Rattansi, A. (1992), *'Race', Culture, and Difference*, London: Sage.

Dozon, J. P., and Fassin, D. (1989), 'Raison épidémiologique et raisons d'Etat. Les enjeux socio-politiques du sida en Afrique', *Sciences Sociales et Santé*, 7 (1): 21–36.

Edwards, N. C., and Boivin, J. F. (1997), 'Ethnocultural predictors of postpartum infant-care behaviours among immigrants in Canada', *Ethnicity and Health*, 2 (3): 163–76.

Elias, N. (1994), *Sport et civilisation. La violence maîtrisée*, Paris: Fayard.

Fassin, D. (1998), 'L'anthropologie entre engagement et distanciation. Essai de sociologie des recherches en sciences sociales sur le sida en Afrique', in C. Becker, J. P. Dozon, and M. Touré (eds.), *Sciences sociales et sida en Afrique*, Paris: Karthala.

—— and Defossez, A. C. (1992), 'Une liaison dangereuse. Sciences sociales et santé publique dans les programmes de réduction de la mortalité maternelle en Equateur', *Cahiers de Sciences Humaines*, 1 (28): 23–36.

—— and Ricard, E. (1996), 'Les immigrés et le sida. Une question mal posée', in S. Hefez (ed.), *Sida et vie psychique*, Paris: La Découverte, pp. 81–90.

Fassin, D., Morice, A., and Quiminal, C. (1997), *Les lois de l'inhospitalité. Les politiques de l'immigration à l'épreuve des sans-papiers*, Paris: La Découverte.

Fassin, E. (1997), 'Du multiculturalisme à la discrimination', *Le Débat*, 97: 131–6.

Geertz, C. (1973), 'Ideology as a cultural system', in *The Interpretation of Cultures*, New York: Basic Books, pp. 193–233.

Giraud, M. (1997), 'Entre particularités épidémiologiques et spécificités culturelles: l'enquête sur les comportements sexuels aux Antilles et en Guyane françaises', *Sciences Sociales et Santé*, 15 (4), 74–93.

Good, B. (1994), *Medicine, Rationality, and Experience. An Anthropological Perspective*, Cambridge: Cambridge University Press.

Grignon, C., Passeron, J. C. (1989), *Le savant et le populaire. Misérabilisme et populisme en sociologie et en littérature*, Paris: Hautes Etudes-Gallimard-Seuil.

Gruénais, M. E. (1992), 'Anthropologies et santé publique. Une rencontre à venir', *Cahiers des Sciences Humaines*, 28 (1): 3–12.

Herzfeld, M. (1992), 'La pratique des stéréotypes', *L'Homme*, 32 (1): 67–77.

Hobart, M. (1993), *An Anthropological Critique of Development. The Growth of Ignorance*, London and New York: Routledge.

Hoggart, R. (1970), *La culture du pauvre*, Paris: Editions de Minuit.

Jackson, W. (1986), 'Melville herskovitz and the search for Afro-American culture', in G. W. Stocking (ed.), *Malinowski, Rivers, Benedikt and Others. Essays on Culture and Personality*, Madison: The University of Wisconsin Press, pp. 95–125.

Lê Thành Khôi (1984), 'Culture et développement', *Revue Tiers Monde*, 25 (97): 9–28.

Lewis, O. (1965), 'The culture of poverty', *Scientific American*, 215 (4): 19–25.

Nathan, T. (1996), *Bilan d'activité du Centre Georges Devereux*, unpublished report, Paris.

Olivier de Sardan, J. P. (1995), *Anthropologie et développement. Essai en socio-anthropologie du changement social*, Paris: Karthala.

Packard, R. M., and Epstein, P. (1991), 'Epidemiologists, social scientists, and the structure of medical research on AIDS in Africa', *Social Science and Medicine*, 33 (7): 771–83.

Pelto, P. J., and Pelto, G. H. (1997), 'Studying knowledge, culture, and behavior in applied medical anthropology', *Medical Anthropology Quarterly*, 11 (2): 147–63.

Pino, M. A., Reascos, N., Vilota, I. *et al.* (1990), Tendencias de los servicios de salud en America Latina, unpublished report, Quito.

Pouchelle, M. C. (1995), 'Transports hospitaliers, extra-vagances de l'âme', in F. Lautman and J. Maître (eds.) *Gestions religieuses de la santé*, Paris: L'Harmattan, pp. 247–99.

Ricoeur, P. (1996), *Lectures on Ideology and Utopia*, New York: Columbia University Press.

Saïd, E. (1978), *Orientalism*, New York: Pantheon Books.

Schnapper, D. (1986), 'Modernité et acculturations. A propos des travailleurs émigrés', *Communications*, 43: 141–68.

Vidal, L. (1995), 'L'anthropologie, la recherche et l'intervention sur le sida en Afrique. Enjeux méthodologiques d'une rencontre', *Sciences Sociales et Santé*, 13 (2): 5–27.

Index

key informants 50, 281
Khattab, H. 5, 13, 186, 289
khi tute 121
Khon Kaen 121
kicking 48
Kimura, R. 266
kindergarten worker 45
Klein, R. 83
Kleinman, A. 58, 97, 235
knowledge 101–2, 117, 223, 257, 268, 277
knowledge, attitudes, and practices (KAP) 105, 277
knowledge–attitudes–beliefs–practices (KABP) 301
kobri kara 51
Koenig, M. 4, 13
Korea 262
Koshland, D. 253
Kunstadter, P. 75
Kusin, J. 38
Kyoto 262
Kyte, R. 277

La Fleur, W. 262
labelling 61
labour force 265
lactation 44, 263
Ladier-Fouladi, M. 156
ladu 52
Lake Victoria 67, 78
Lane, S. 91
languages 201
Last, Murray 70
late modernity 117
latent illness 104, 119
Lavely, W. 131
laws 95, 135, 146, 157
lay beliefs 58
lay models 4–6
lay referral networks 59, 68–70
least-squares regressions 206
Lebowa 197–200
Lebra, T. 261
legislation 226, 243
legitimation 75
legitimization 222
Leitch, I. 40
Leninism 134, 140
Leslie, J. 65
Lesthaeghe, R. 193
Li Peng 142
Li Xiaorong 131

life cycle 164, 198, 200, 208–12, 216, 284
life expectancy 155
lime 47
Lindenbaum, S. 256
literacy 16, 39
live birth 53
living standards 137
Lloyd, C. 278
local beliefs 49–50
local notion 53
local practices 40–2
Lockwood, M. 213
Logan, M. 244
London Economist 155
longitudinal study 39
love marriages 269
low birth weight (LBW) 40, 233
low income 237
low-income neighbourhood 158
Low, S. 58
Luo 60
Luo women 58, 76, 79
Lutz, Wolfgang 216
Lyttleton, C. 113

mabiki see infanticide
MacGaffey, J. 216
Maghreb 306
magic power 77
Maine, D. 102, 289
Malaysia 280
male preachers 173
male–female interactions 278
Malek-Afzali 158
Malhotra 286
malnutrition 237
Malthus' thesis 262
mantear 305
Maoist thought 134, 139–40
Marathi 15–16
March, K. 69
Margolix, A. 184
marital dynamics 94
marital status 201, 213
Marks, S. 194
marriage 16, 94, 155, 212, 265, 269
Martin Hilber 291
Martínez, B. 238
Marumoto, Y. 272
Marxism 131, 134, 139
Maseualpajti Organization 235, 245
massage(s) 51, 53, 178, 239, 246

neem 43
neglect 223–8
negotiated entitlement 283
negotiation 225, 242
neo-Buddhist 15–16
neoeugenics 255
nervosa 79
Netherlands Interdisciplinary Demographic
    Institute (NIDI) 39
network partners 68, 71
network size 68
neurofibromatosis 260, 274
'new geography' 119
new reproductive technologies (NRTs) 83,
    90–1, 95, 254, 274
Newberger, E. 233
Nichter, M. 38, 64
Niehaus, I. 213
Nigeria 156, 280
non-governmental organizations 158, 234
Norfloxin 121
Norplant 290
Northern Sotho 206, 217
nuclear families 42, 208, 264, 272
nurses 72
nutrition 14, 26, 36, 38–55
Nwakoby 5
nyach 64
nyamrerwa 59, 62, 69, 74, 77
Nyamwaya, D. 59

O'Keefe, P. 32
Obermeyer 2
Obeyesekere, G. 70
Obisa 60, 71, 78
objective fact 101
obstetric care 302
    see also maternal mortality
odds ratios 109
Odhiambo, E. 60
Ohkura, K. 266
Okoth-Owiro, A. 70
Olaniran, N. 5
'old' reproductive technologies 93
Oman 55
Omran 176
one-child policy 7, 131, 133, 135,
    137–9
Oomman, N. 13–14
Open Letter 140, 145
openness 282
Oreomycin 113

Organization of Volunteer Women Health
    Workers 158
organizations 289
Orientalism 311
Ortiz, O. 287
Orubuloye, I. 278
Osaka 262
Osakue, G. 291
Osero, J. 70, 75
ostracism 93
'Other' 271, 273
'otherness' 306, 311
ova 95–6
overweight 222
overwork 19
Owich 60, 78
Oyugis 78

paganism 208
Paidar, P. 154
pain control medication 183
Paiva, V. 278
Palmer 146
pan 18
Panadol 70, 74
Pangman, W. 225
Paolisso, M. 65
papaya 43–4
paracetamol 70, 113
parity 39, 42, 50, 181
Parkin, D. 60
Parra, P. 240
Parsons, T. 62
parteras 305
participatory training 158
partners 73, 118–19, 201, 210, 255, 268
Pattaravanich, U. 114
'pass laws' 195
passion play 171
Patel, P. 14
patriarchy 95, 142, 187, 216, 221, 227
Paxman, J. M. 294
peanut 44
peasantry 137, 139–45
Pedi 217
pelvic inflammatory disease (PID) 63, 72
Peng Peiyun 143–5
penile discharge 119
perceptions 39, 114, 117, 122, 235–6
peritonitis 183
'permissibility' 176
Pescosolido, B. 62

Printed in the United States
62493LVS00002B/63

9 780199 246892